Are you Saken, too?

WIGGLE...
WIGGLE...

Ken-ichi Sakura

Dragon Drive has been so busy, what with the cards, anime, games and capsule toys. Is everyone keeping up?
I hope you're catching it all without missing anything! I am!
While we're at it, don't forget the manga.

And don't forget to take out the trash...

Ken-ichi Sakura's manga debut was *Fabre Tanteiki*, which was published in a special edition of *Monthly Shonen Jump* in 2000. Serialization of *Dragon Drive* began in the March 2001 issue of *Monthly Shonen Jump* and the hugely successful series has inspired video games and an animated TV show. Sakura's latest title, *Kotokuri*, began running in the March 2006 issue of *Monthly Shonen Jump*. *Dragon Drive* and *Kotokuri* have both become tremendously popular in Japan because of Sakura's unique sense of humor and dynamic portrayal of feisty teen characters.

DRAGON DRIVE™

DRAGON DRIVE
VOLUME 5

The SHONEN JUMP Manga Edition

STORY AND ART BY
KEN-ICHI SAKURA

Translation/Martin Hunt, HC Language Solutions, Inc.
English Adaptation/Ian Reid, HC Language Solutions, Inc.
Touch-up Art & Lettering/Jim Keefe
Design/Sam Elzway
Editor/Shaenon K. Garrity

Editor in Chief, Books/Alvin Lu
Editor in Chief, Magazines/Marc Weidenbaum
VP of Publishing Licensing/Rika Inouye
VP of Sales/Gonzalo Ferreyra
Sr. VP of Marketing/Liza Coppola
Publisher/Hyoe Narita

Printed in the U.S.A.

Published by VIZ Media, LLC
P.O. Box 77010
San Francisco, CA 94107

SHONEN JUMP Manga Edition
10 9 8 7 6 5 4 3 2 1
First printing, December 2007

viz media™
www.viz.com

RATED A FOR ALL AGES
PARENTAL ADVISORY
DRAGON DRIVE is rated A and is suitable for readers of all ages.
ratings.viz.com

THE WORLD'S MOST POPULAR MANGA
SHONEN JUMP™
www.shonenjump.com

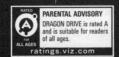

SHONEN JUMP MANGA EDITION

DRAGON DRIVE

Vol. 5
MISSION

STORY & ART BY
KEN-ICHI SAKURA

IN COLLABORATION WITH BANDAI • CHAN'S • ORG

CHARACTERS

Reiji Ozora

A JUNIOR HIGH SCHOOL STUDENT WHO NEVER APPLIED HIMSELF, BUT HE'S TOTALLY GETTING INTO DRAGON DRIVE.

Maiko Yukino

SHE'S ALWAYS GETTING TICKED OFF BY HER UNRELIABLE CHILDHOOD PAL REIJI, BUT SHE SECRETLY CARES ABOUT HIM.

Chibi

REIJI'S DRAGON PARTNER. IN RIKYU, HE'S KNOWN AS SENKOKURA.

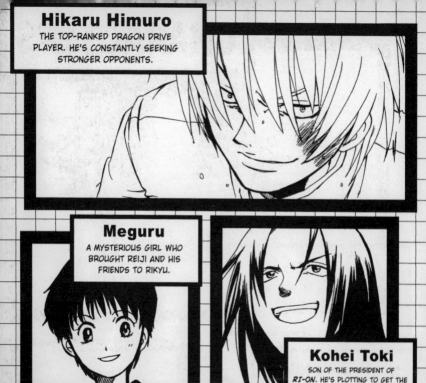

Hikaru Himuro

THE TOP-RANKED DRAGON DRIVE PLAYER. HE'S CONSTANTLY SEEKING STRONGER OPPONENTS.

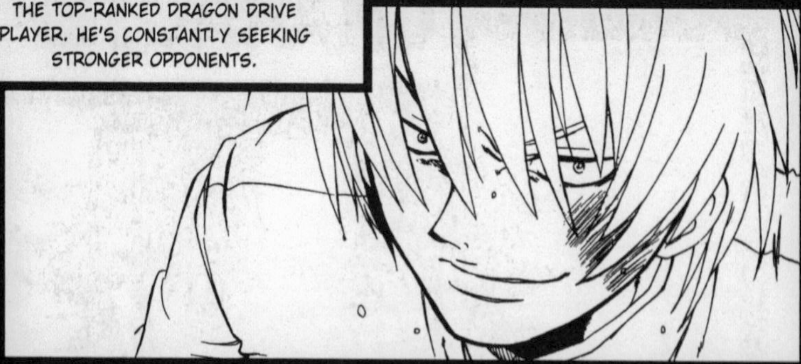

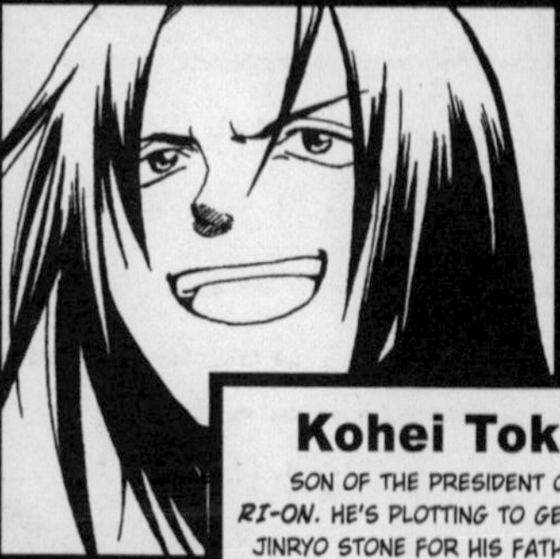

Kohei Toki

SON OF THE PRESIDENT OF *RI-ON*. HE'S PLOTTING TO GET THE JINRYO STONE FOR HIS FATHER.

Meguru

A MYSTERIOUS GIRL WHO BROUGHT REIJI AND HIS FRIENDS TO RIKYU.

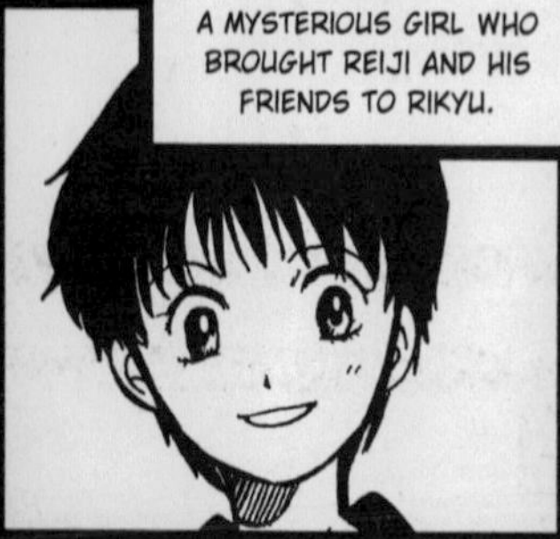

STORY

DRAGON DRIVE IS A VIRTUAL REALITY GAME THAT ONLY KIDS CAN PLAY. THE THRILL OF THE GAME GRIPS REIJI, A BOY WHO WAS NEVER REALLY GOOD AT ANYTHING. WHILE TRAINING IN A SPECIAL ROOM ONE DAY, REIJI AND HIS FRIENDS ARE WHISKED AWAY TO RIKYU, AN ALTERNATE EARTH. THERE, HE LEARNS THAT *RI-ON*, THE ORGANIZATION RUNNING D.D., IS PLOTTING TO CONQUER BOTH RIKYU AND EARTH. *RI-ON* IS USING CHILDREN TO GET THE JINRYU STONE, WHICH HAS THE POWER TO CONTROL DRAGONS. TO SAVE BOTH WORLDS, REIJI JOINS ROKKAKU TO ENTER THE DRAGONIC HEAVEN COMPETITION IN RIKYU. THE BATTLE FOR THE GRAND PRIZE, THE JINRYU STONE, ENDS WITH KOHEI TOKI SEIZING THE STONE THROUGH UNDERHANDED TACTICS. REIJI MANAGES TO GET IN ONE HIT AS KOHEI IS TRANSPORTED BACK TO EARTH, BUT THE STONE APPEARS TO BE LOST...

Vol. 5 MISSION
CONTENTS

STAGE 17   **MISSION**
→ → → → → → → → → → → → 7

STAGE 18   **PROMISE**
→ → → → → → → → → → → → 59

STAGE 19   **HYSTERIC ROSE**
→ → → → → → → → → → → → 107

STAGE 20   **AUCTION**
→ → → → → → → → → → → → 153

DRAGON DRIVE

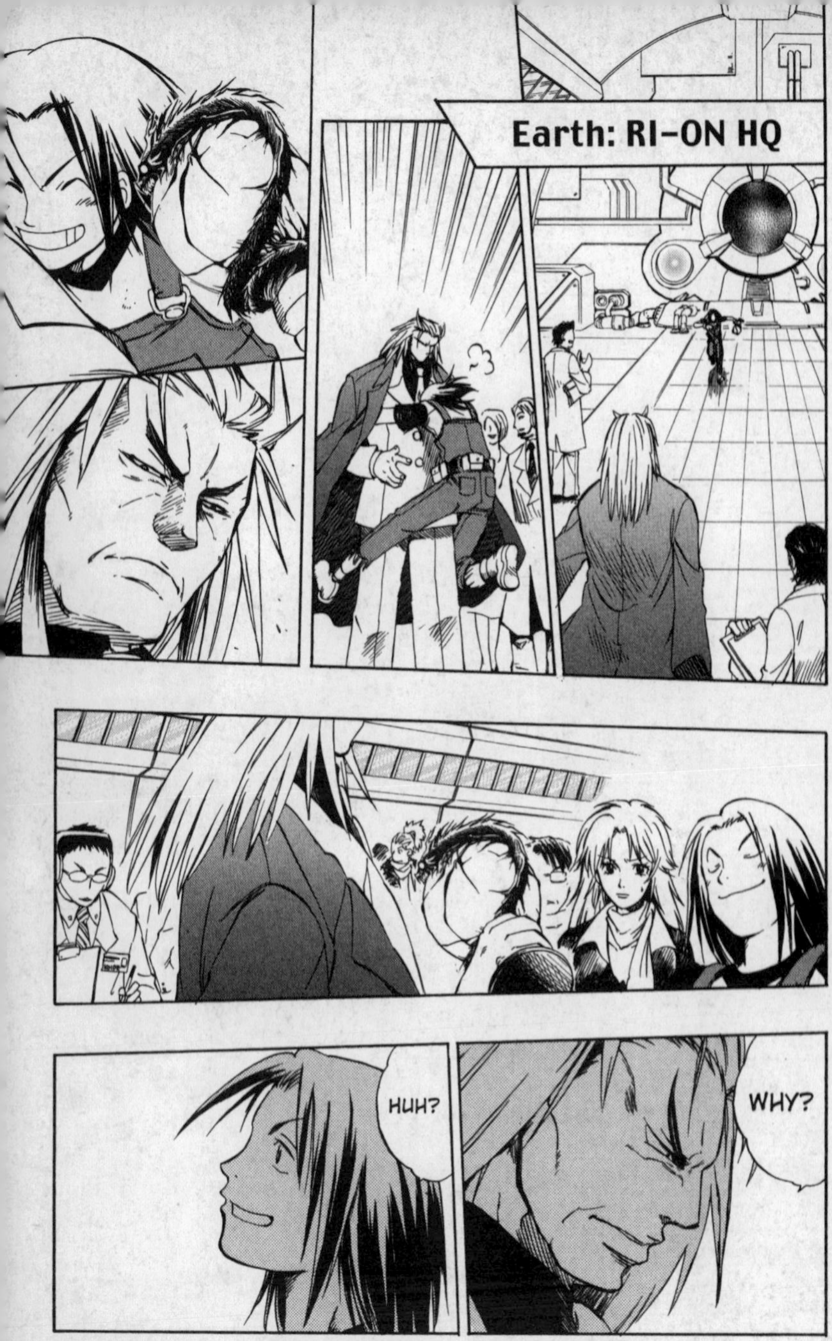
Earth: RI-ON HQ
WHY?
HUH?

STAGE17 MISSION

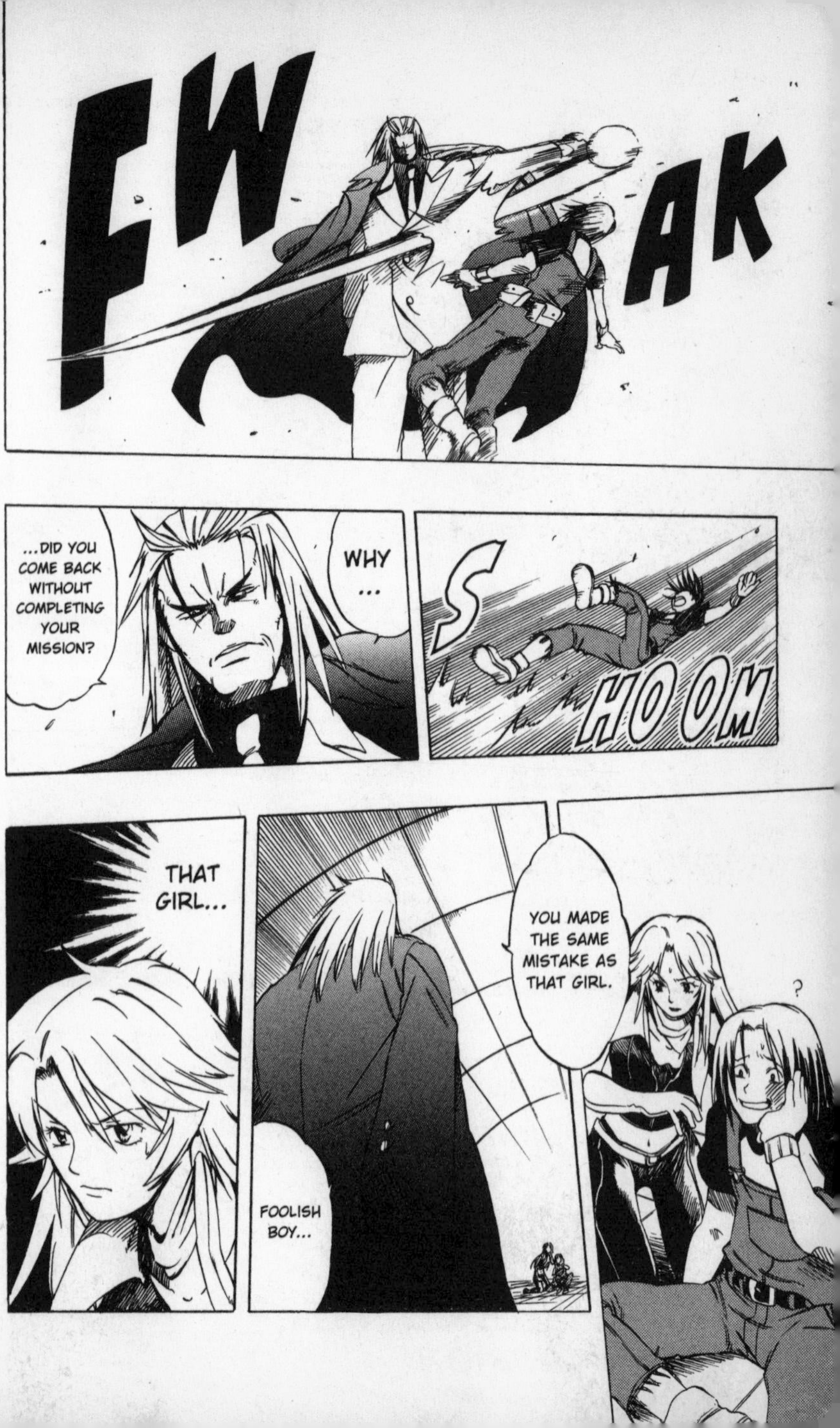
FWAK
SHOOM
WHY ...
...DID YOU COME BACK WITHOUT COMPLETING YOUR MISSION?
YOU MADE THE SAME MISTAKE AS THAT GIRL.
?
FOOLISH BOY...
THAT GIRL...

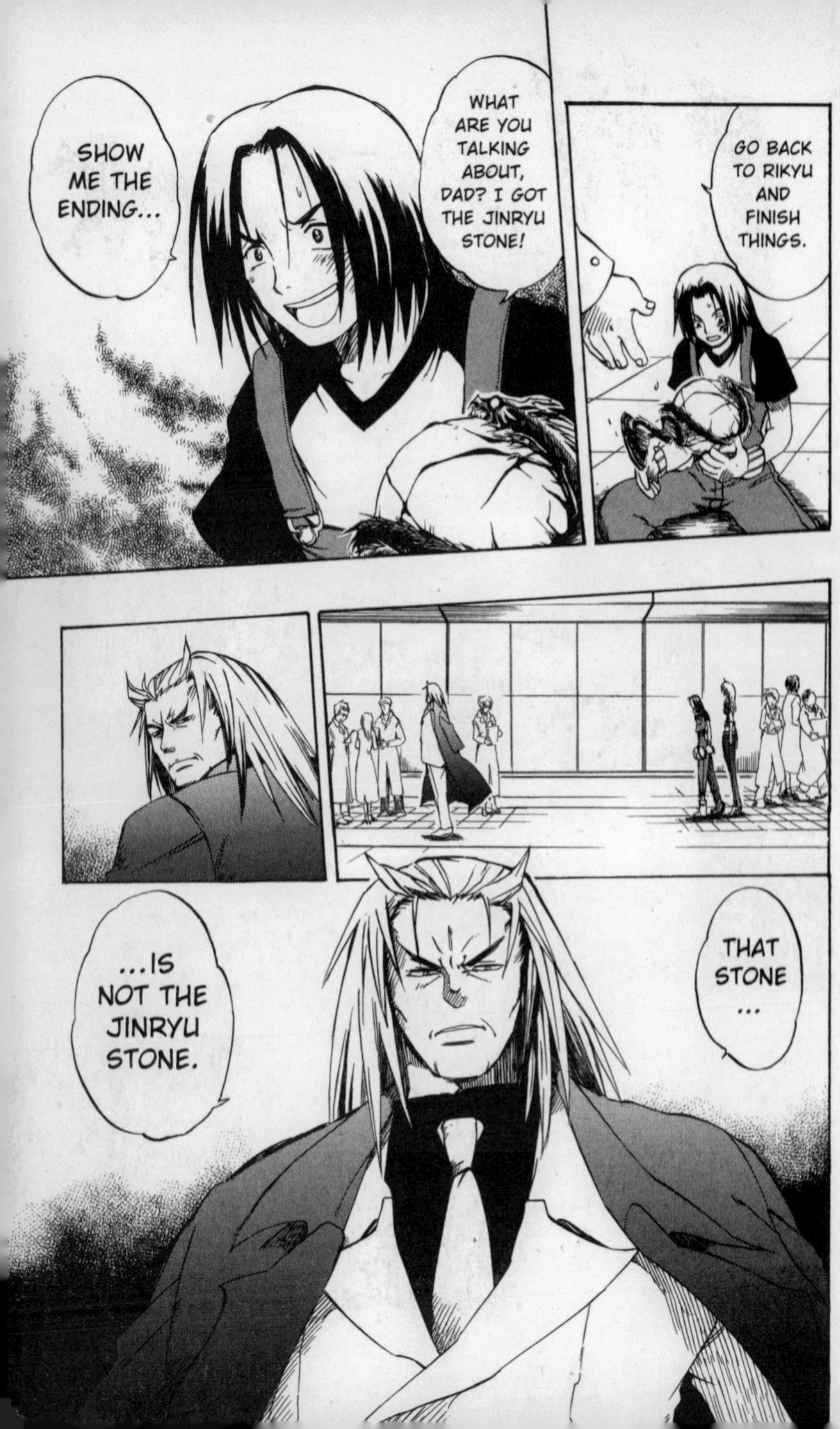
GO BACK TO RIKYU AND FINISH THINGS.
WHAT ARE YOU TALKING ABOUT, DAD? I GOT THE JINRYU STONE!
SHOW ME THE ENDING...
THAT STONE...
...IS NOT THE JINRYU STONE.

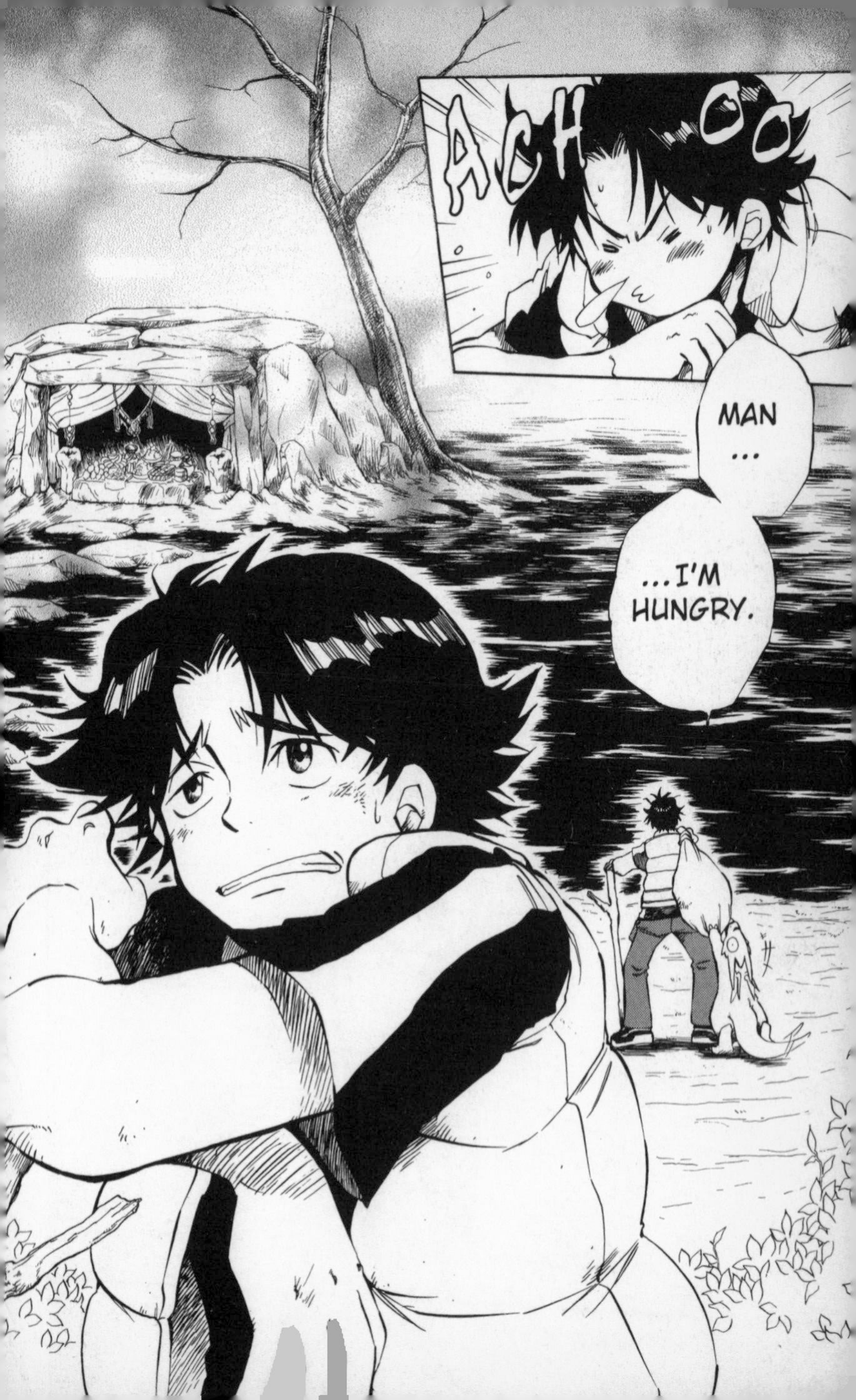
ACH-OO
MAN ...
...I'M HUNGRY.

STAGE17 MISSION

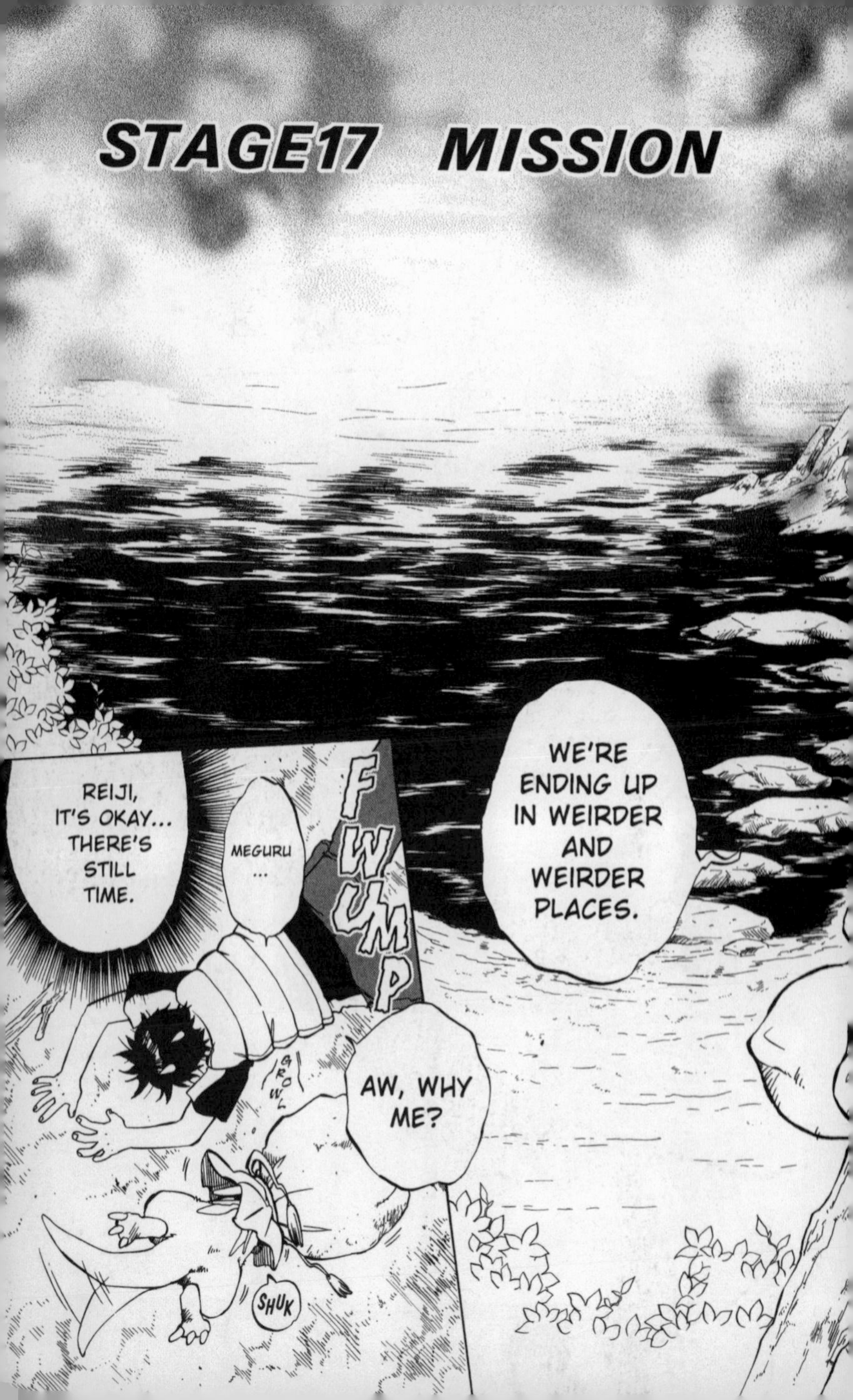
WE'RE ENDING UP IN WEIRDER AND WEIRDER PLACES.
FWUMP
MEGURU...
REIJI, IT'S OKAY... THERE'S STILL TIME.
AW, WHY ME?
GROWL
SHUK

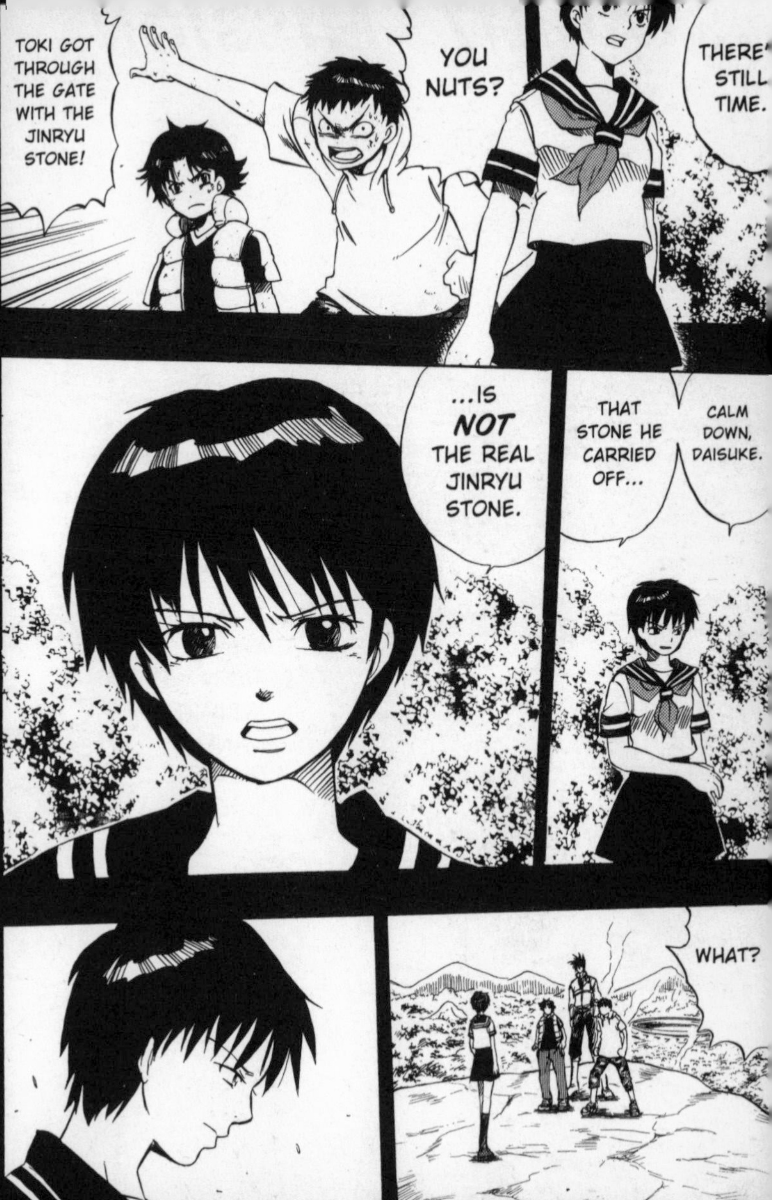
THERE' STILL TIME.
YOU NUTS?
TOKI GOT THROUGH THE GATE WITH THE JINRYU STONE!
CALM DOWN, DAISUKE.
THAT STONE HE CARRIED OFF...
...IS NOT THE REAL JINRYU STONE.
WHAT?

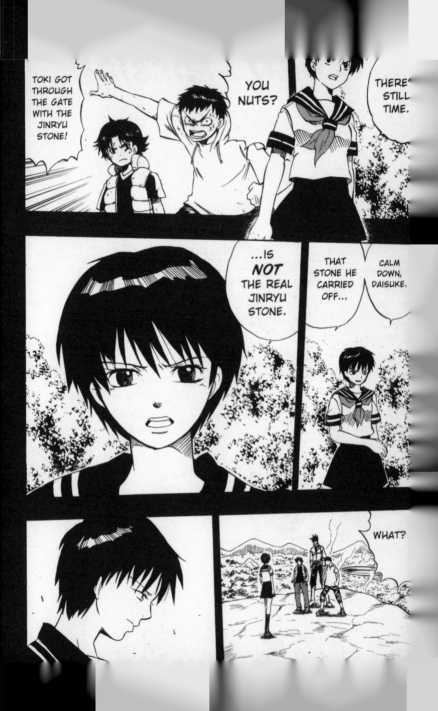

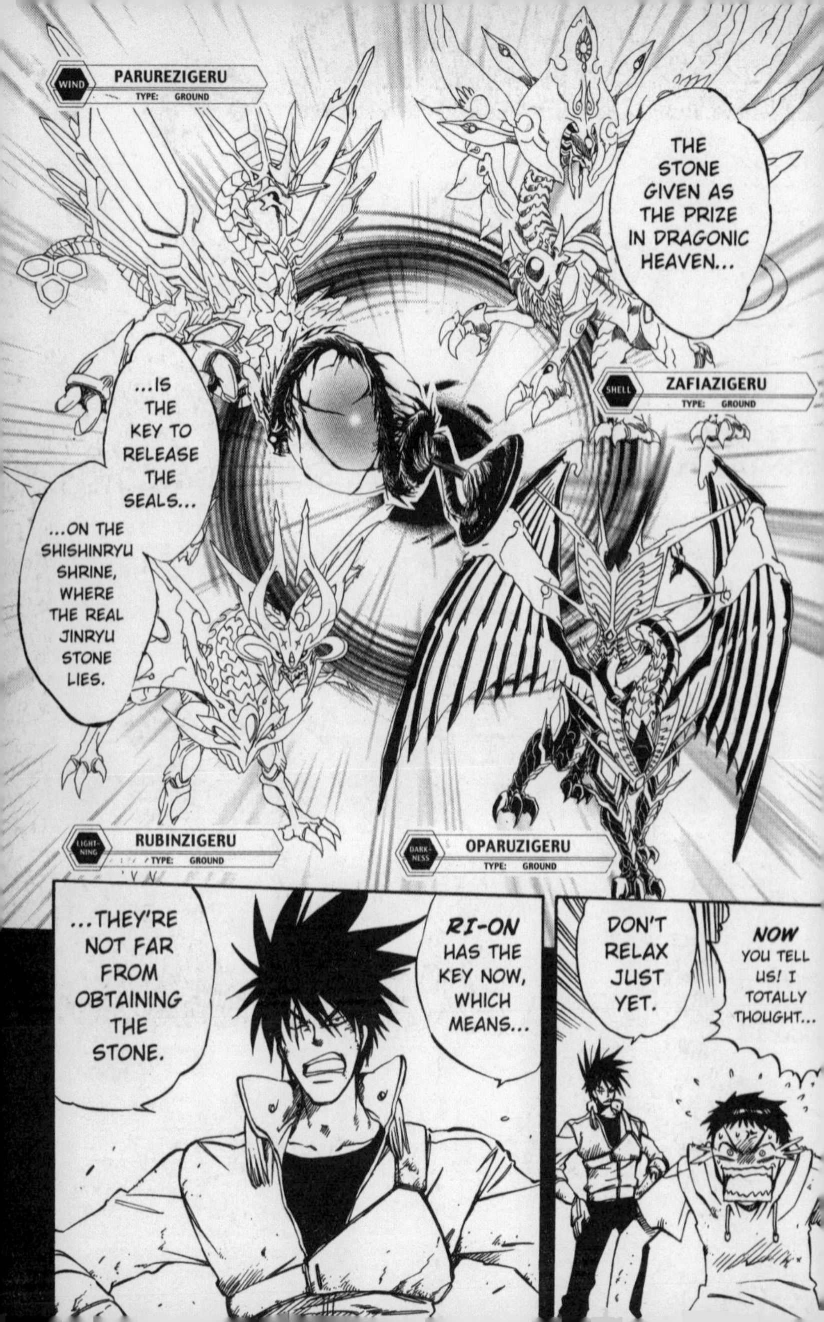
THE STONE GIVEN AS THE PRIZE IN DRAGONIC HEAVEN...
...IS THE KEY TO RELEASE THE SEALS...
...ON THE SHISHINRYU SHRINE, WHERE THE REAL JINRYU STONE LIES.
SHELL ZAFIAZIGERU TYPE: GROUND
WIND PARUREZIGERU TYPE: GROUND
DARKNESS OPARUZIGERU TYPE: GROUND
LIGHTNING RUBINZIGERU TYPE: GROUND
DON'T RELAX JUST YET.
NOW YOU TELL US! I TOTALLY THOUGHT...
RI-ON HAS THE KEY NOW, WHICH MEANS...
...THEY'RE NOT FAR FROM OBTAINING THE STONE.

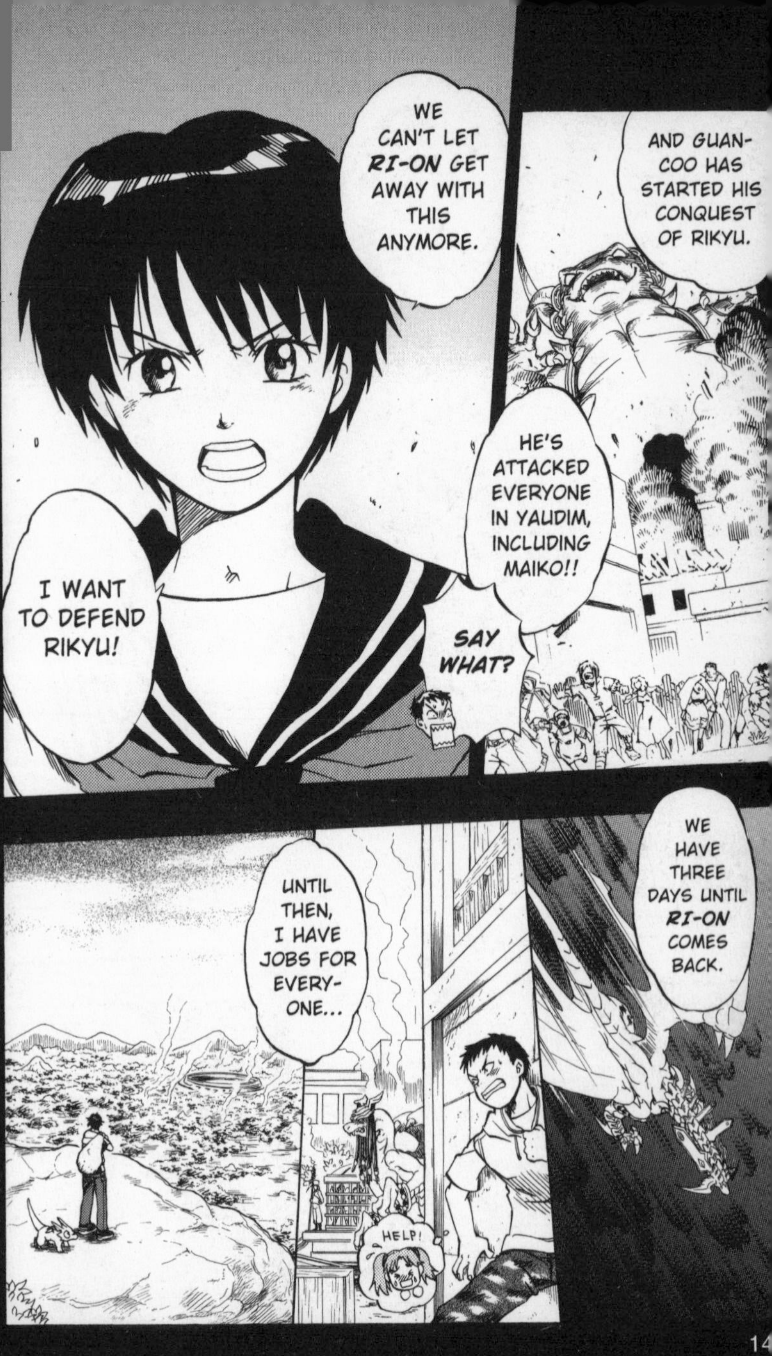
AND GUAN-COO HAS STARTED HIS CONQUEST OF RIKYU.
HE'S ATTACKED EVERYONE IN YAUDIM, INCLUDING MAIKO!!
WE CAN'T LET RI-ON GET AWAY WITH THIS ANYMORE.
SAY WHAT?
I WANT TO DEFEND RIKYU!
WE HAVE THREE DAYS UNTIL RI-ON COMES BACK.
UNTIL THEN, I HAVE JOBS FOR EVERY-ONE...
HELP!

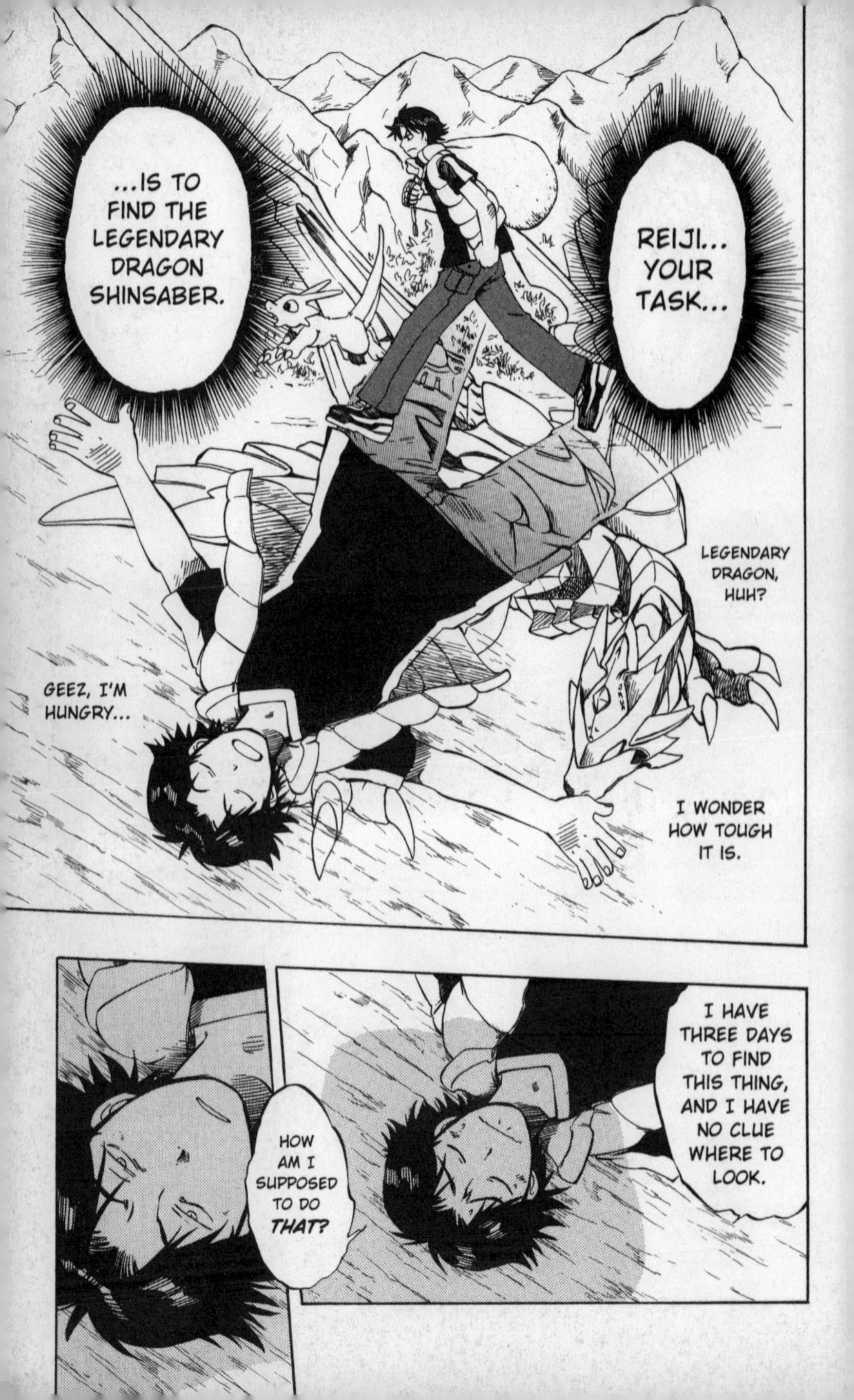
REIJI... YOUR TASK...
...IS TO FIND THE LEGENDARY DRAGON SHINSABER.
LEGENDARY DRAGON, HUH?
GEEZ, I'M HUNGRY...
I WONDER HOW TOUGH IT IS.
I HAVE THREE DAYS TO FIND THIS THING, AND I HAVE NO CLUE WHERE TO LOOK.
HOW AM I SUPPOSED TO DO *THAT?*

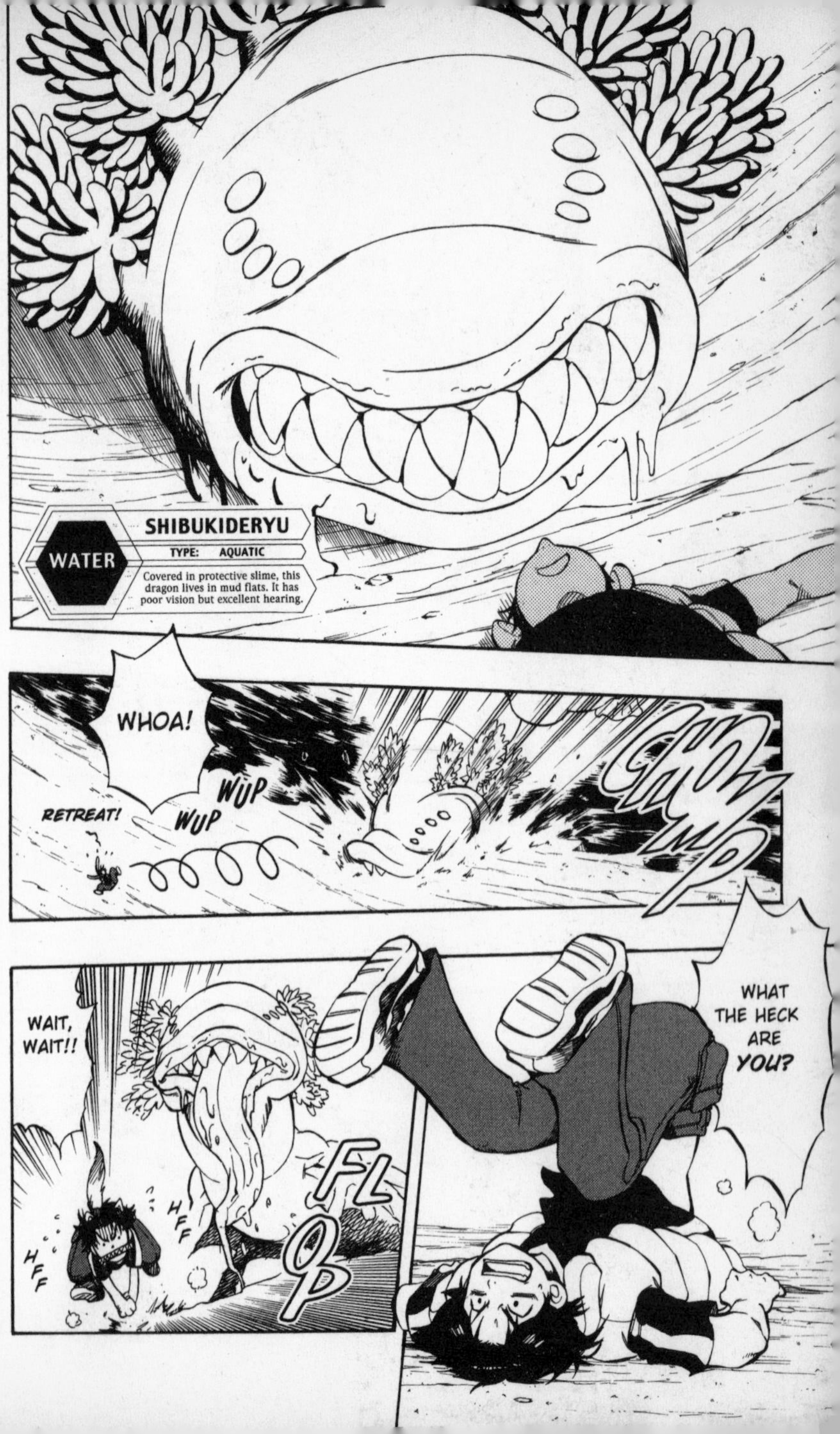
SHIBUKIDERYU
WATER
TYPE: AQUATIC
Covered in protective slime, this dragon lives in mud flats. It has poor vision but excellent hearing.
CHOMP
WHOA!
WUP
WUP
RETREAT!
WHAT THE HECK ARE YOU?
WAIT, WAIT!!
FLOP
HFF
HFF

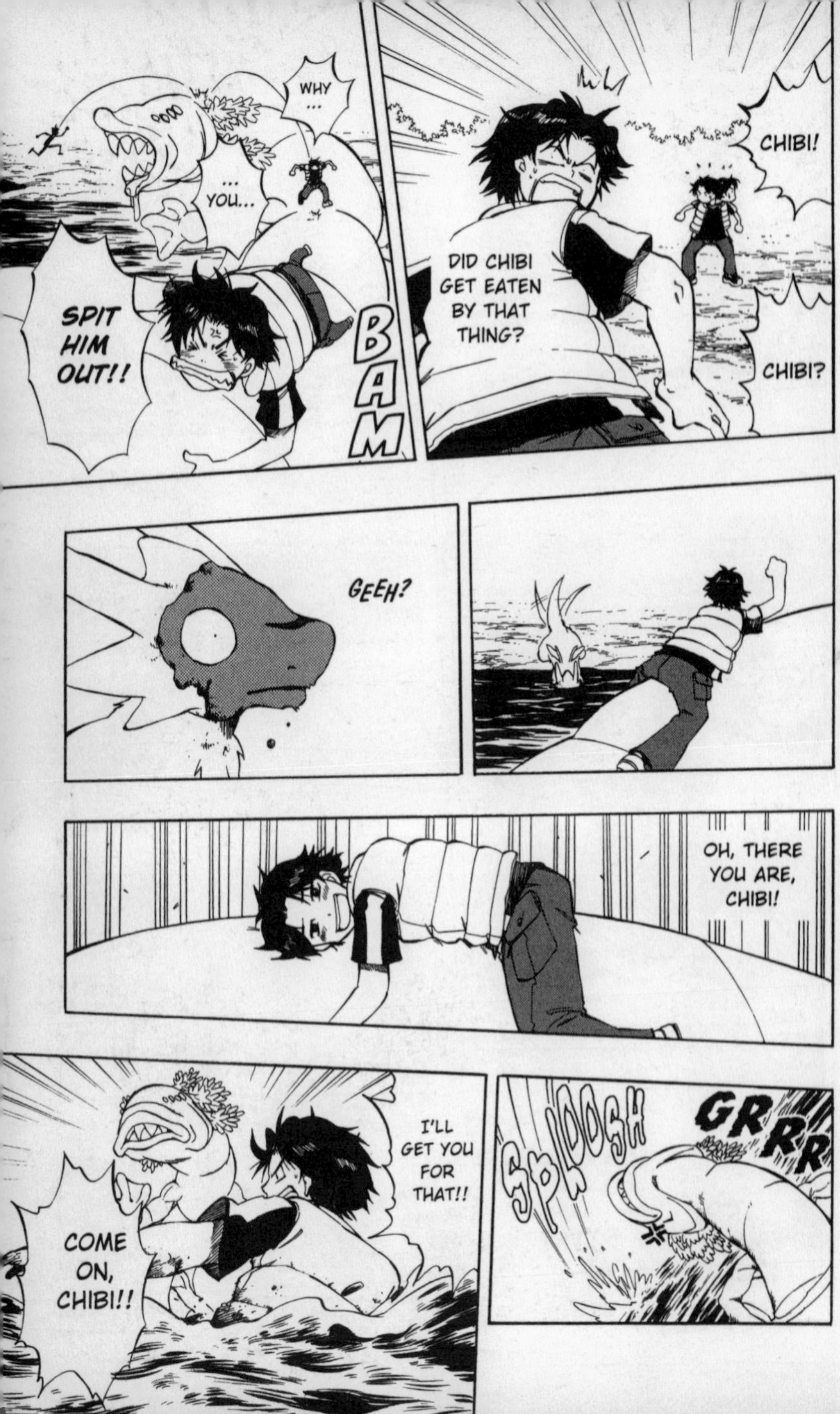
CHIBI!
CHIBI?
DID CHIBI GET EATEN BY THAT THING?
WHY ...
... YOU...
BAM
SPIT HIM OUT!!
GEEH?
OH, THERE YOU ARE, CHIBI!
GRRR
SPLOOSH
I'LL GET YOU FOR THAT!!
COME ON, CHIBI!!

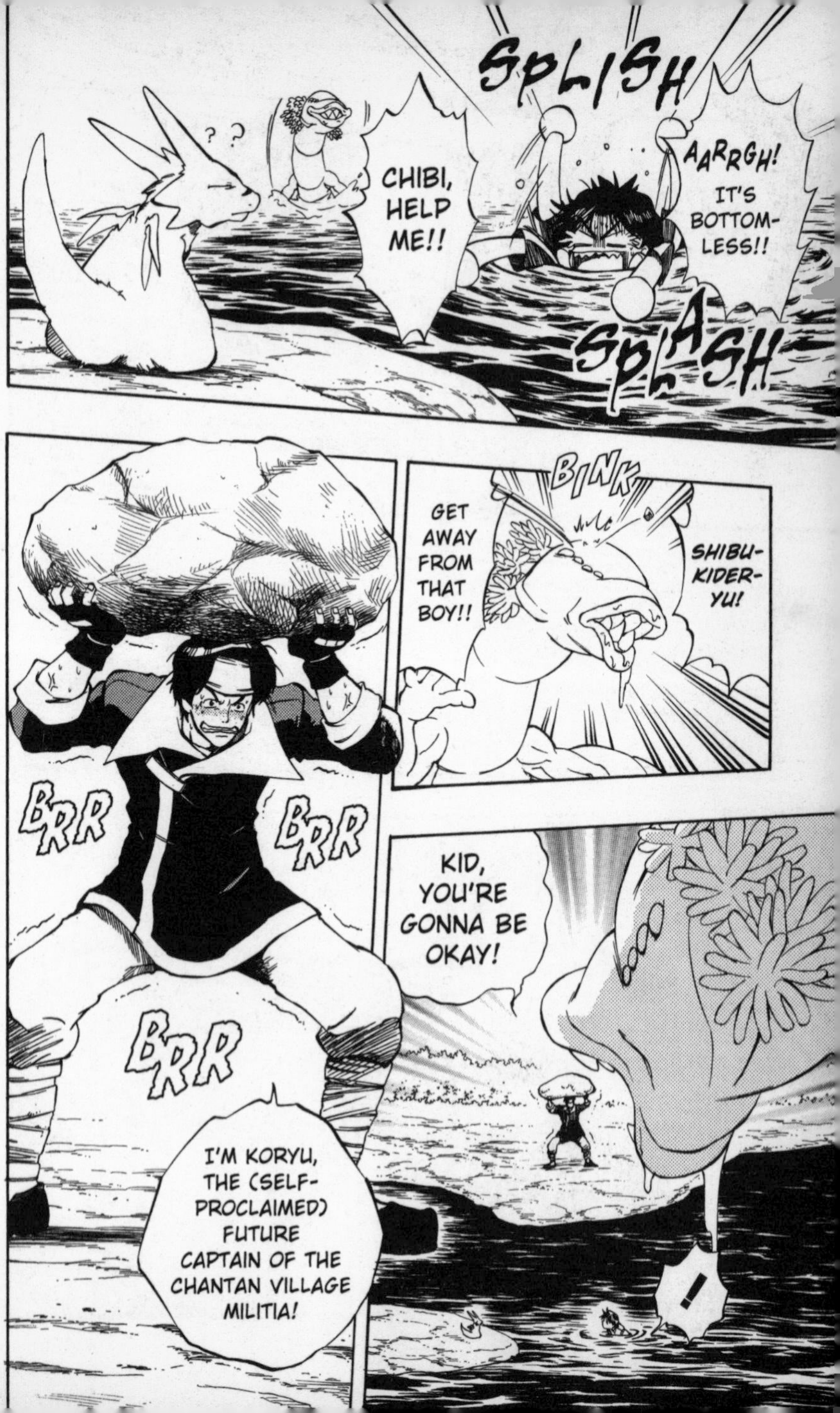
SPLISH
AARRGH! IT'S BOTTOMLESS!!
SPLASH
CHIBI, HELP ME!!
? ?
BINK
SHIBUKIDERYU!
GET AWAY FROM THAT BOY!!
KID, YOU'RE GONNA BE OKAY!
!
BRR
BRR
BRR
I'M KORYU, THE (SELF-PROCLAIMED) FUTURE CAPTAIN OF THE CHANTAN VILLAGE MILITIA!

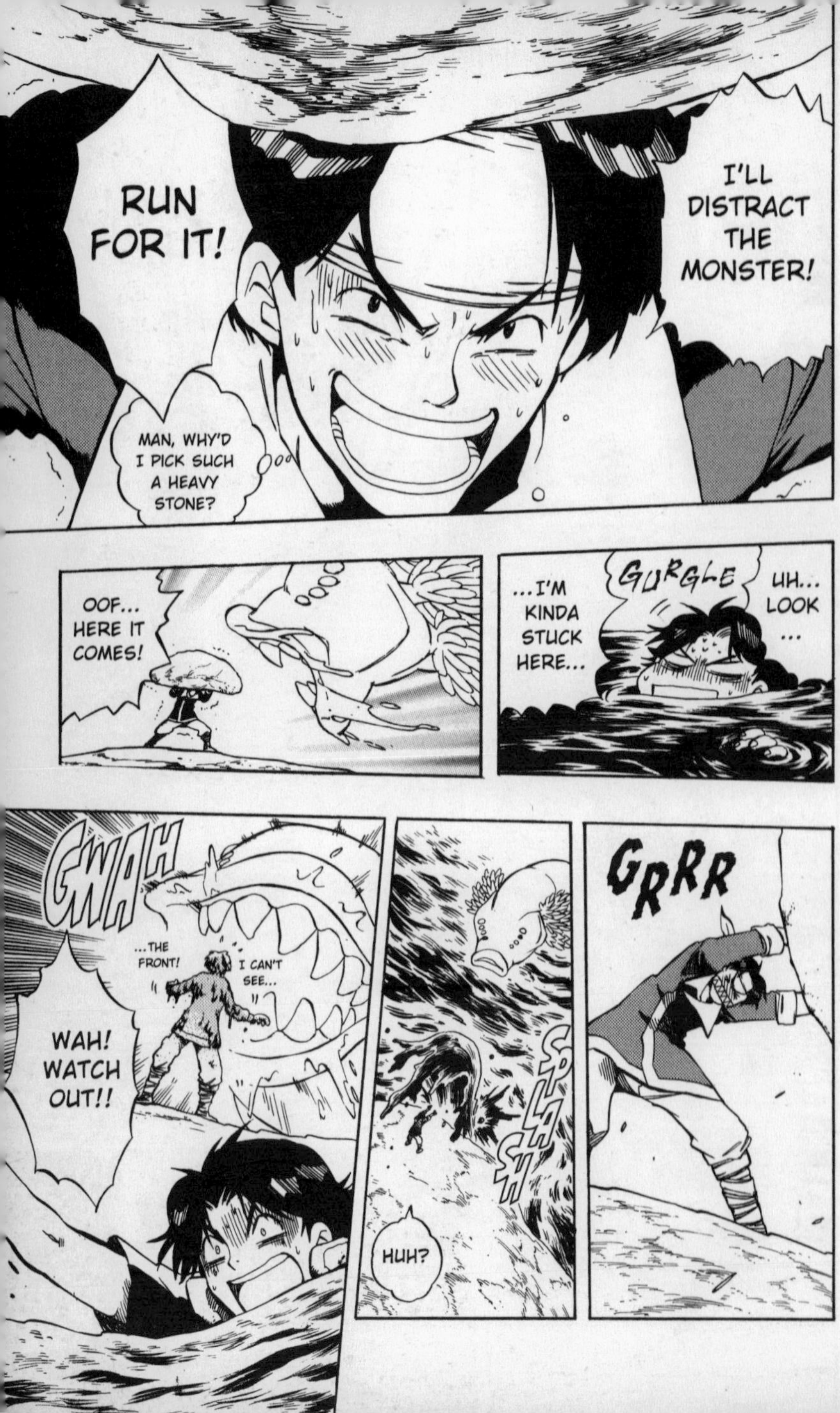
I'LL DISTRACT THE MONSTER!
RUN FOR IT!
MAN, WHY'D I PICK SUCH A HEAVY STONE?
UH... LOOK ...
GURGLE
...I'M KINDA STUCK HERE...
OOF... HERE IT COMES!
GRRR
SPLASH
HUH?
GWAH
I CAN'T SEE...
...THE FRONT!
WAH! WATCH OUT!!

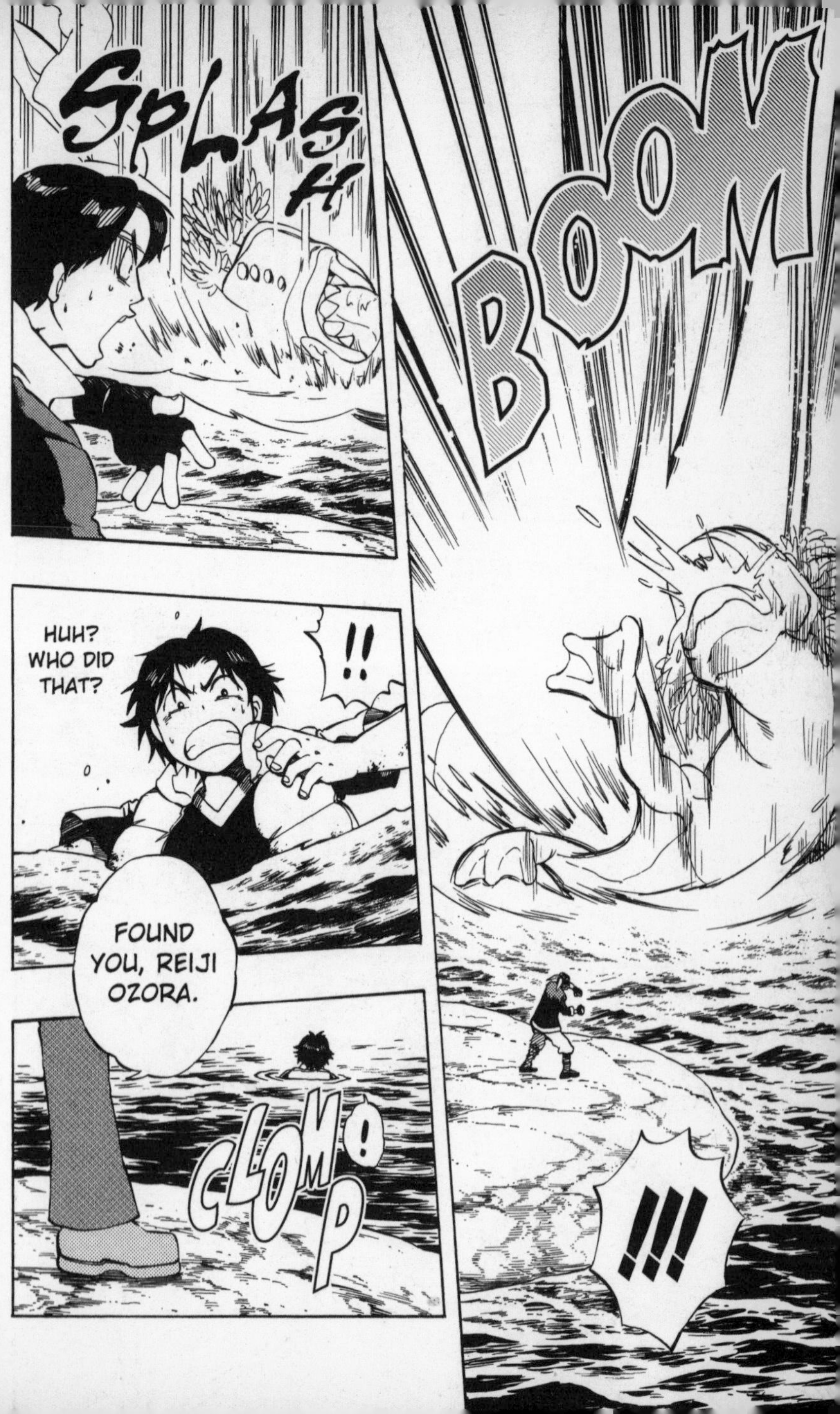
BOOM
!!!
SPLASH
!!
HUH? WHO DID THAT?
FOUND YOU, REIJI OZORA.
CLOMP

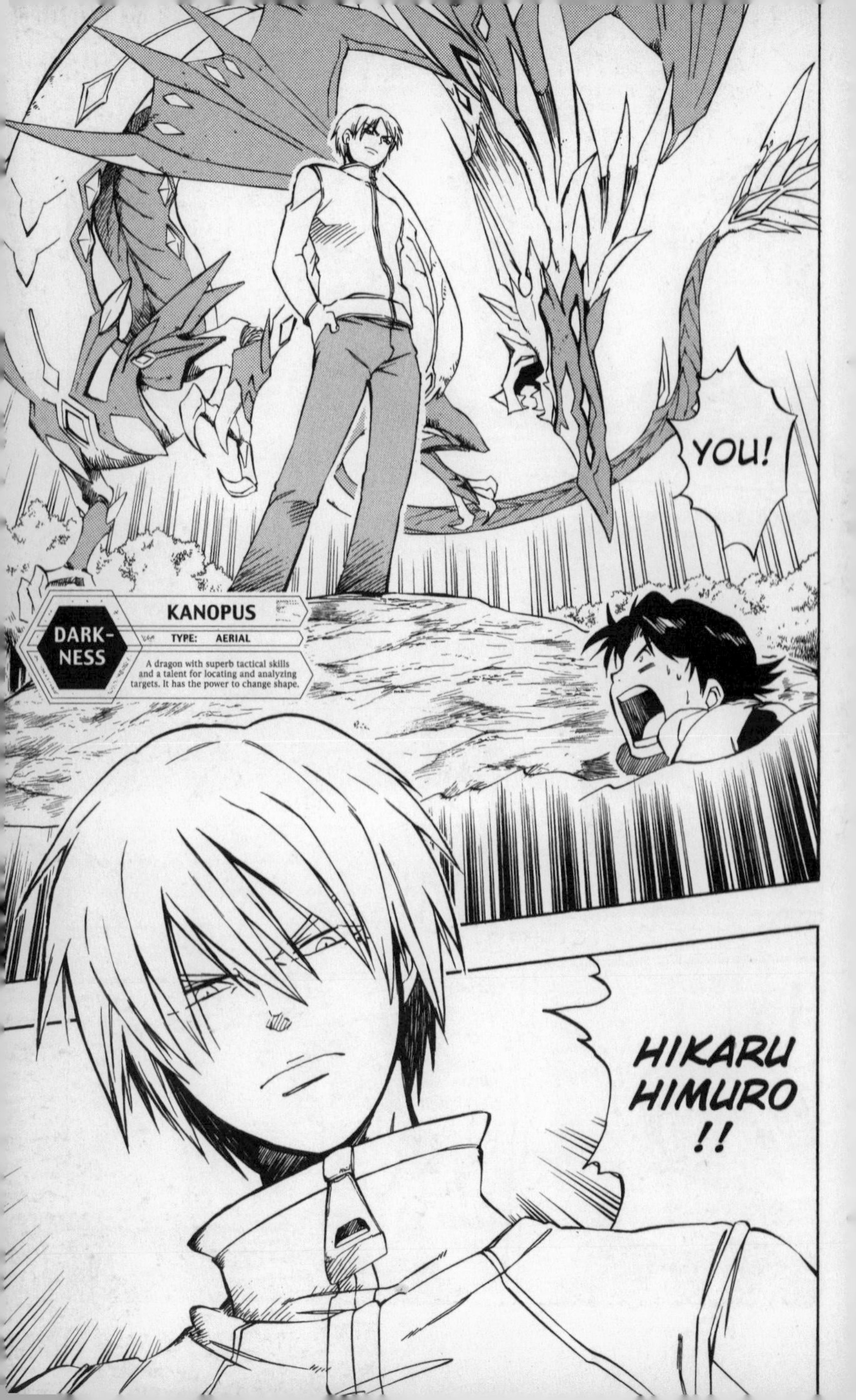
YOU!
KANOPUS
DARK-NESS
TYPE: AERIAL
A dragon with superb tactical skills and a talent for locating and analyzing targets. It has the power to change shape.
HIKARU HIMURO !!

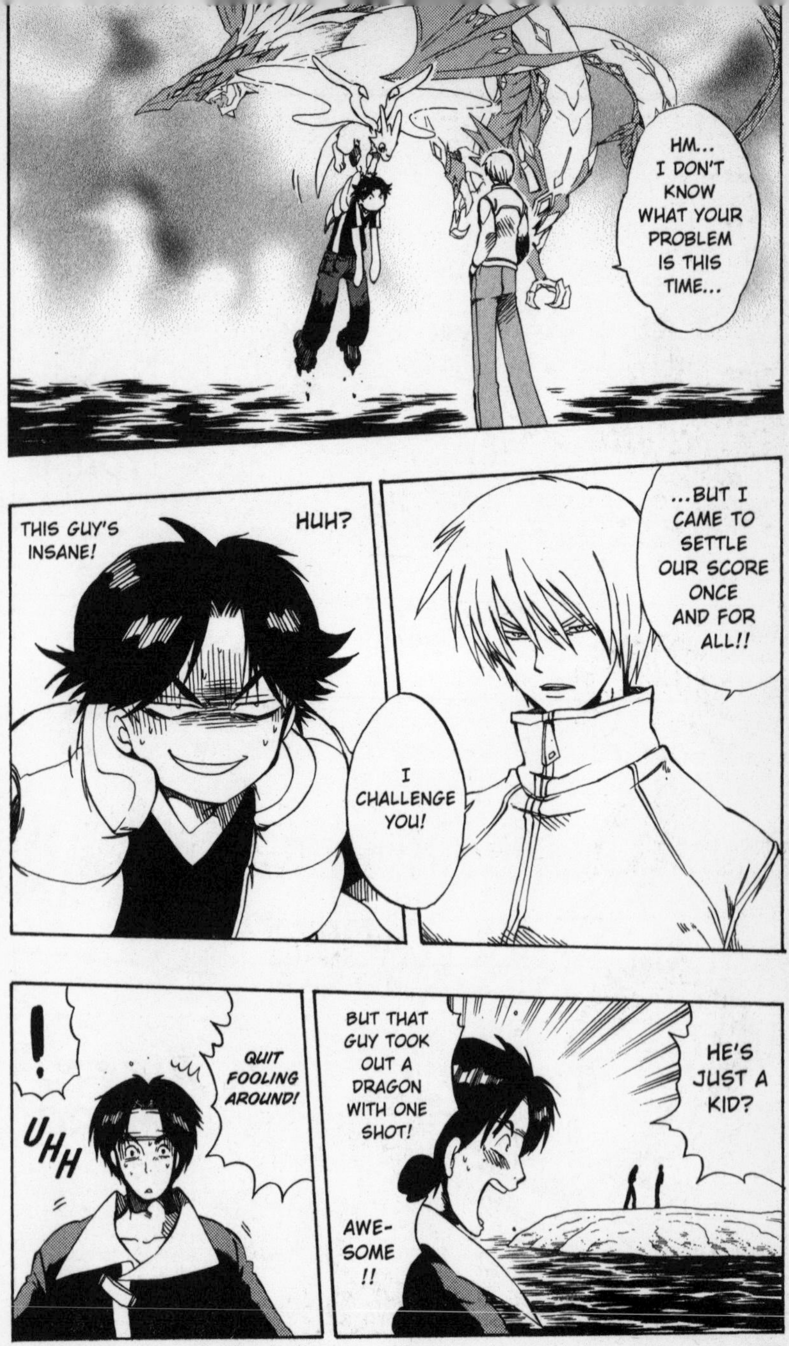
HM... I DON'T KNOW WHAT YOUR PROBLEM IS THIS TIME...
...BUT I CAME TO SETTLE OUR SCORE ONCE AND FOR ALL!!
I CHALLENGE YOU!
HUH?
THIS GUY'S INSANE!
HE'S JUST A KID?
BUT THAT GUY TOOK OUT A DRAGON WITH ONE SHOT!
AWE-SOME!!
!
QUIT FOOLING AROUND!
UHH

READ THIS WAY

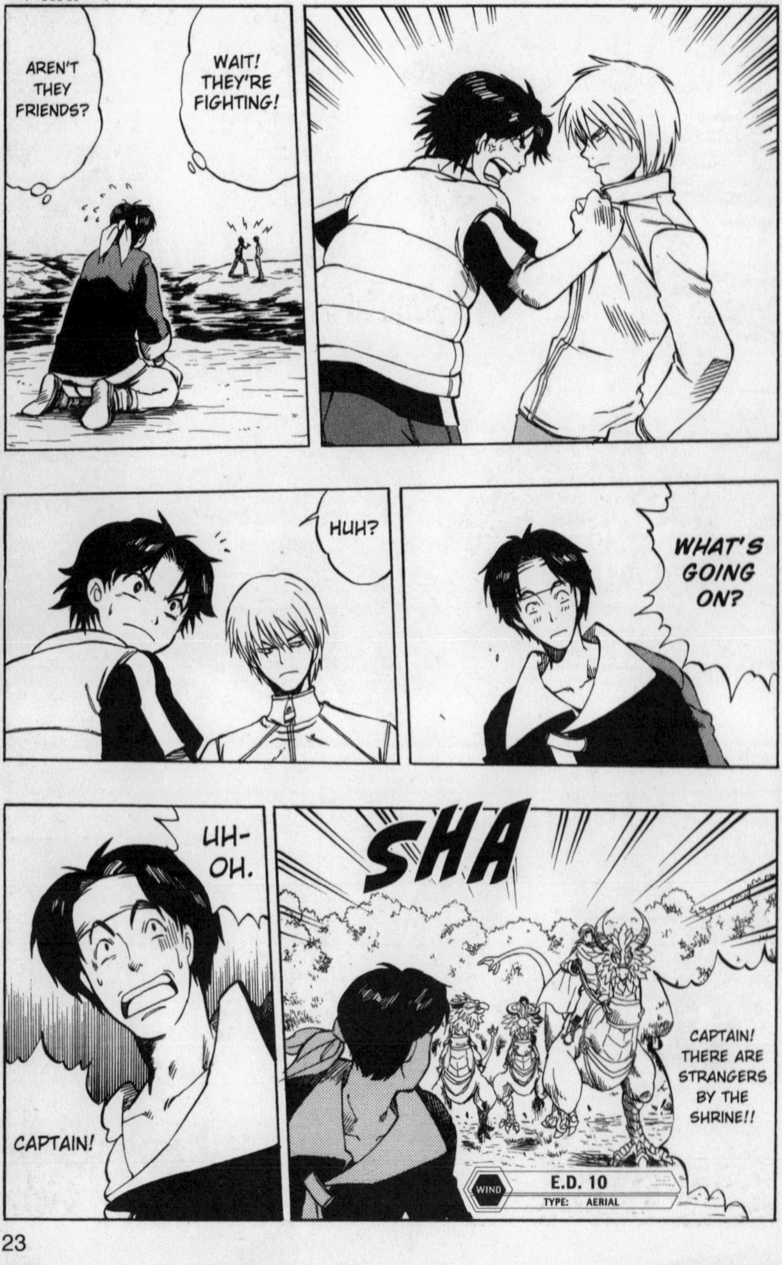

WAIT! THEY'RE FIGHTING!
AREN'T THEY FRIENDS?
WHAT'S GOING ON?
HUH?
SHA
CAPTAIN! THERE ARE STRANGERS BY THE SHRINE!!
WIND
E.D. 10
TYPE: AERIAL
UH-OH.
CAPTAIN!

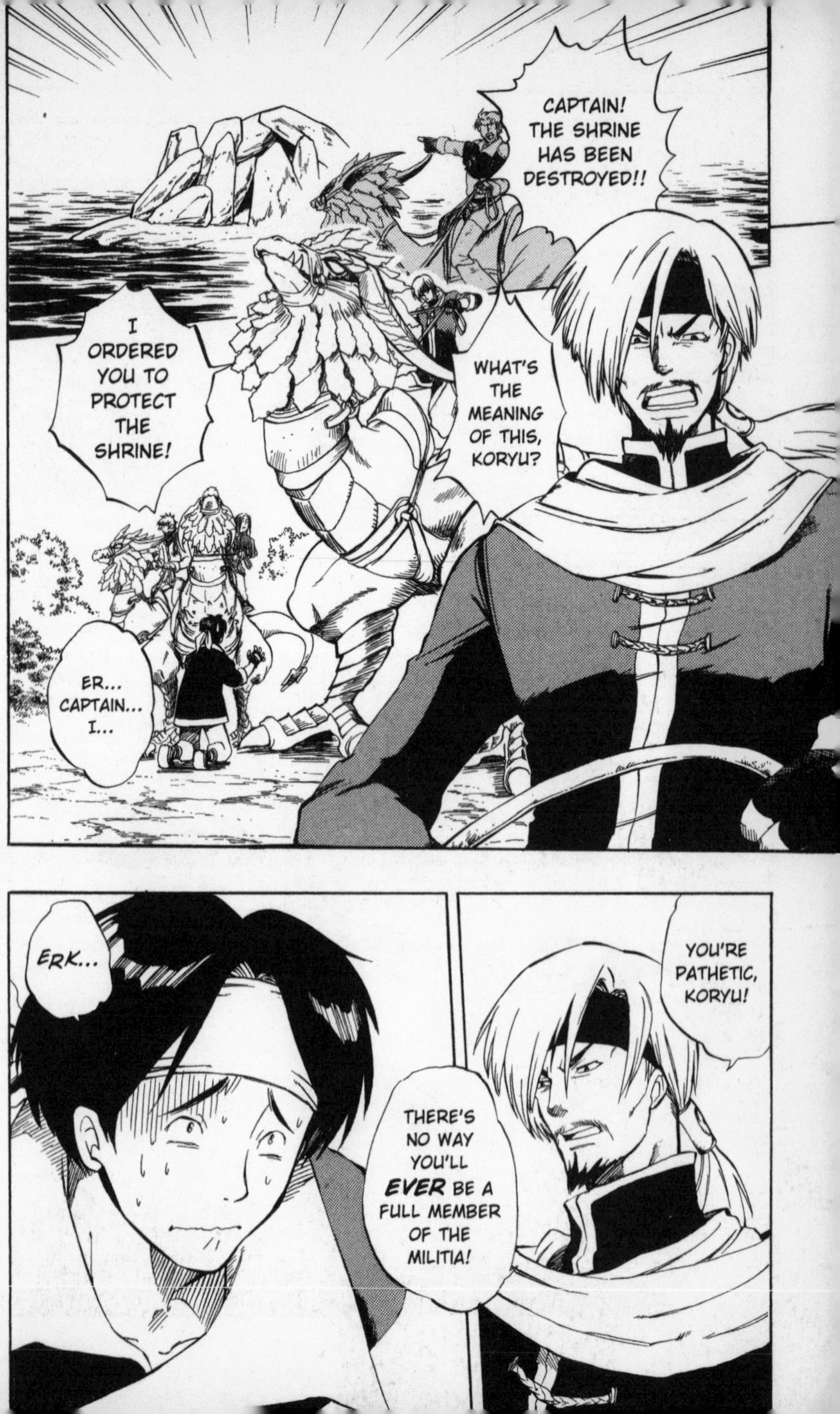
CAPTAIN! THE SHRINE HAS BEEN DESTROYED!!
WHAT'S THE MEANING OF THIS, KORYU?
I ORDERED YOU TO PROTECT THE SHRINE!
ER... CAPTAIN... I...
YOU'RE PATHETIC, KORYU!
THERE'S NO WAY YOU'LL ***EVER*** BE A FULL MEMBER OF THE MILITIA!
ERK...

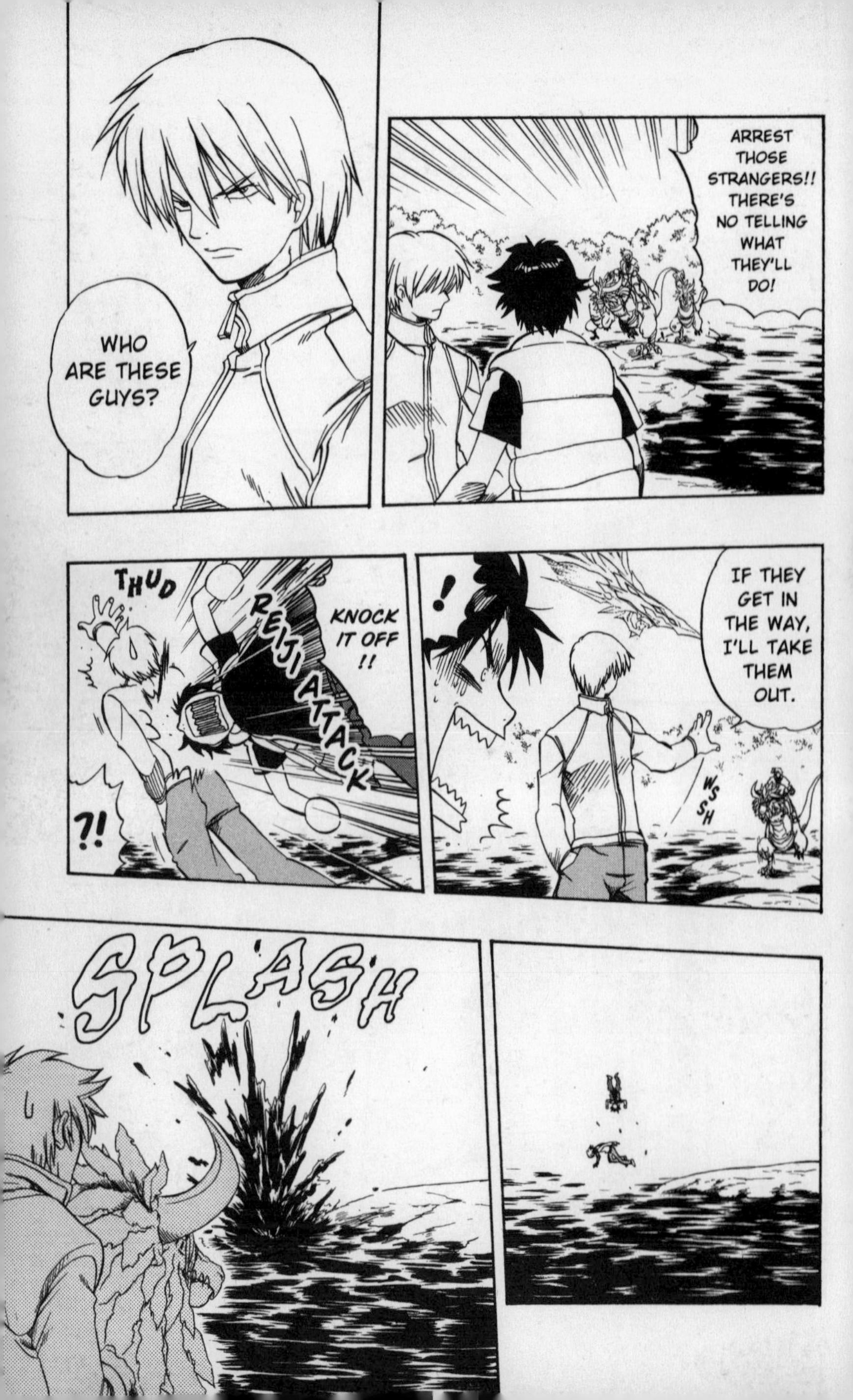
ARREST THOSE STRANGERS!! THERE'S NO TELLING WHAT THEY'LL DO!
WHO ARE THESE GUYS?
!
IF THEY GET IN THE WAY, I'LL TAKE THEM OUT.
WSSH
THUD
REIJI ATTACK
KNOCK IT OFF!!
?!
SPLASH

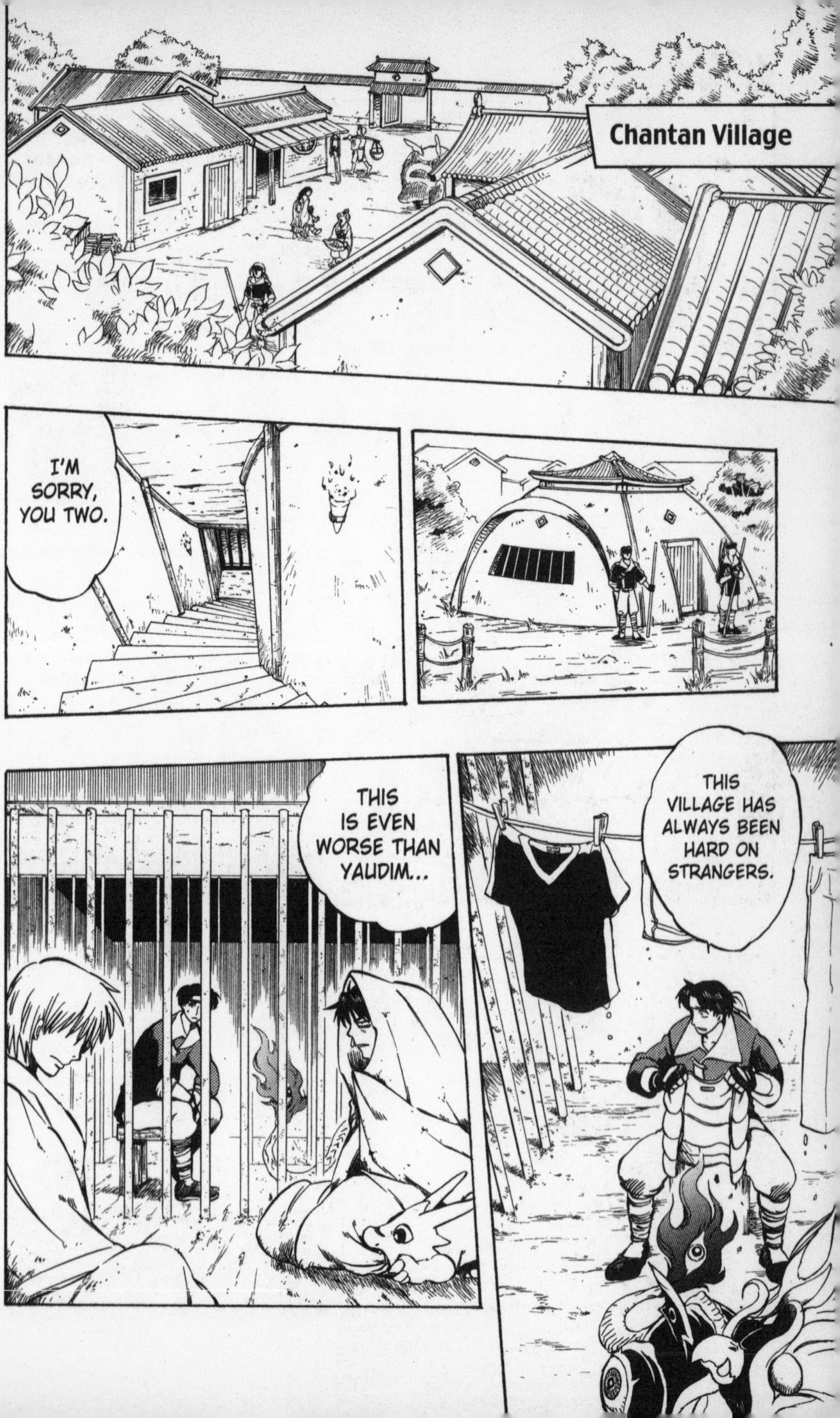
Chantan Village
I'M SORRY, YOU TWO.
THIS VILLAGE HAS ALWAYS BEEN HARD ON STRANGERS.
THIS IS EVEN WORSE THAN YAUDIM...

READ THIS WAY

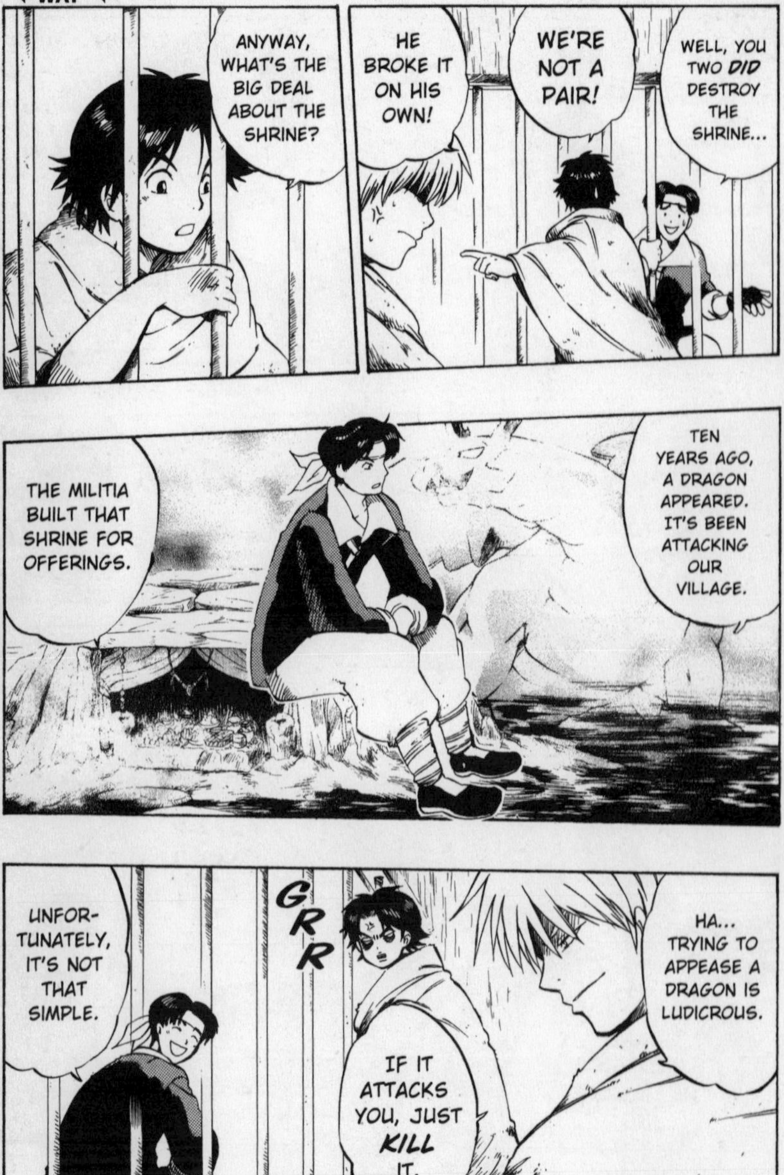
WELL, YOU TWO *DID* DESTROY THE SHRINE...
WE'RE NOT A PAIR!
HE BROKE IT ON HIS OWN!
ANYWAY, WHAT'S THE BIG DEAL ABOUT THE SHRINE?
TEN YEARS AGO, A DRAGON APPEARED. IT'S BEEN ATTACKING OUR VILLAGE.
THE MILITIA BUILT THAT SHRINE FOR OFFERINGS.
HA... TRYING TO APPEASE A DRAGON IS LUDICROUS.
IF IT ATTACKS YOU, JUST *KILL* IT.
GRR
UNFORTUNATELY, IT'S NOT THAT SIMPLE.

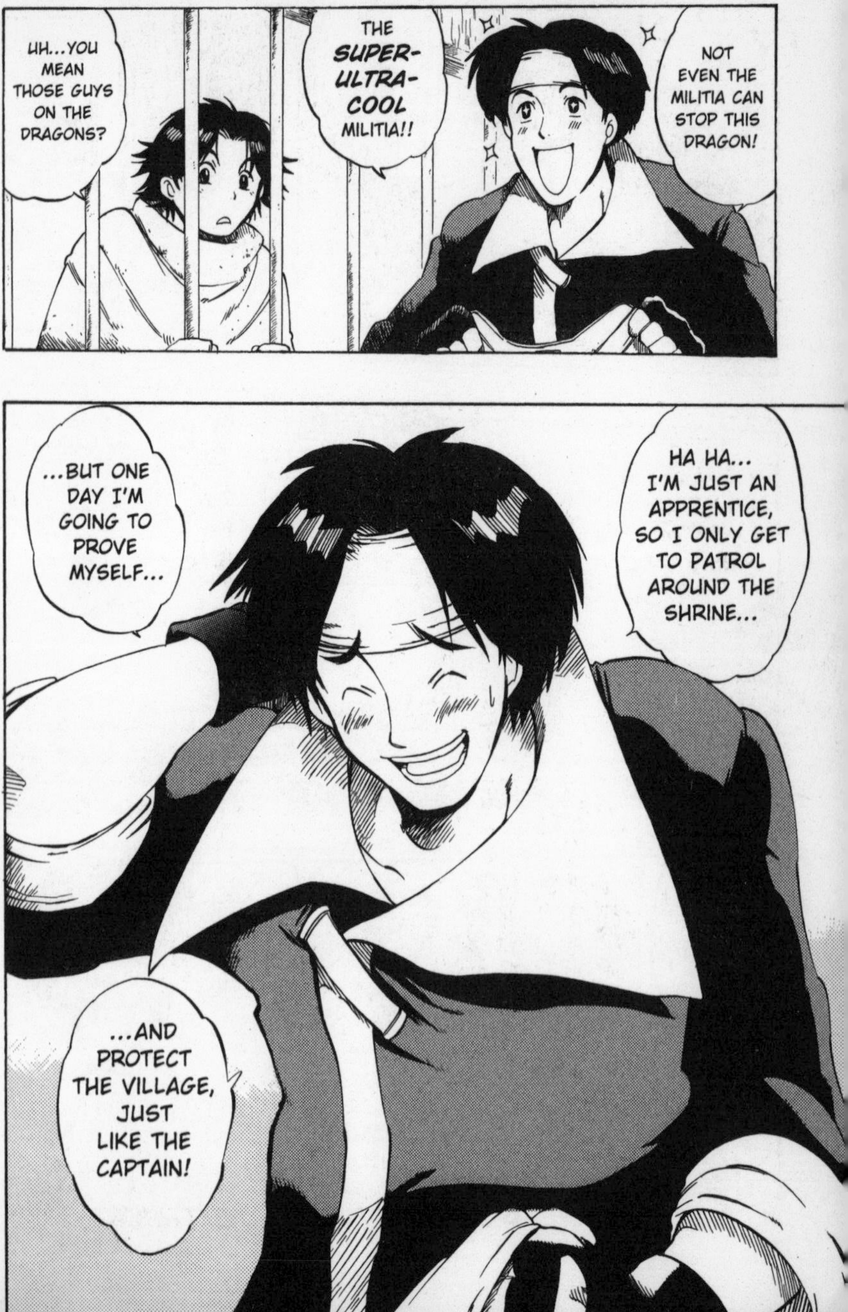
NOT EVEN THE MILITIA CAN STOP THIS DRAGON!
THE SUPER-ULTRA-COOL MILITIA!!
UH...YOU MEAN THOSE GUYS ON THE DRAGONS?
HA HA... I'M JUST AN APPRENTICE, SO I ONLY GET TO PATROL AROUND THE SHRINE...
...BUT ONE DAY I'M GOING TO PROVE MYSELF...
...AND PROTECT THE VILLAGE, JUST LIKE THE CAPTAIN!

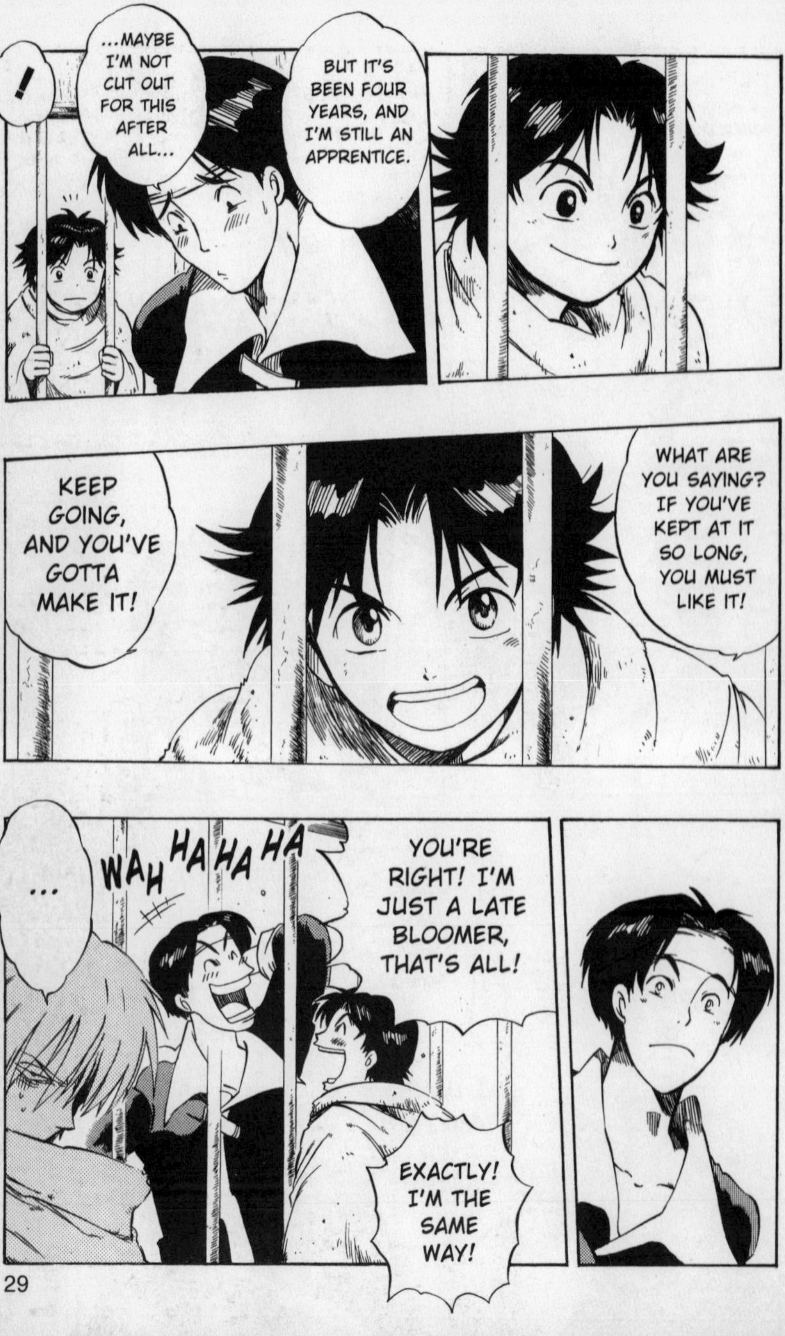
BUT IT'S BEEN FOUR YEARS, AND I'M STILL AN APPRENTICE.
...MAYBE I'M NOT CUT OUT FOR THIS AFTER ALL...
!
WHAT ARE YOU SAYING? IF YOU'VE KEPT AT IT SO LONG, YOU MUST LIKE IT!
KEEP GOING, AND YOU'VE GOTTA MAKE IT!
YOU'RE RIGHT! I'M JUST A LATE BLOOMER, THAT'S ALL!
WAH HA HA HA HA
...
EXACTLY! I'M THE SAME WAY!

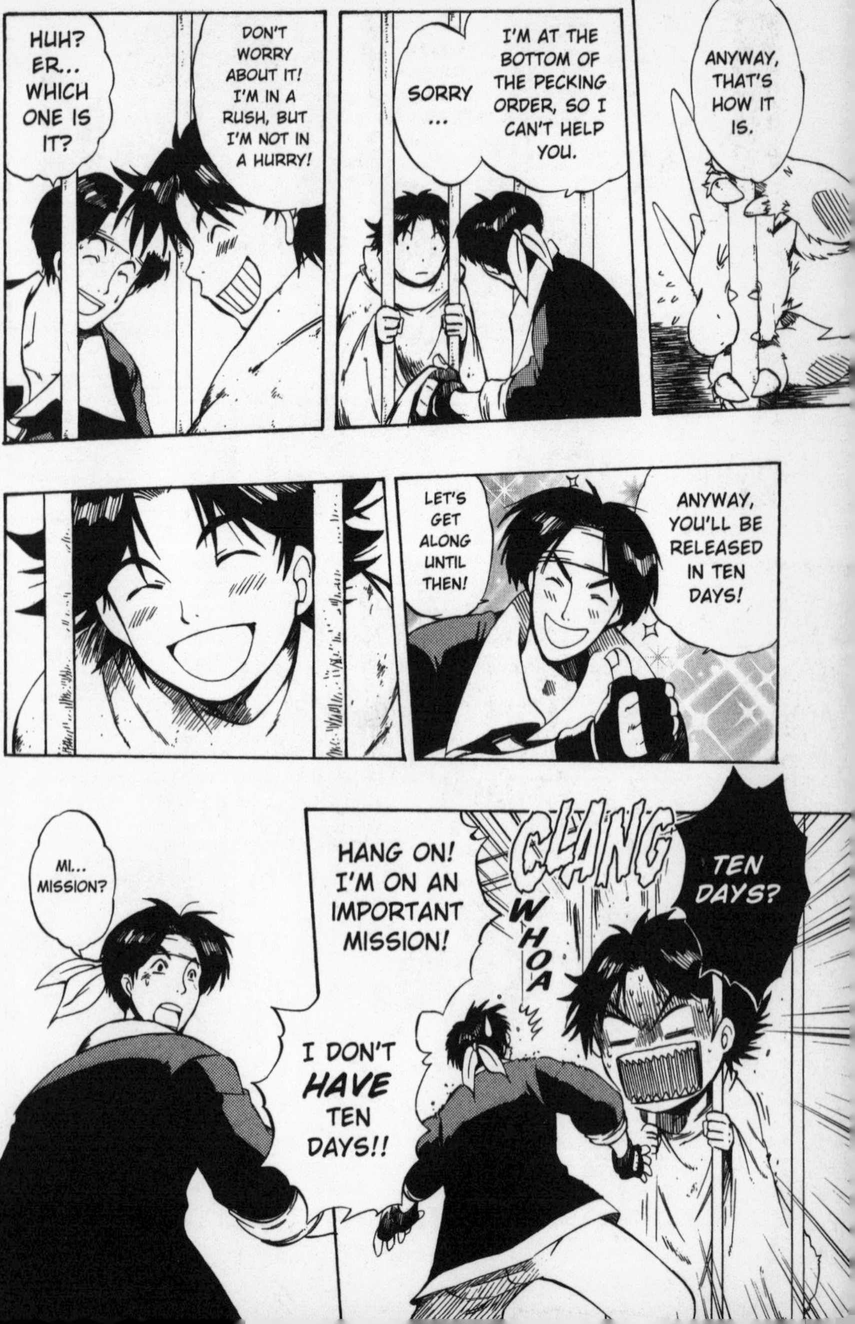

ANYWAY, THAT'S HOW IT IS.
I'M AT THE BOTTOM OF THE PECKING ORDER, SO I CAN'T HELP YOU.
SORRY...
DON'T WORRY ABOUT IT! I'M IN A RUSH, BUT I'M NOT IN A HURRY!
HUH? ER... WHICH ONE IS IT?
ANYWAY, YOU'LL BE RELEASED IN TEN DAYS!
LET'S GET ALONG UNTIL THEN!
TEN DAYS?
CLANG
WHOA
HANG ON! I'M ON AN IMPORTANT MISSION!
I DON'T HAVE TEN DAYS!!
MI... MISSION?

READ THIS WAY

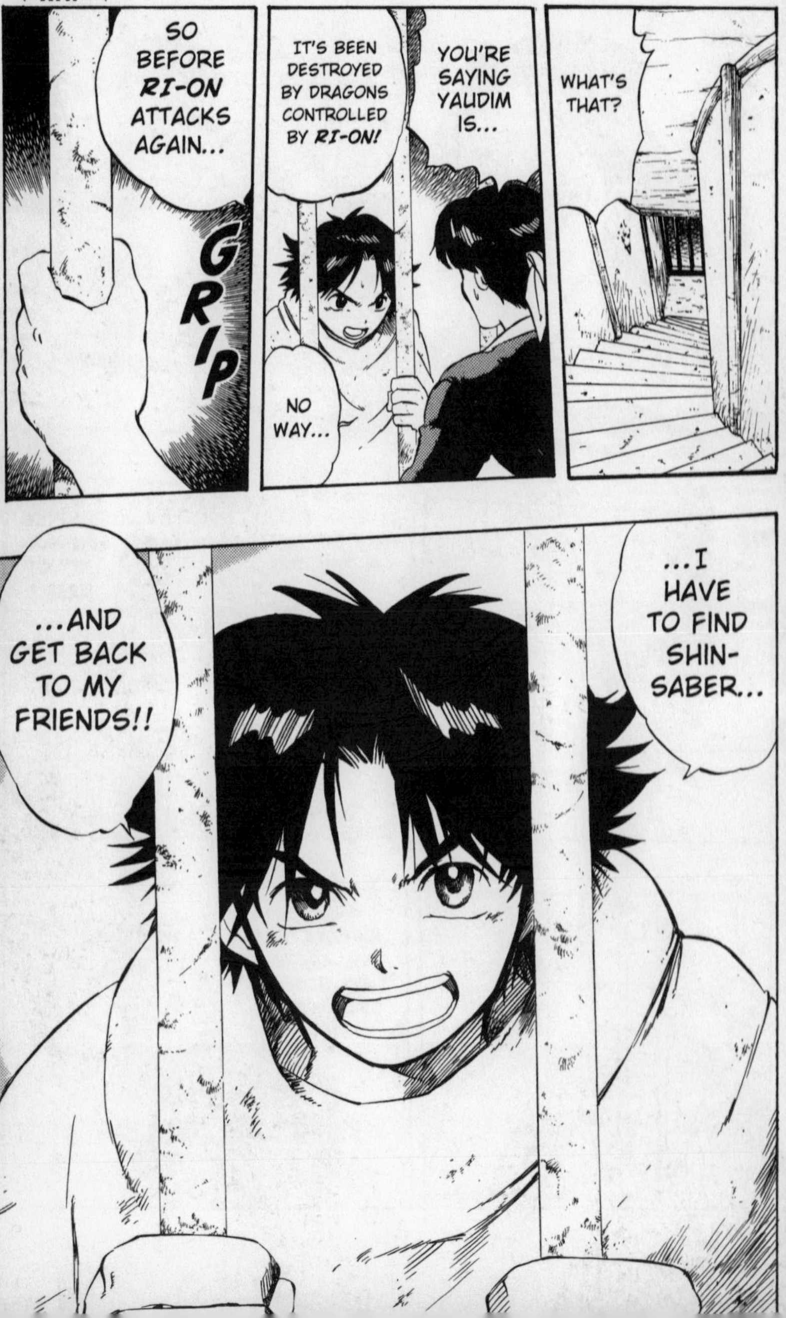
WHAT'S THAT?
YOU'RE SAYING YAUDIM IS...
IT'S BEEN DESTROYED BY DRAGONS CONTROLLED BY RI-ON!
NO WAY...
SO BEFORE RI-ON ATTACKS AGAIN...
GRIP
...I HAVE TO FIND SHIN-SABER...
...AND GET BACK TO MY FRIENDS!!

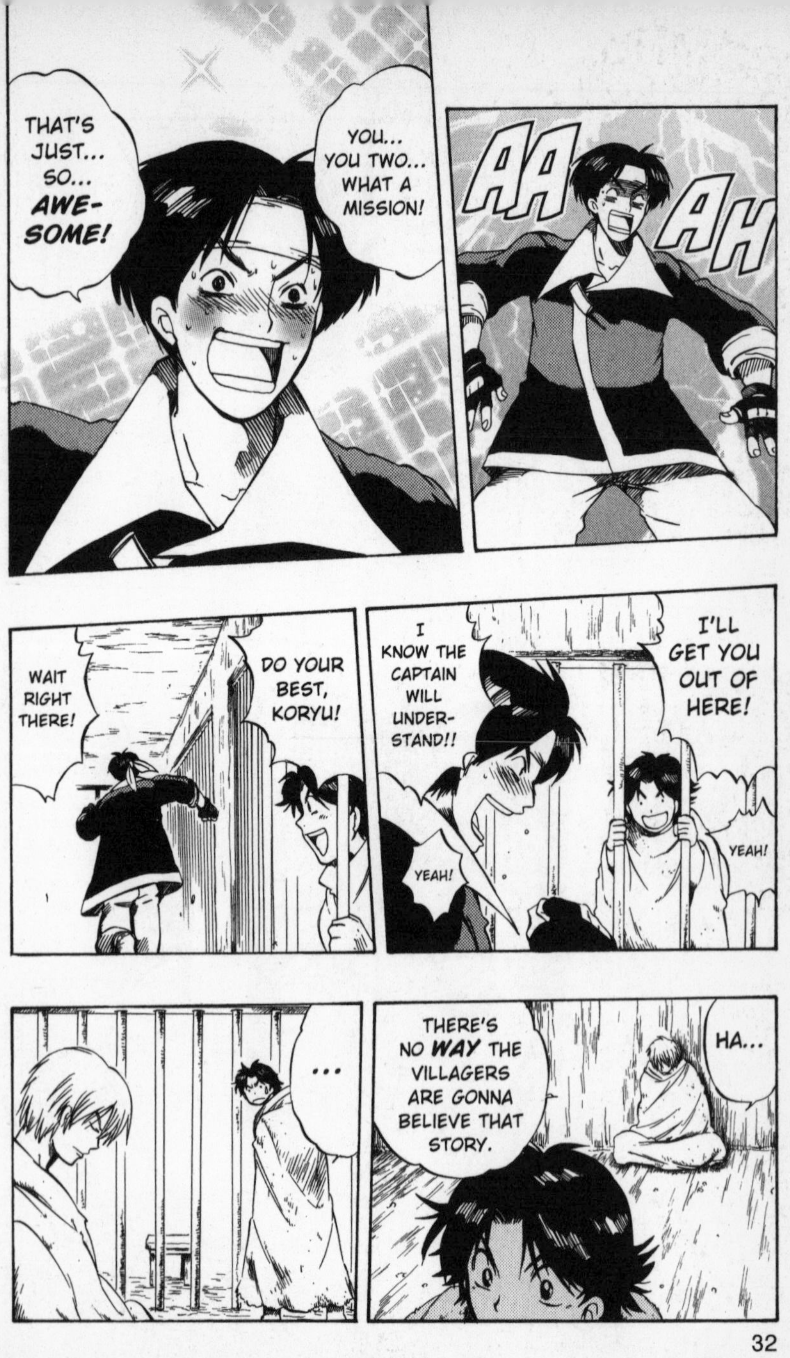
AA AH
YOU... YOU TWO... WHAT A MISSION!
THAT'S JUST... SO... **AWE-SOME!**
I'LL GET YOU OUT OF HERE!
YEAH!
I KNOW THE CAPTAIN WILL UNDER-STAND!!
YEAH!
DO YOUR BEST, KORYU!
WAIT RIGHT THERE!
HA...
THERE'S NO ***WAY*** THE VILLAGERS ARE GONNA BELIEVE THAT STORY.
...

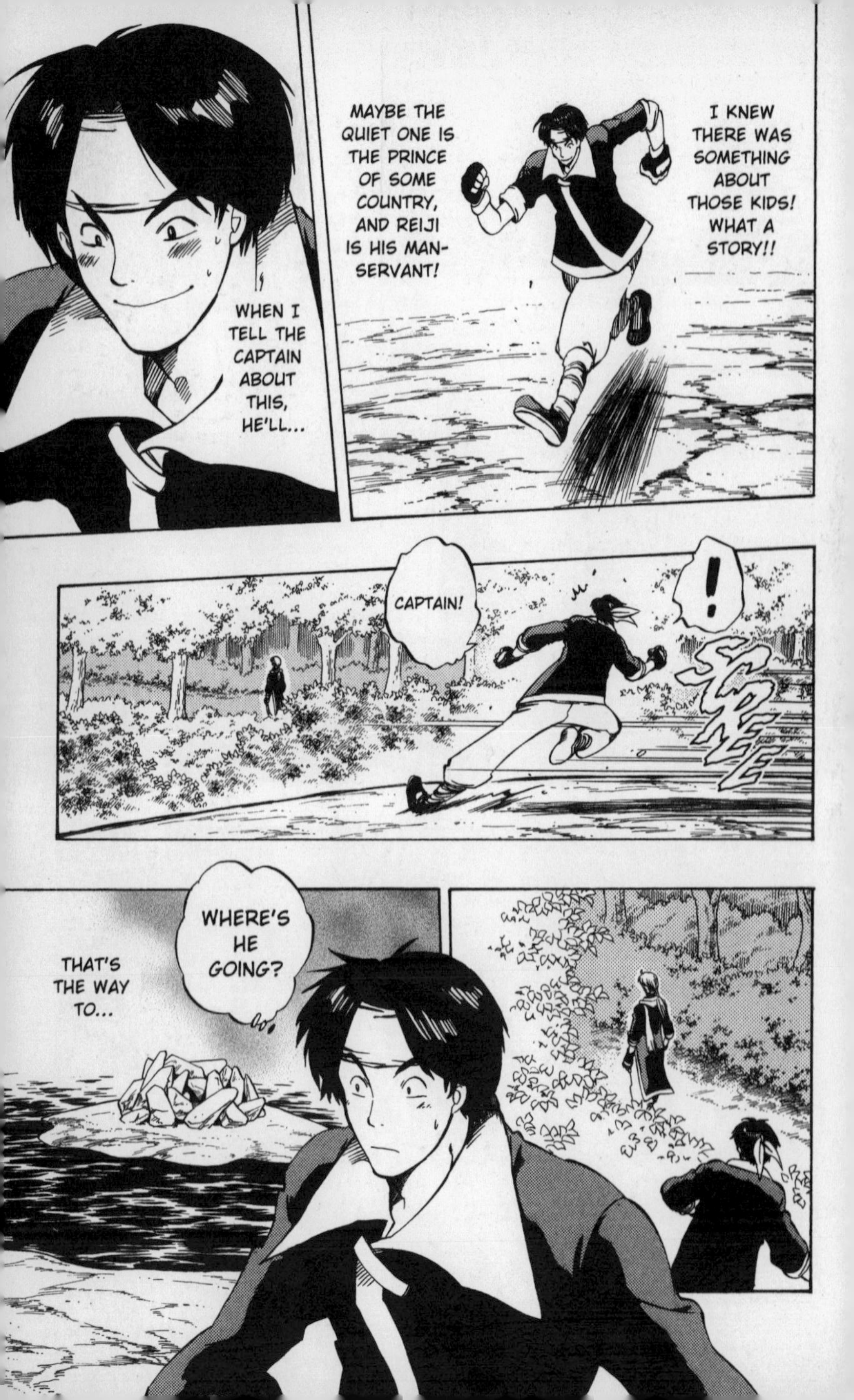
I KNEW THERE WAS SOMETHING ABOUT THOSE KIDS! WHAT A STORY!!
MAYBE THE QUIET ONE IS THE PRINCE OF SOME COUNTRY, AND REIJI IS HIS MAN-SERVANT!
WHEN I TELL THE CAPTAIN ABOUT THIS, HE'LL...
!
CAPTAIN!
SKREE
WHERE'S HE GOING?
THAT'S THE WAY TO...

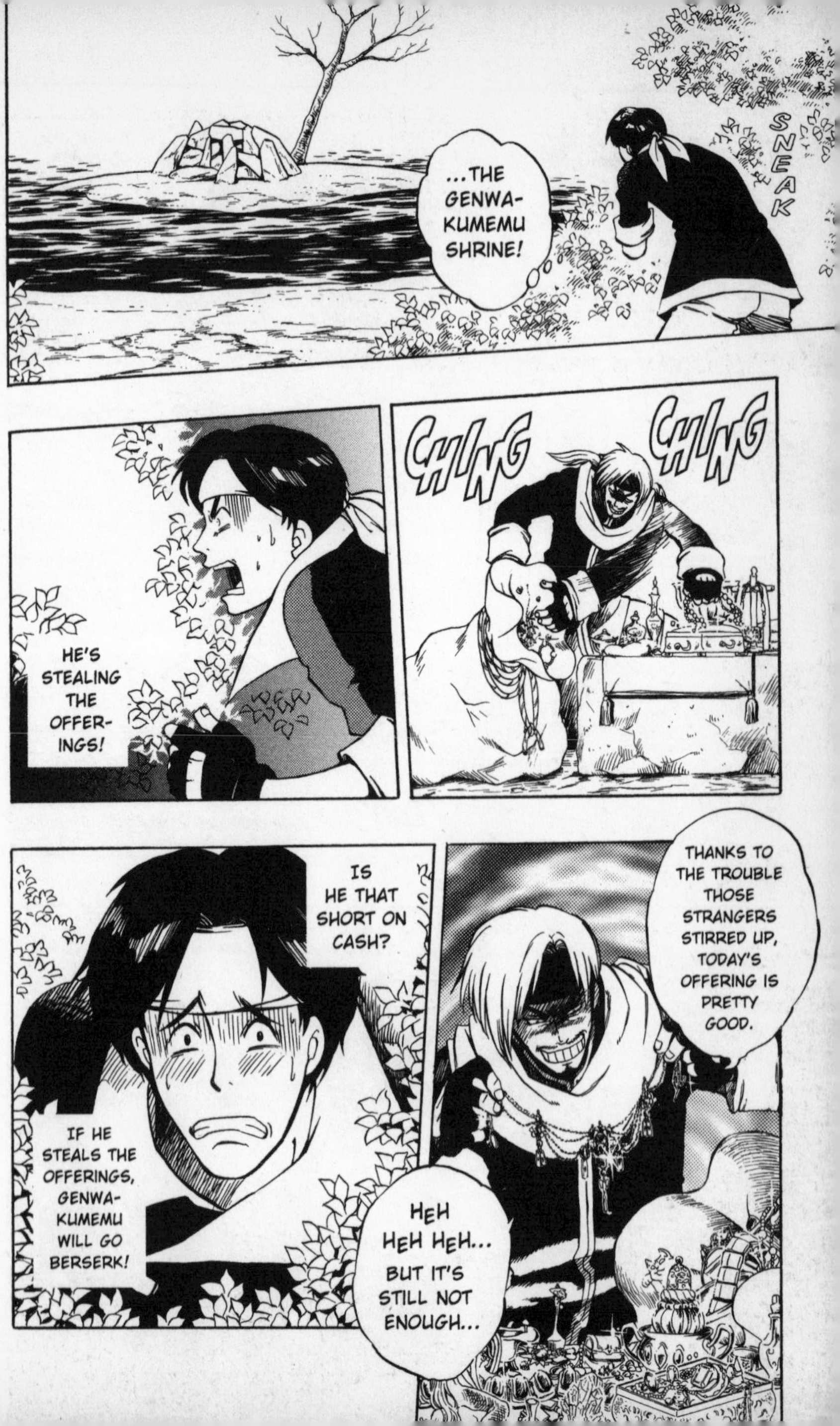
SNEAK
...THE GENWA-KUMEMU SHRINE!
CHING
CHING
HE'S STEALING THE OFFERINGS!
THANKS TO THE TROUBLE THOSE STRANGERS STIRRED UP, TODAY'S OFFERING IS PRETTY GOOD.
HEH HEH HEH... BUT IT'S STILL NOT ENOUGH...
IS HE THAT SHORT ON CASH?
IF HE STEALS THE OFFERINGS, GENWA-KUMEMU WILL GO BERSERK!

TOMP TOMP

PHEEp

SHOOOOM

MY LOVELY GENWA-KUMEMU.

TONIGHT, LET'S TERRIFY THE VILLAGE AGAIN AND MAKE OUR-SELVES RICH!!

GENWAKUMEMU

TYPE: AERIAL

WIND

This dragon creates a thick fog to confuse enemies. Its armor-like wings are impervious to almost any attack.

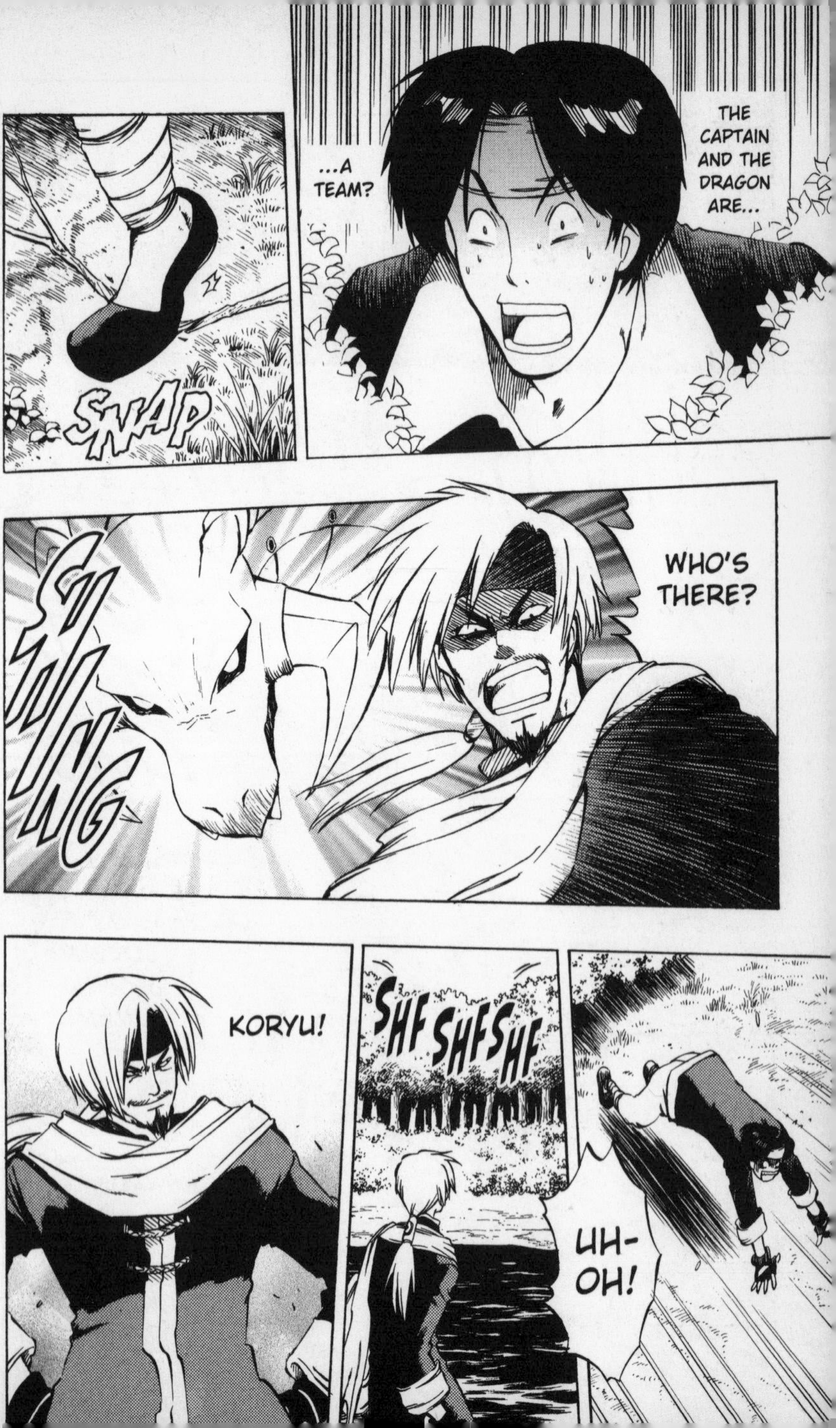
THE CAPTAIN AND THE DRAGON ARE...
...A TEAM?
SNAP
WHO'S THERE?
SHING
UH-OH!
SHF SHF SHF
KORYU!

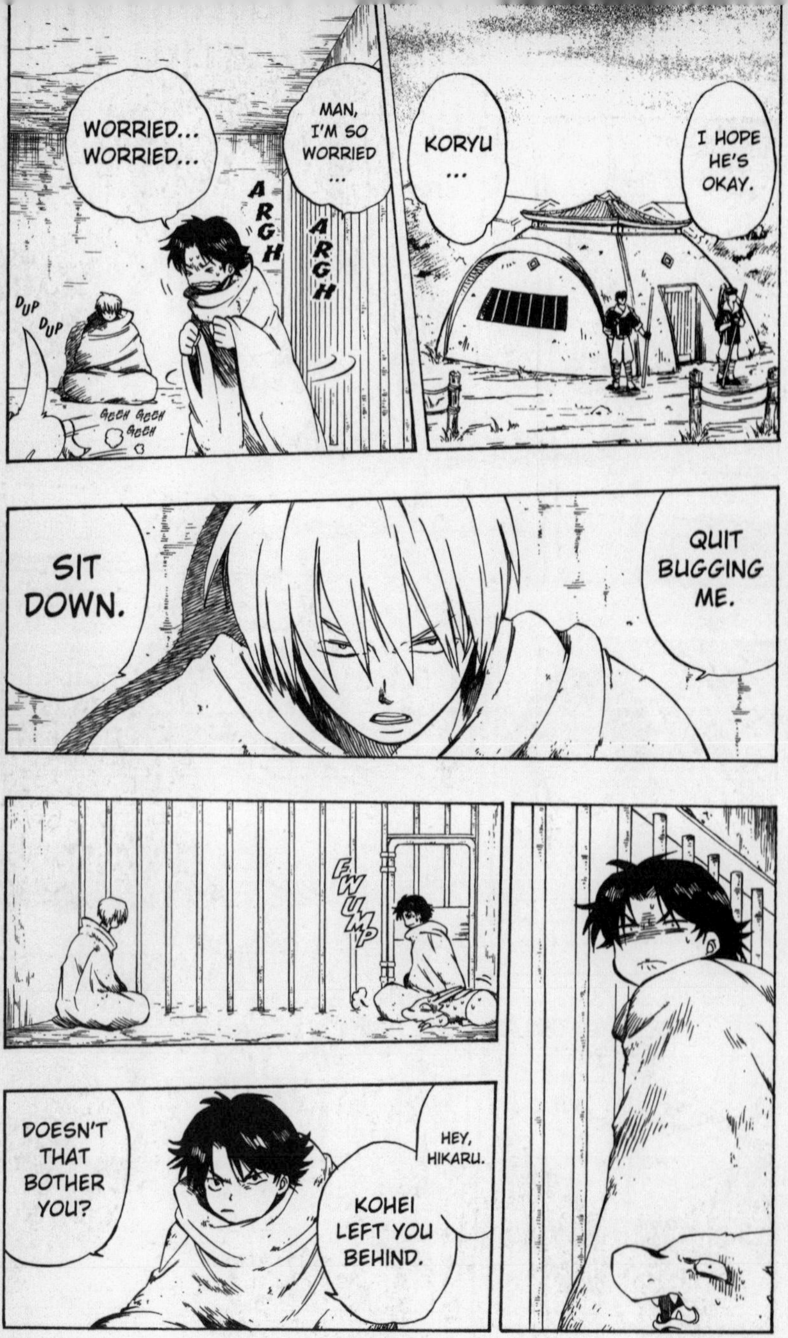
I HOPE HE'S OKAY.
KORYU ...
MAN, I'M SO WORRIED ...
ARGH
ARGH
WORRIED... WORRIED...
DUP DUP
GEEH GEEH GEEH
QUIT BUGGING ME.
SIT DOWN.
FWUMP
HEY, HIKARU.
KOHEI LEFT YOU BEHIND.
DOESN'T THAT BOTHER YOU?

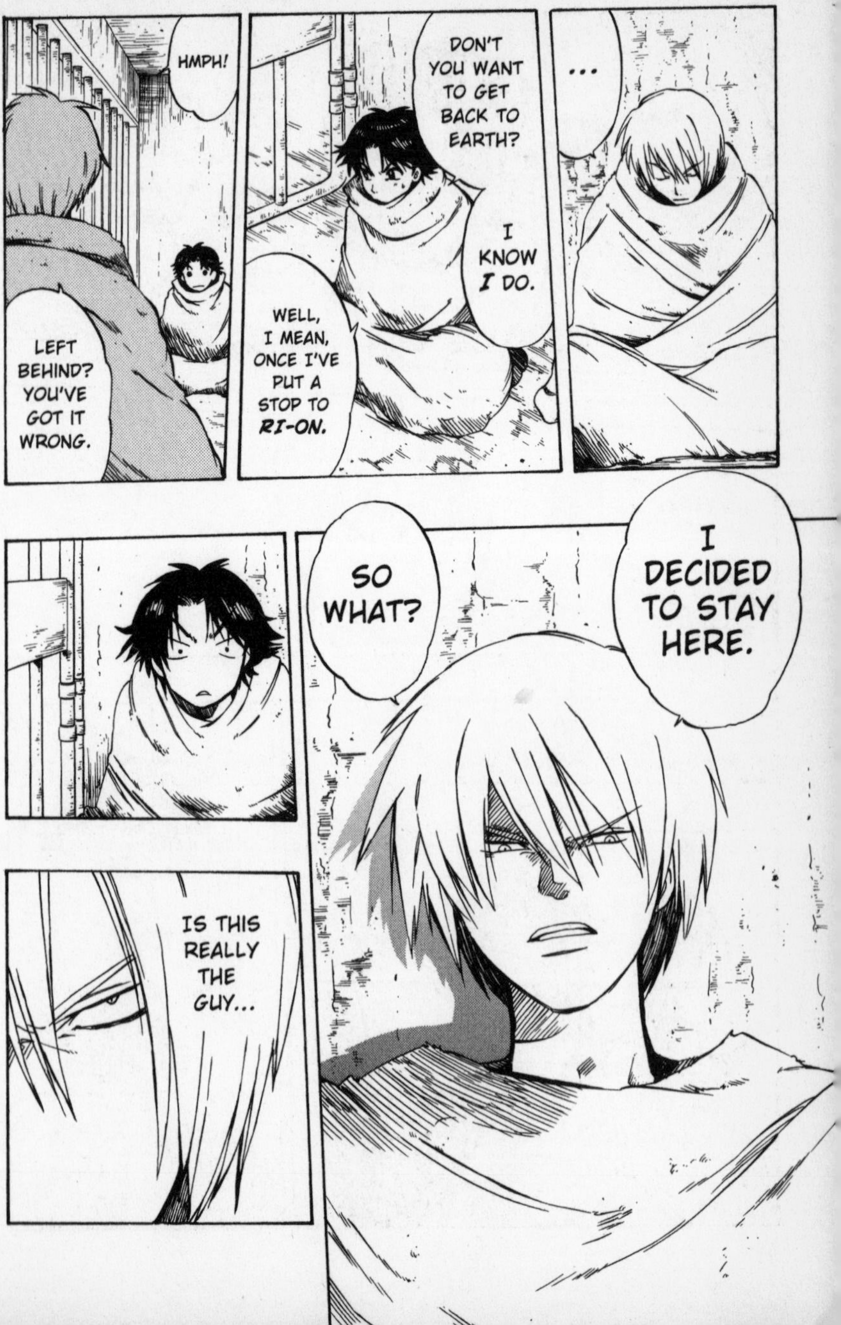
...
DON'T YOU WANT TO GET BACK TO EARTH?
I KNOW *I* DO.
WELL, I MEAN, ONCE I'VE PUT A STOP TO *RI-ON.*
HMPH!
LEFT BEHIND? YOU'VE GOT IT WRONG.
I DECIDED TO STAY HERE.
SO WHAT?
IS THIS REALLY THE GUY...

READ THIS WAY

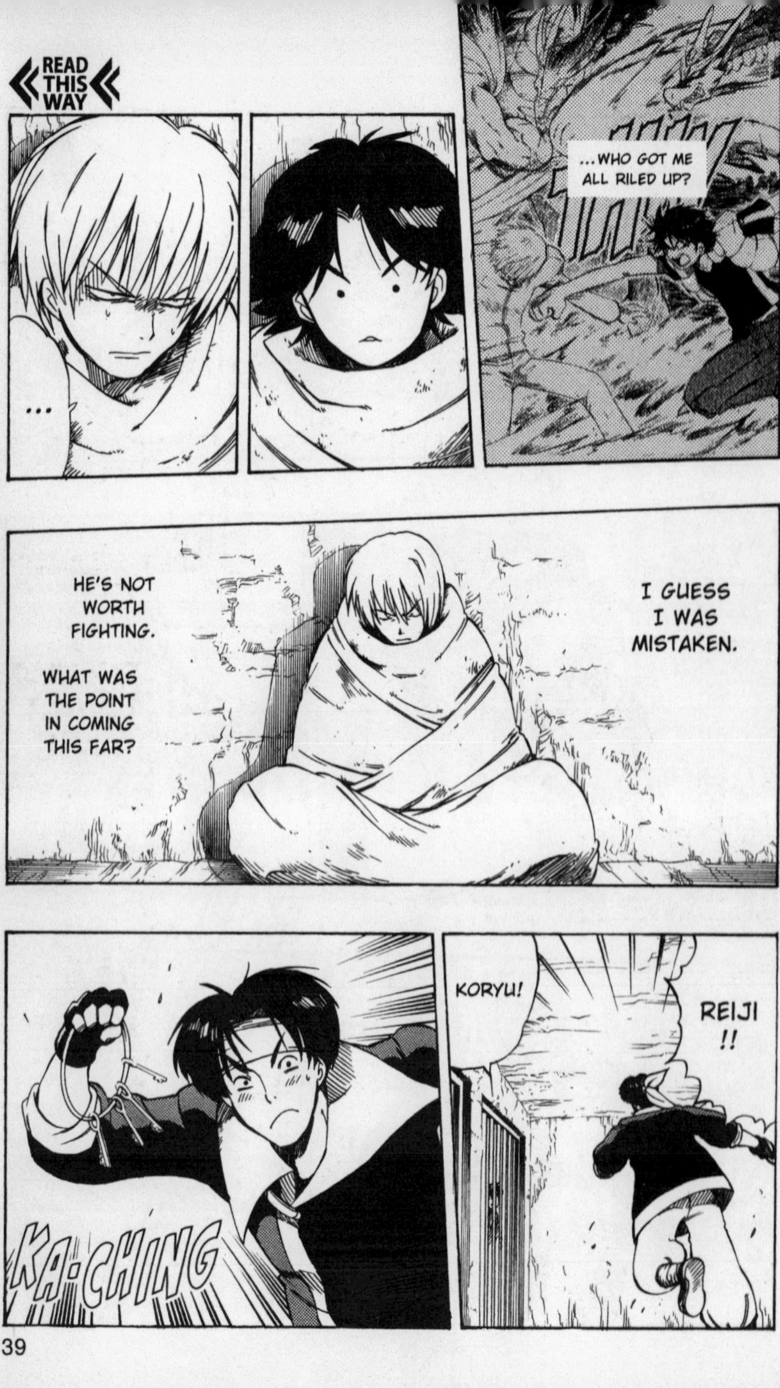
...WHO GOT ME ALL RILED UP?
...
I GUESS I WAS MISTAKEN.
HE'S NOT WORTH FIGHTING.
WHAT WAS THE POINT IN COMING THIS FAR?
REIJI !!
KORYU!
KA-CHING

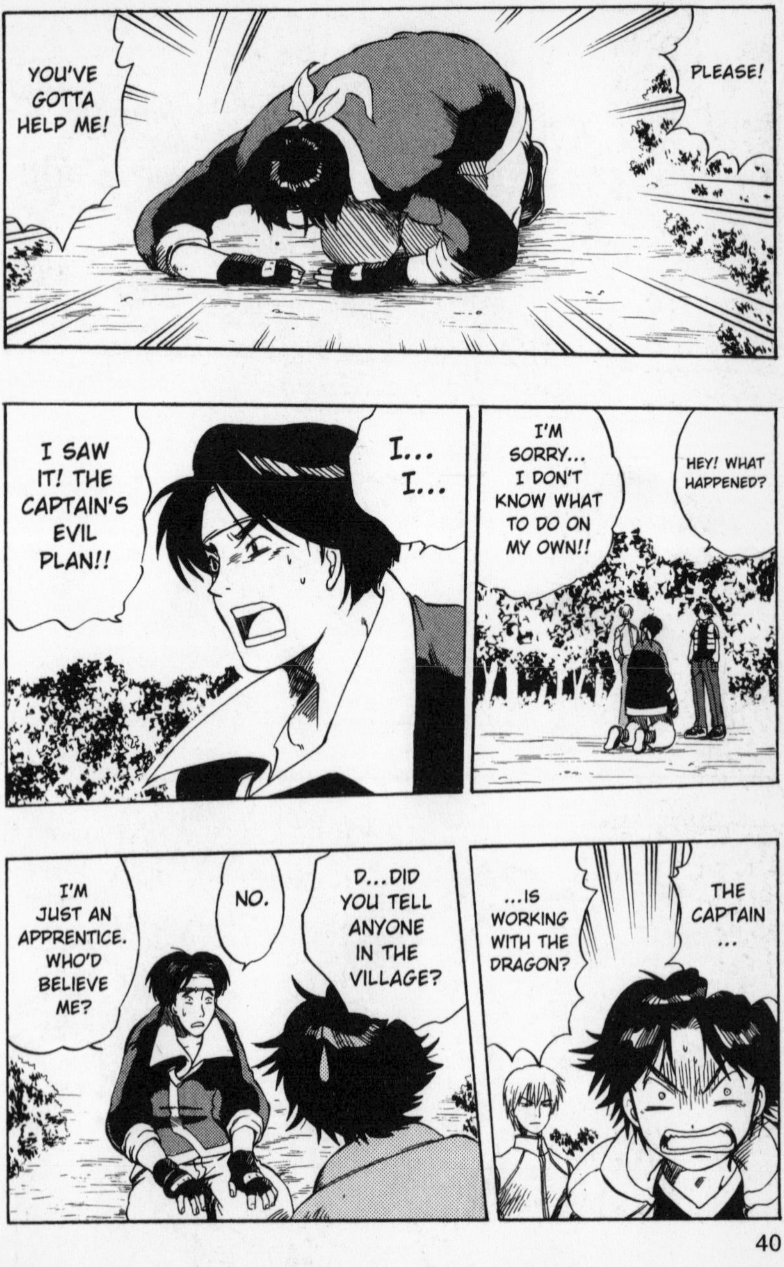
PLEASE!
YOU'VE GOTTA HELP ME!
HEY! WHAT HAPPENED?
I'M SORRY... I DON'T KNOW WHAT TO DO ON MY OWN!!
I... I...
I SAW IT! THE CAPTAIN'S EVIL PLAN!!
THE CAPTAIN...
...IS WORKING WITH THE DRAGON?
D...DID YOU TELL ANYONE IN THE VILLAGE?
NO.
I'M JUST AN APPRENTICE. WHO'D BELIEVE ME?

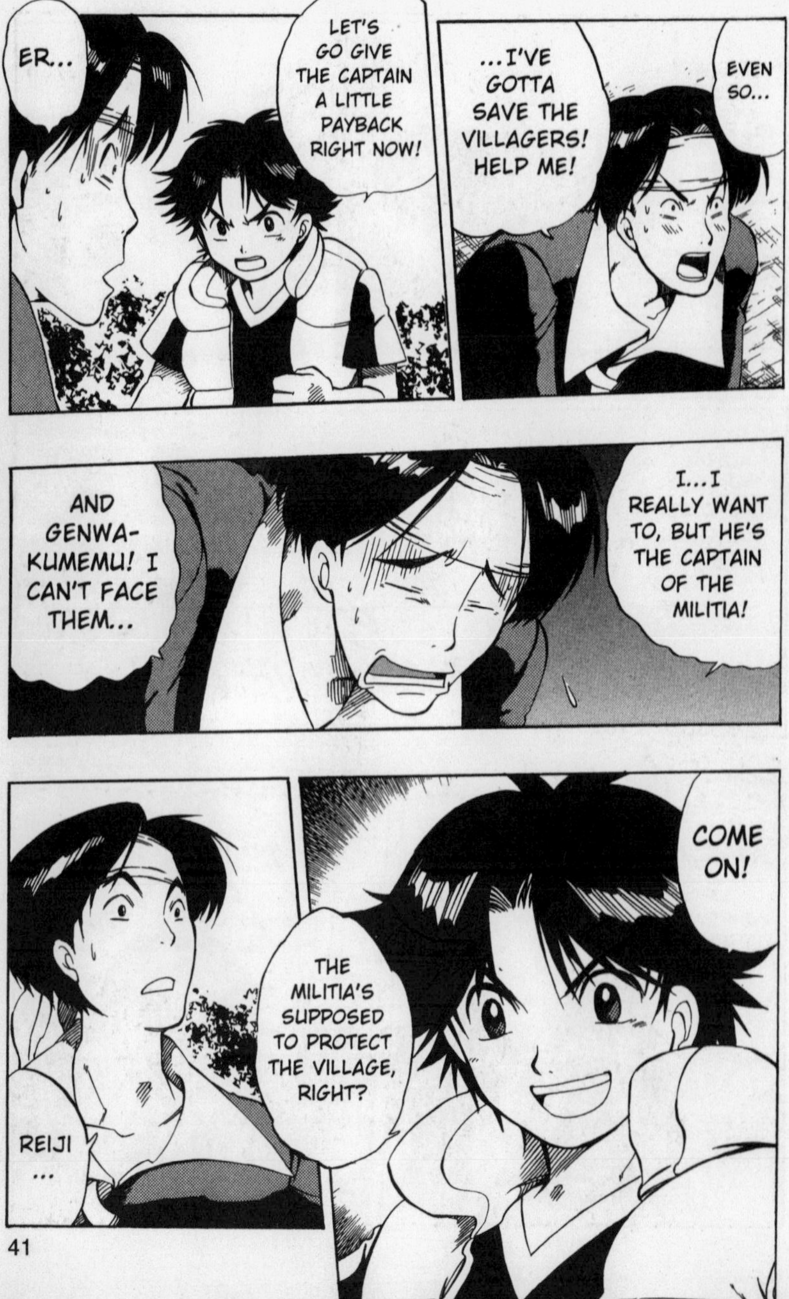
EVEN SO...
...I'VE GOTTA SAVE THE VILLAGERS! HELP ME!
LET'S GO GIVE THE CAPTAIN A LITTLE PAYBACK RIGHT NOW!
ER...
I...I REALLY WANT TO, BUT HE'S THE CAPTAIN OF THE MILITIA!
AND GENWA-KUMEMU! I CAN'T FACE THEM...
COME ON!
THE MILITIA'S SUPPOSED TO PROTECT THE VILLAGE, RIGHT?
REIJI...

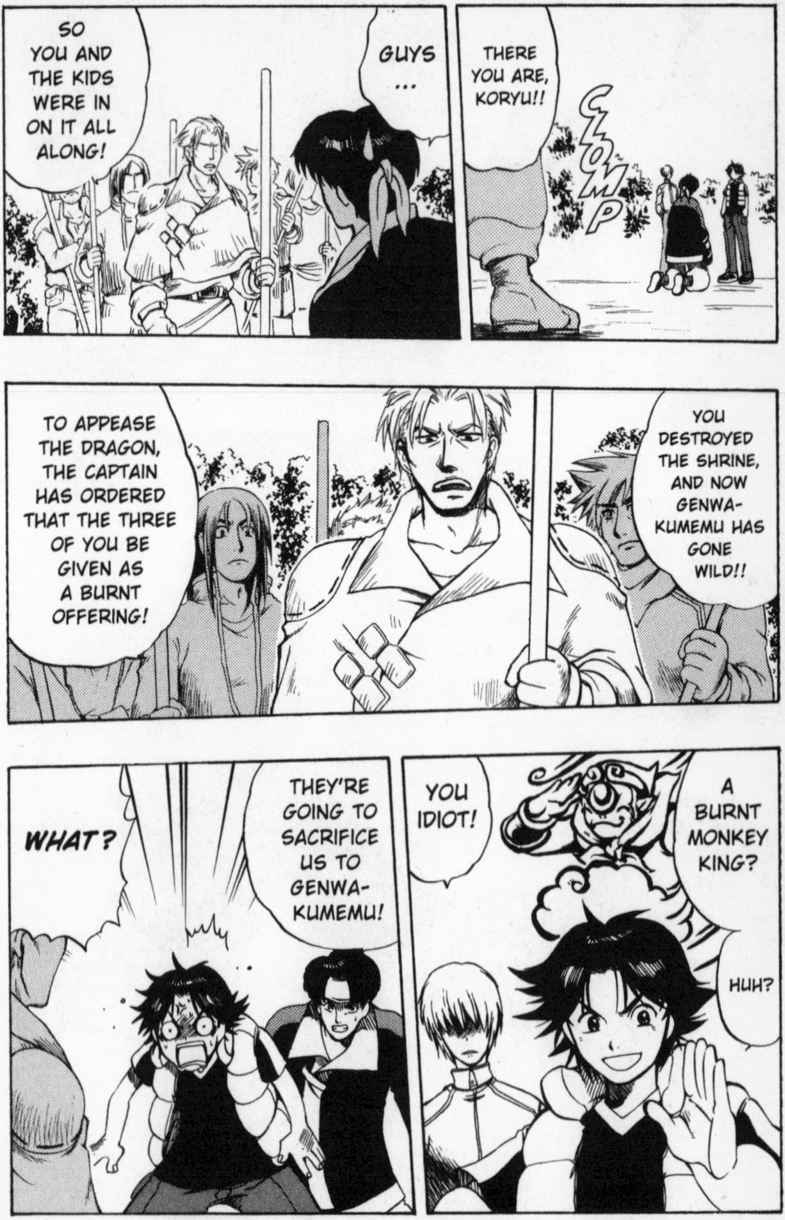
THERE YOU ARE, KORYU!!
CLOMP
GUYS ...
SO YOU AND THE KIDS WERE IN ON IT ALL ALONG!
YOU DESTROYED THE SHRINE, AND NOW GENWA-KUMEMU HAS GONE WILD!!
TO APPEASE THE DRAGON, THE CAPTAIN HAS ORDERED THAT THE THREE OF YOU BE GIVEN AS A BURNT OFFERING!
A BURNT MONKEY KING?
YOU IDIOT!
HUH?
THEY'RE GOING TO SACRIFICE US TO GENWA-KUMEMU!
WHAT?

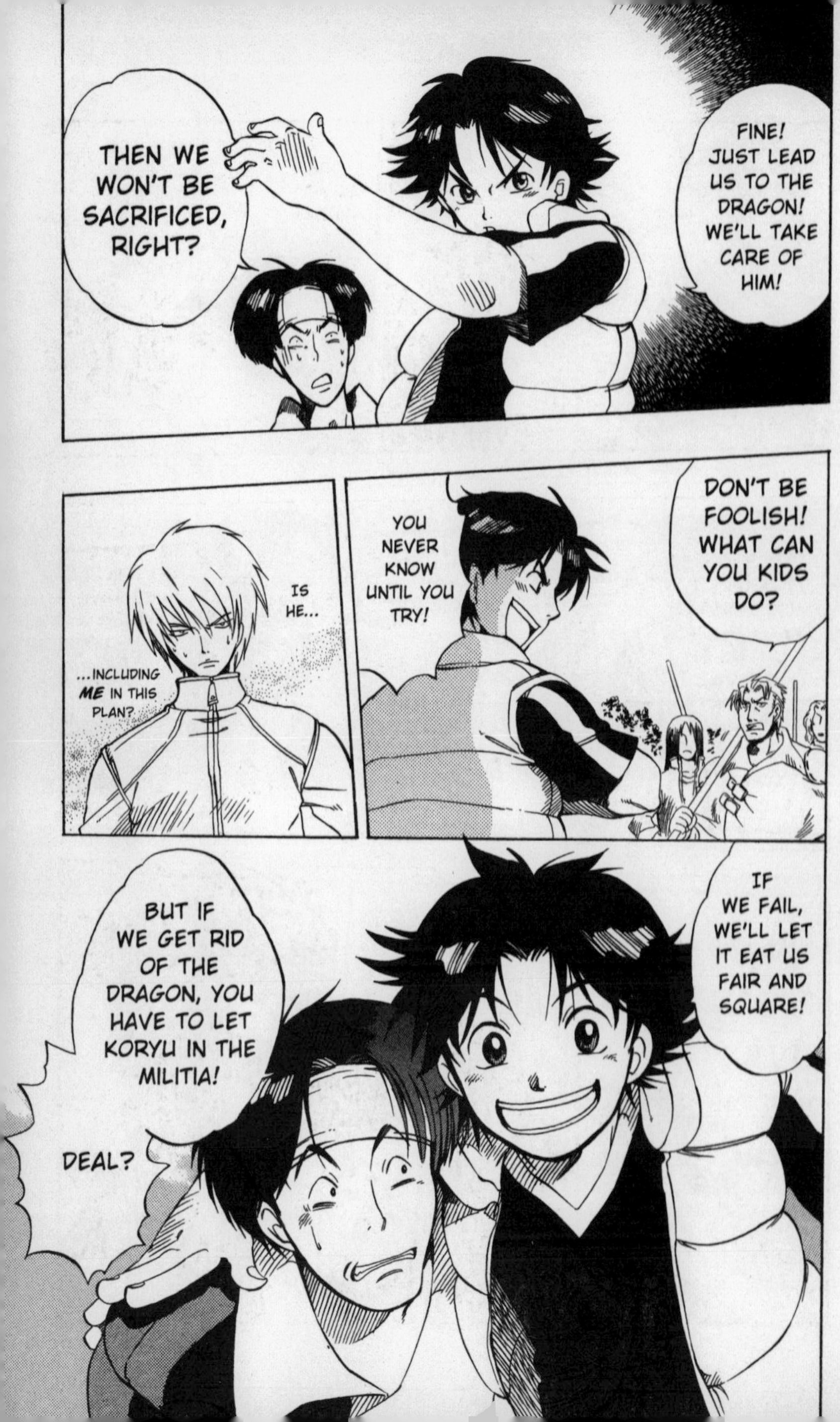
FINE! JUST LEAD US TO THE DRAGON! WE'LL TAKE CARE OF HIM!
THEN WE WON'T BE SACRIFICED, RIGHT?
DON'T BE FOOLISH! WHAT CAN YOU KIDS DO?
YOU NEVER KNOW UNTIL YOU TRY!
IS HE...
...INCLUDING *ME* IN THIS PLAN?
IF WE FAIL, WE'LL LET IT EAT US FAIR AND SQUARE!
BUT IF WE GET RID OF THE DRAGON, YOU HAVE TO LET KORYU IN THE MILITIA!
DEAL?

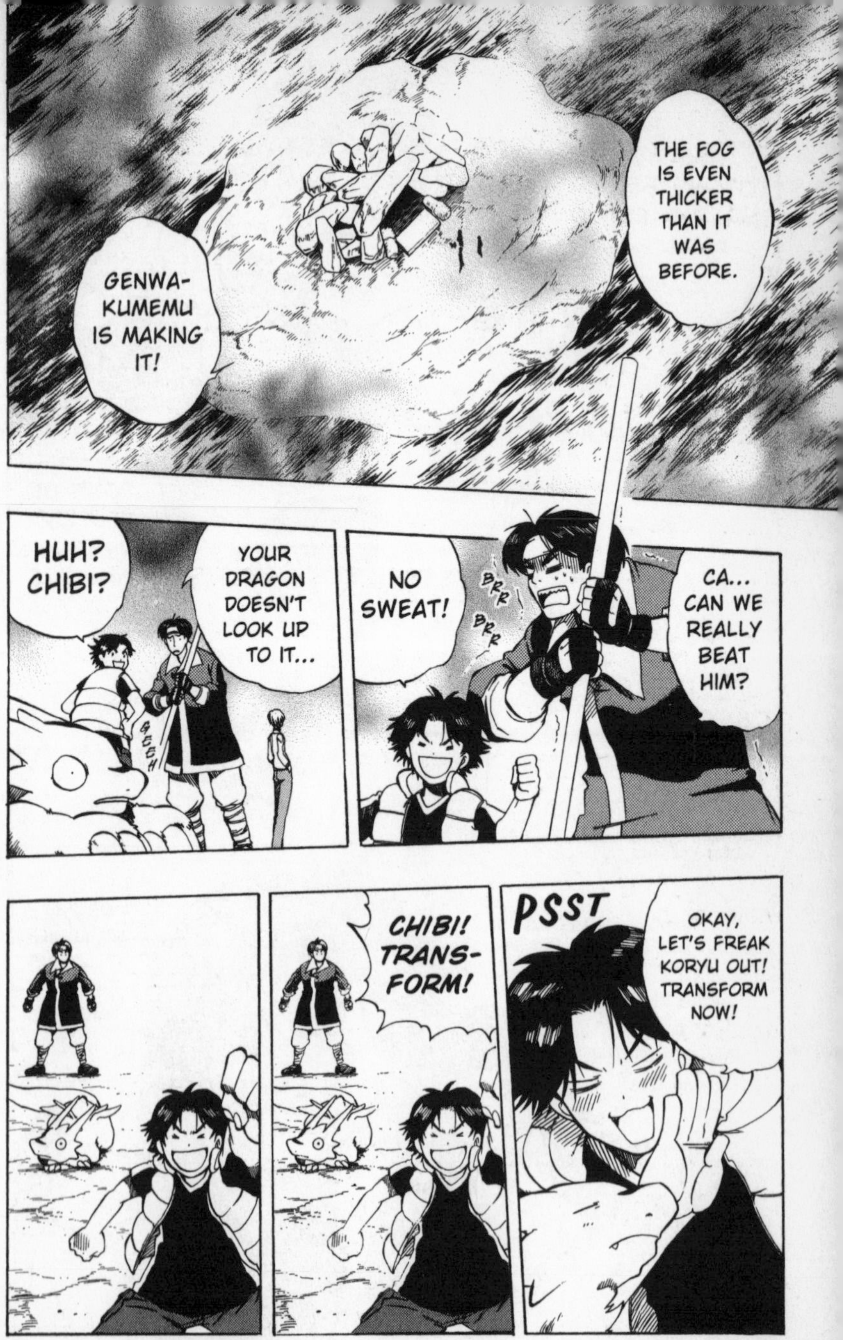
THE FOG IS EVEN THICKER THAN IT WAS BEFORE.
GENWA-KUMEMU IS MAKING IT!
CA... CAN WE REALLY BEAT HIM?
BRR BRR
NO SWEAT!
YOUR DRAGON DOESN'T LOOK UP TO IT...
HUH? CHIBI?
PSST
OKAY, LET'S FREAK KORYU OUT! TRANSFORM NOW!
CHIBI! TRANS-FORM!

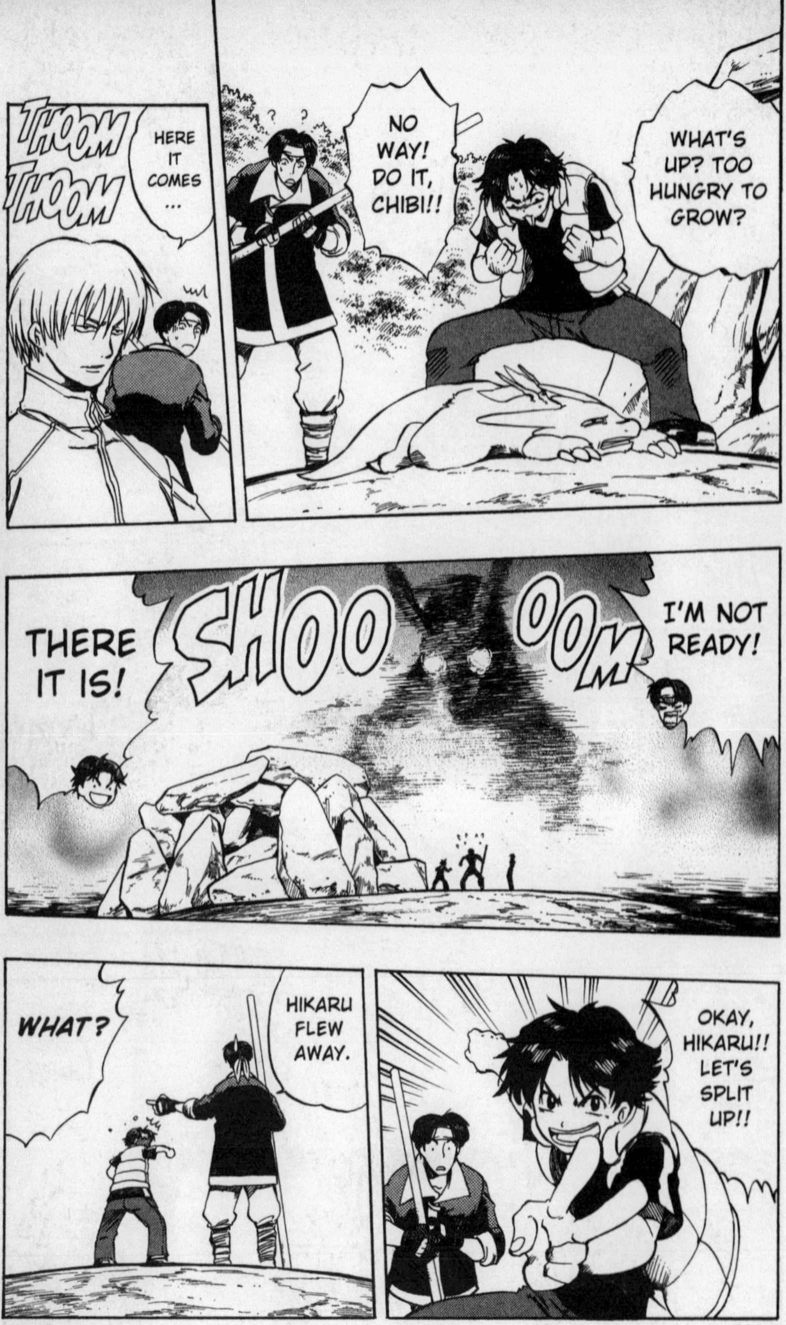
...
WHAT'S UP? TOO HUNGRY TO GROW?
NO WAY! DO IT, CHIBI!!
THOOM THOOM
HERE IT COMES ...
I'M NOT READY!
SHOO OOM
THERE IT IS!
OKAY, HIKARU!! LET'S SPLIT UP!!
HIKARU FLEW AWAY.
WHAT?

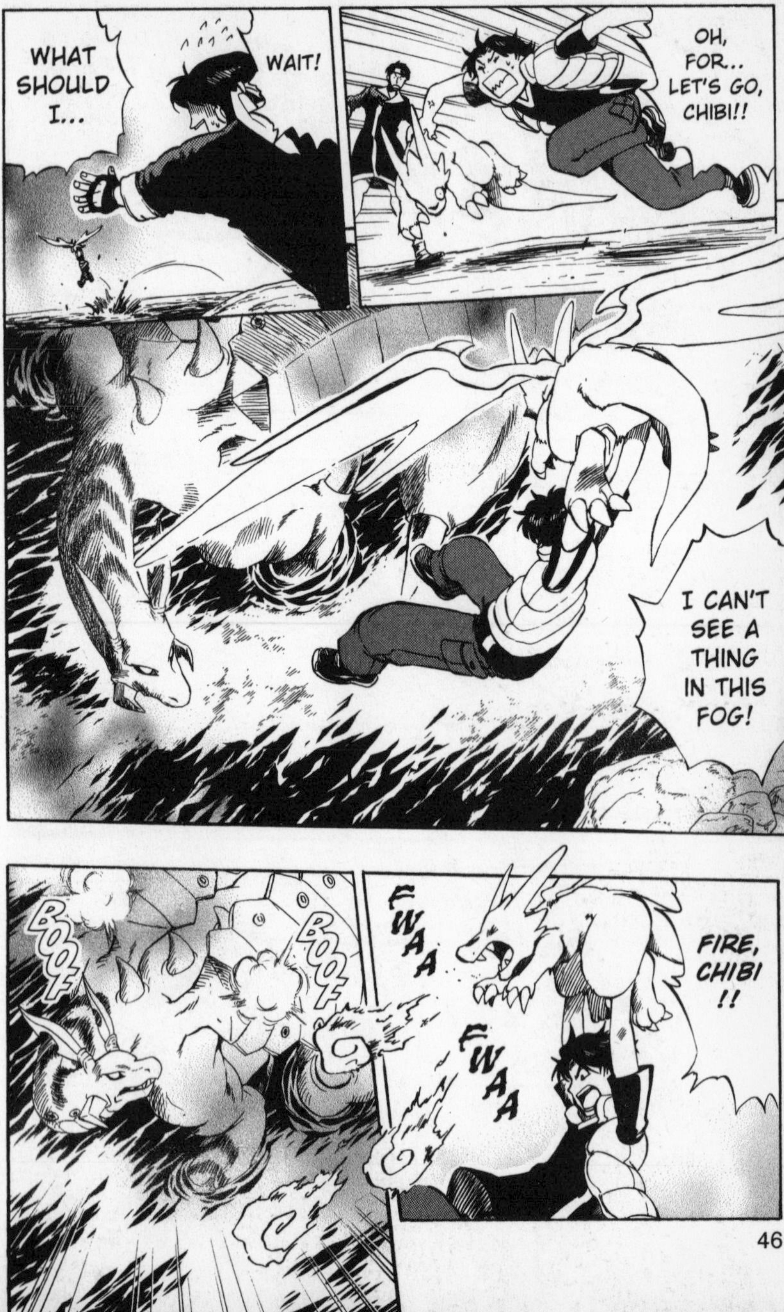
OH, FOR.. LET'S GO, CHIBI!!
WAIT!
WHAT SHOULD I...
I CAN'T SEE A THING IN THIS FOG!
FIRE, CHIBI !!
FWAA
FWAA
BOOF
BOOF

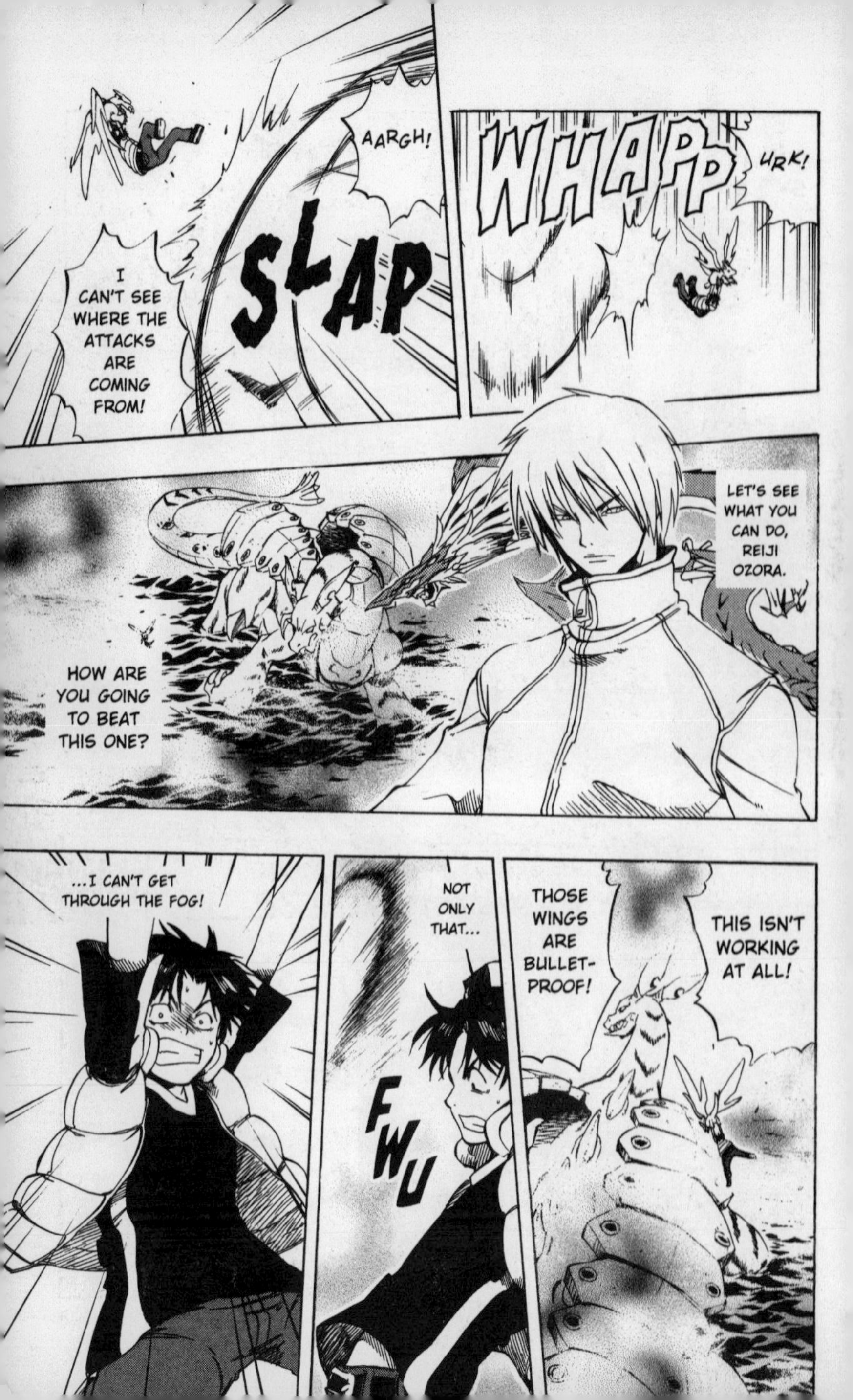
WHAPP
URK!
AARGH!
SLAP
I CAN'T SEE WHERE THE ATTACKS ARE COMING FROM!
LET'S SEE WHAT YOU CAN DO, REIJI OZORA.
HOW ARE YOU GOING TO BEAT THIS ONE?
THIS ISN'T WORKING AT ALL!
THOSE WINGS ARE BULLET-PROOF!
NOT ONLY THAT...
FWU
...I CAN'T GET THROUGH THE FOG!

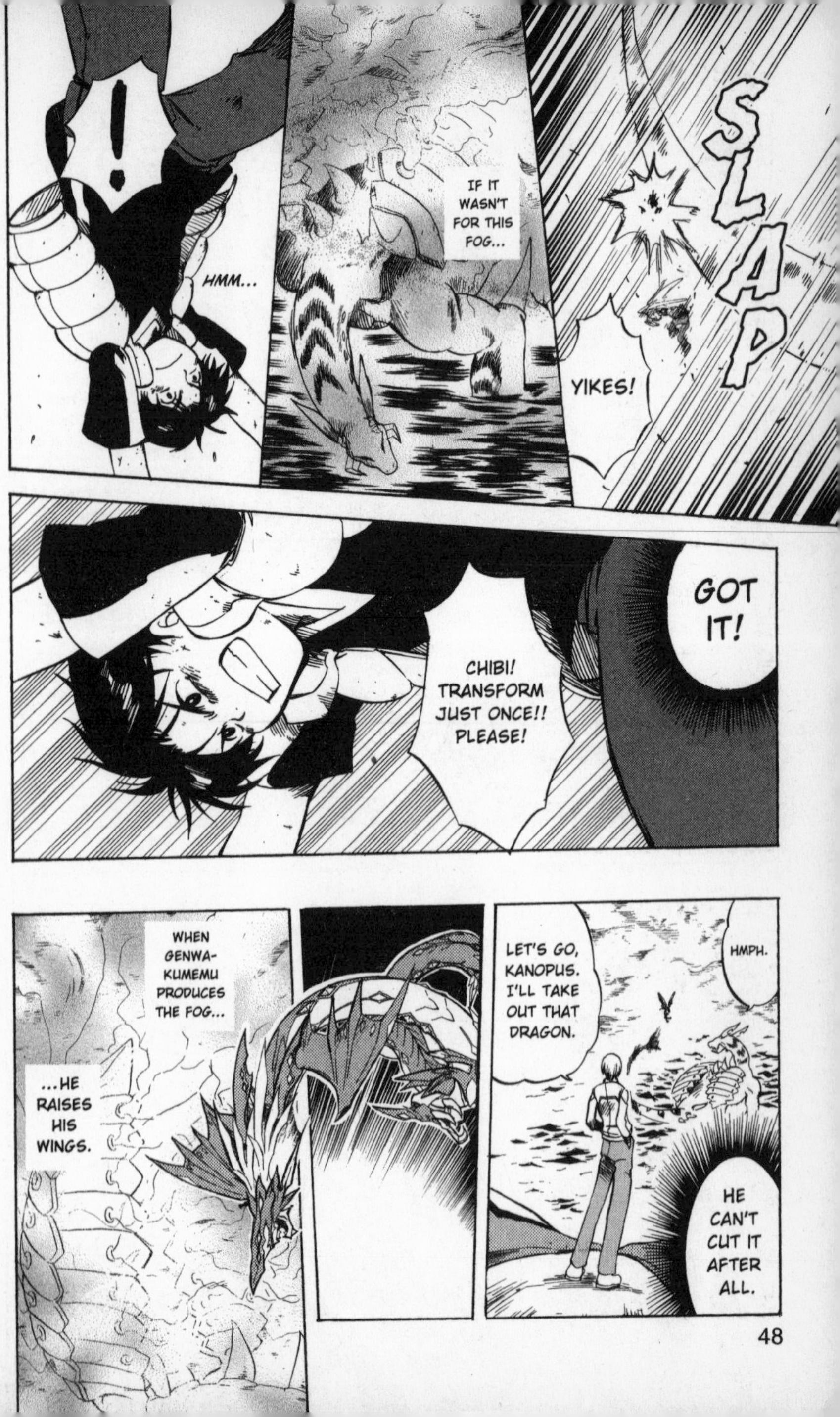
SLAP
YIKES!
IF IT WASN'T FOR THIS FOG...
!
HMM...
GOT IT!
CHIBI! TRANSFORM JUST ONCE!! PLEASE!
HMPH.
LET'S GO, KANOPUS. I'LL TAKE OUT THAT DRAGON.
HE CAN'T CUT IT AFTER ALL.
WHEN GENWA-KUMEMU PRODUCES THE FOG...
...HE RAISES HIS WINGS.

READ THIS WAY

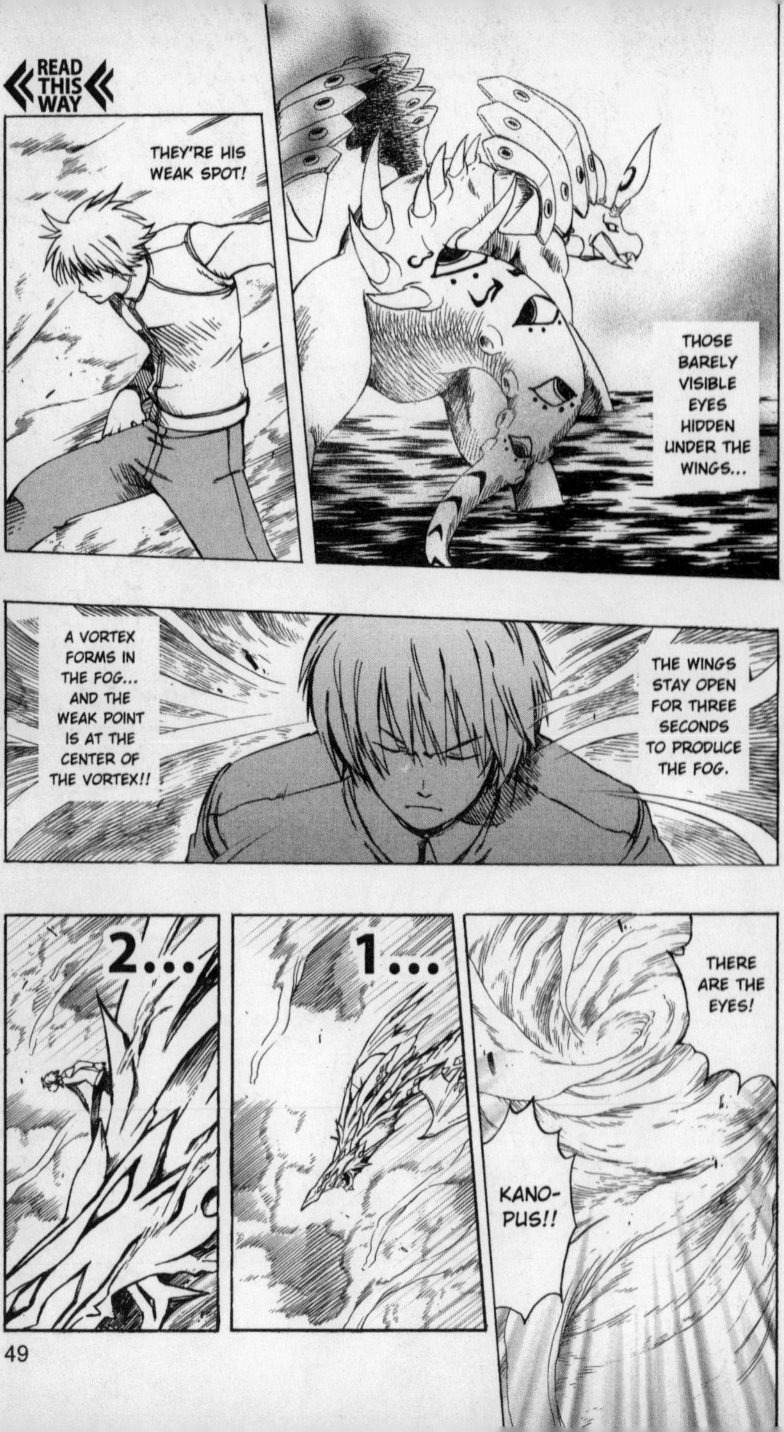
THOSE BARELY VISIBLE EYES HIDDEN UNDER THE WINGS...
THEY'RE HIS WEAK SPOT!
THE WINGS STAY OPEN FOR THREE SECONDS TO PRODUCE THE FOG.
A VORTEX FORMS IN THE FOG... AND THE WEAK POINT IS AT THE CENTER OF THE VORTEX!!
THERE ARE THE EYES!
KANO-PUS!!
1...
2...

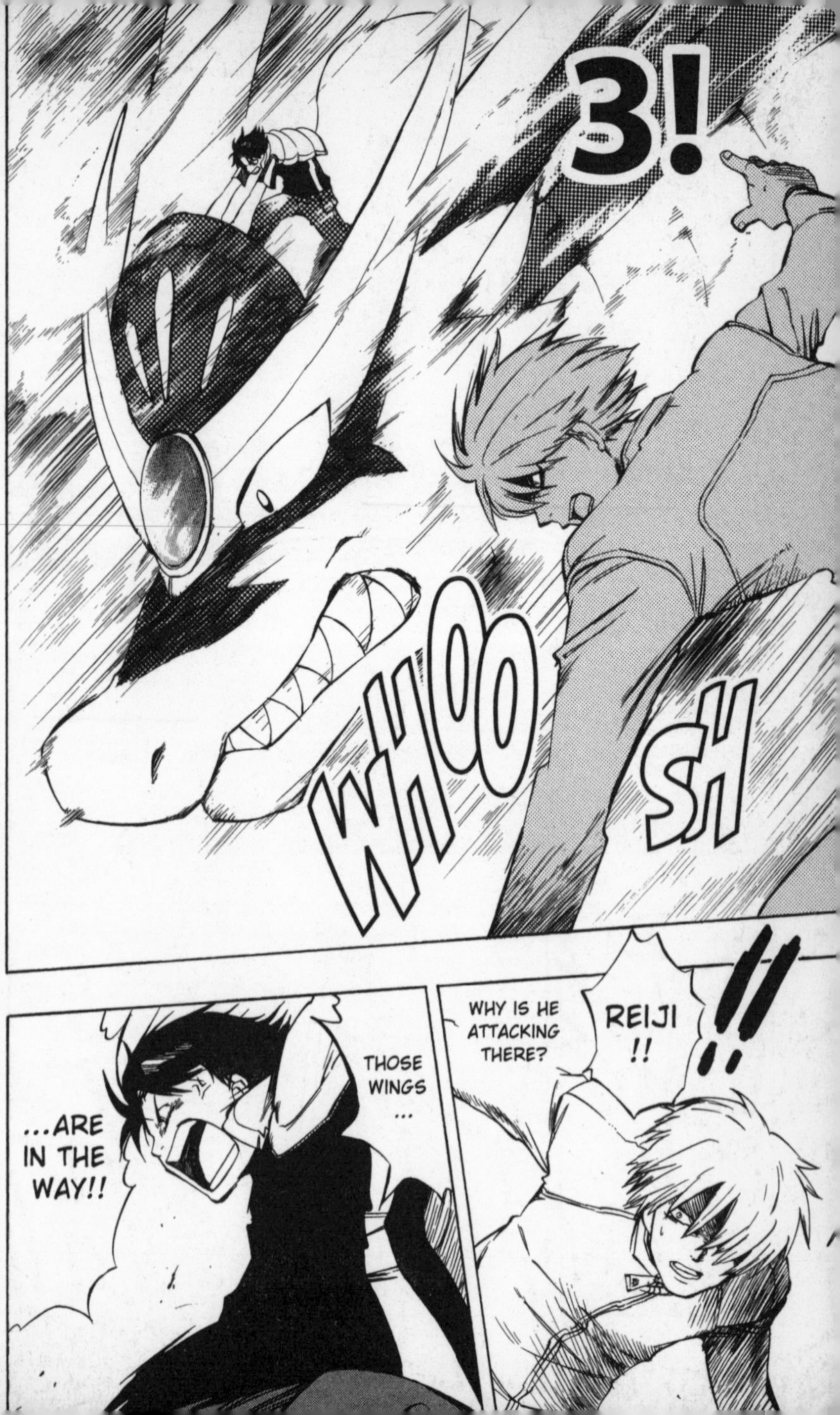
3!
WHOOSH
!!
REIJI !!
WHY IS HE ATTACKING THERE?
THOSE WINGS ...
...ARE IN THE WAY!!

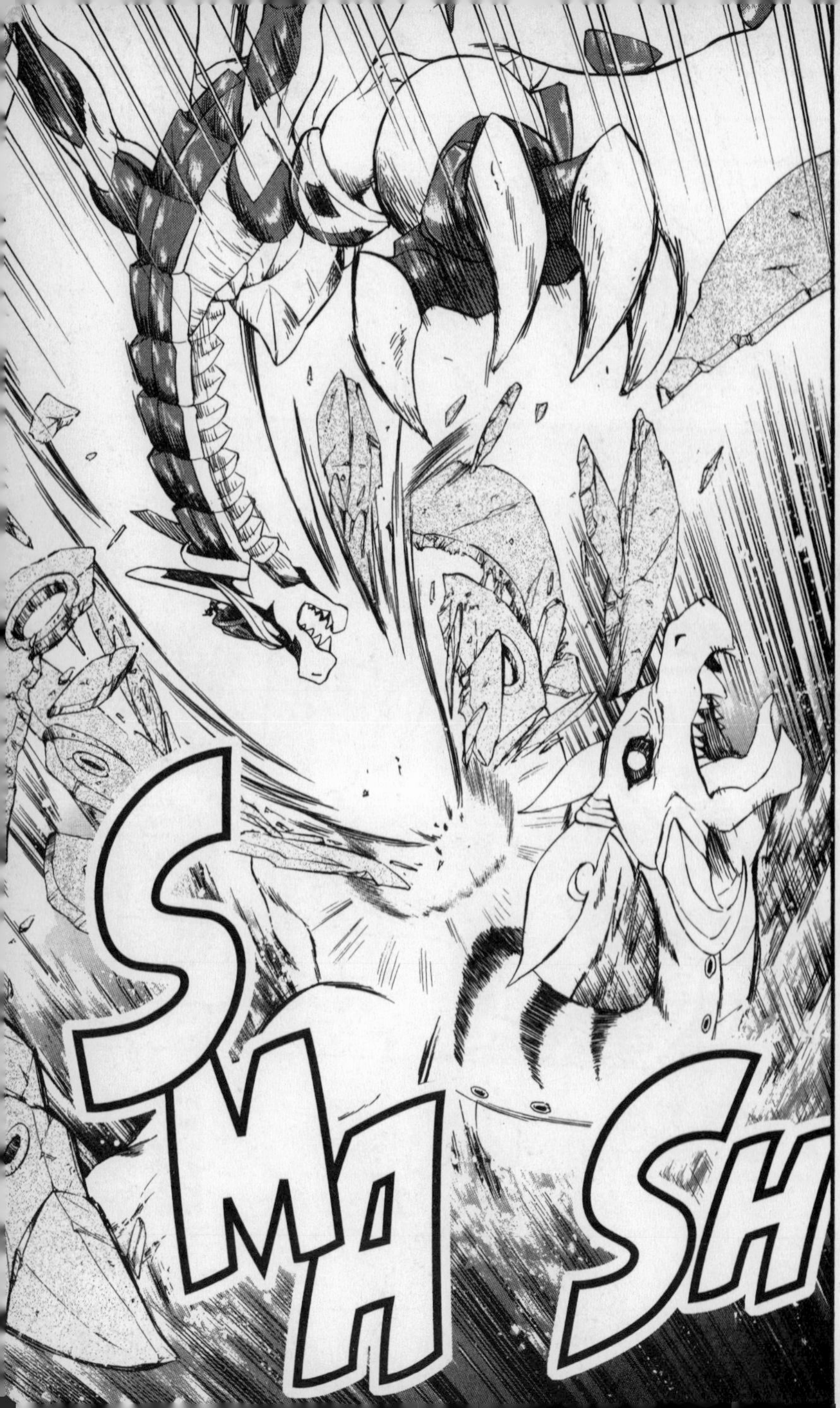
SMASH

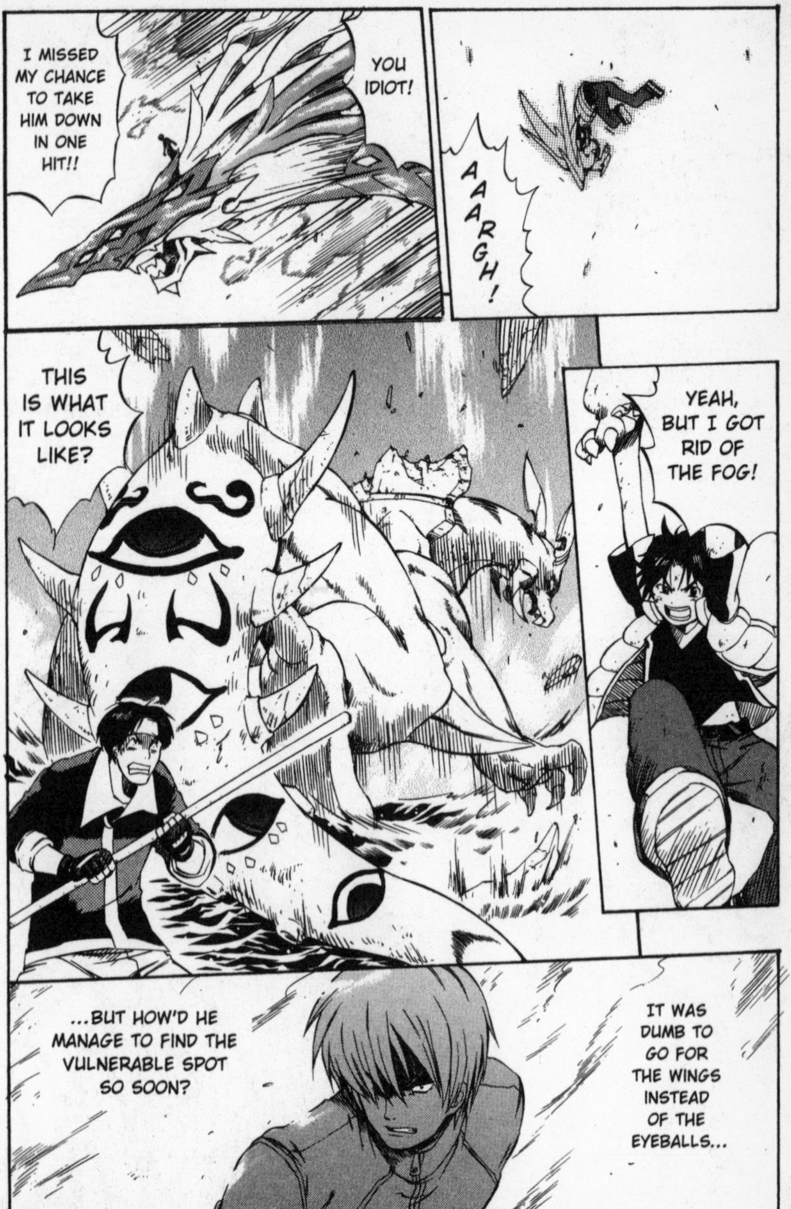
AAARGH!
YOU IDIOT!
I MISSED MY CHANCE TO TAKE HIM DOWN IN ONE HIT!!
YEAH, BUT I GOT RID OF THE FOG!
THIS IS WHAT IT LOOKS LIKE?
IT WAS DUMB TO GO FOR THE WINGS INSTEAD OF THE EYEBALLS...
...BUT HOW'D HE MANAGE TO FIND THE VULNERABLE SPOT SO SOON?

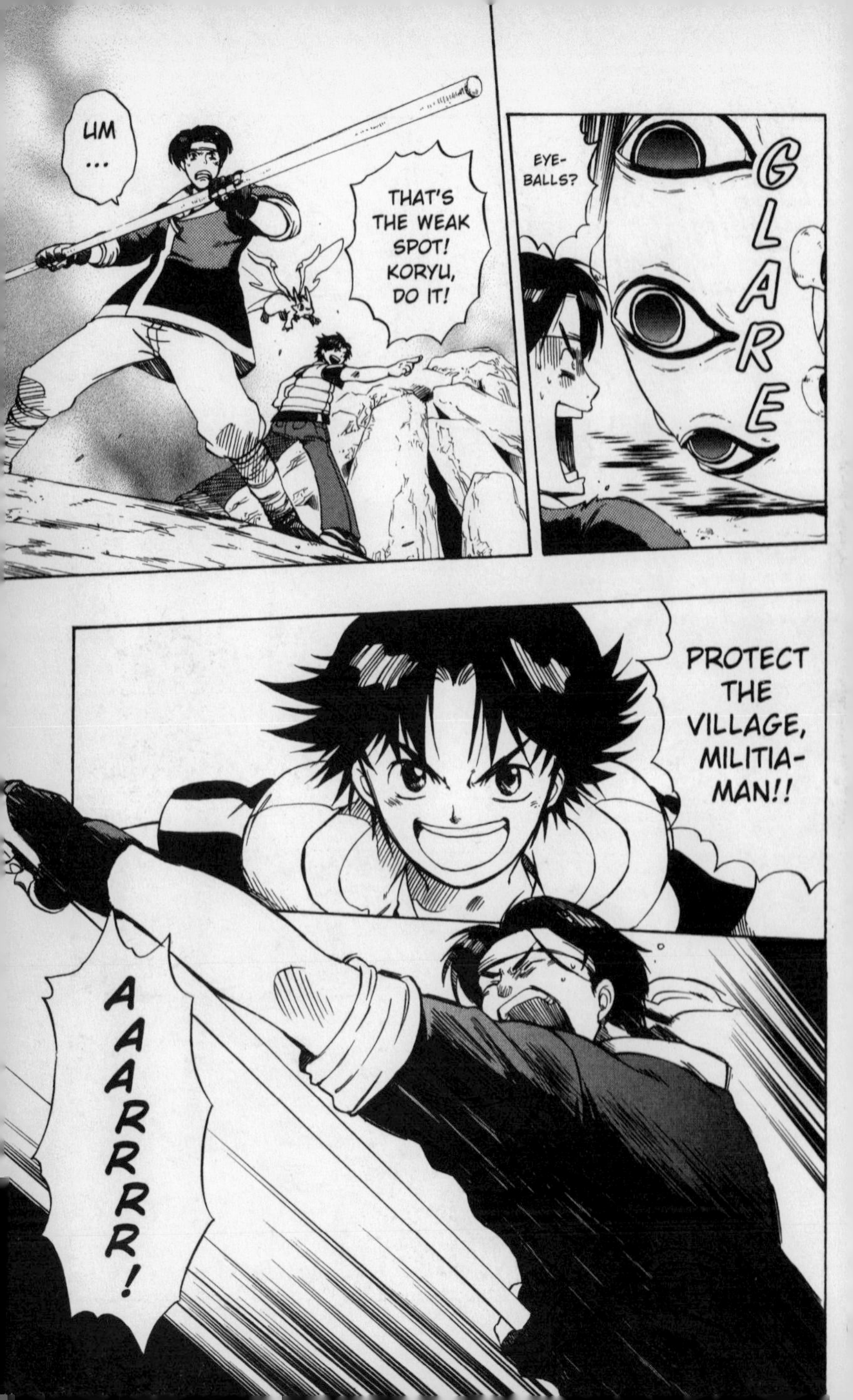
EYE-BALLS?
GLARE
THAT'S THE WEAK SPOT! KORYU, DO IT!
UM ...
PROTECT THE VILLAGE, MILITIA-MAN!!
AAARRRR!

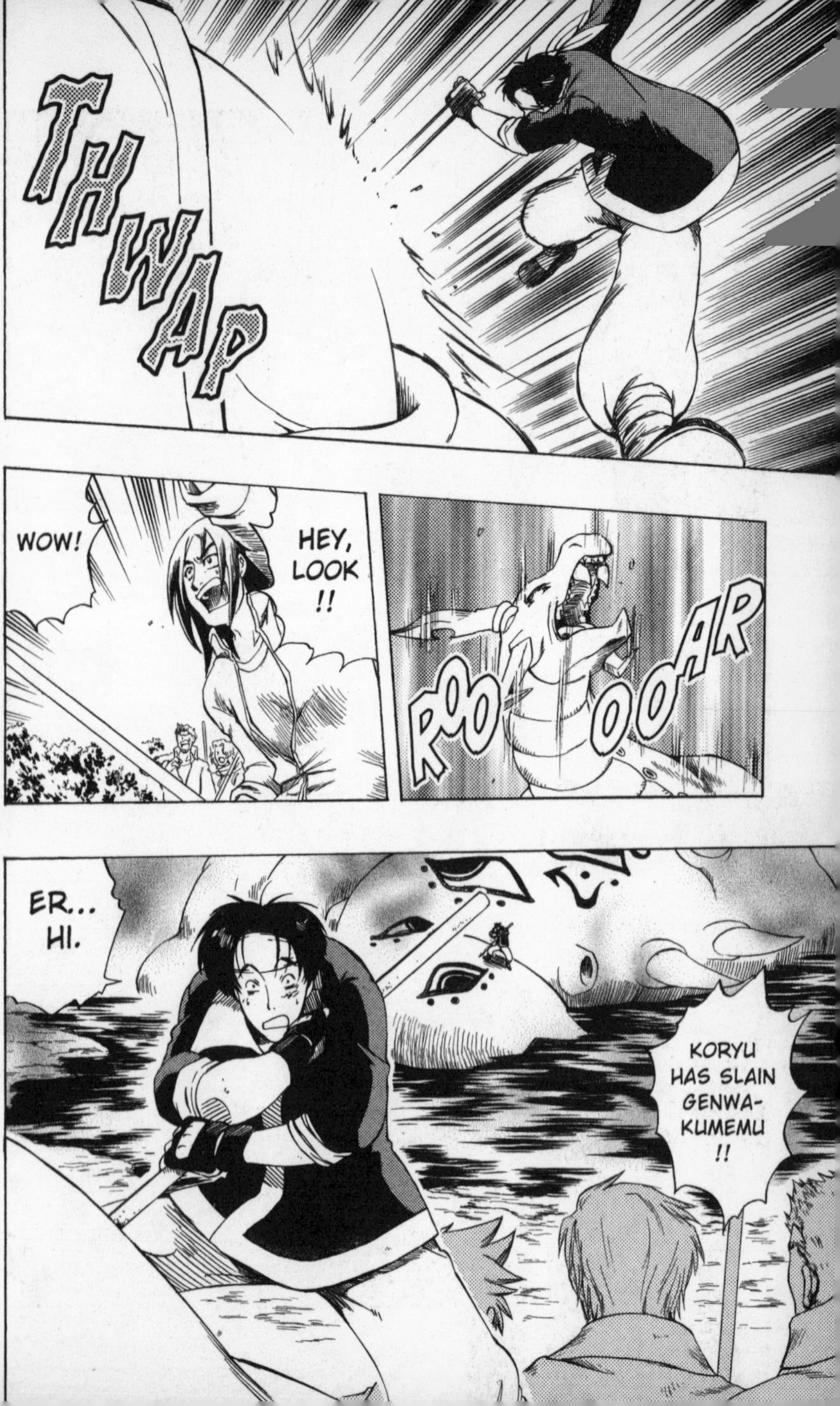
THWAP
ROOOOOAR
HEY, LOOK !!
WOW!
KORYU HAS SLAIN GENWA-KUMEMU !!
ER... HI.

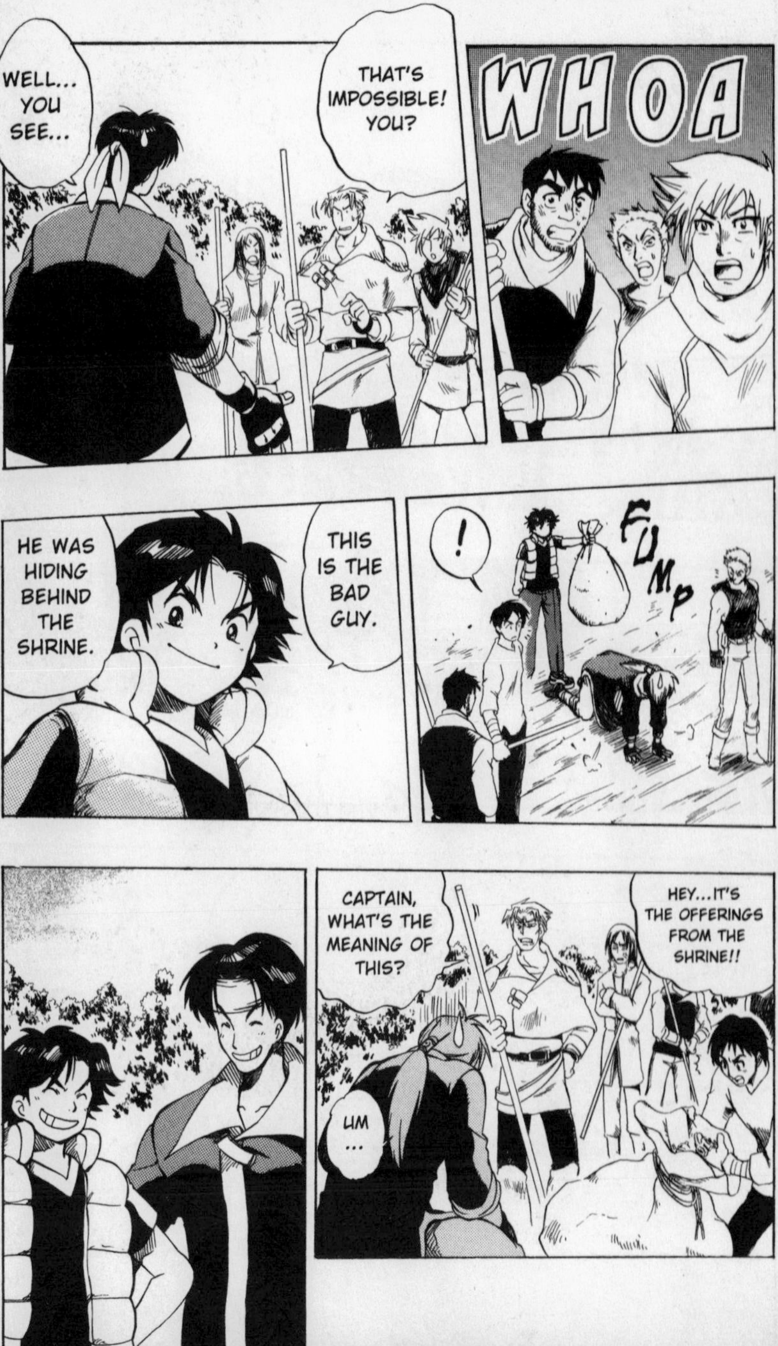
WHOA
THAT'S IMPOSSIBLE! YOU?
WELL... YOU SEE...
!
FUMP
THIS IS THE BAD GUY.
HE WAS HIDING BEHIND THE SHRINE.
HEY...IT'S THE OFFERINGS FROM THE SHRINE!!
CAPTAIN, WHAT'S THE MEANING OF THIS?
UM ...

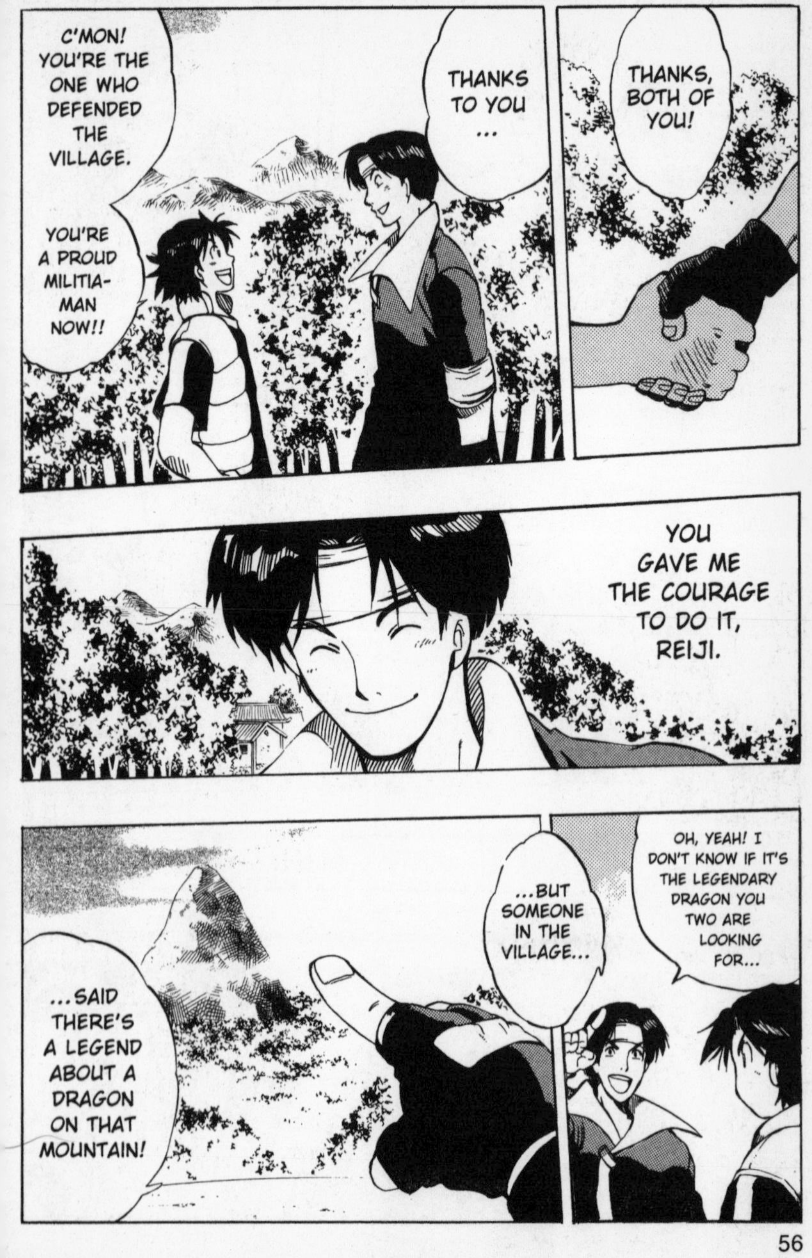
THANKS, BOTH OF YOU!
THANKS TO YOU ...
C'MON! YOU'RE THE ONE WHO DEFENDED THE VILLAGE.
YOU'RE A PROUD MILITIA-MAN NOW!!
YOU GAVE ME THE COURAGE TO DO IT, REIJI.
OH, YEAH! I DON'T KNOW IF IT'S THE LEGENDARY DRAGON YOU TWO ARE LOOKING FOR...
...BUT SOMEONE IN THE VILLAGE...
...SAID THERE'S A LEGEND ABOUT A DRAGON ON THAT MOUNTAIN!

READ THIS WAY

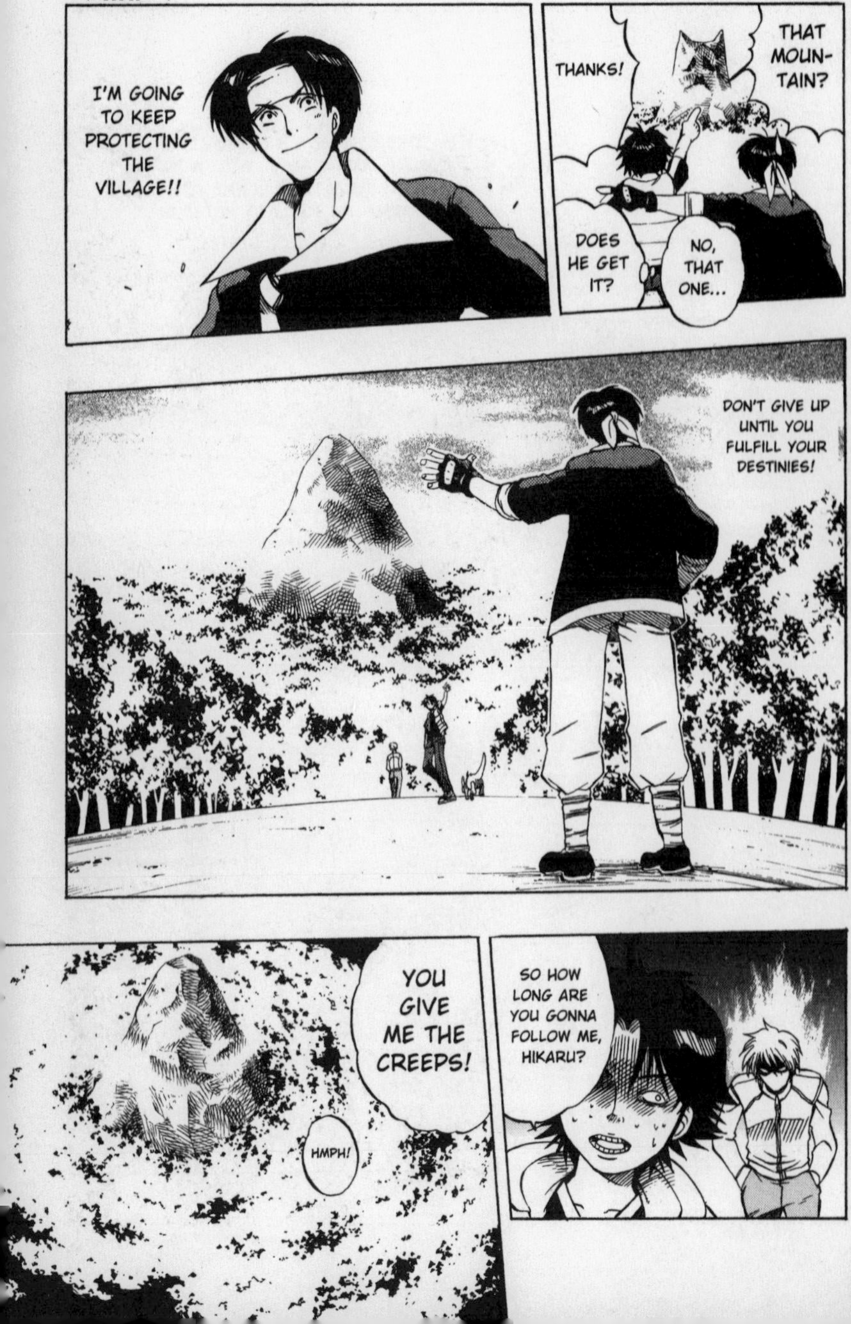
THAT MOUN-TAIN?
THANKS!
NO, THAT ONE...
DOES HE GET IT?
I'M GOING TO KEEP PROTECTING THE VILLAGE!!
DON'T GIVE UP UNTIL YOU FULFILL YOUR DESTINIES!
SO HOW LONG ARE YOU GONNA FOLLOW ME, HIKARU?
YOU GIVE ME THE CREEPS!
HMPH!

THIS CHARACTER IS BASED ON
YUSUKE MATSUSHIMA, WHO WON THE
RIGHT TO APPEAR IN THE COMIC.
SORRY IT'S SO LATE, YUSUKE!!

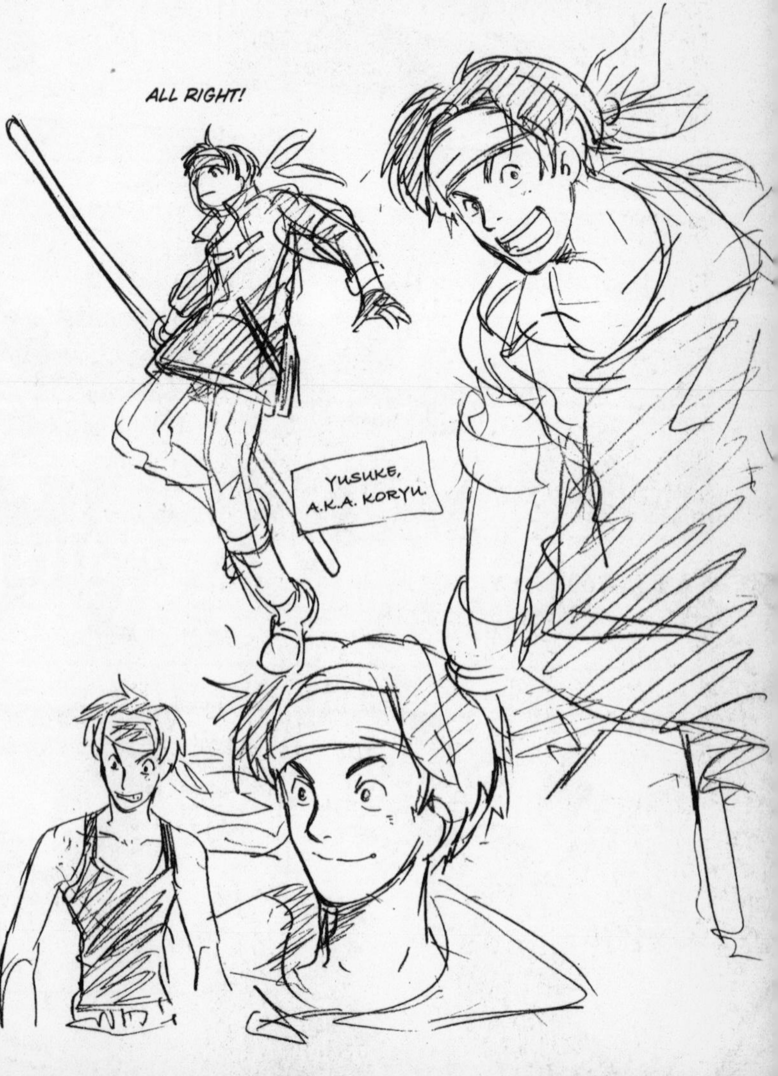
YUSUKE, A.K.A. KORYU.
ALL RIGHT!

STAGE18 PROMISE

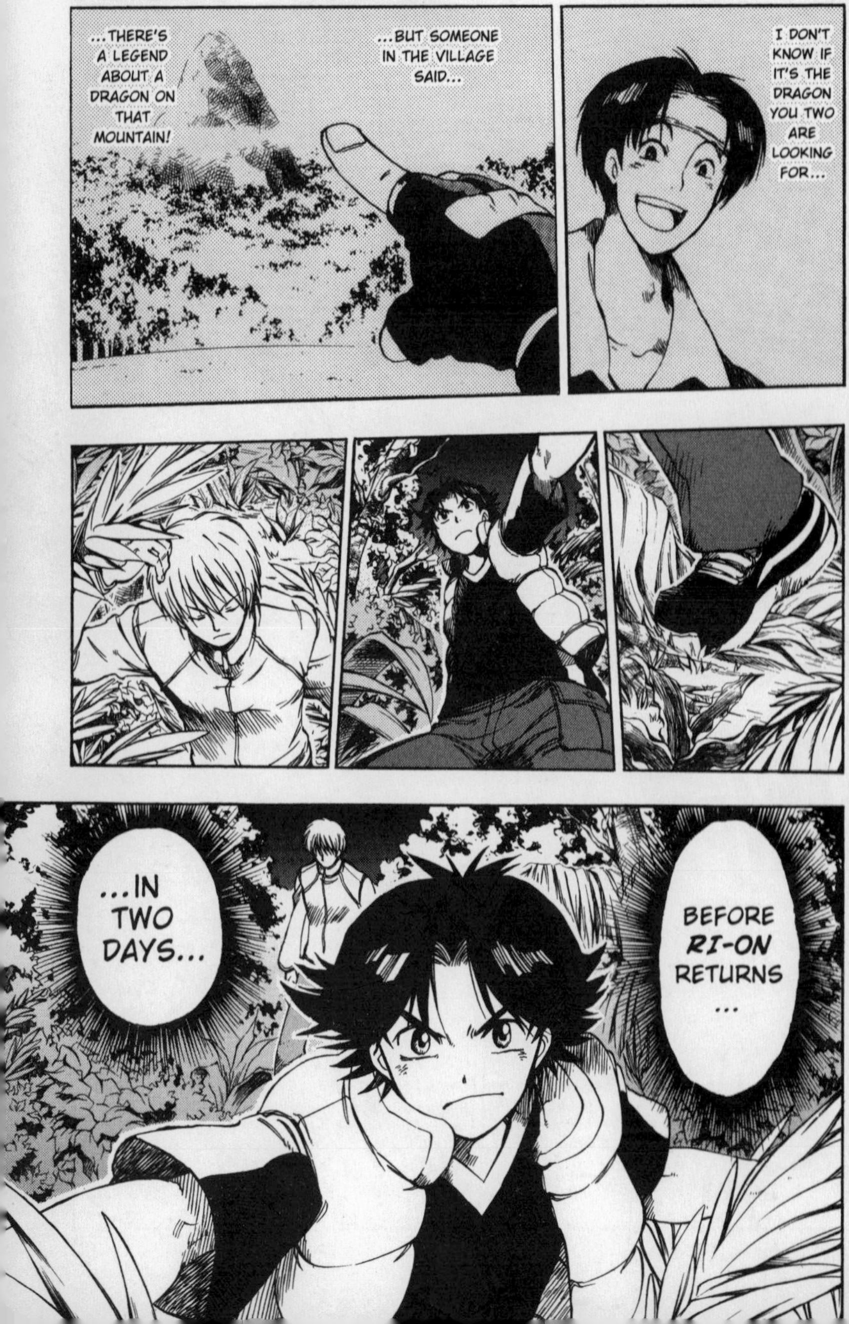
I DON'T KNOW IF IT'S THE DRAGON YOU TWO ARE LOOKING FOR...
...BUT SOMEONE IN THE VILLAGE SAID...
...THERE'S A LEGEND ABOUT A DRAGON ON THAT MOUNTAIN!
BEFORE *RI-ON* RETURNS ...
...IN TWO DAYS...

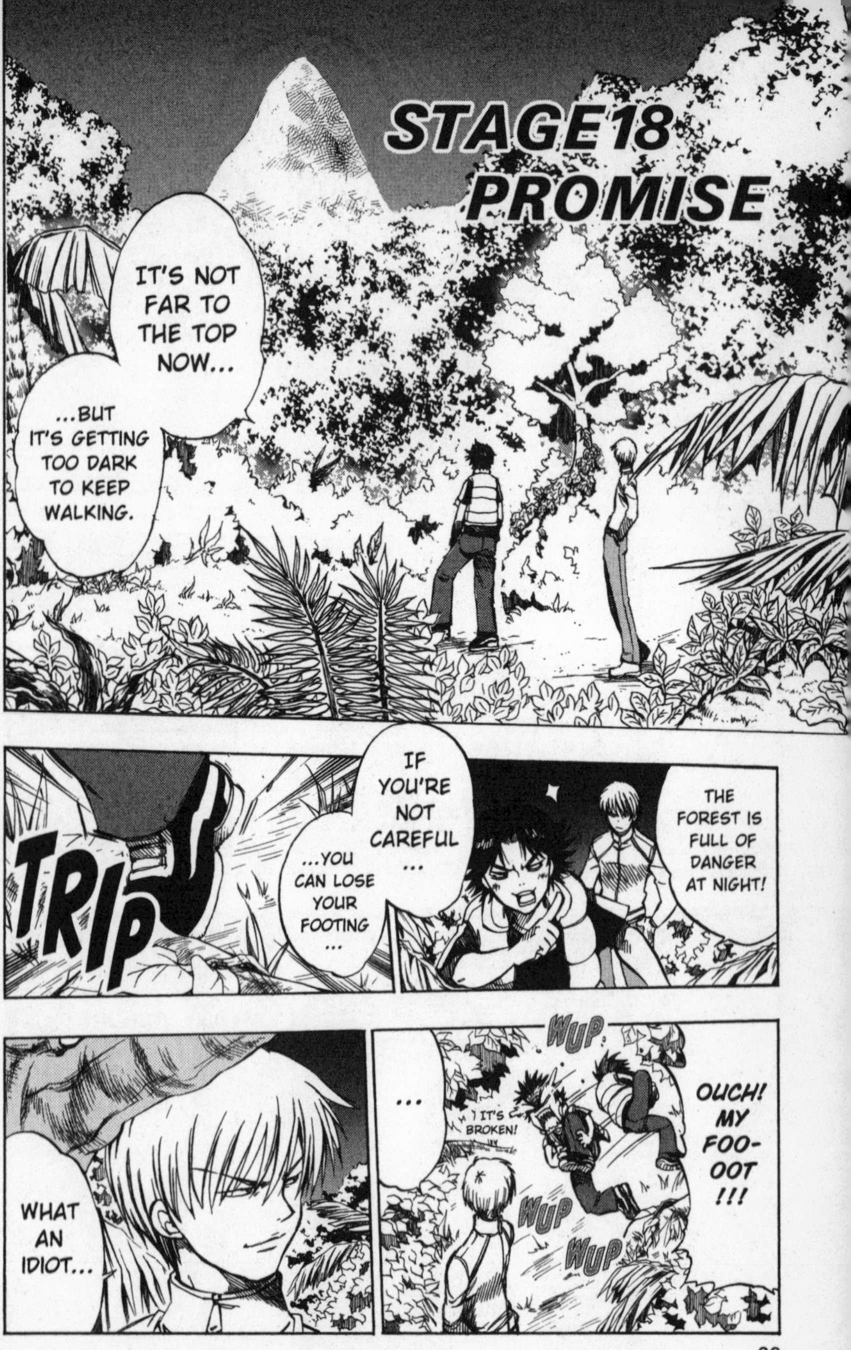
STAGE18
PROMISE
IT'S NOT FAR TO THE TOP NOW...
...BUT IT'S GETTING TOO DARK TO KEEP WALKING.
THE FOREST IS FULL OF DANGER AT NIGHT!
IF YOU'RE NOT CAREFUL...
...YOU CAN LOSE YOUR FOOTING...
TRIP
WUP
OUCH! MY FOO-OOT!!!
IT'S BROKEN!
WUP
WUP
...
WHAT AN IDIOT...

READ THIS WAY

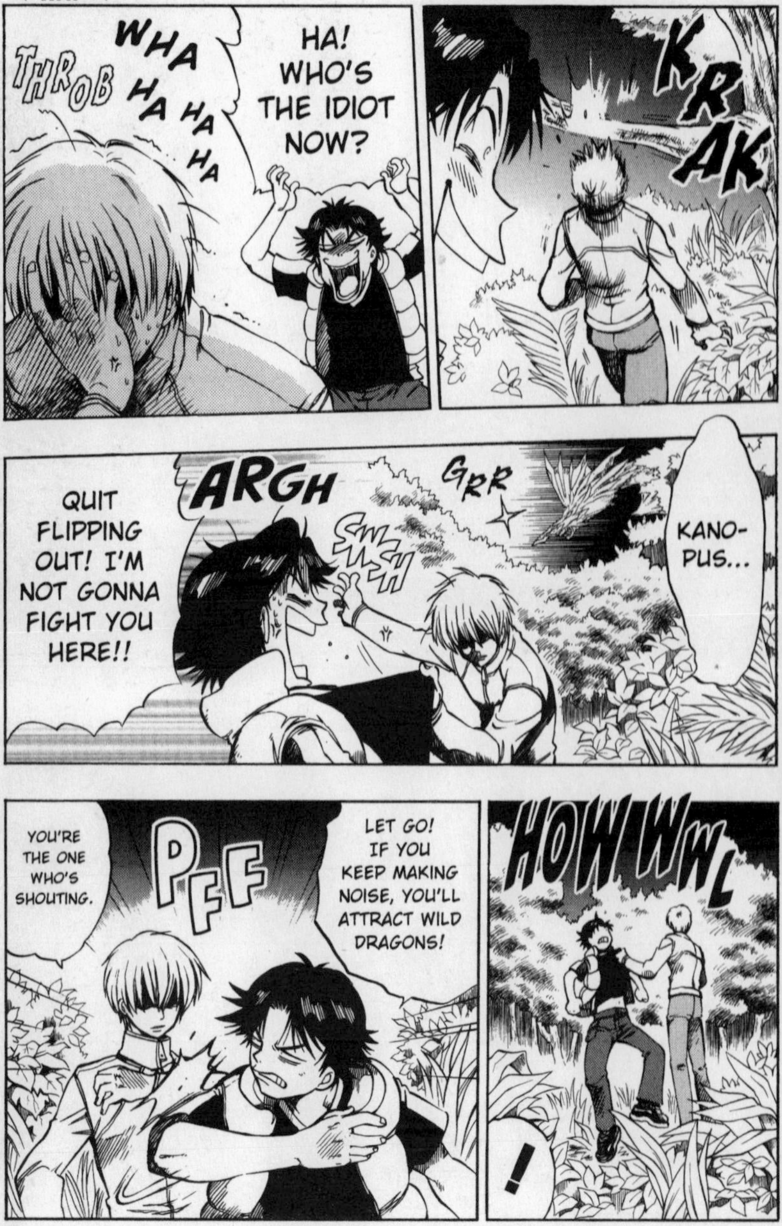

KRAK
WHA HA HA HA HA
HA! WHO'S THE IDIOT NOW?
THROB
KANO-PUS...
GRR
SWISH
ARGH
QUIT FLIPPING OUT! I'M NOT GONNA FIGHT YOU HERE!!
HOWWWL
!
LET GO! IF YOU KEEP MAKING NOISE, YOU'LL ATTRACT WILD DRAGONS!
PFF
YOU'RE THE ONE WHO'S SHOUTING.

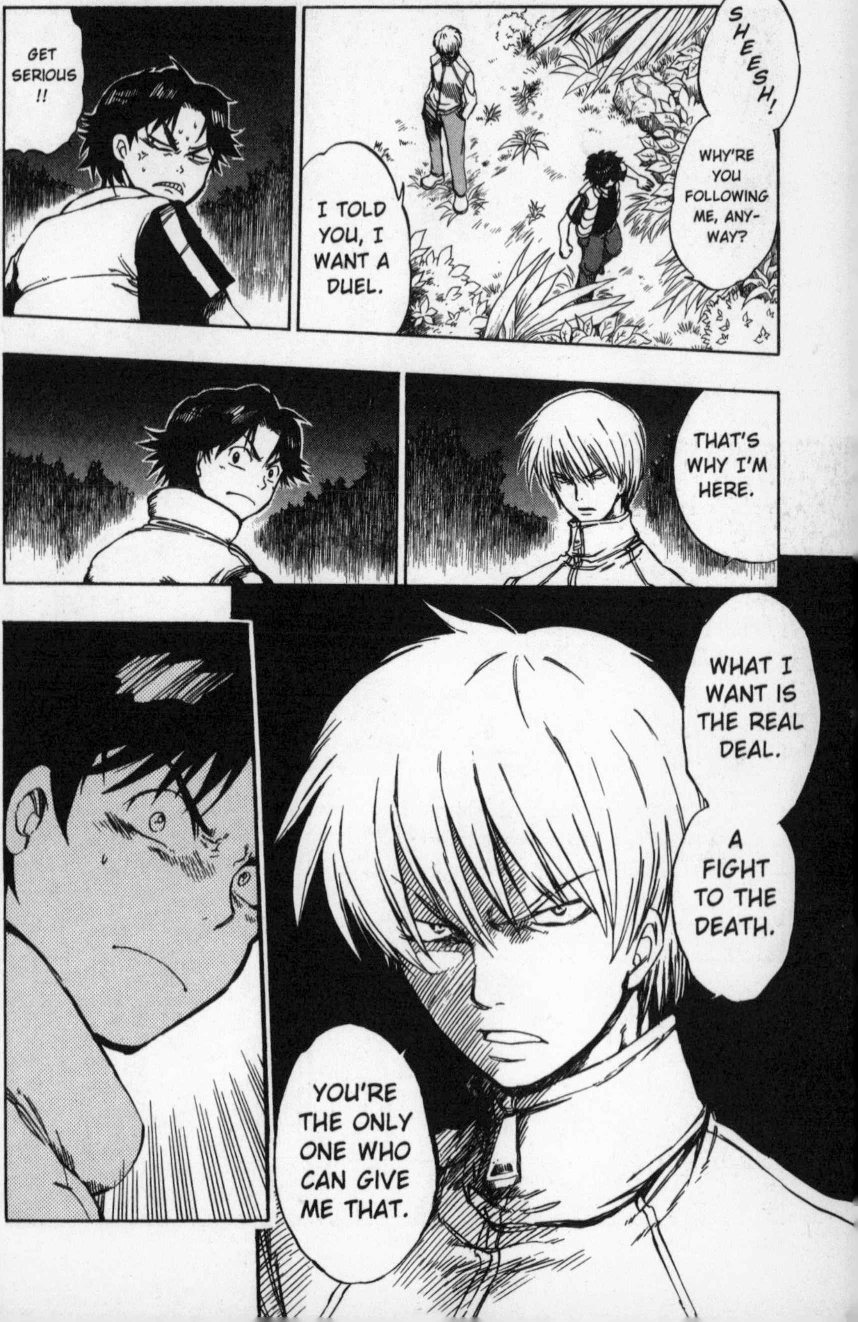
SHEESH!
WHY'RE YOU FOLLOWING ME, ANYWAY?
I TOLD YOU, I WANT A DUEL.
GET SERIOUS!!
THAT'S WHY I'M HERE.
WHAT I WANT IS THE REAL DEAL.
A FIGHT TO THE DEATH.
YOU'RE THE ONLY ONE WHO CAN GIVE ME THAT.

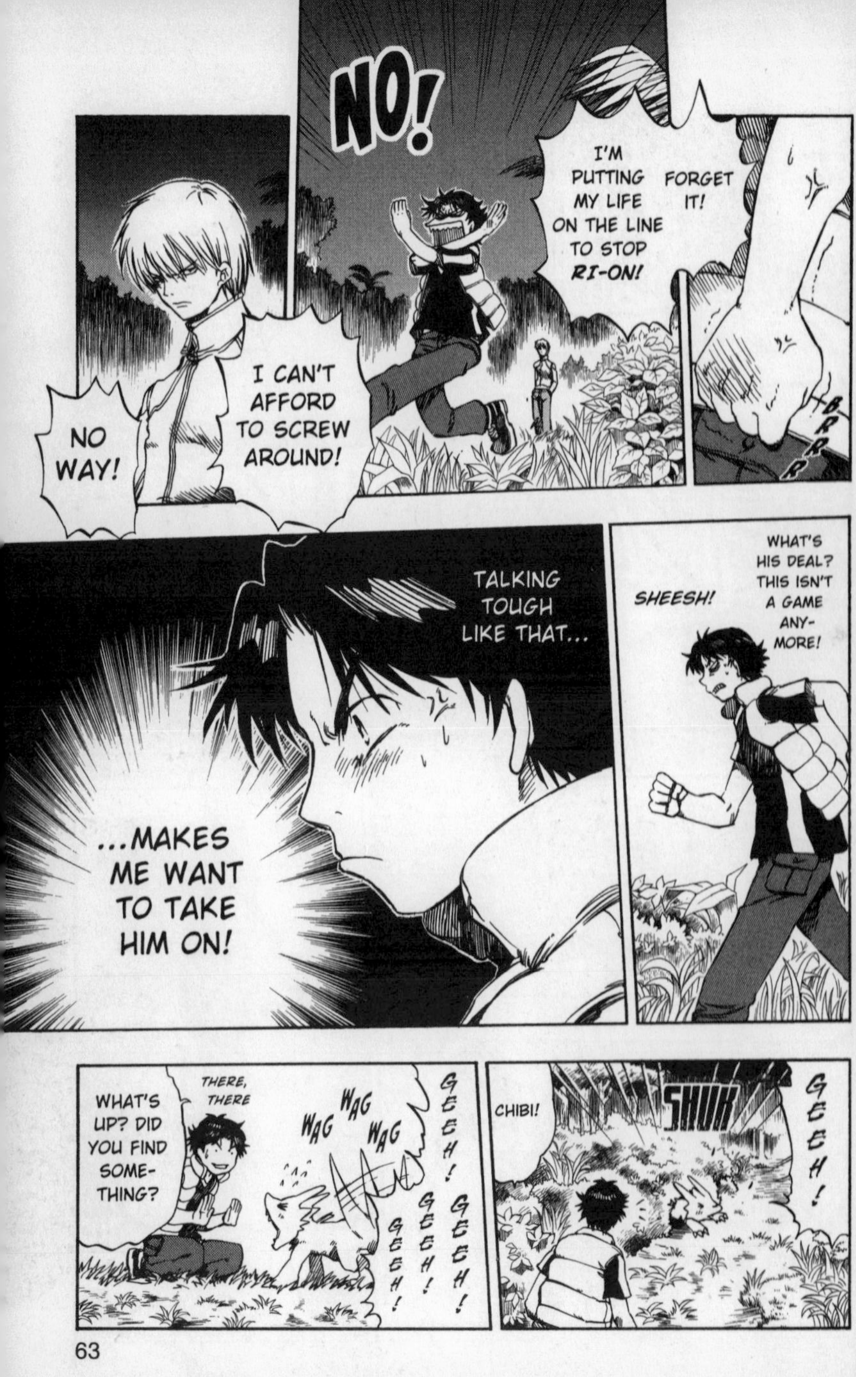
FORGET IT!
I'M PUTTING MY LIFE ON THE LINE TO STOP RI-ON!
BRRRR
NO!
I CAN'T AFFORD TO SCREW AROUND!
NO WAY!
WHAT'S HIS DEAL? THIS ISN'T A GAME ANYMORE!
SHEESH!
TALKING TOUGH LIKE THAT...
...MAKES ME WANT TO TAKE HIM ON!
GEEH!
SHUK
CHIBI!
GEEH! GEEH! GEEH!
WAG WAG WAG
THERE, THERE
WHAT'S UP? DID YOU FIND SOMETHING?

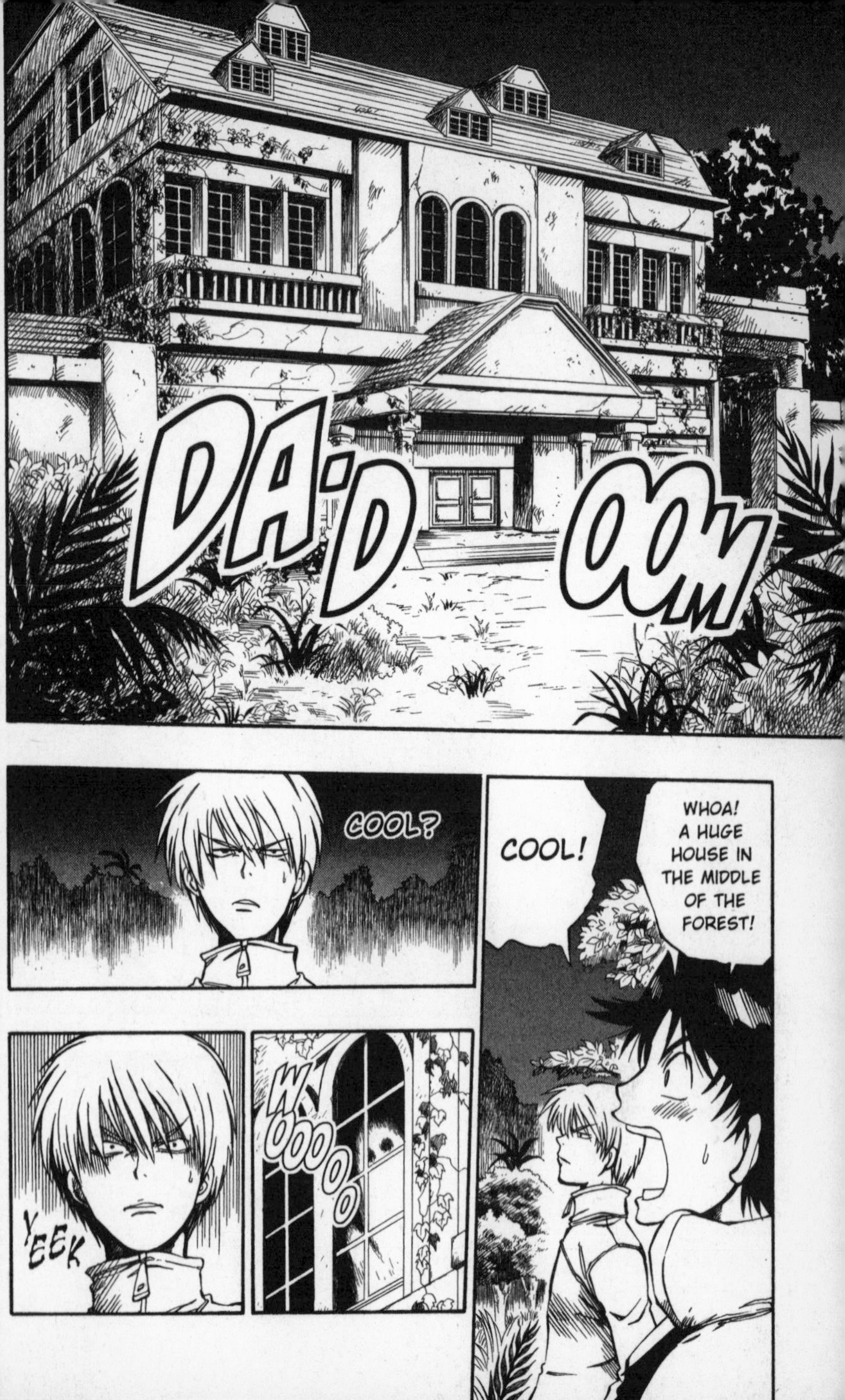
DA-DOOM
WHOA! A HUGE HOUSE IN THE MIDDLE OF THE FOREST!
COOL!
COOL?
WOOOOOO
YEEK

READ THIS WAY

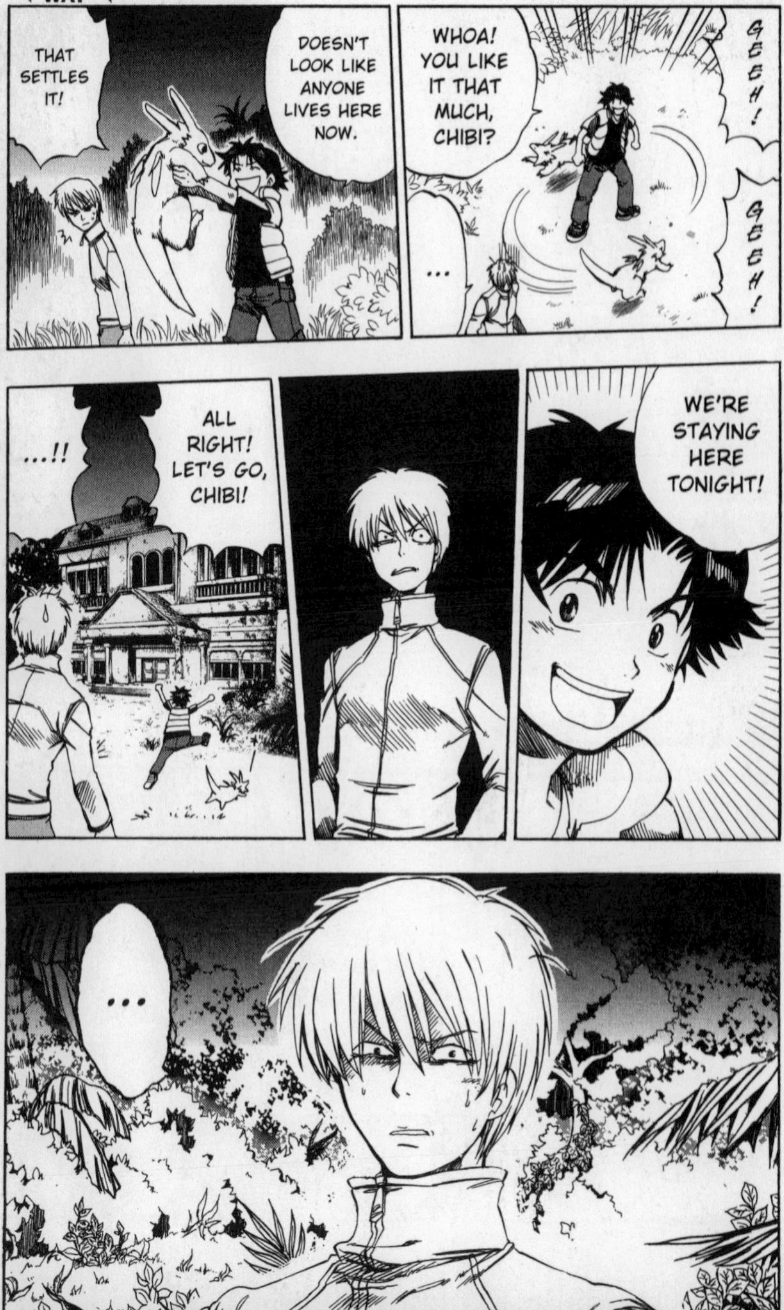
GEEH! GEEH!
WHOA! YOU LIKE IT THAT MUCH, CHIBI?
...
DOESN'T LOOK LIKE ANYONE LIVES HERE NOW.
THAT SETTLES IT!
WE'RE STAYING HERE TONIGHT!
ALL RIGHT! LET'S GO, CHIBI!
...!!
...

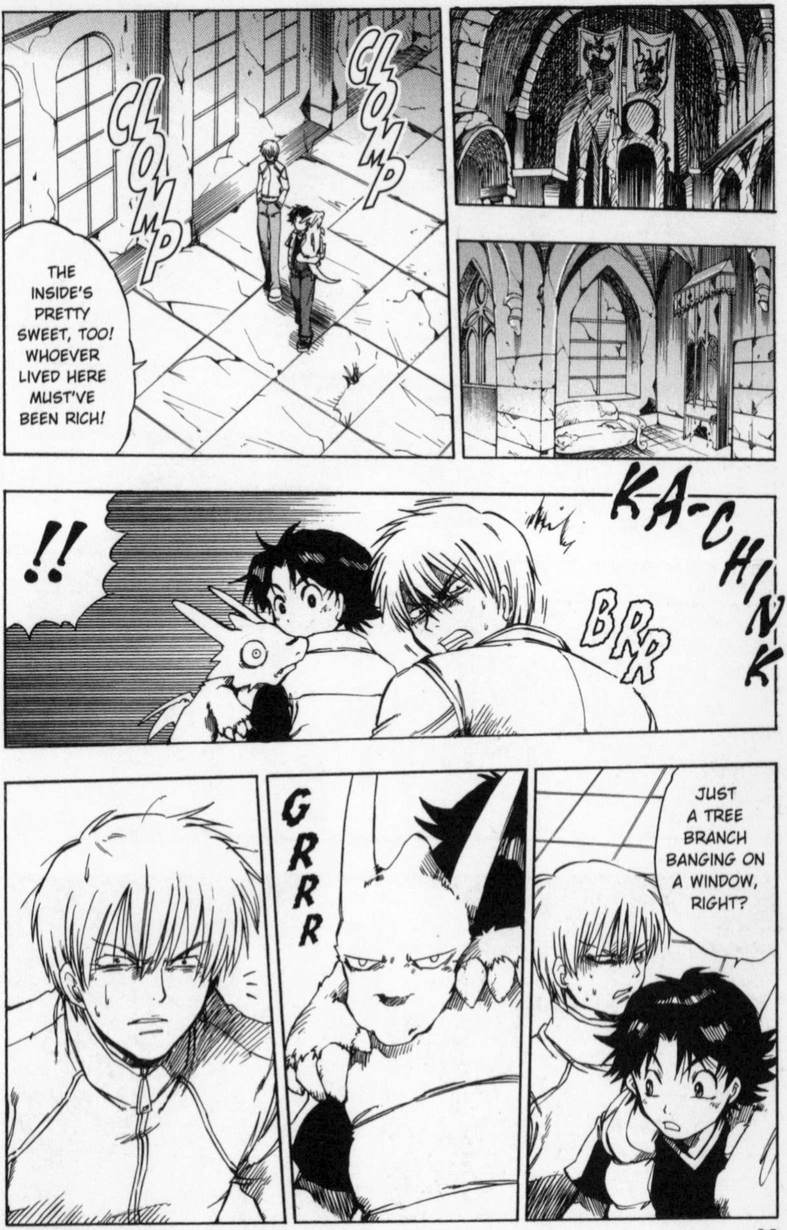
CLOMP
CLOMP
THE INSIDE'S PRETTY SWEET, TOO! WHOEVER LIVED HERE MUST'VE BEEN RICH!
KA-CHINK
BRR
!!
JUST A TREE BRANCH BANGING ON A WINDOW, RIGHT?
GRRR

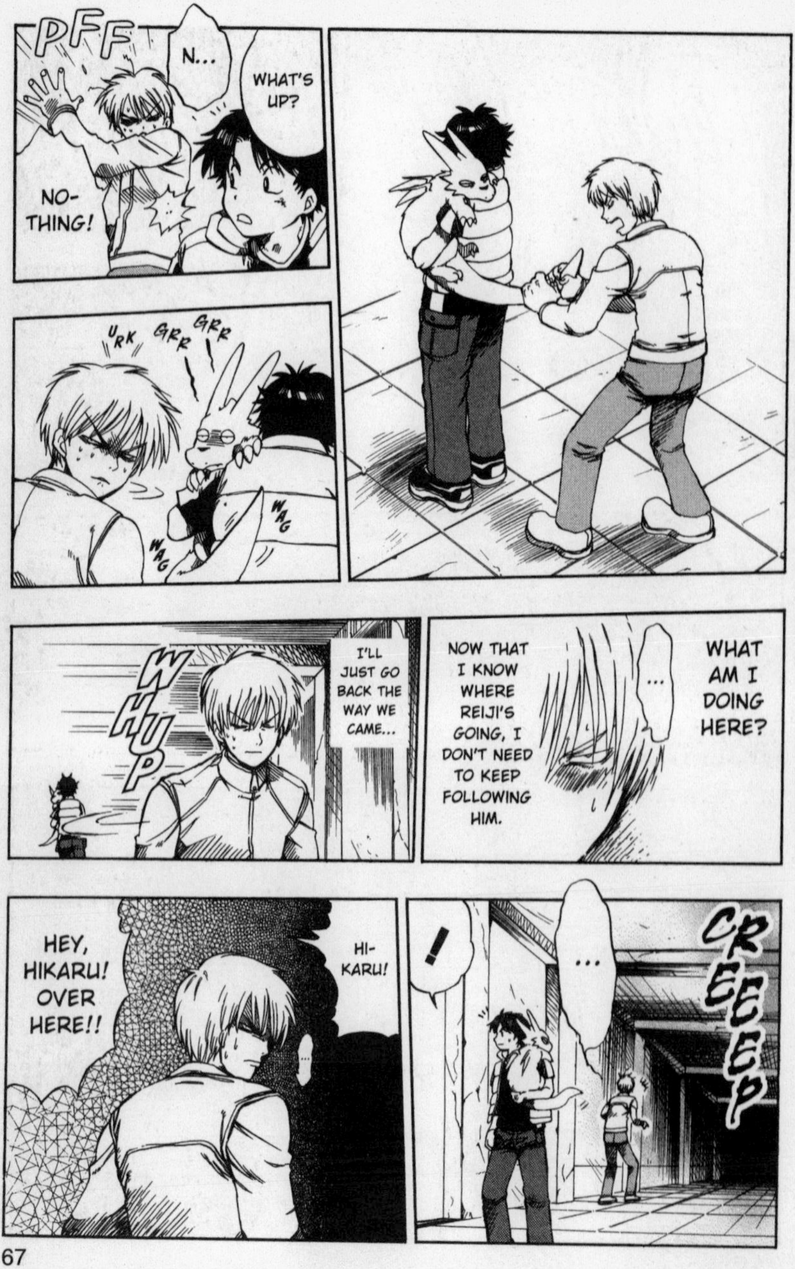
WHAT'S UP?
N...
PFF
NO-THING!
GRR GRR
URK
WAG
WAG
WHAT AM I DOING HERE?
...
NOW THAT I KNOW WHERE REIJI'S GOING, I DON'T NEED TO KEEP FOLLOWING HIM.
I'LL JUST GO BACK THE WAY WE CAME...
WHUP
CREEEP
...
!
HI-KARU!
HEY, HIKARU! OVER HERE!!
...

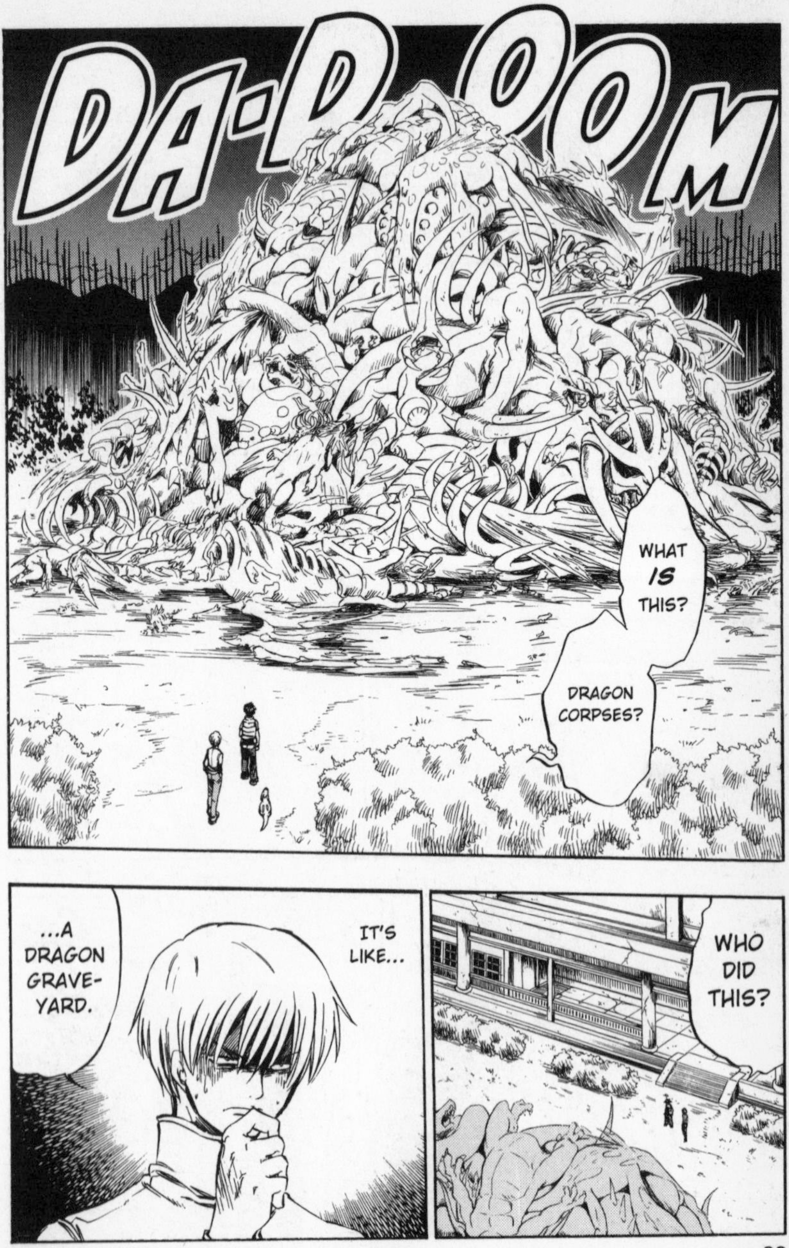
DA-DOOM
WHAT IS THIS?
DRAGON CORPSES?
WHO DID THIS?
IT'S LIKE...
...A DRAGON GRAVEYARD.

READ THIS WAY

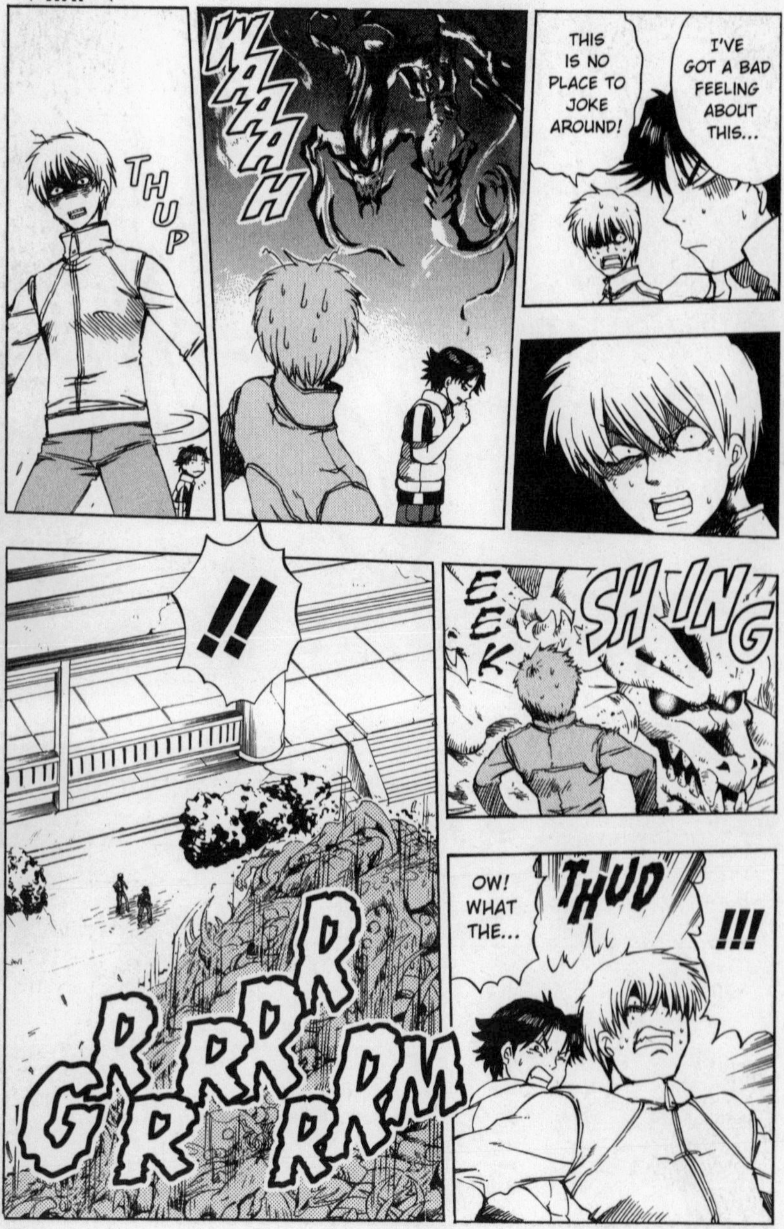
I'VE GOT A BAD FEELING ABOUT THIS...
THIS IS NO PLACE TO JOKE AROUND!
WAAAAH
THUP
SHING
EEK
THUD
!!!
OW! WHAT THE...
!!
GRRRRRRM

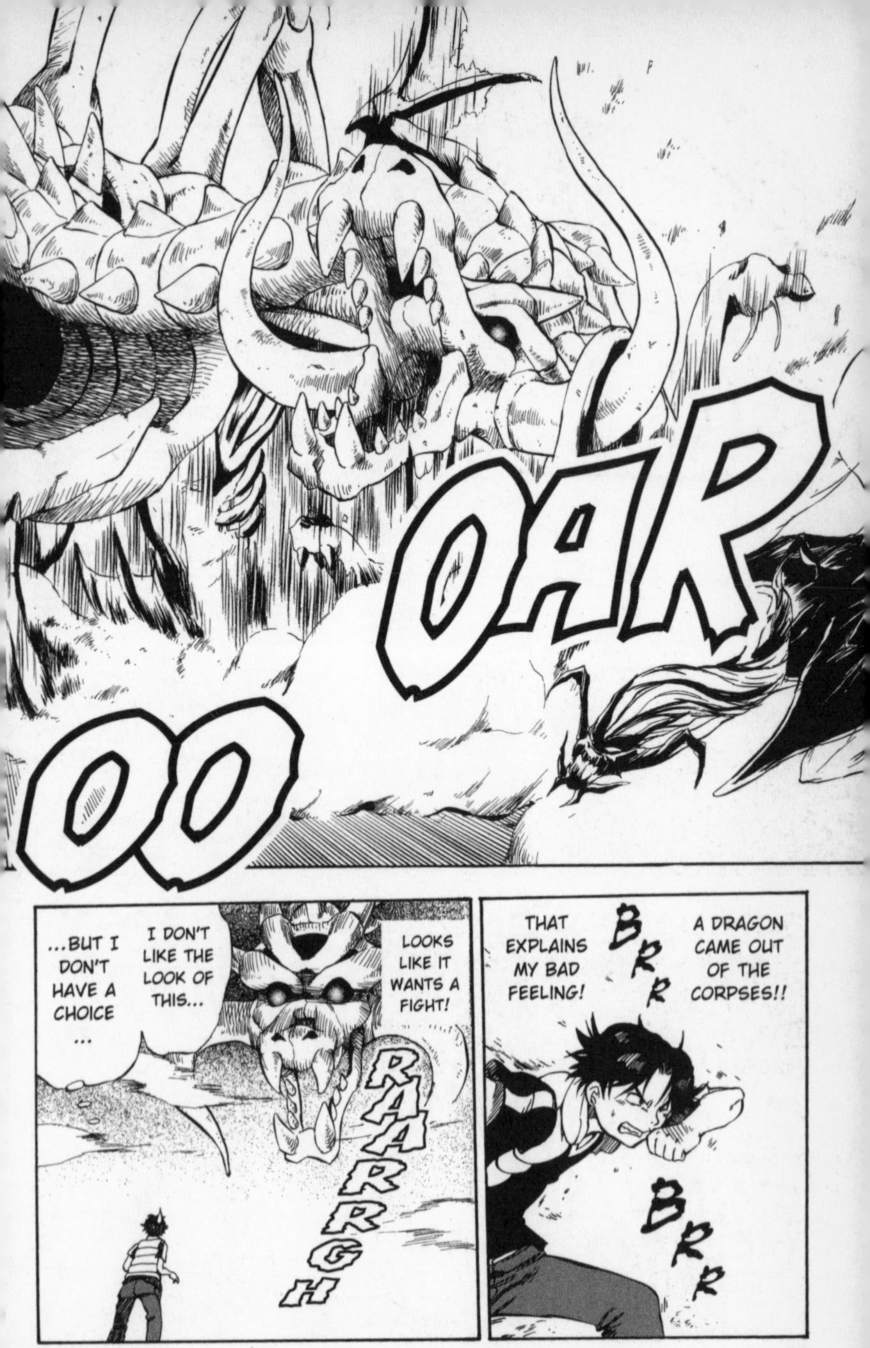
OOOAR
A DRAGON CAME OUT OF THE CORPSES!!
BRRR
THAT EXPLAINS MY BAD FEELING!
BRRR
LOOKS LIKE IT WANTS A FIGHT!
RAARRGH
I DON'T LIKE THE LOOK OF THIS...
...BUT I DON'T HAVE A CHOICE ...

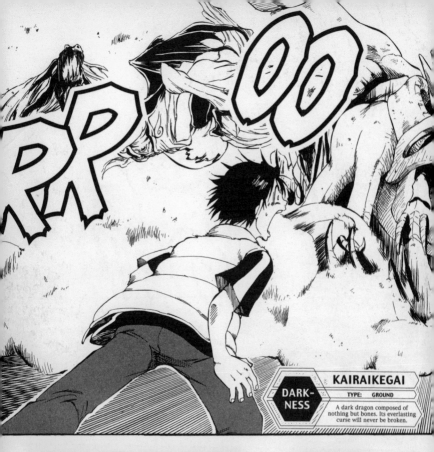

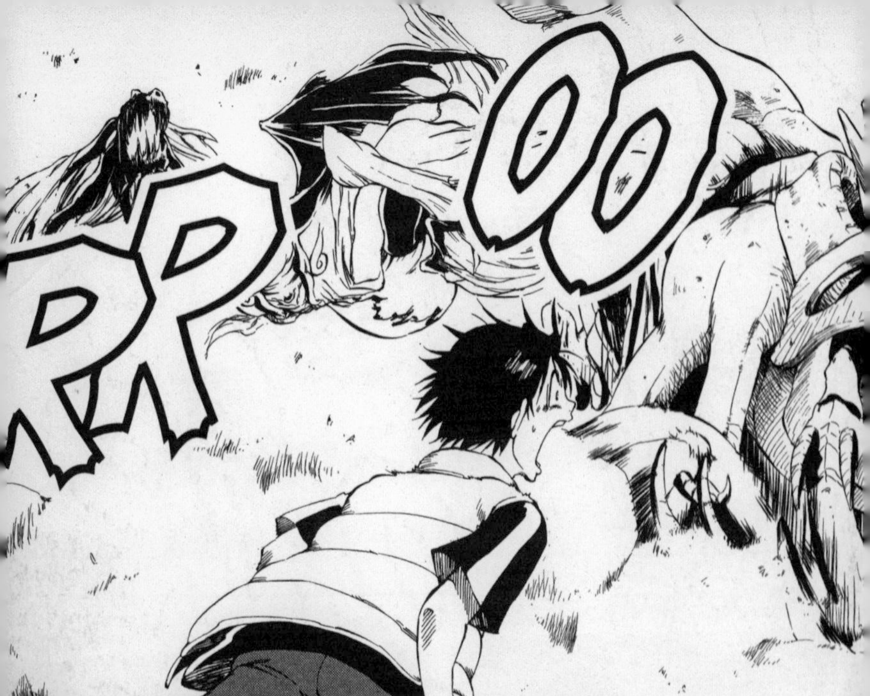
RROOO
KAIRAIKEGAI
DARK-NESS
TYPE: GROUND
A dark dragon composed of nothing but bones. Its everlasting curse will never be broken.

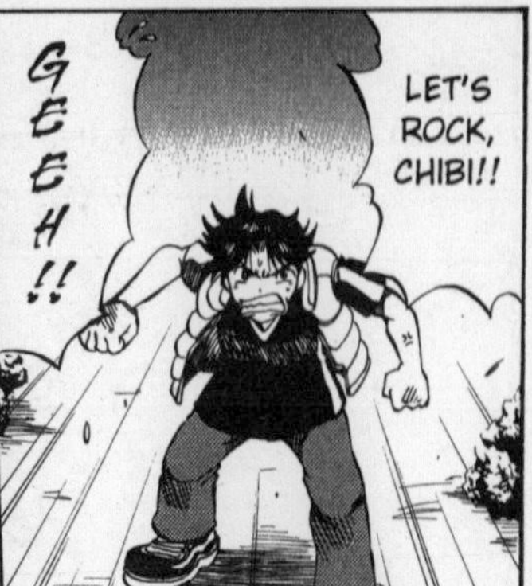
LET'S ROCK, CHIBI!!
GEEH!!

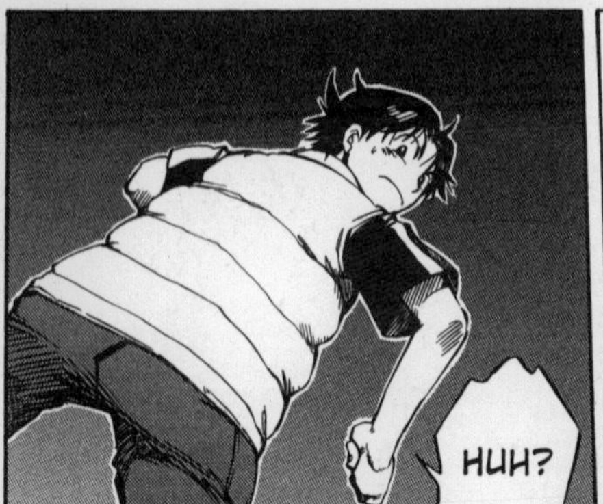
HUH?

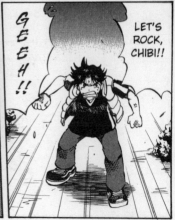

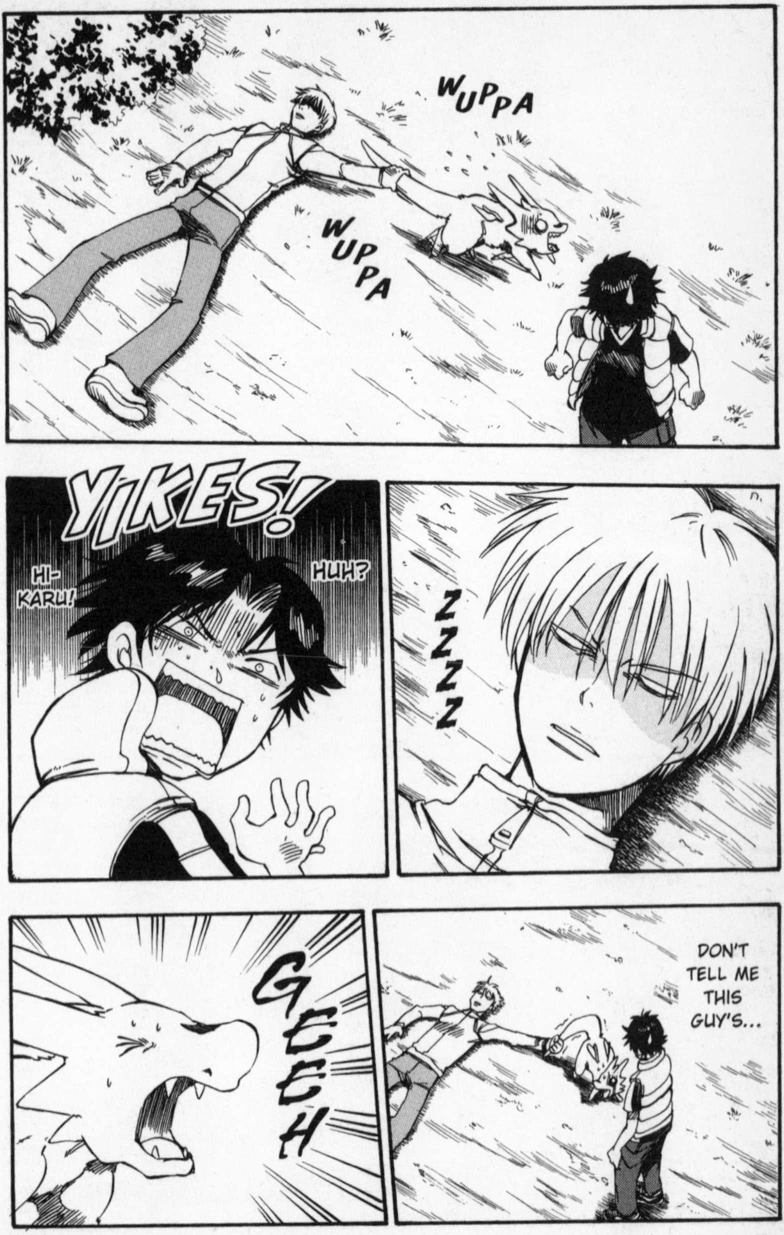
WUPPA
WUPPA
ZZZZ
YIKES!
HUH?
HI-KARU!
DON'T TELL ME THIS GUY'S...
GEEH

READ THIS WAY

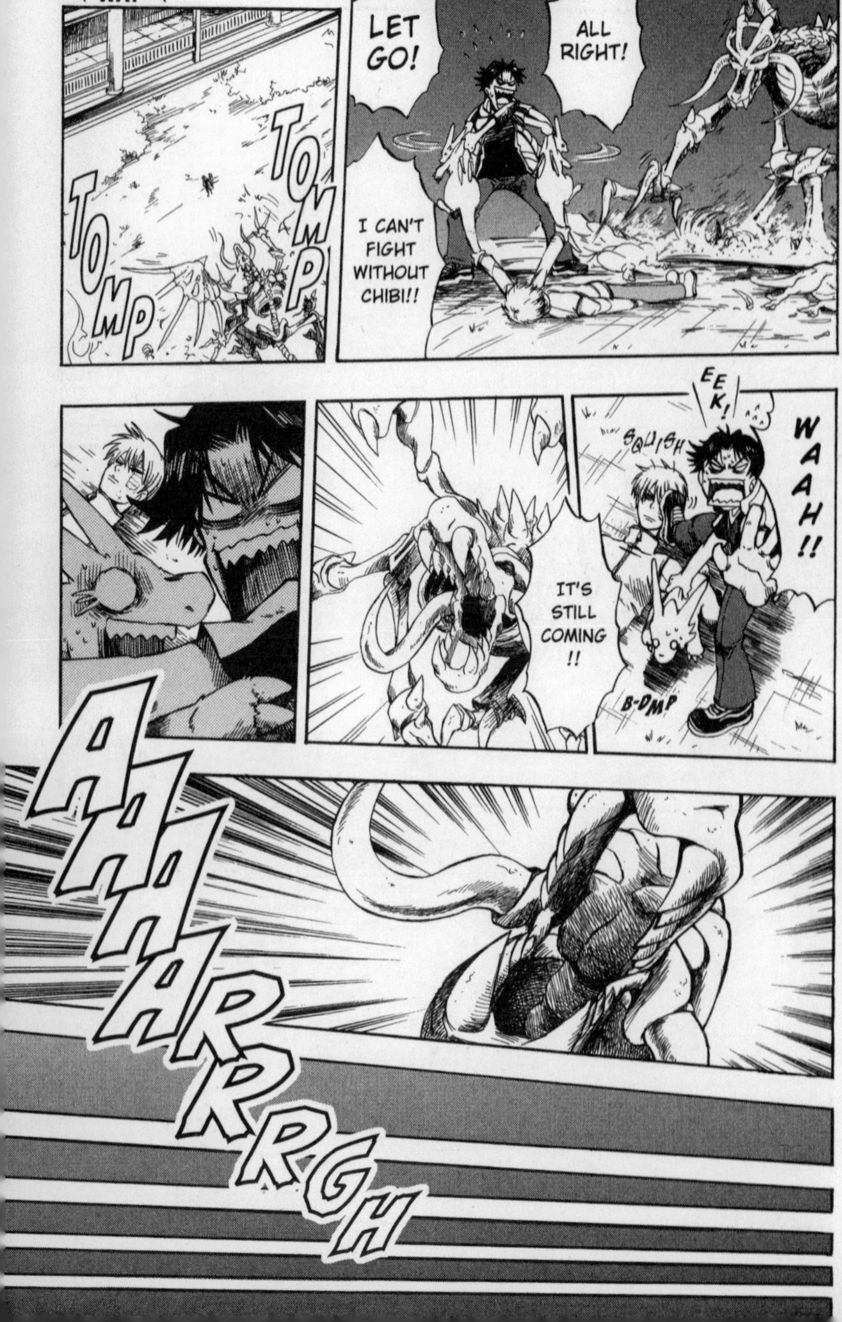
ALL RIGHT!
LET GO!
I CAN'T FIGHT WITHOUT CHIBI!!
TOMP TOMP
EEK!
WAAH!!
SQUISH
IT'S STILL COMING!!
B-DMP
AAHARRGH

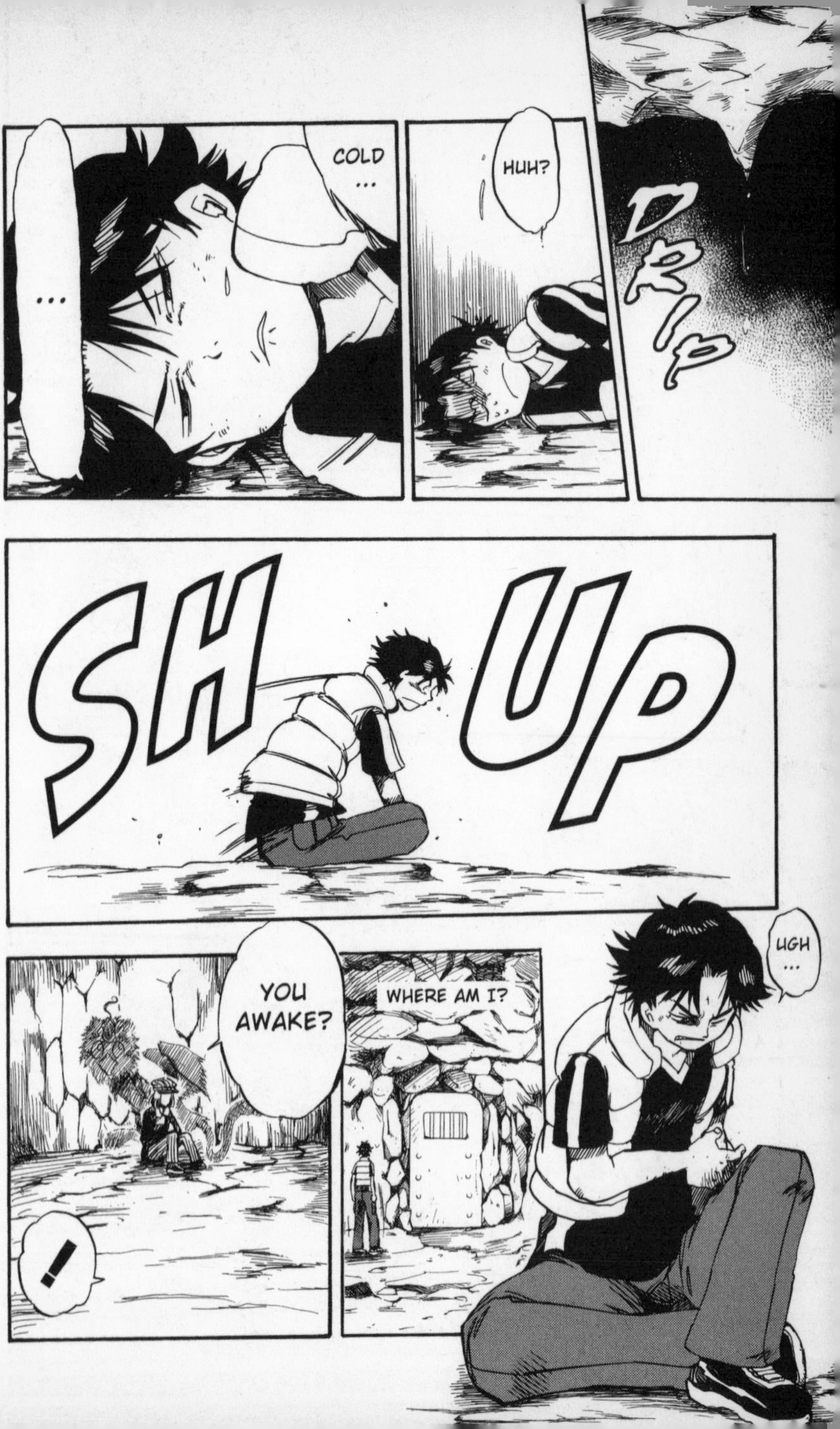
DRIP
HUH?
COLD ...
...
SH UP
UGH ...
WHERE AM I?
YOU AWAKE?
!

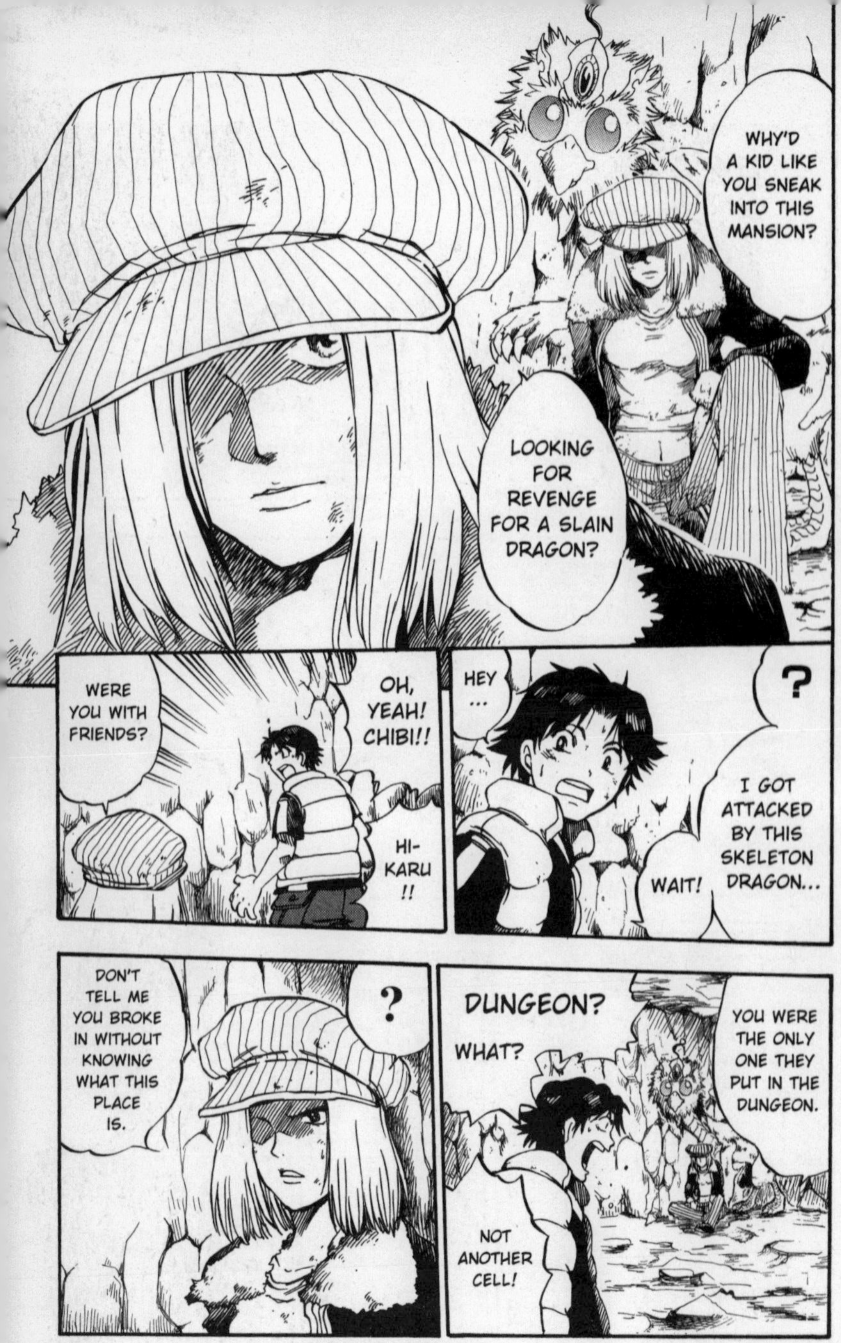
WHY'D A KID LIKE YOU SNEAK INTO THIS MANSION?
LOOKING FOR REVENGE FOR A SLAIN DRAGON?
?
HEY ...
I GOT ATTACKED BY THIS SKELETON DRAGON...
WAIT!
OH, YEAH! CHIBI!!
WERE YOU WITH FRIENDS?
HI-KARU !!
YOU WERE THE ONLY ONE THEY PUT IN THE DUNGEON.
DUNGEON?
WHAT?
NOT ANOTHER CELL!
?
DON'T TELL ME YOU BROKE IN WITHOUT KNOWING WHAT THIS PLACE IS.

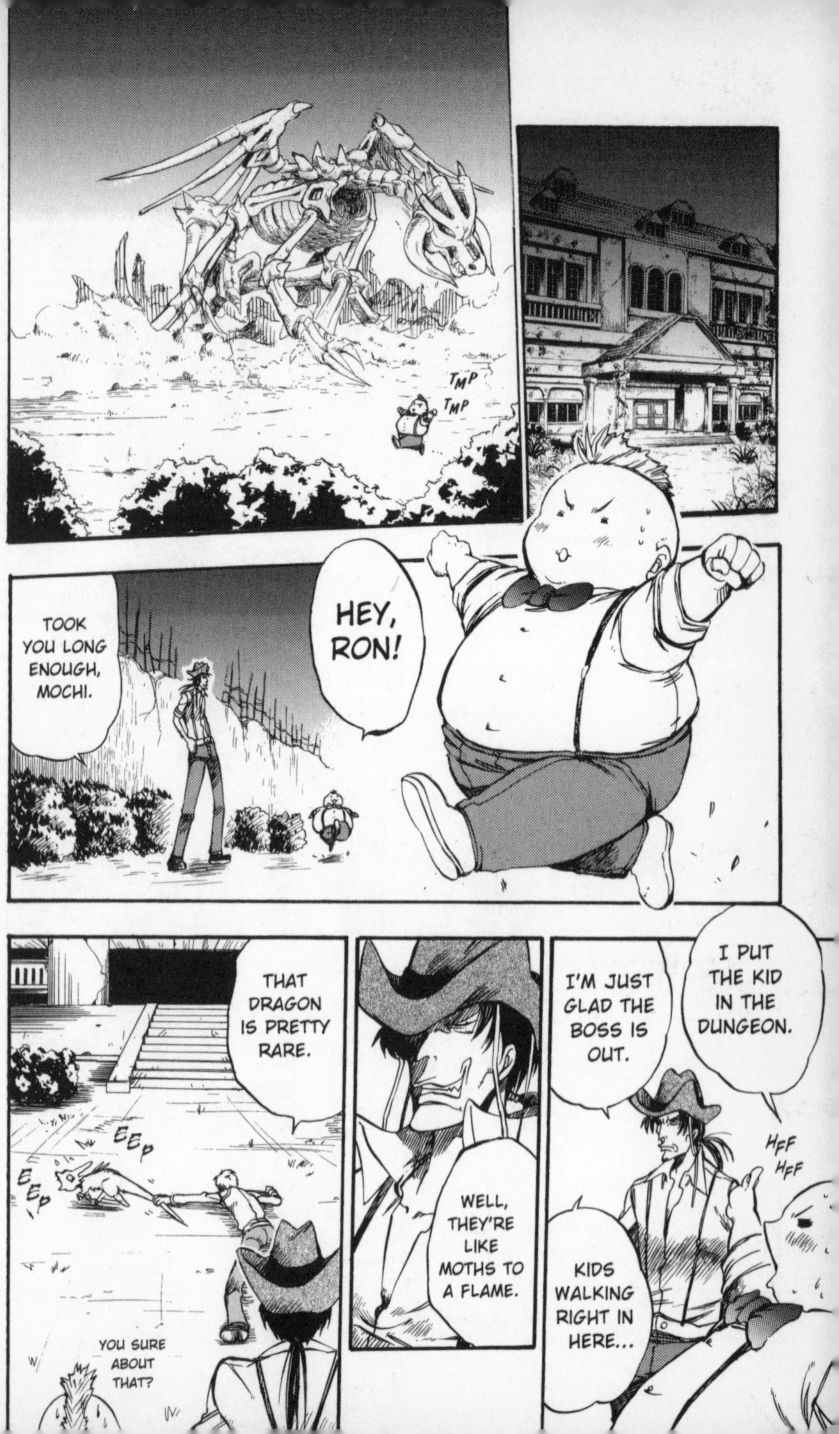
TMP
TMP
HEY, RON!
TOOK YOU LONG ENOUGH, MOCHI.
I PUT THE KID IN THE DUNGEON.
I'M JUST GLAD THE BOSS IS OUT.
HFF HFF
KIDS WALKING RIGHT IN HERE...
WELL, THEY'RE LIKE MOTHS TO A FLAME.
THAT DRAGON IS PRETTY RARE.
EEP
EEP
YOU SURE ABOUT THAT?

READ THIS WAY

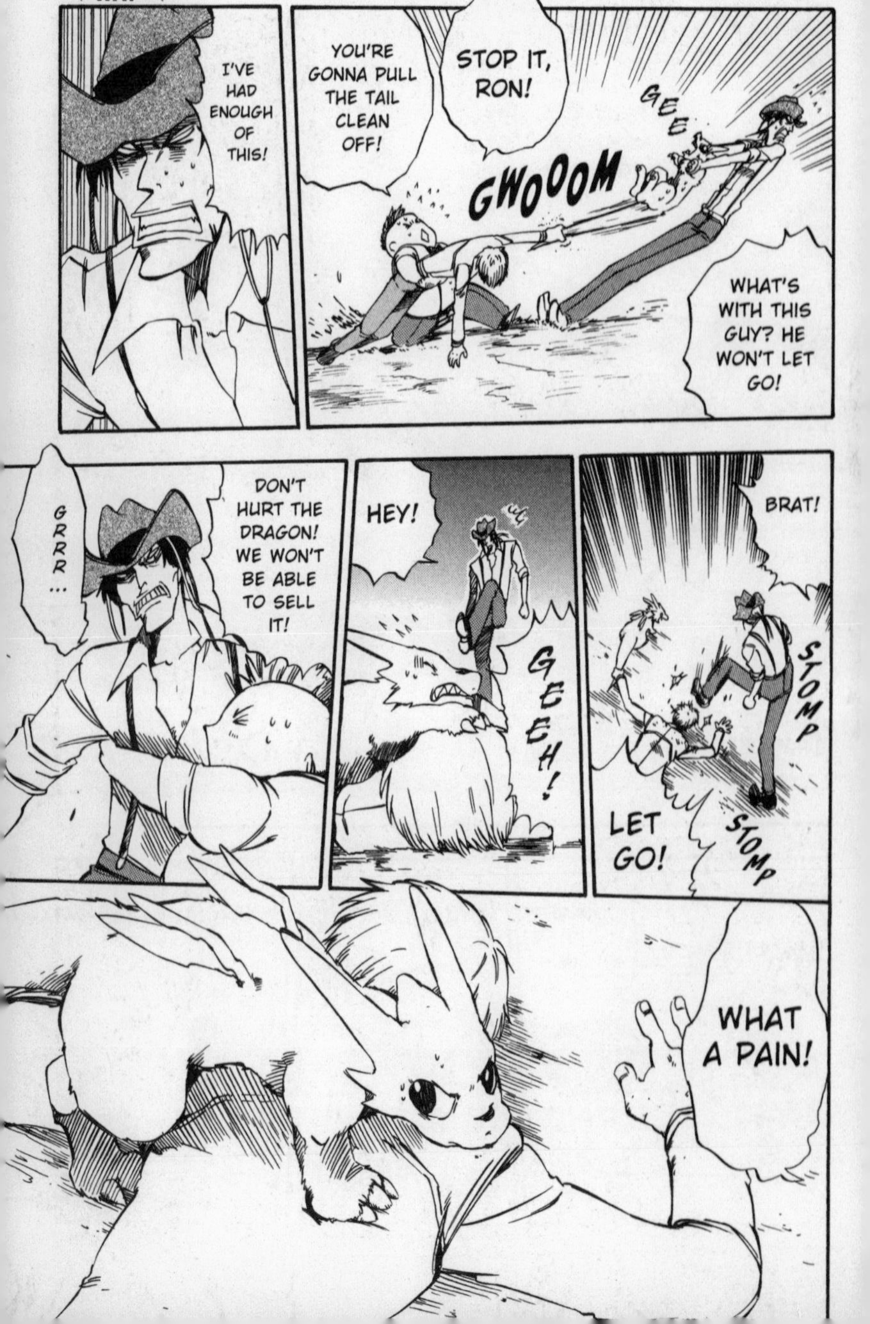
STOP IT, RON!
YOU'RE GONNA PULL THE TAIL CLEAN OFF!
GEE
GWOOOM
WHAT'S WITH THIS GUY? HE WON'T LET GO!
I'VE HAD ENOUGH OF THIS!
BRAT!
STOMP
LET GO!
STOMP
HEY!
GEEH!
DON'T HURT THE DRAGON! WE WON'T BE ABLE TO SELL IT!
GRRR...
WHAT A PAIN!

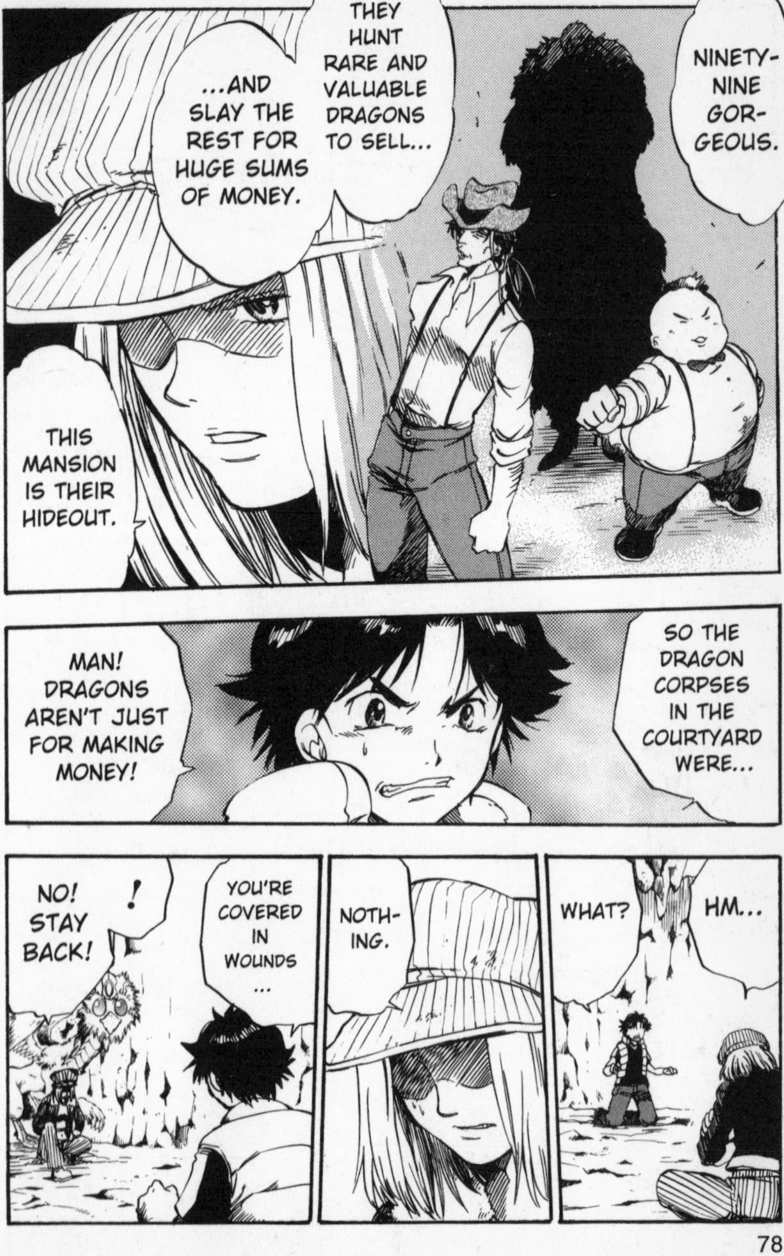
NINETY-NINE GORGEOUS.
THEY HUNT RARE AND VALUABLE DRAGONS TO SELL...
...AND SLAY THE REST FOR HUGE SUMS OF MONEY.
THIS MANSION IS THEIR HIDEOUT.
SO THE DRAGON CORPSES IN THE COURTYARD WERE...
MAN! DRAGONS AREN'T JUST FOR MAKING MONEY!
HM...
WHAT?
NOTH-ING.
YOU'RE COVERED IN WOUNDS ...
!
NO! STAY BACK!

READ THIS WAY

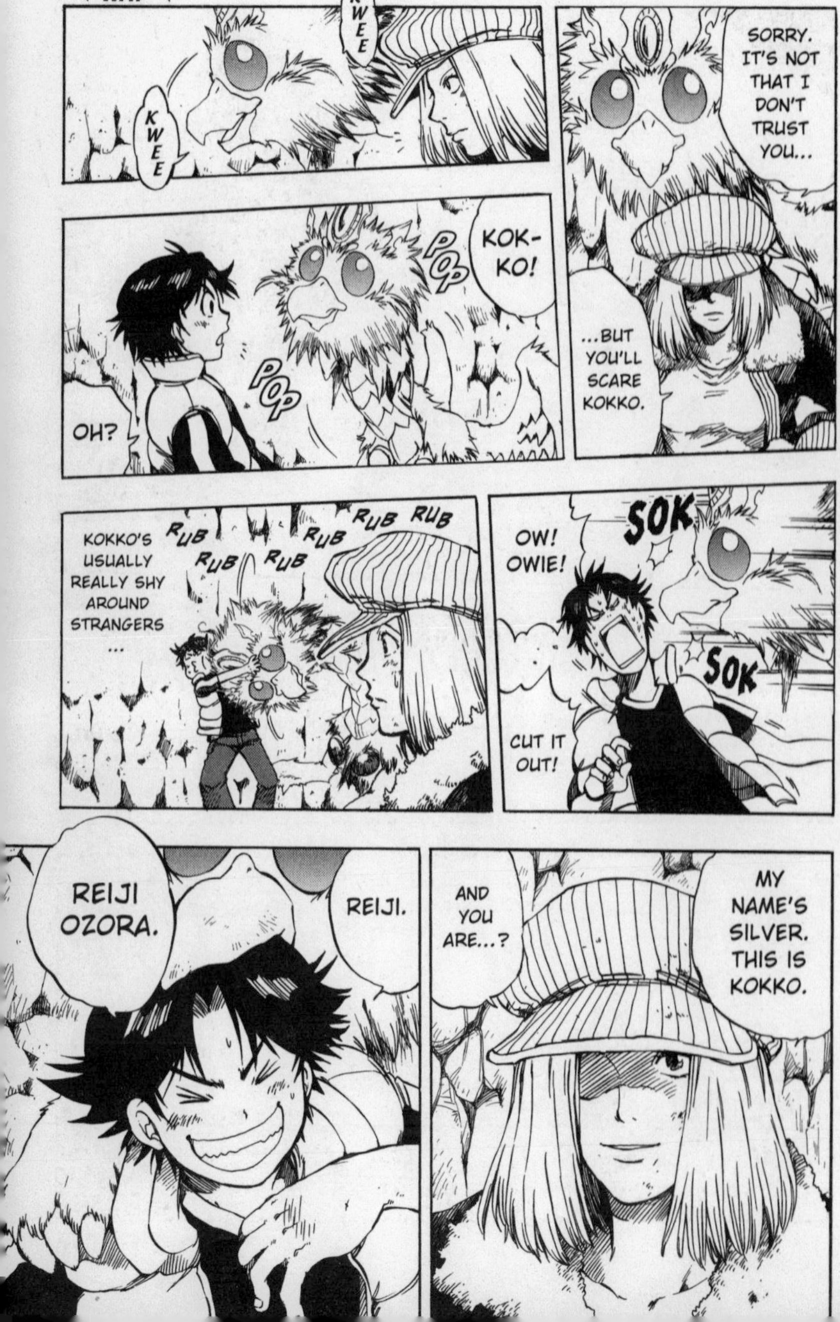
SORRY. IT'S NOT THAT I DON'T TRUST YOU...
...BUT YOU'LL SCARE KOKKO.
KWEE
KWEE
KOK-KO!
POP
POP
OH?
SOK
OW! OWIE!
SOK
CUT IT OUT!
RUB RUB RUB RUB RUB RUB
KOKKO'S USUALLY REALLY SHY AROUND STRANGERS ...
MY NAME'S SILVER. THIS IS KOKKO.
AND YOU ARE...?
REIJI.
REIJI OZORA.

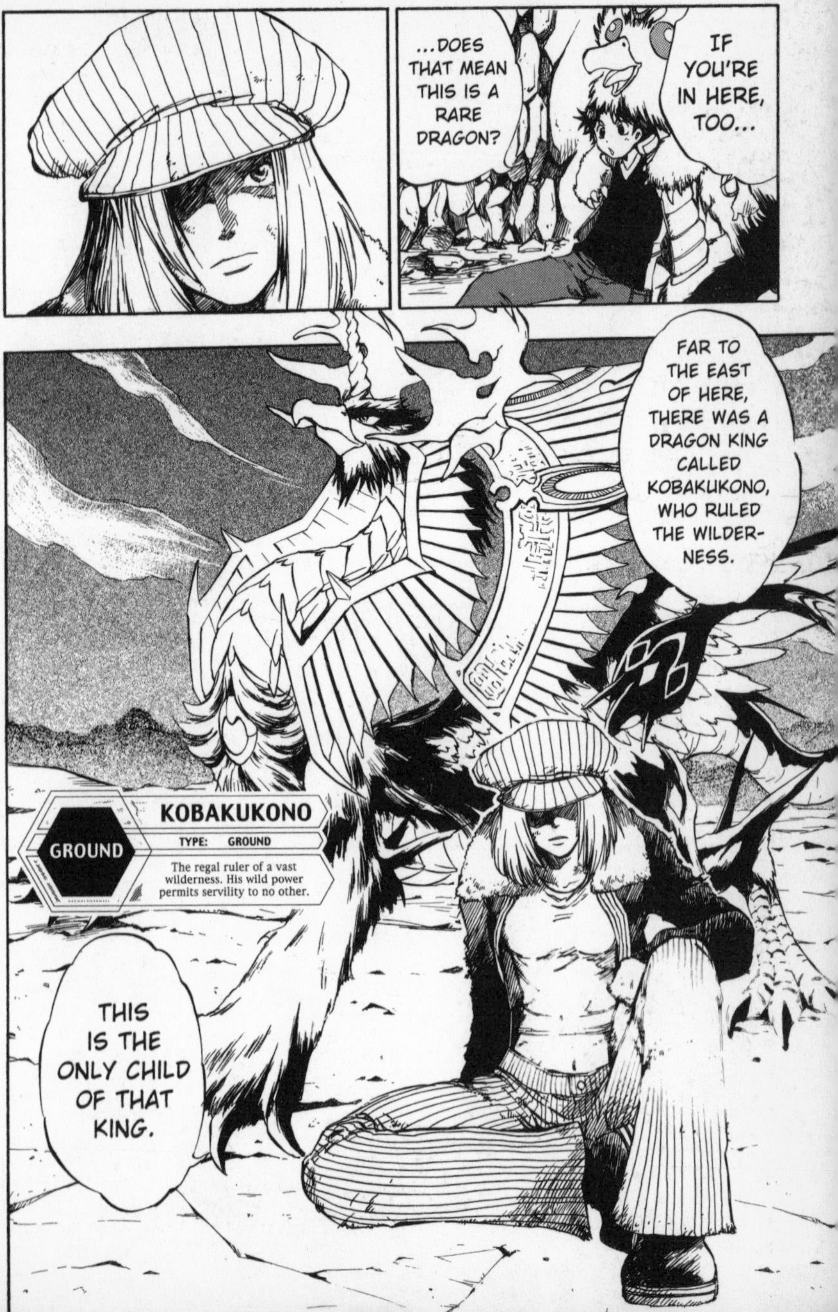
IF YOU'RE IN HERE, TOO...
...DOES THAT MEAN THIS IS A RARE DRAGON?
FAR TO THE EAST OF HERE, THERE WAS A DRAGON KING CALLED KOBAKUKONO, WHO RULED THE WILDERNESS.
KOBAKUKONO
GROUND
TYPE: GROUND
The regal ruler of a vast wilderness. His wild power permits servility to no other.
THIS IS THE ONLY CHILD OF THAT KING.

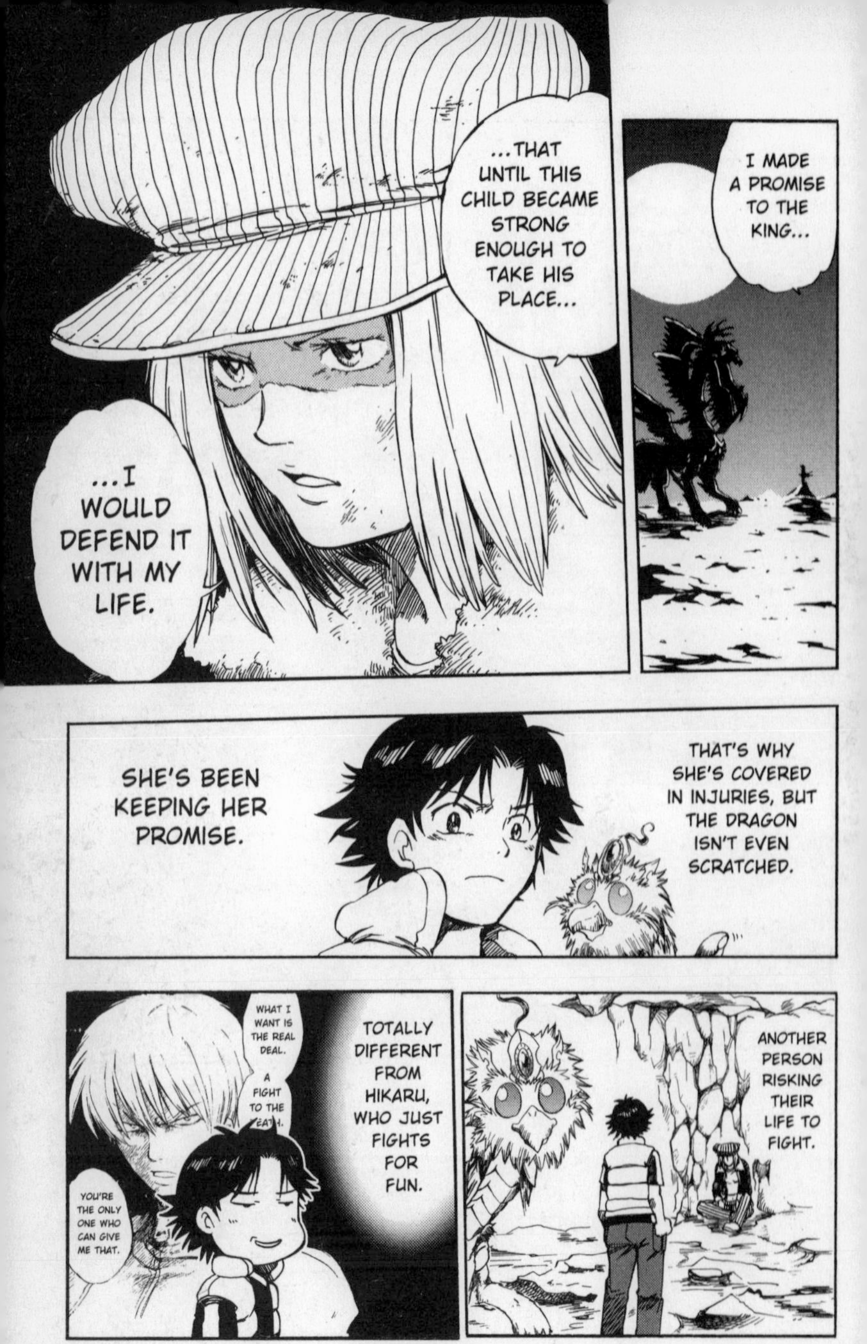
I MADE A PROMISE TO THE KING...
...THAT UNTIL THIS CHILD BECAME STRONG ENOUGH TO TAKE HIS PLACE...
...I WOULD DEFEND IT WITH MY LIFE.
THAT'S WHY SHE'S COVERED IN INJURIES, BUT THE DRAGON ISN'T EVEN SCRATCHED.
SHE'S BEEN KEEPING HER PROMISE.
ANOTHER PERSON RISKING THEIR LIFE TO FIGHT.
TOTALLY DIFFERENT FROM HIKARU, WHO JUST FIGHTS FOR FUN.
WHAT I WANT IS THE REAL DEAL.
A FIGHT TO THE DEATH.
YOU'RE THE ONLY ONE WHO CAN GIVE ME THAT.

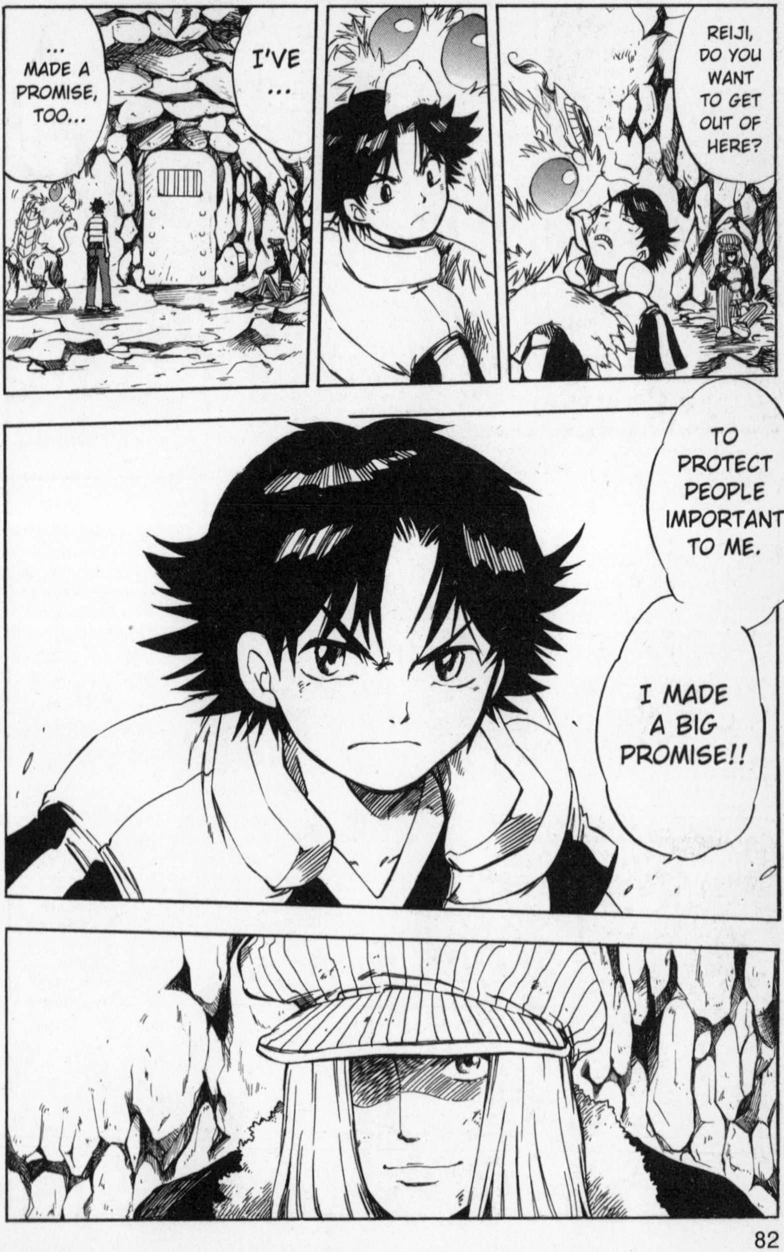
REIJI, DO YOU WANT TO GET OUT OF HERE?
I'VE ...
... MADE A PROMISE, TOO...
TO PROTECT PEOPLE IMPORTANT TO ME.
I MADE A BIG PROMISE!!

READ THIS WAY

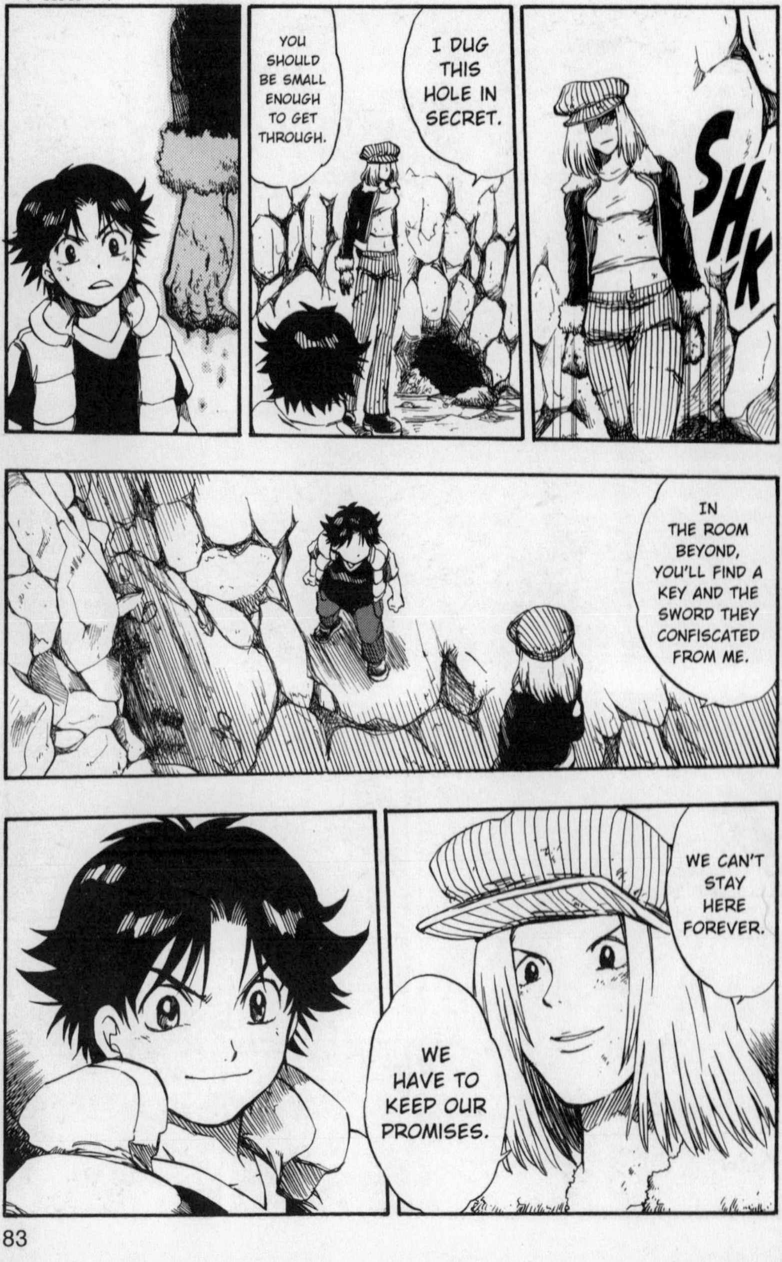
SHK
I DUG THIS HOLE IN SECRET.
YOU SHOULD BE SMALL ENOUGH TO GET THROUGH.
IN THE ROOM BEYOND, YOU'LL FIND A KEY AND THE SWORD THEY CONFISCATED FROM ME.
WE CAN'T STAY HERE FOREVER.
WE HAVE TO KEEP OUR PROMISES.

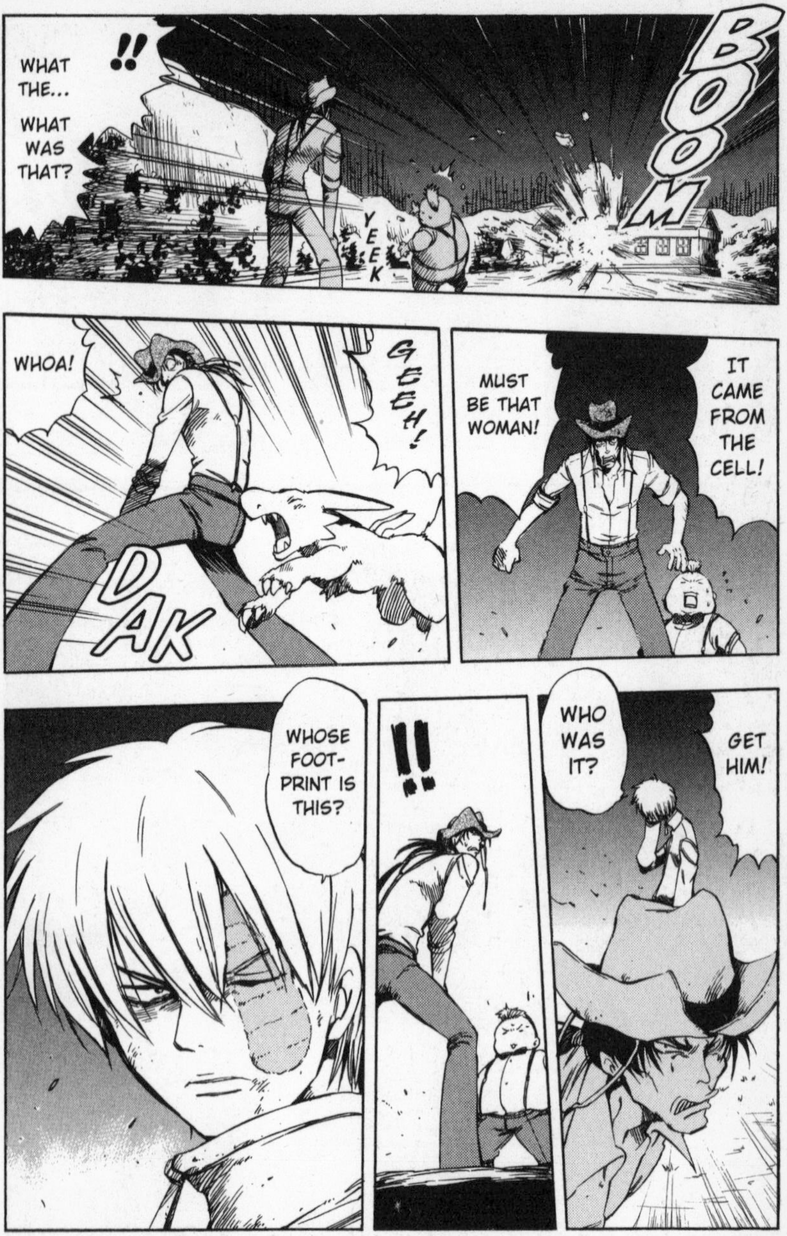
BOOM
YEEK
!!
WHAT THE...
WHAT WAS THAT?
IT CAME FROM THE CELL!
MUST BE THAT WOMAN!
GEEH!
WHOA!
DAK
GET HIM!
WHO WAS IT?
!!
WHOSE FOOT-PRINT IS THIS?

READ THIS WAY

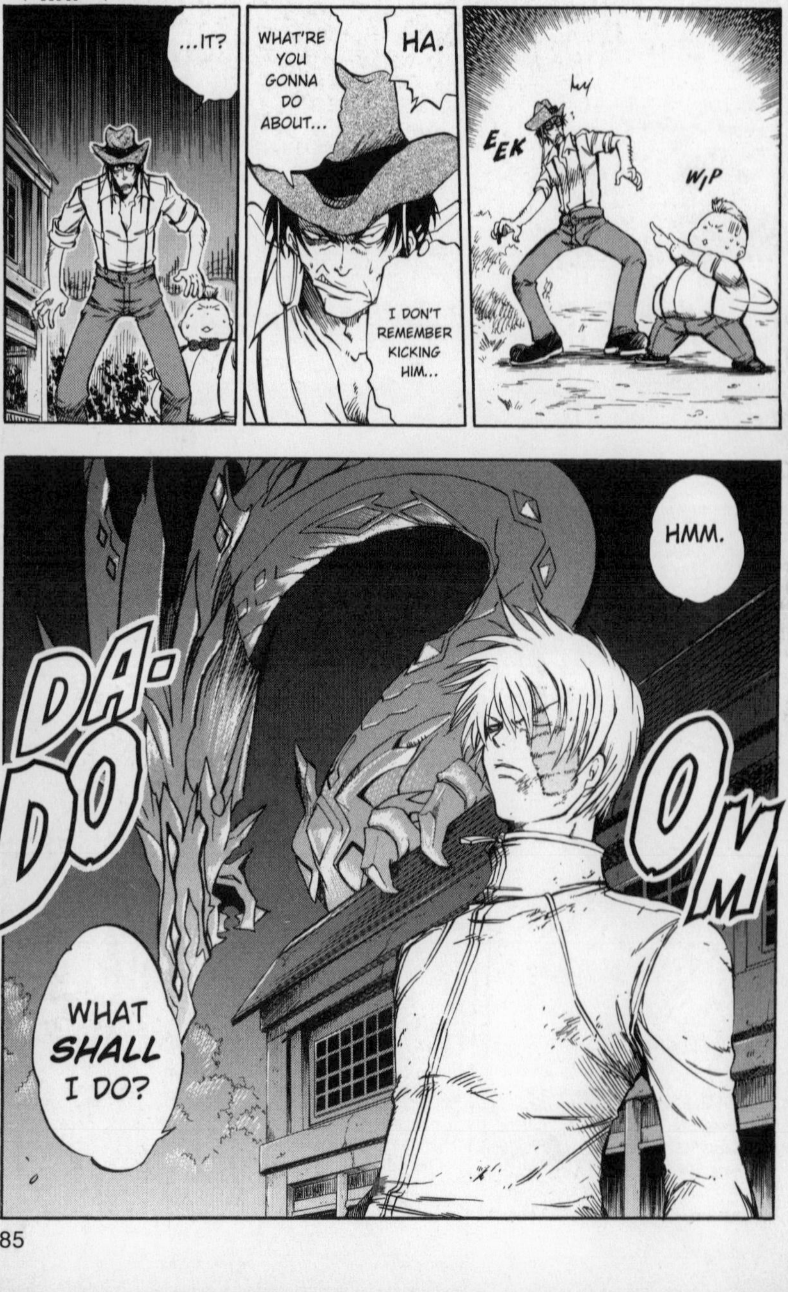
EEK
WIP
HA.
WHAT'RE YOU GONNA DO ABOUT...
I DON'T REMEMBER KICKING HIM...
...IT?
HMM.
DA-DOOM
WHAT **SHALL** I DO?

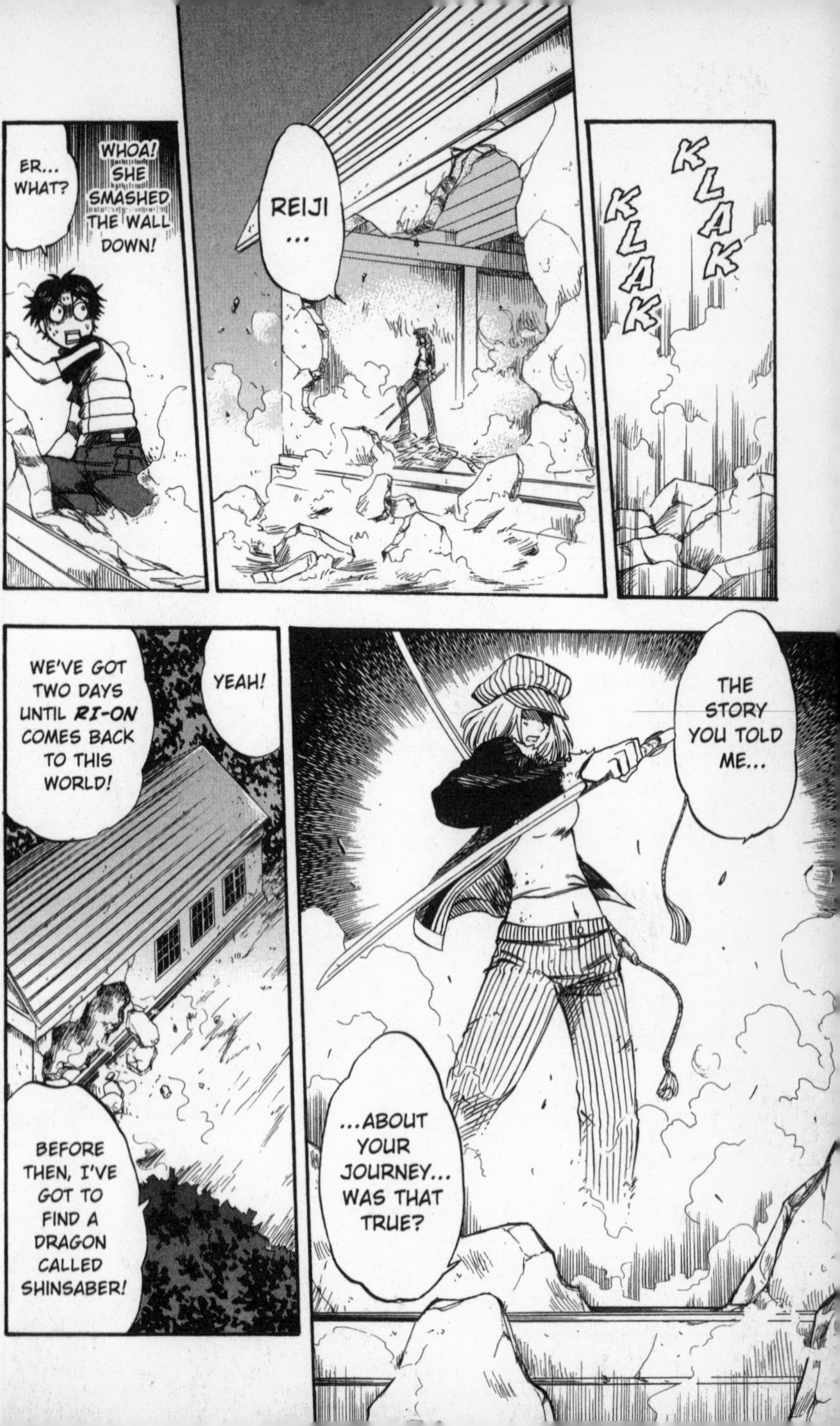
KLAK
KLAK
REIJI...
WHOA! SHE SMASHED THE WALL DOWN!
ER... WHAT?
THE STORY YOU TOLD ME...
...ABOUT YOUR JOURNEY... WAS THAT TRUE?
YEAH!
WE'VE GOT TWO DAYS UNTIL *RI-ON* COMES BACK TO THIS WORLD!
BEFORE THEN, I'VE GOT TO FIND A DRAGON CALLED SHINSABER!

READ THIS WAY

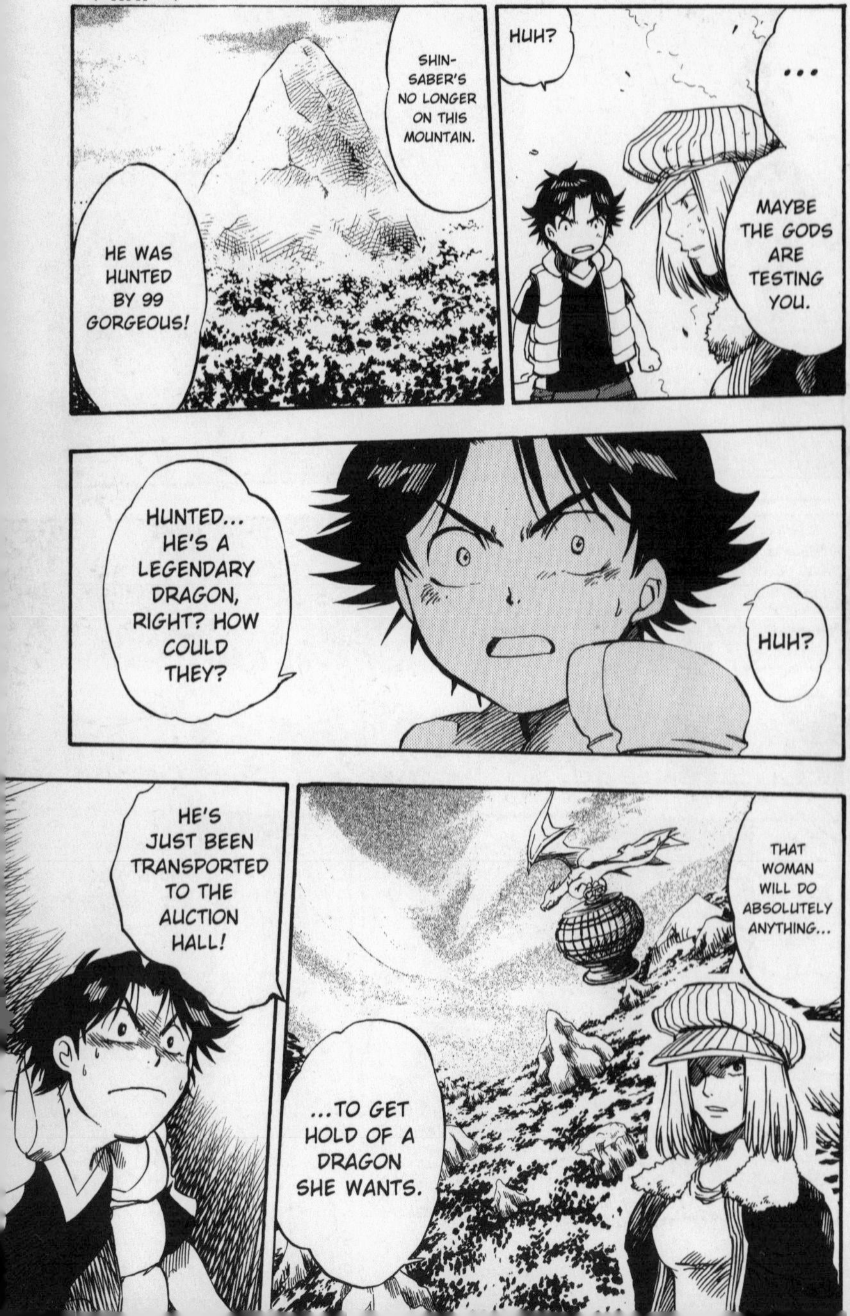
...
MAYBE THE GODS ARE TESTING YOU.
HUH?
SHIN-SABER'S NO LONGER ON THIS MOUNTAIN.
HE WAS HUNTED BY 99 GORGEOUS!
HUH?
HUNTED... HE'S A LEGENDARY DRAGON, RIGHT? HOW COULD THEY?
THAT WOMAN WILL DO ABSOLUTELY ANYTHING...
...TO GET HOLD OF A DRAGON SHE WANTS.
HE'S JUST BEEN TRANSPORTED TO THE AUCTION HALL!

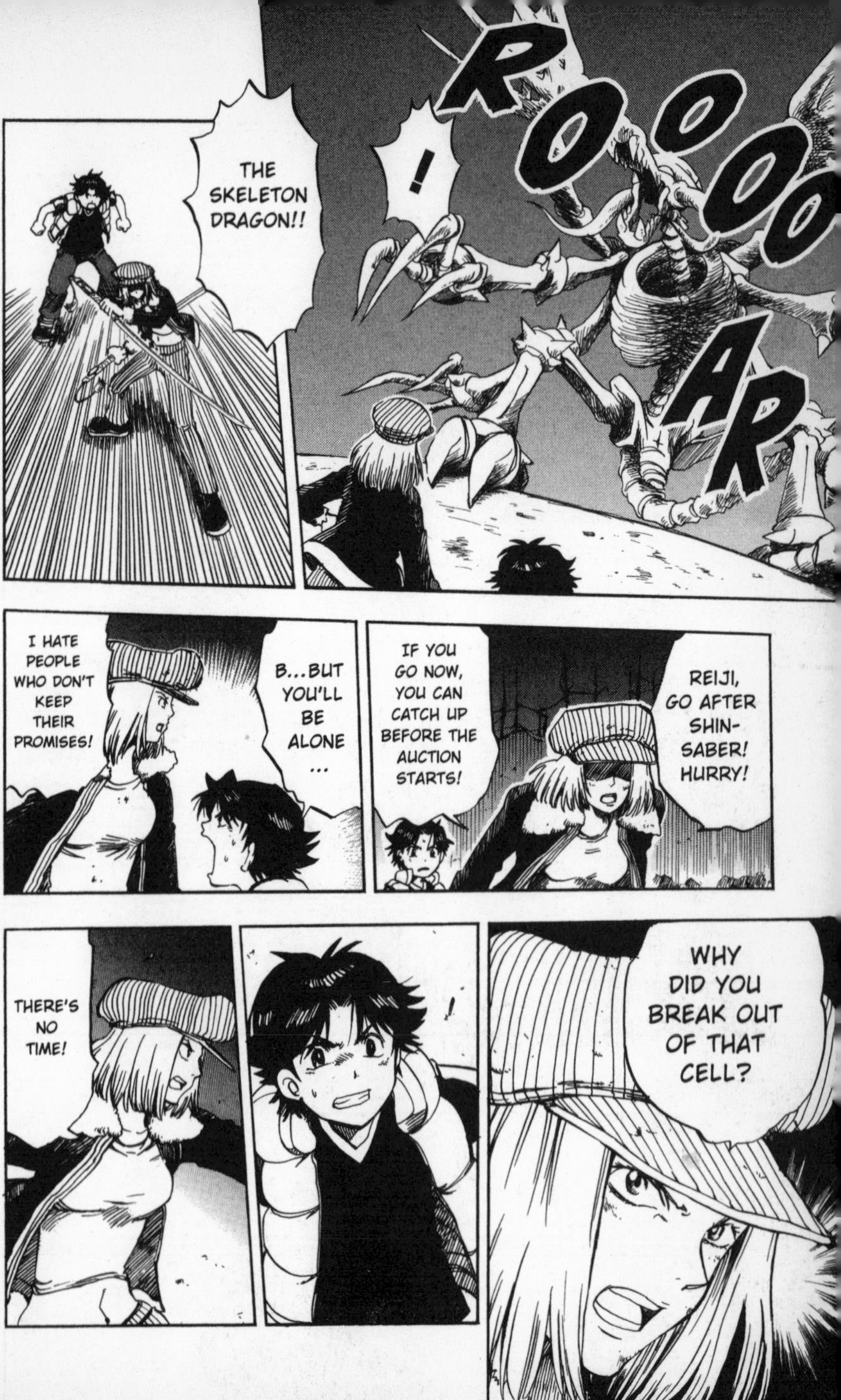
ROOOOAR
!
THE SKELETON DRAGON!!
REIJI, GO AFTER SHIN-SABER! HURRY!
IF YOU GO NOW, YOU CAN CATCH UP BEFORE THE AUCTION STARTS!
B...BUT YOU'LL BE ALONE...
I HATE PEOPLE WHO DON'T KEEP THEIR PROMISES!
WHY DID YOU BREAK OUT OF THAT CELL?
!
THERE'S NO TIME!

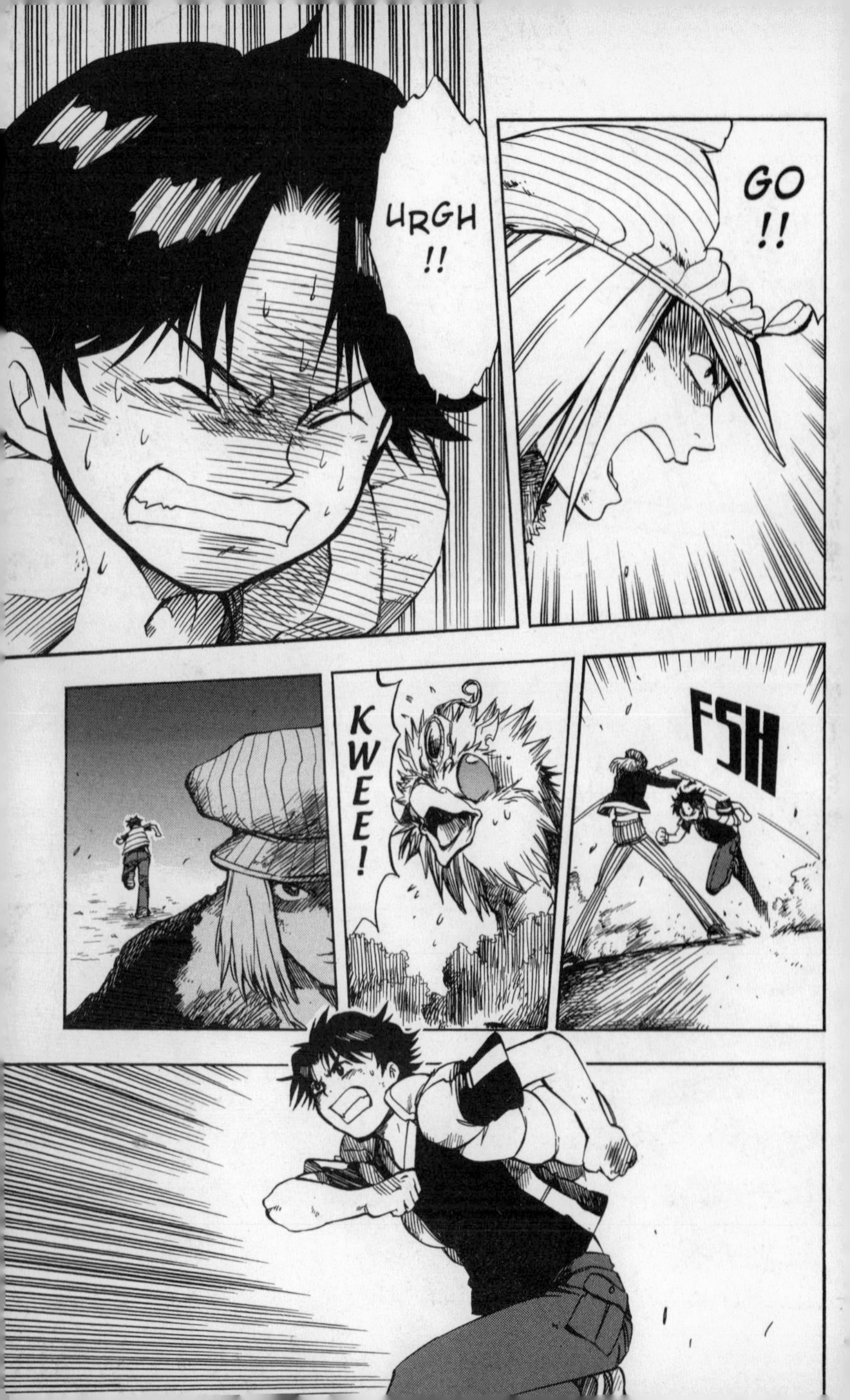
GO!!
URGH!!
FSH
KWEE!

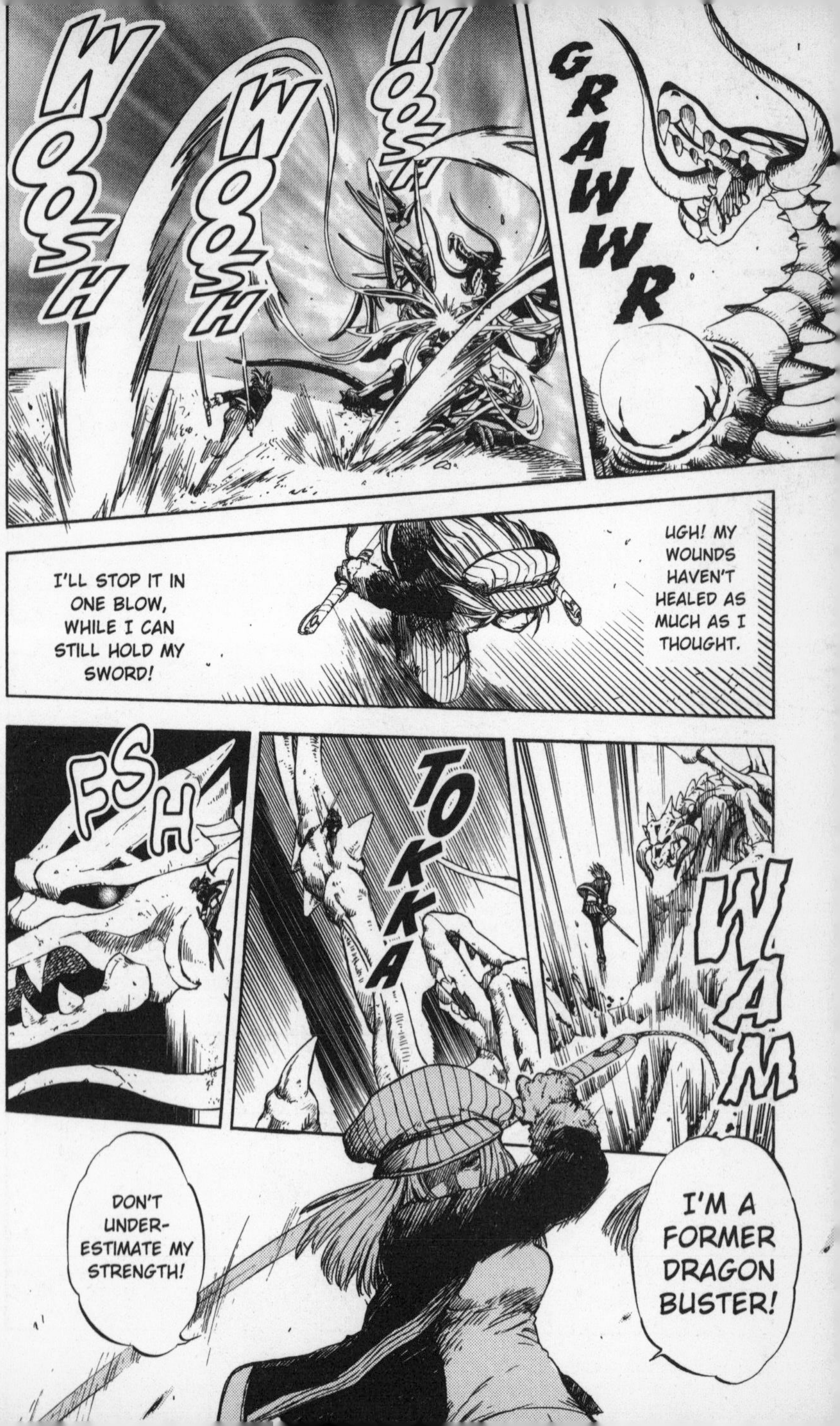
GRAWWR
WOOSH
WOOSH
WOOSH
UGH! MY WOUNDS HAVEN'T HEALED AS MUCH AS I THOUGHT.
I'LL STOP IT IN ONE BLOW, WHILE I CAN STILL HOLD MY SWORD!
WAM
TOKKA
FSH
I'M A FORMER DRAGON BUSTER!
DON'T UNDER-ESTIMATE MY STRENGTH!

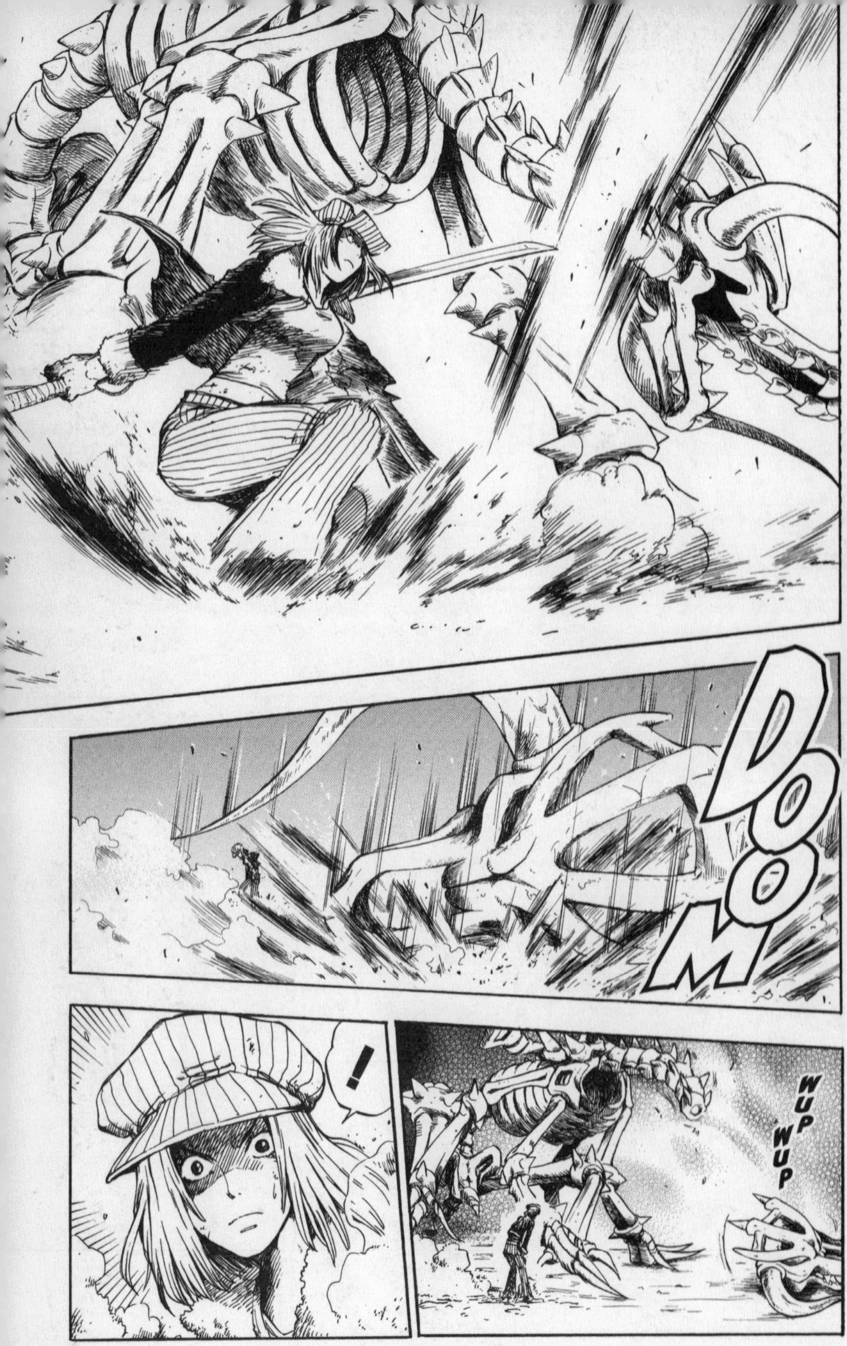
DOOOM
WUP
WUP
!

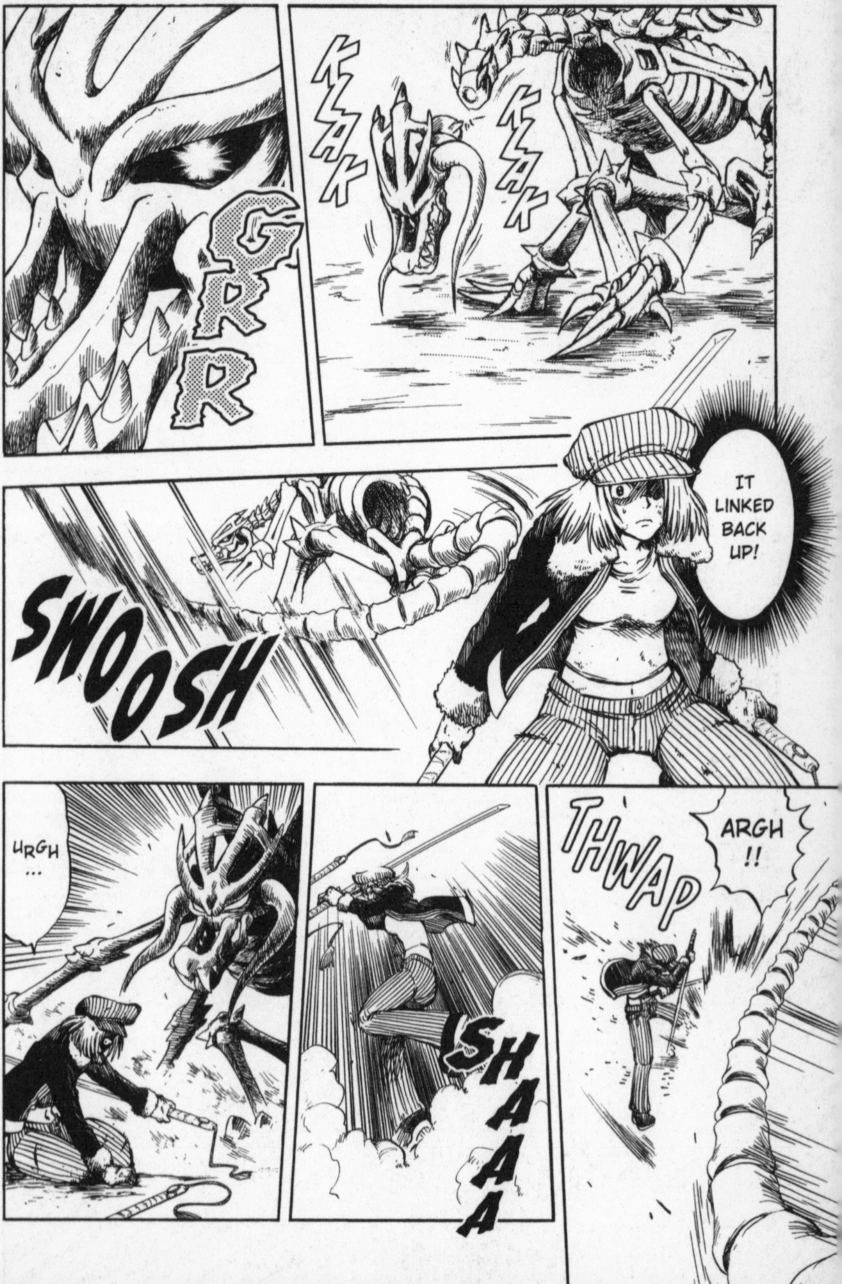
KLAK
KLAK
GRR
IT LINKED BACK UP!
SWOOSH
THWAP
ARGH !!
SHAAAA
URGH ...

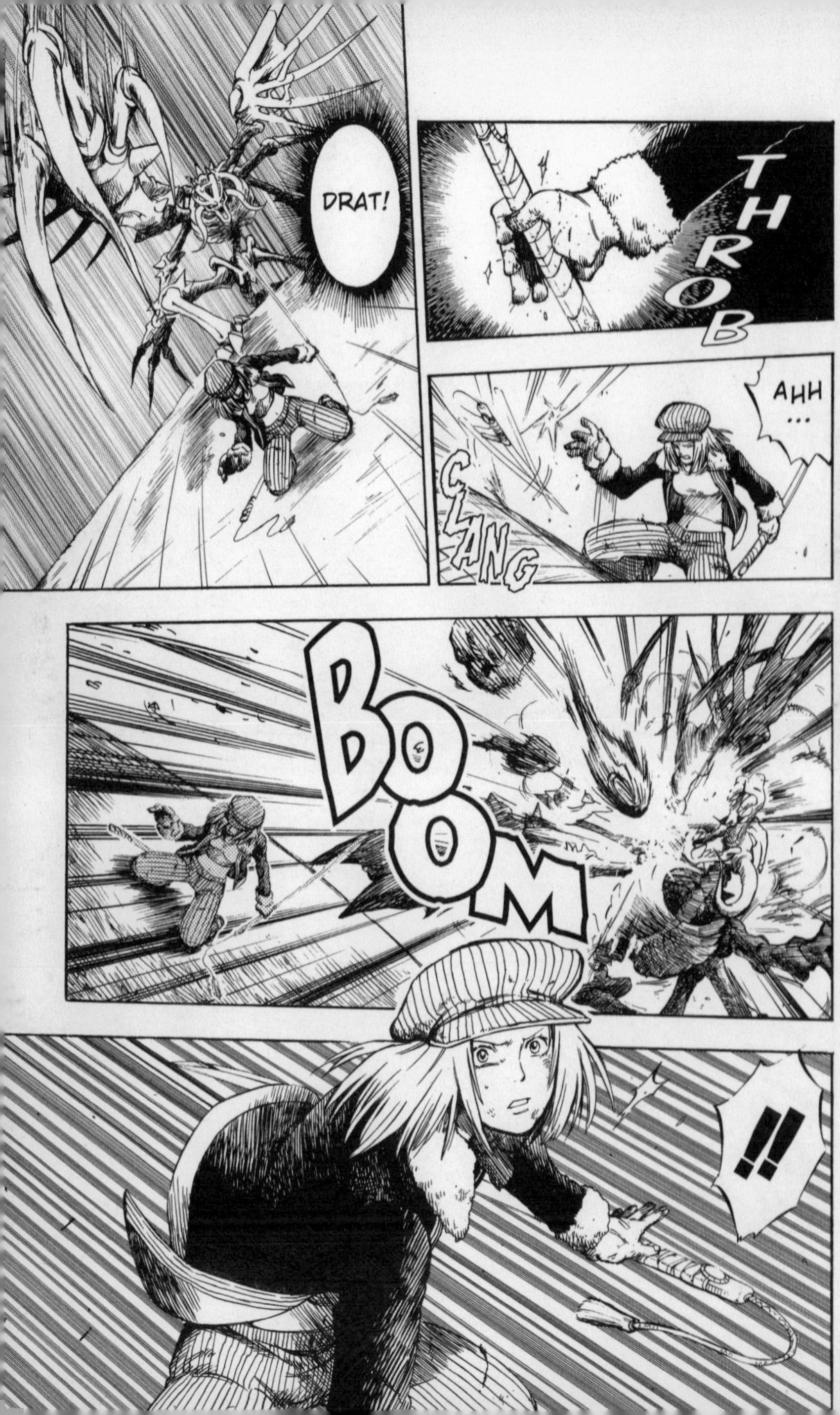
THROB
AHH ...
CLANG
DRAT!
BOOM
!!

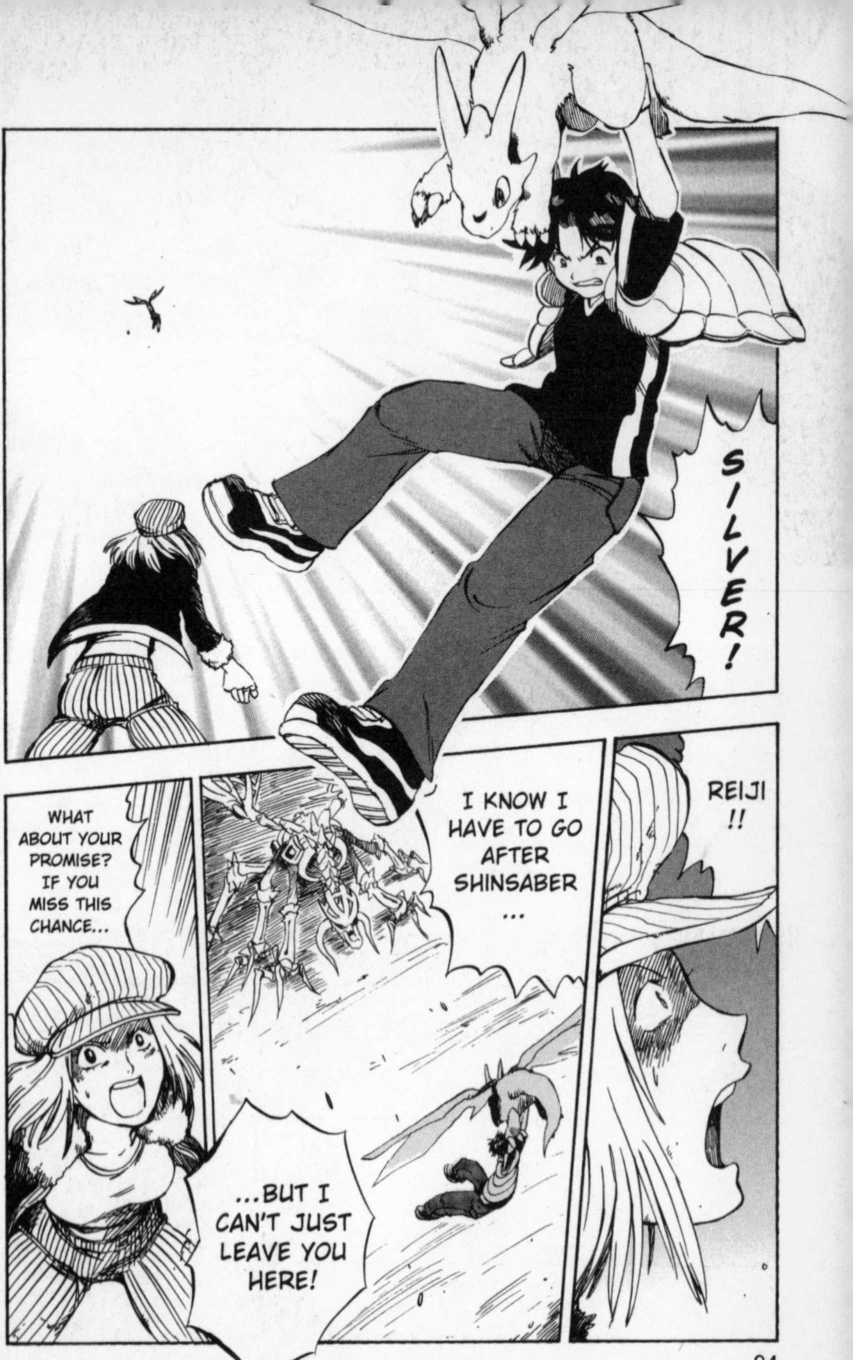
SILVER!
REIJI !!
I KNOW I HAVE TO GO AFTER SHINSABER ...
...BUT I CAN'T JUST LEAVE YOU HERE!
WHAT ABOUT YOUR PROMISE? IF YOU MISS THIS CHANCE...

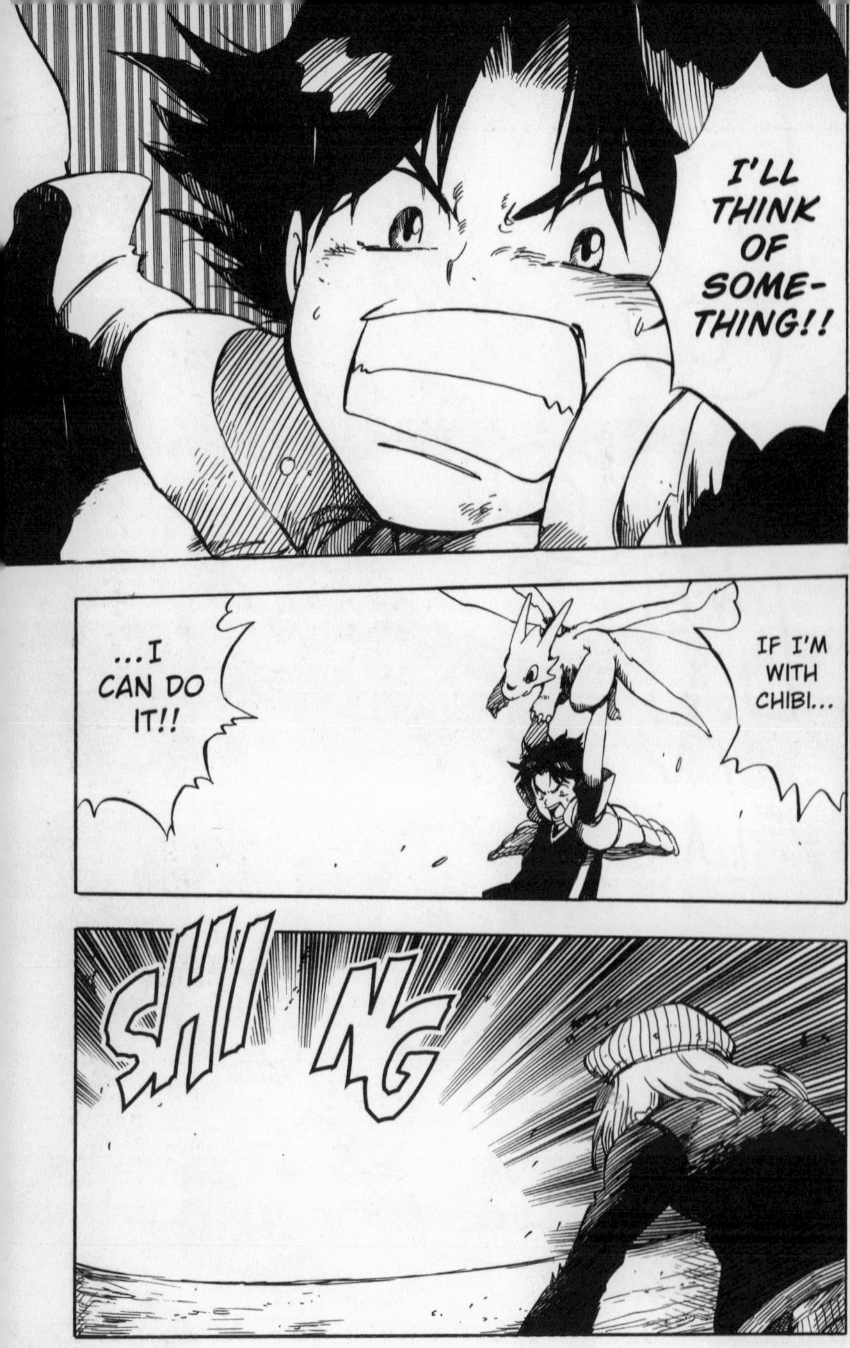
I'LL THINK OF SOMETHING!!
IF I'M WITH CHIBI...
...I CAN DO IT!!
CHING

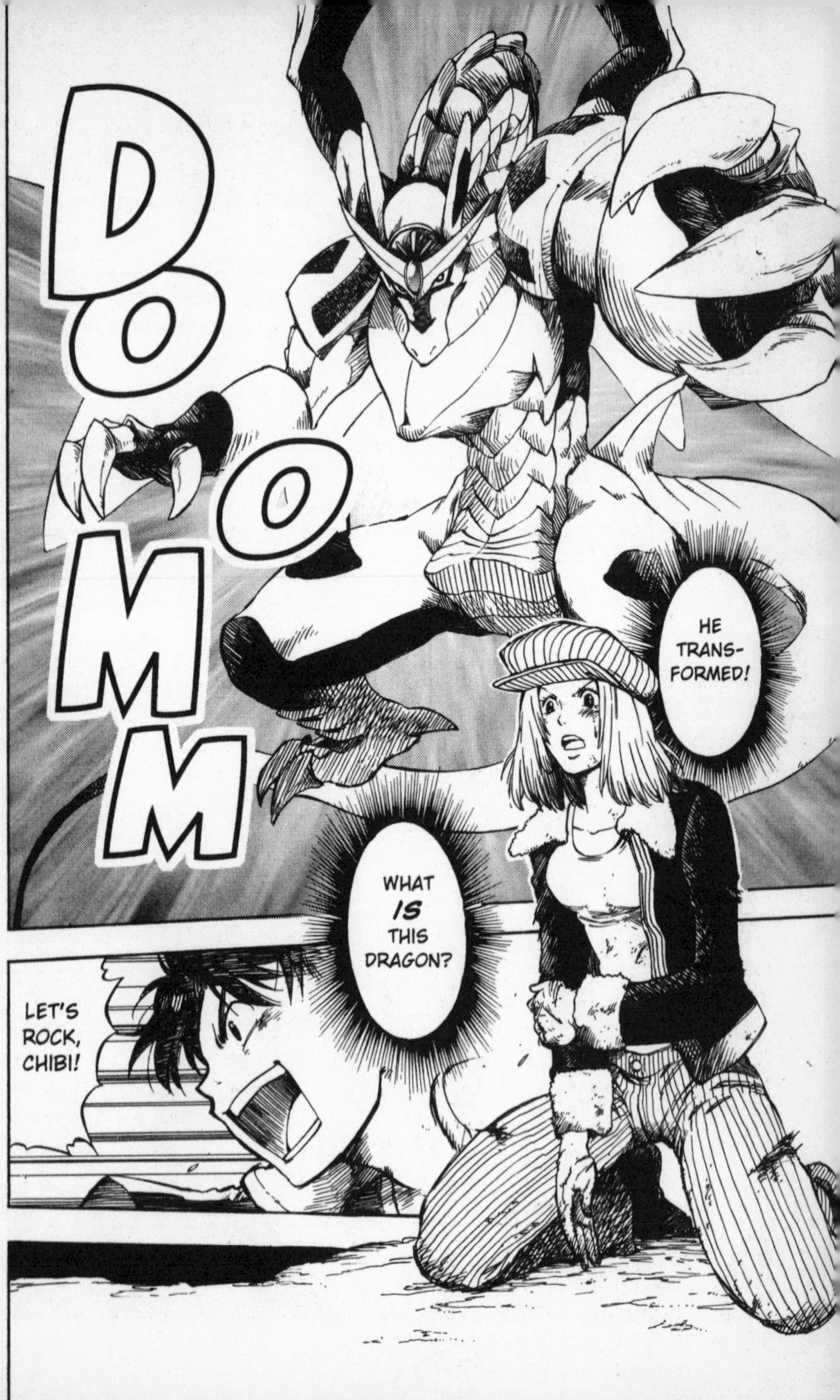
DOMM
HE TRANS-FORMED!
WHAT *IS* THIS DRAGON?
LET'S ROCK, CHIBI!

READ THIS WAY

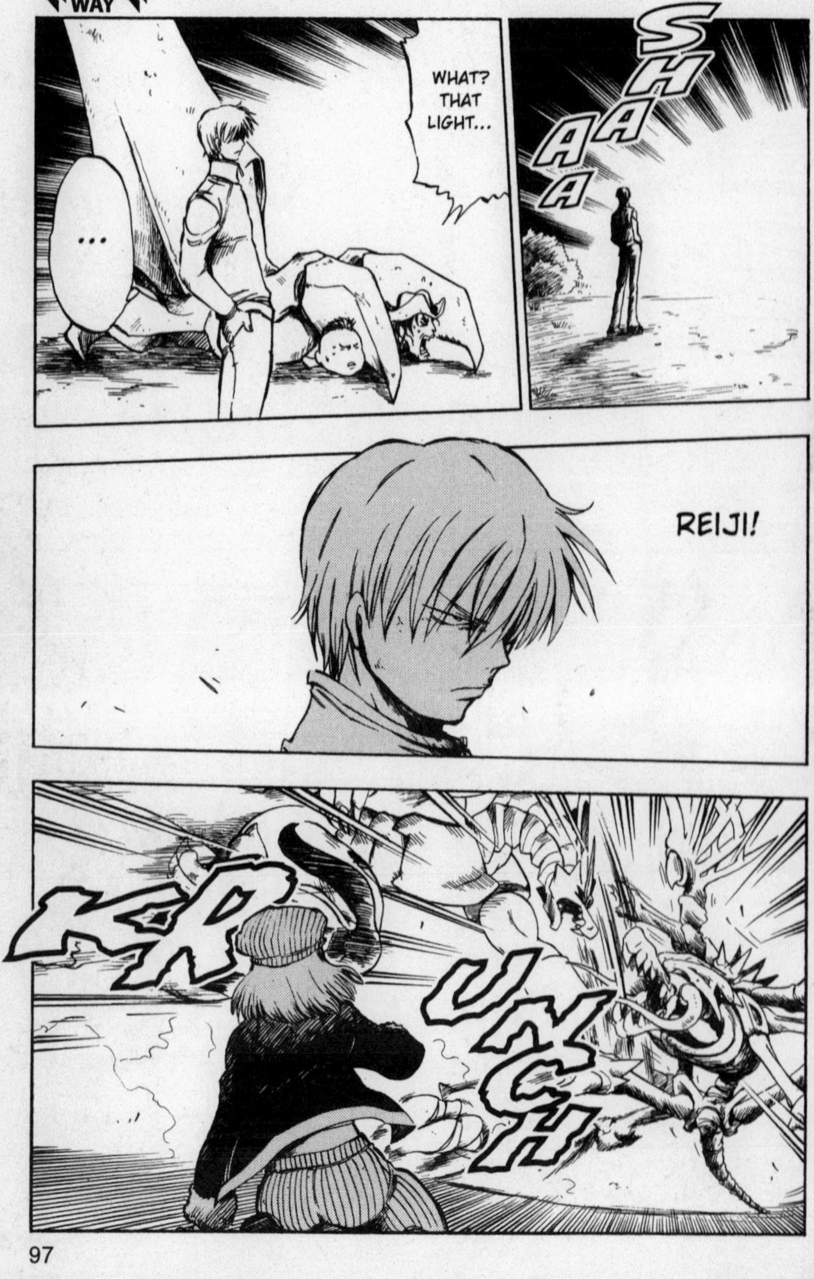
SHAAAA
WHAT? THAT LIGHT...
...
REIJI!
KRUNCH

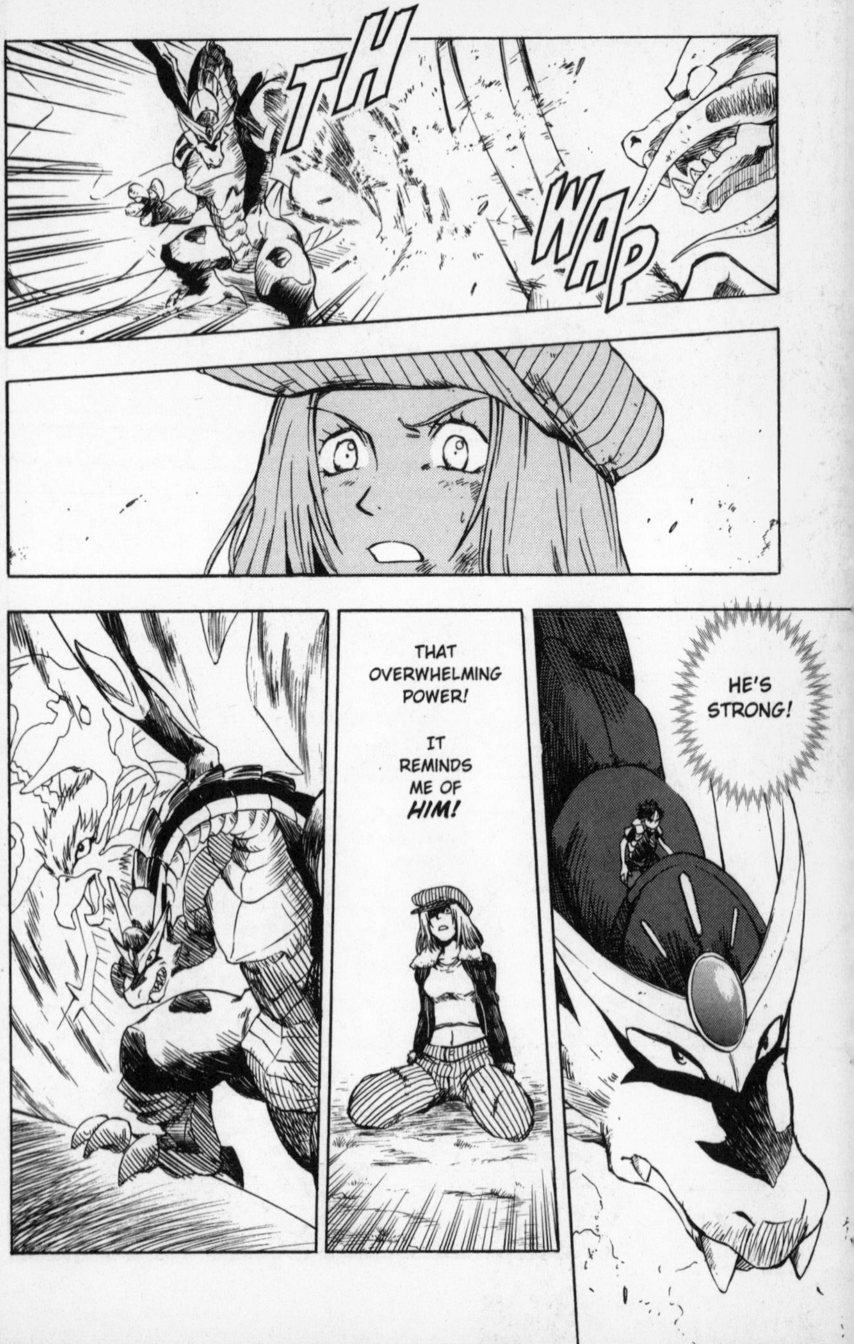
THWAP
HE'S STRONG!
THAT OVERWHELMING POWER!
IT REMINDS ME OF HIM!

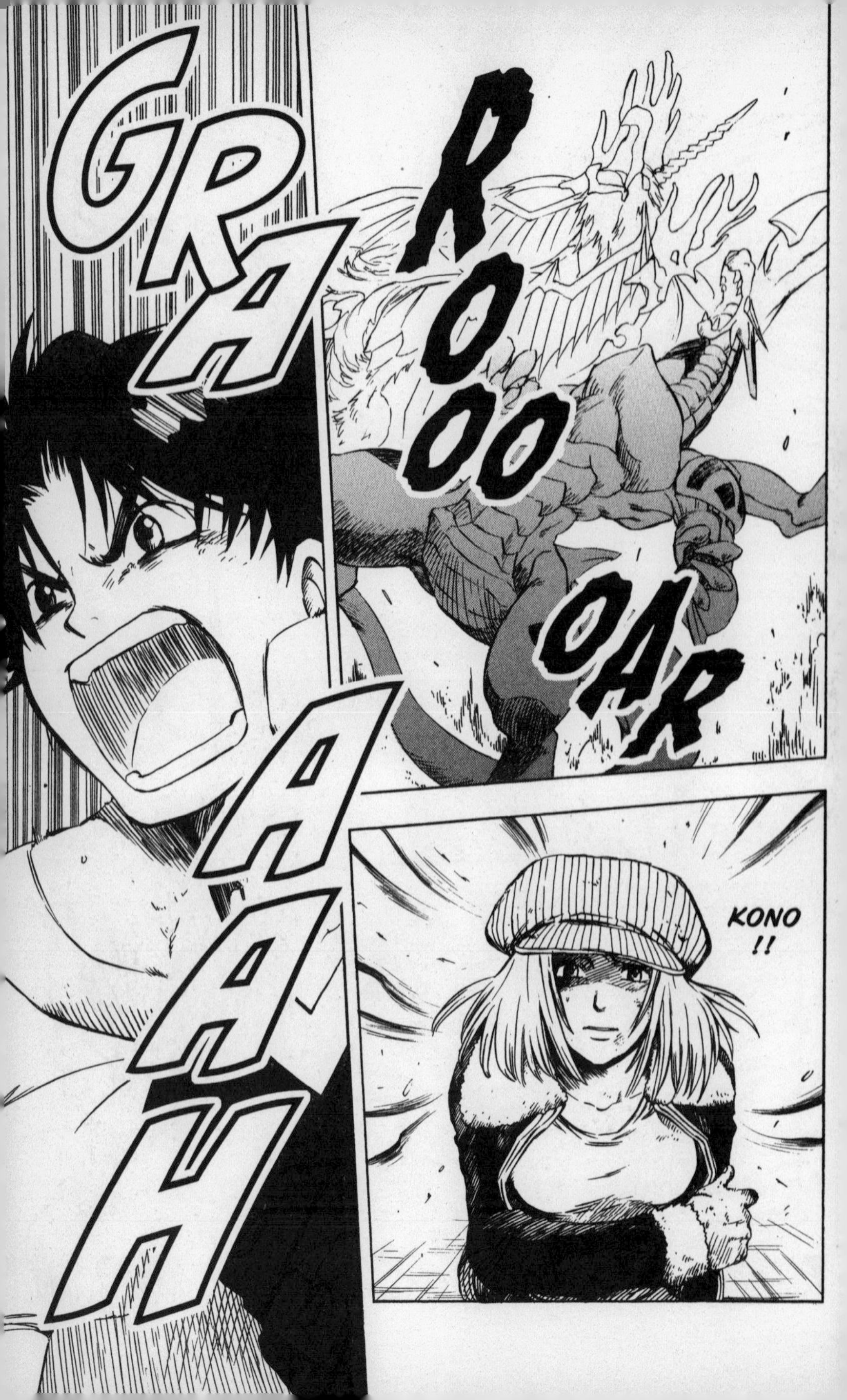
ROOOOAR
KONO !!
GRAAAH

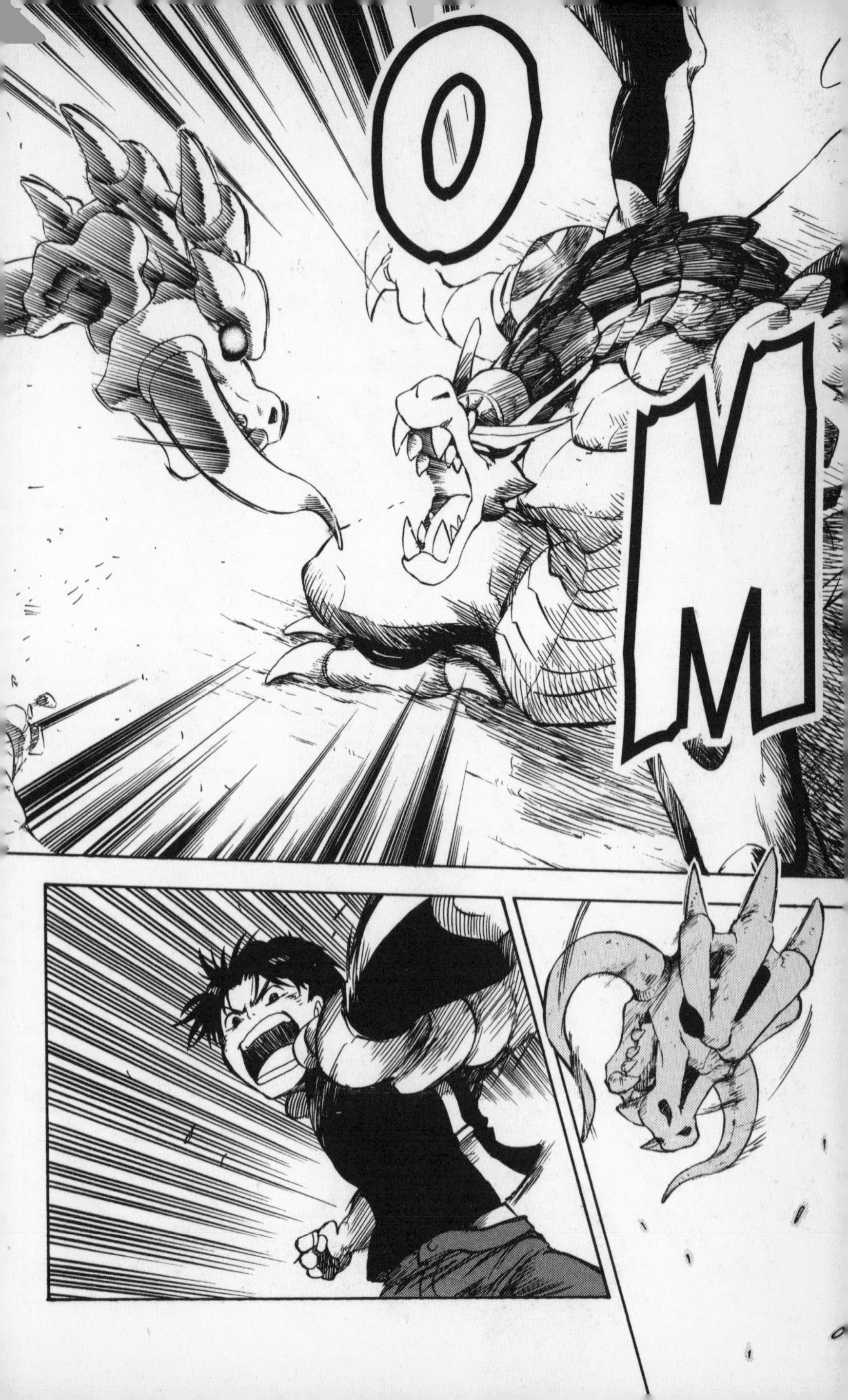
OOMM

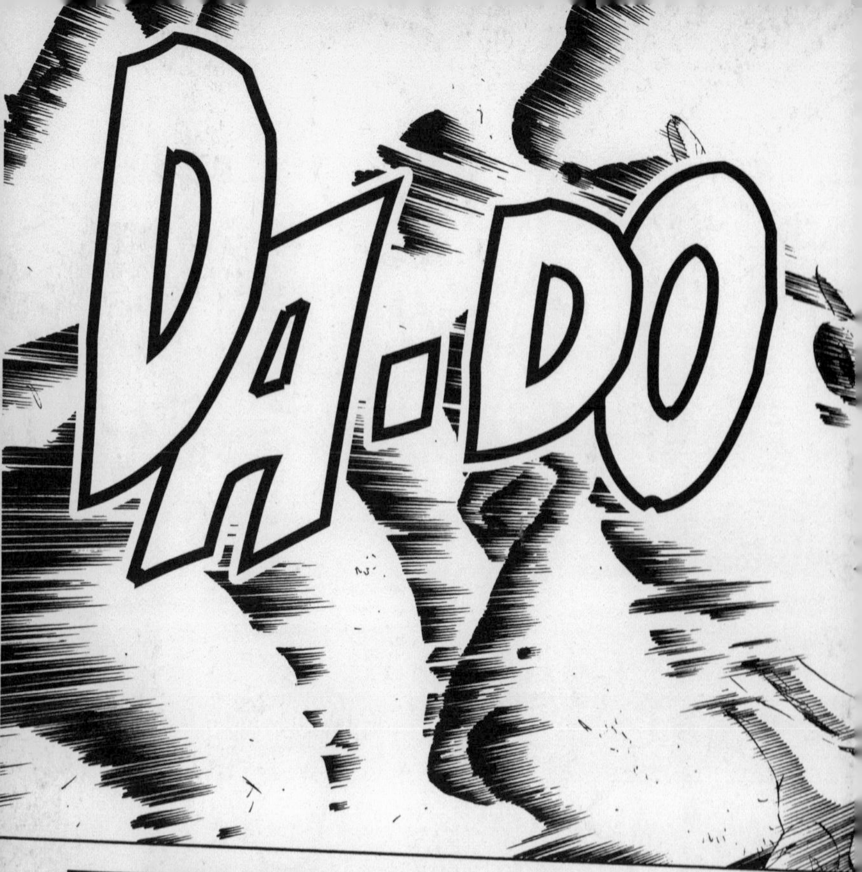
DA-DO
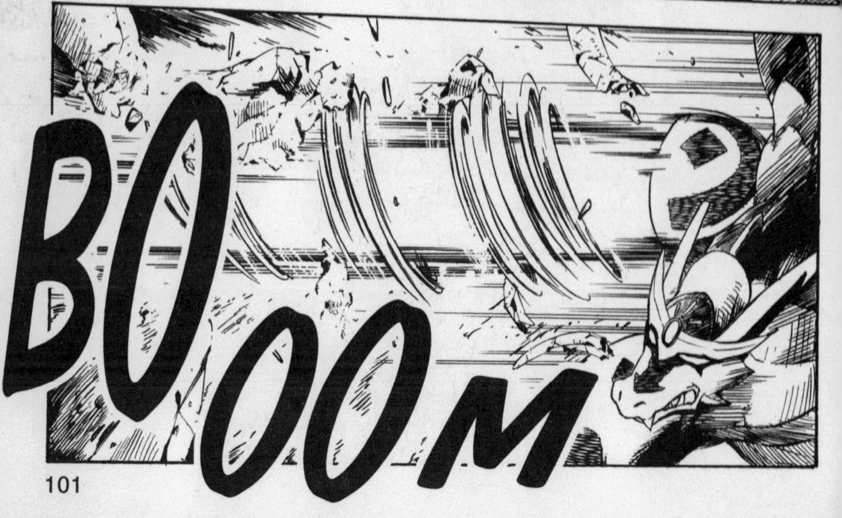
BOOOM

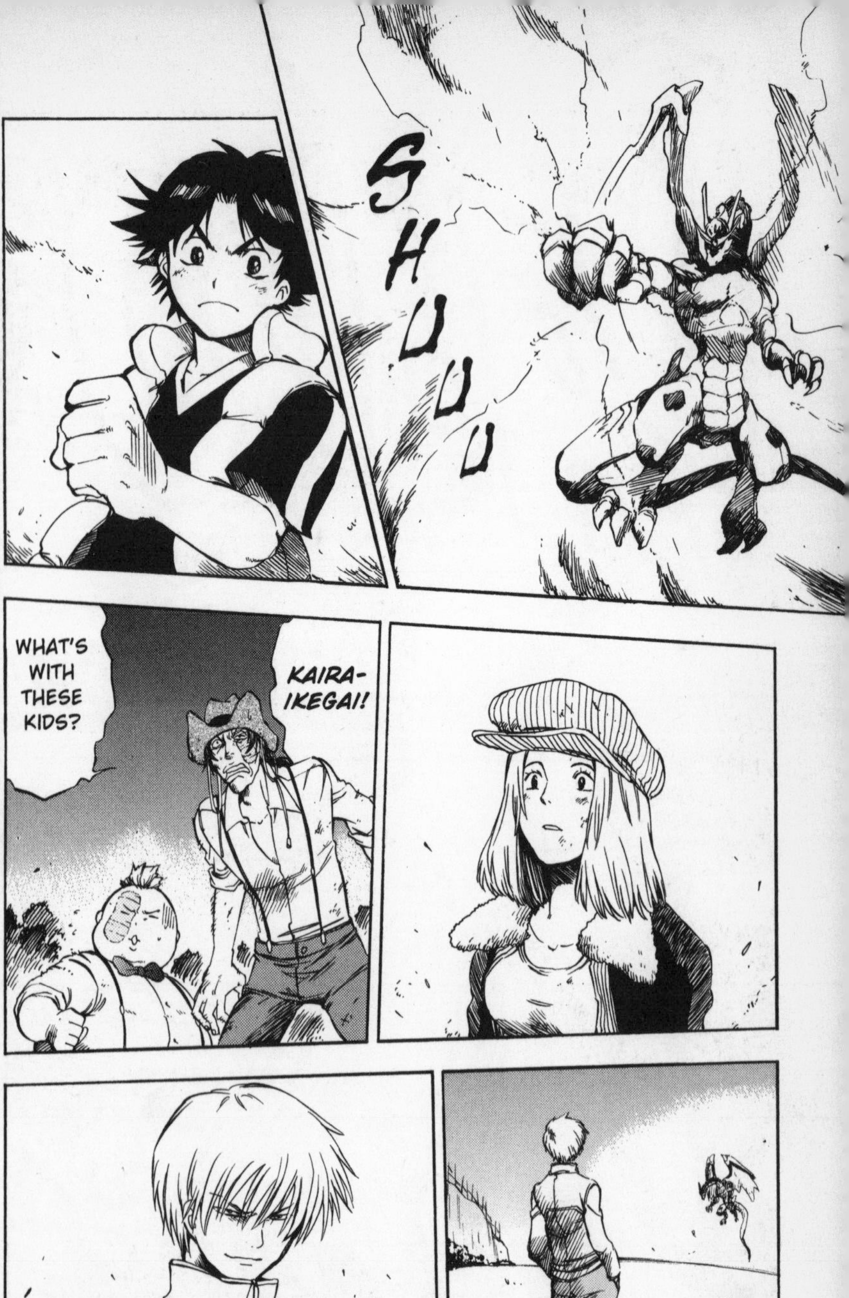
SHUUU
KAIRA-IKEGAI!
WHAT'S WITH THESE KIDS?

READ THIS WAY

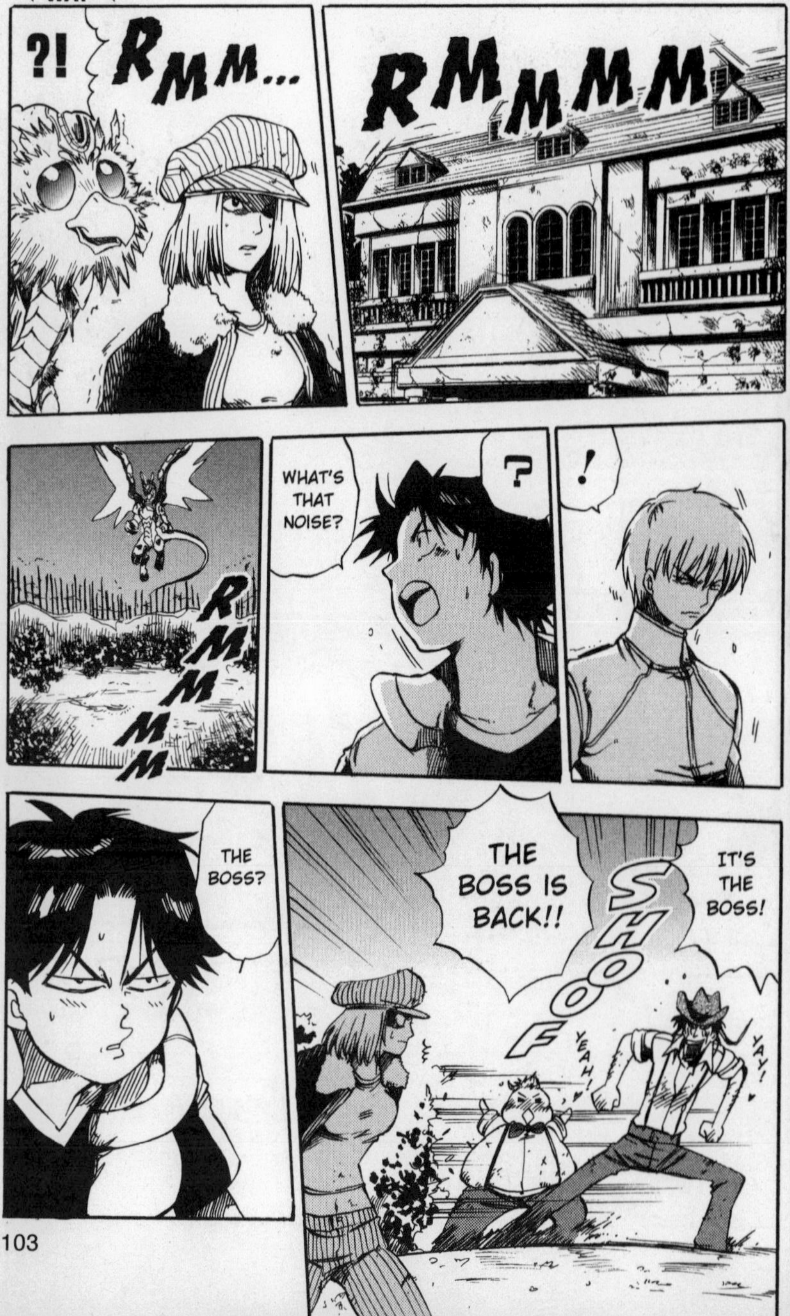
RMMMMM
?!
RMM...
!
?
WHAT'S THAT NOISE?
RMMMMM
IT'S THE BOSS!
THE BOSS IS BACK!!
SHOOOF
YAY!
YEAH!
THE BOSS?

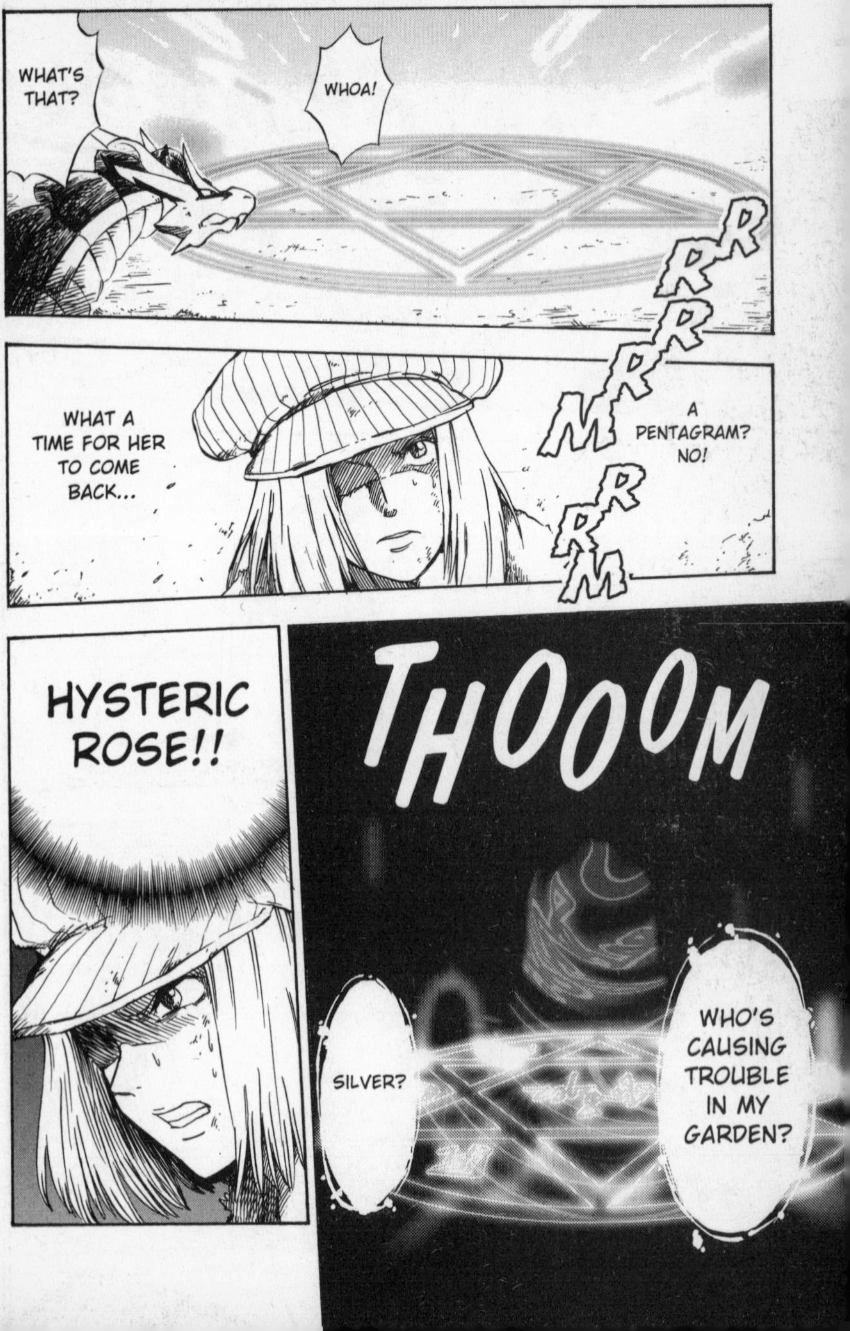
WHOA!
WHAT'S THAT?
RRRRMRRM
A PENTAGRAM? NO!
WHAT A TIME FOR HER TO COME BACK...
THOOOM
WHO'S CAUSING TROUBLE IN MY GARDEN?
SILVER?
HYSTERIC ROSE!!

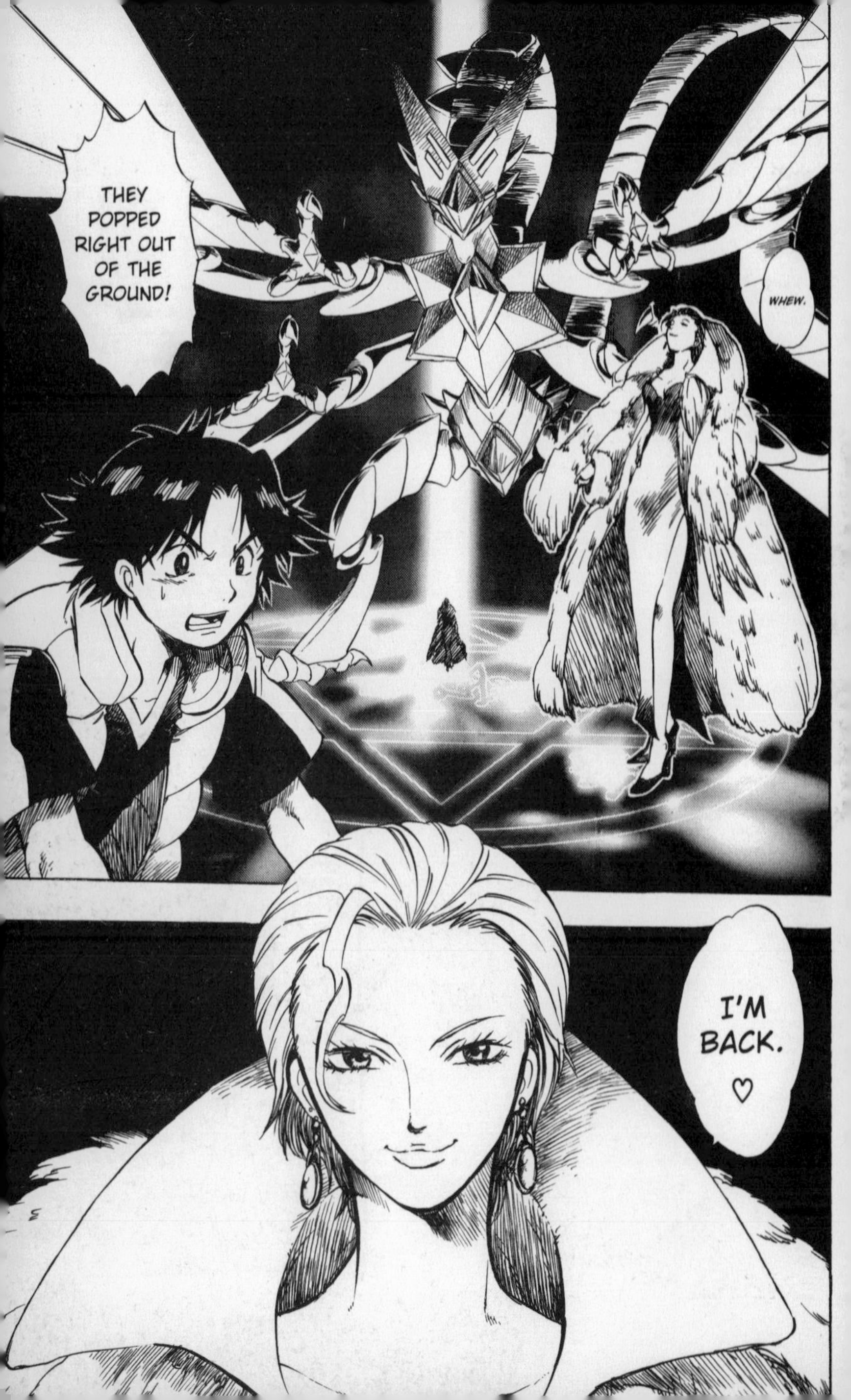
WHEW.
THEY POPPED RIGHT OUT OF THE GROUND!
I'M BACK. ♡

Spaced-Out Silver ①

BY TORA-SAN

GUESS WHAT?
I BLEW OFF WORK TODAY...
WHERE TO?
I'LL GO LOOK FOR IT.
LET'S TRY AGAIN.
LOOK, TIME FLIES!
GEEH
WHAT KIND OF FLIES ARE THOSE?
THEY SURE ARE FAST...

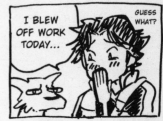

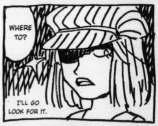

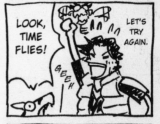

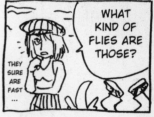

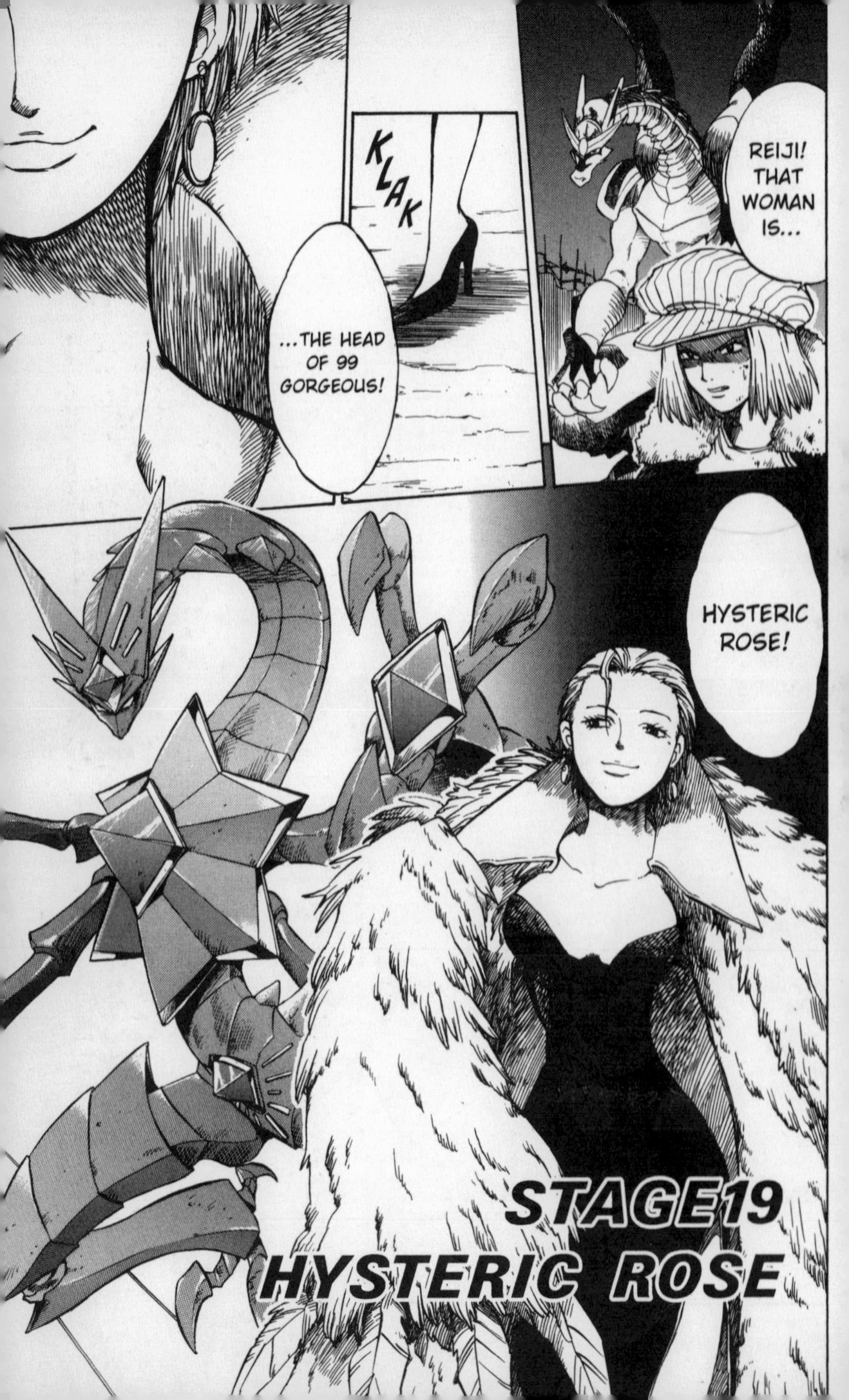
REIJI! THAT WOMAN IS...
KLAK
...THE HEAD OF 99 GORGEOUS!
HYSTERIC ROSE!
STAGE19 HYSTERIC ROSE

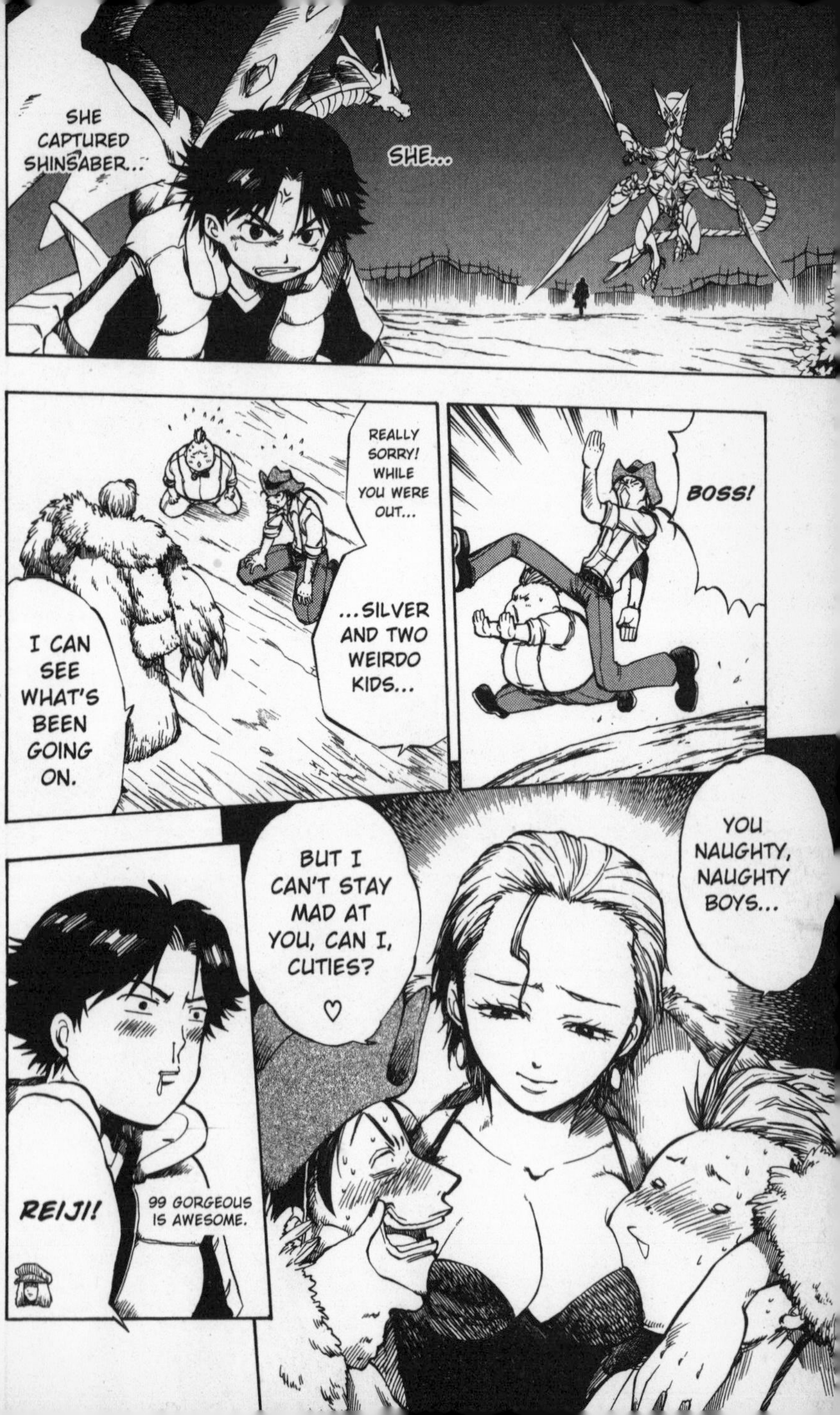
SHE...
SHE CAPTURED SHINSABER...
BOSS!
REALLY SORRY! WHILE YOU WERE OUT...
...SILVER AND TWO WEIRDO KIDS...
I CAN SEE WHAT'S BEEN GOING ON.
YOU NAUGHTY, NAUGHTY BOYS...
BUT I CAN'T STAY MAD AT YOU, CAN I, CUTIES?
♡
99 GORGEOUS IS AWESOME.
REIJI!

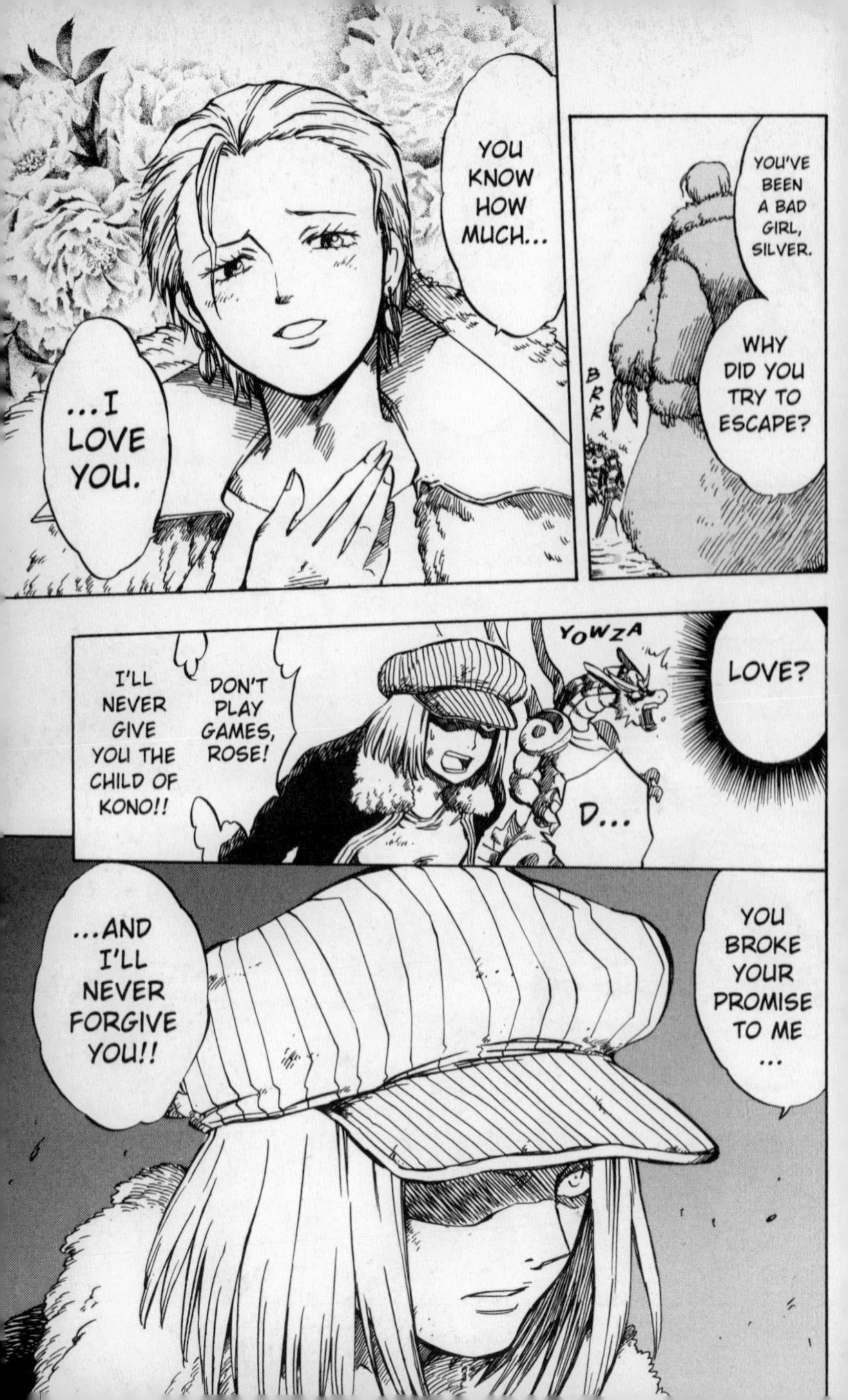
YOU'VE BEEN A BAD GIRL, SILVER.
WHY DID YOU TRY TO ESCAPE?
BRR
YOU KNOW HOW MUCH...
...I LOVE YOU.
LOVE?
YOWZA
D...
DON'T PLAY GAMES, ROSE!
I'LL NEVER GIVE YOU THE CHILD OF KONO!!
YOU BROKE YOUR PROMISE TO ME ...
...AND I'LL NEVER FORGIVE YOU!!

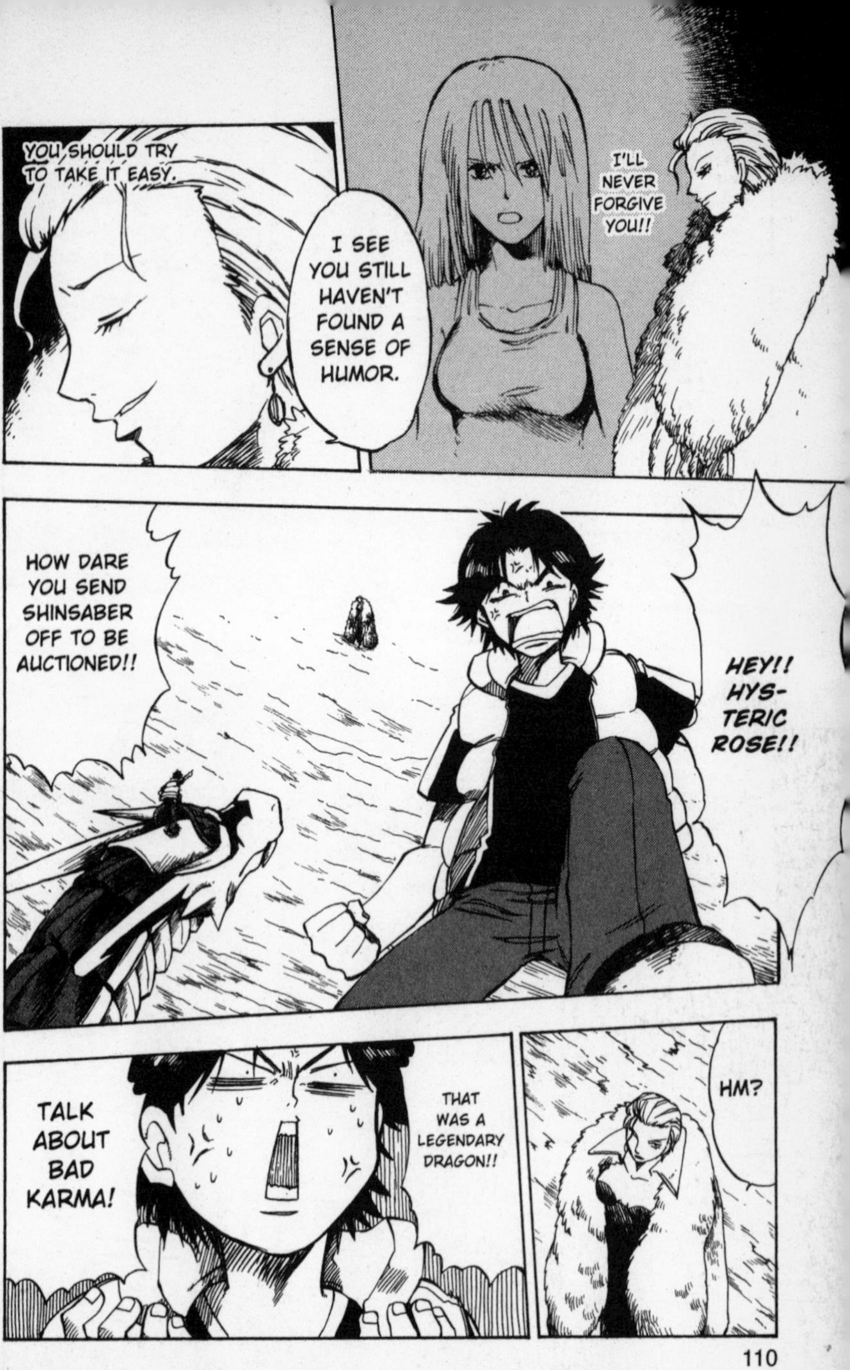
I'LL NEVER FORGIVE YOU!!
I SEE YOU STILL HAVEN'T FOUND A SENSE OF HUMOR.
YOU SHOULD TRY TO TAKE IT EASY.
HEY!! HYS-TERIC ROSE!!
HOW DARE YOU SEND SHINSABER OFF TO BE AUCTIONED!!
HM?
THAT WAS A LEGENDARY DRAGON!!
TALK ABOUT BAD KARMA!

READ THIS WAY

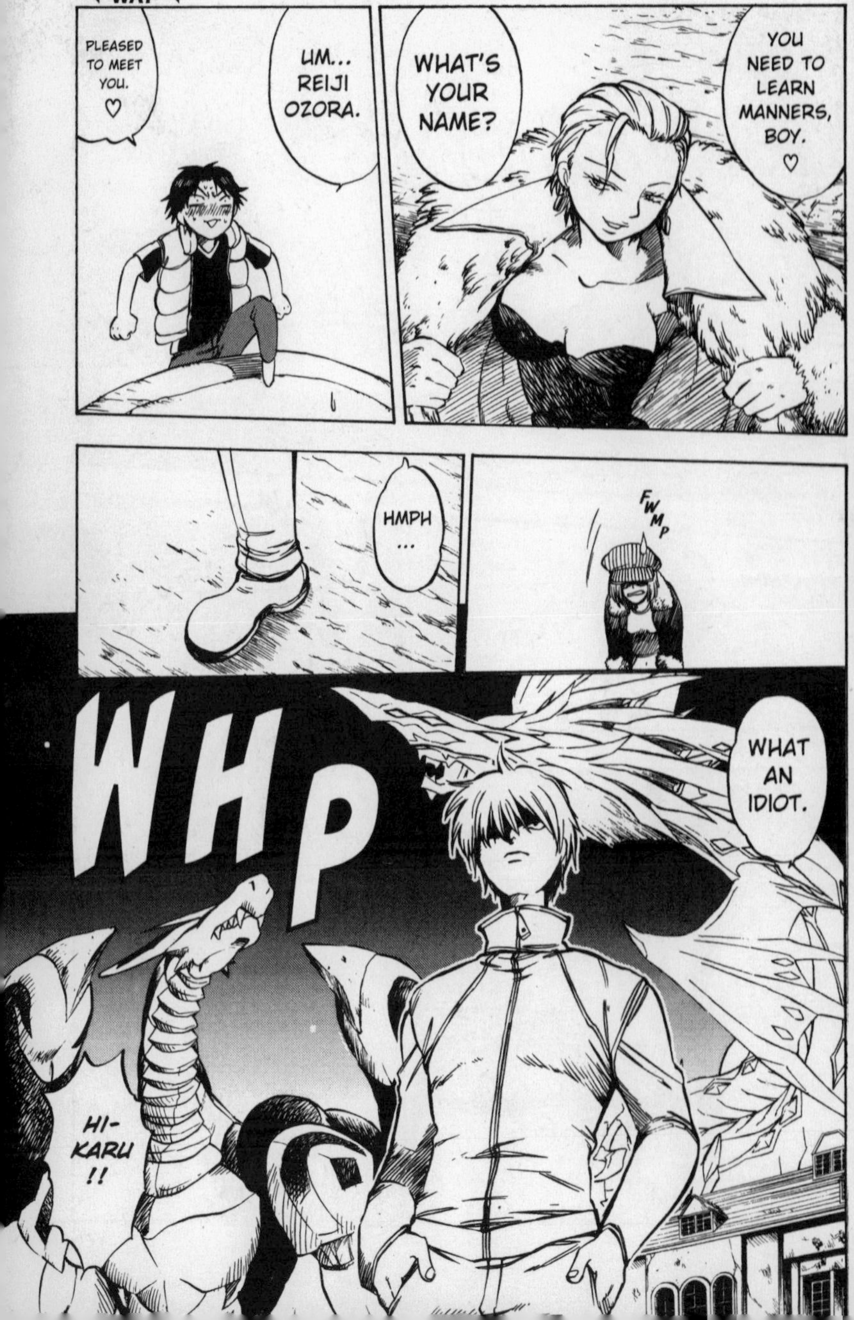
YOU NEED TO LEARN MANNERS, BOY. ♡
WHAT'S YOUR NAME?
UM... REIJI OZORA.
PLEASED TO MEET YOU. ♡
FWMP
HMPH ...
WHAT AN IDIOT.
WHP
HI-KARU !!

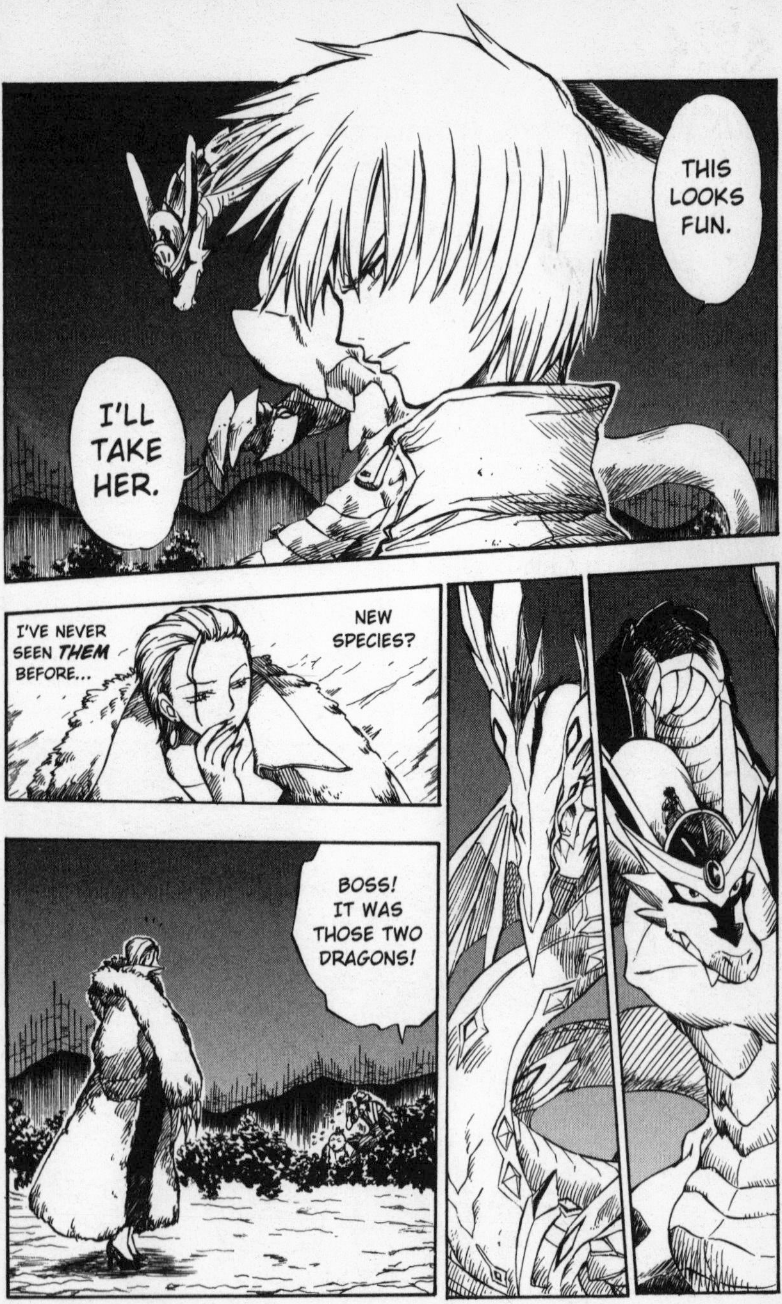
THIS LOOKS FUN.
I'LL TAKE HER.
NEW SPECIES?
I'VE NEVER SEEN *THEM* BEFORE...
BOSS! IT WAS THOSE TWO DRAGONS!

READ THIS WAY

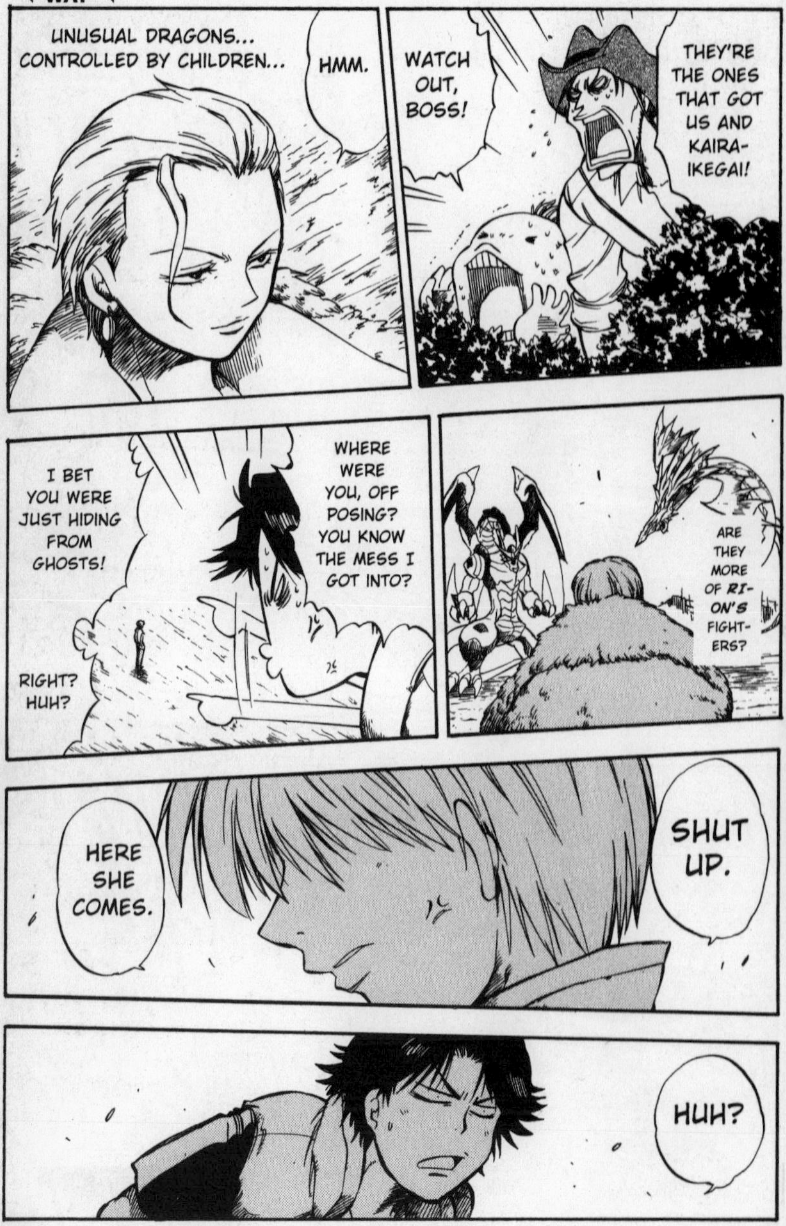

THEY'RE THE ONES THAT GOT US AND KAIRA-IKEGAI!
WATCH OUT, BOSS!
HMM.
UNUSUAL DRAGONS... CONTROLLED BY CHILDREN...
ARE THEY MORE OF RI-ON'S FIGHTERS?
WHERE WERE YOU, OFF POSING? YOU KNOW THE MESS I GOT INTO?
I BET YOU WERE JUST HIDING FROM GHOSTS!
RIGHT? HUH?
SHUT UP.
HERE SHE COMES.
HUH?

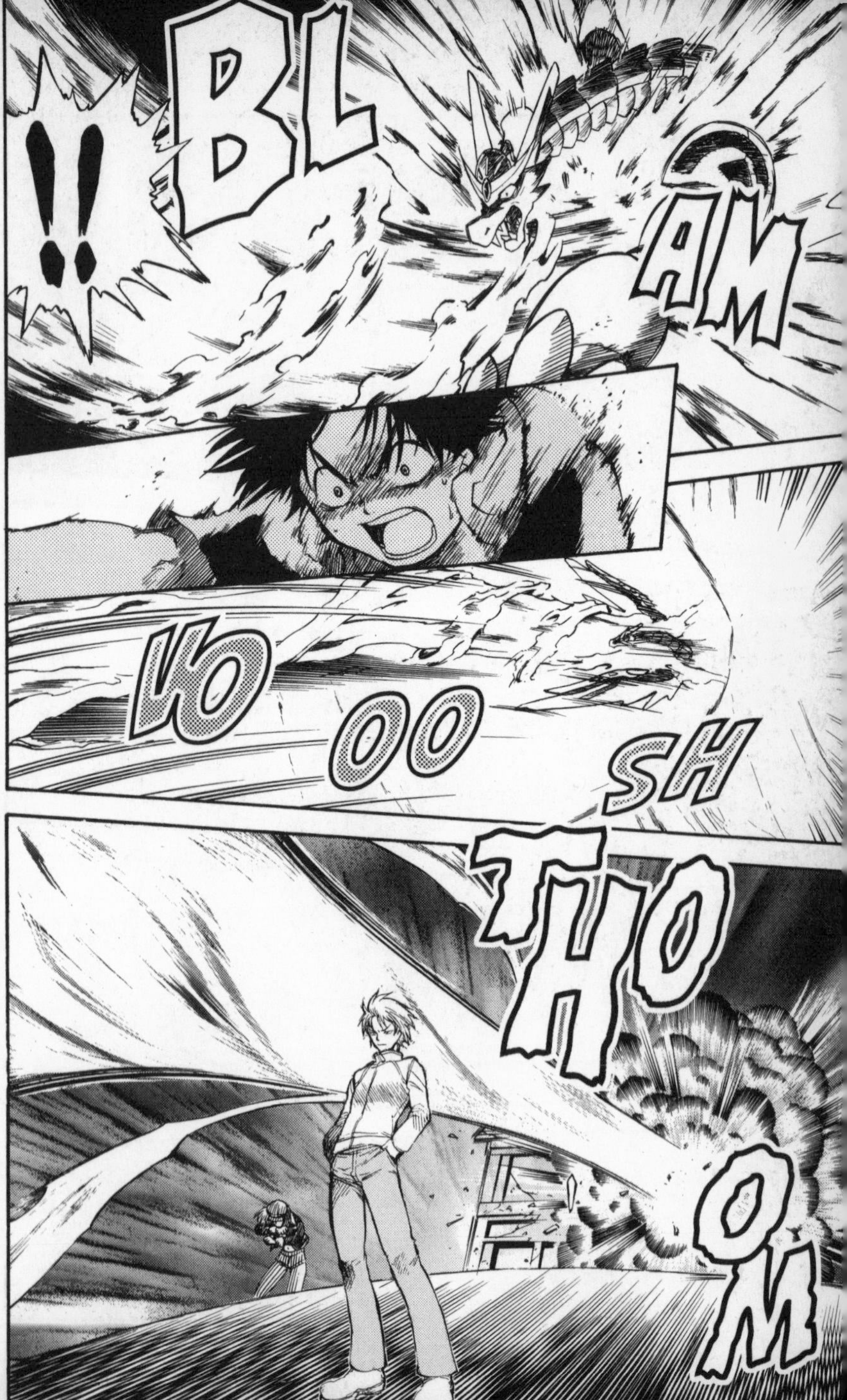
BLAM
!!
WOOOSH
THOOM

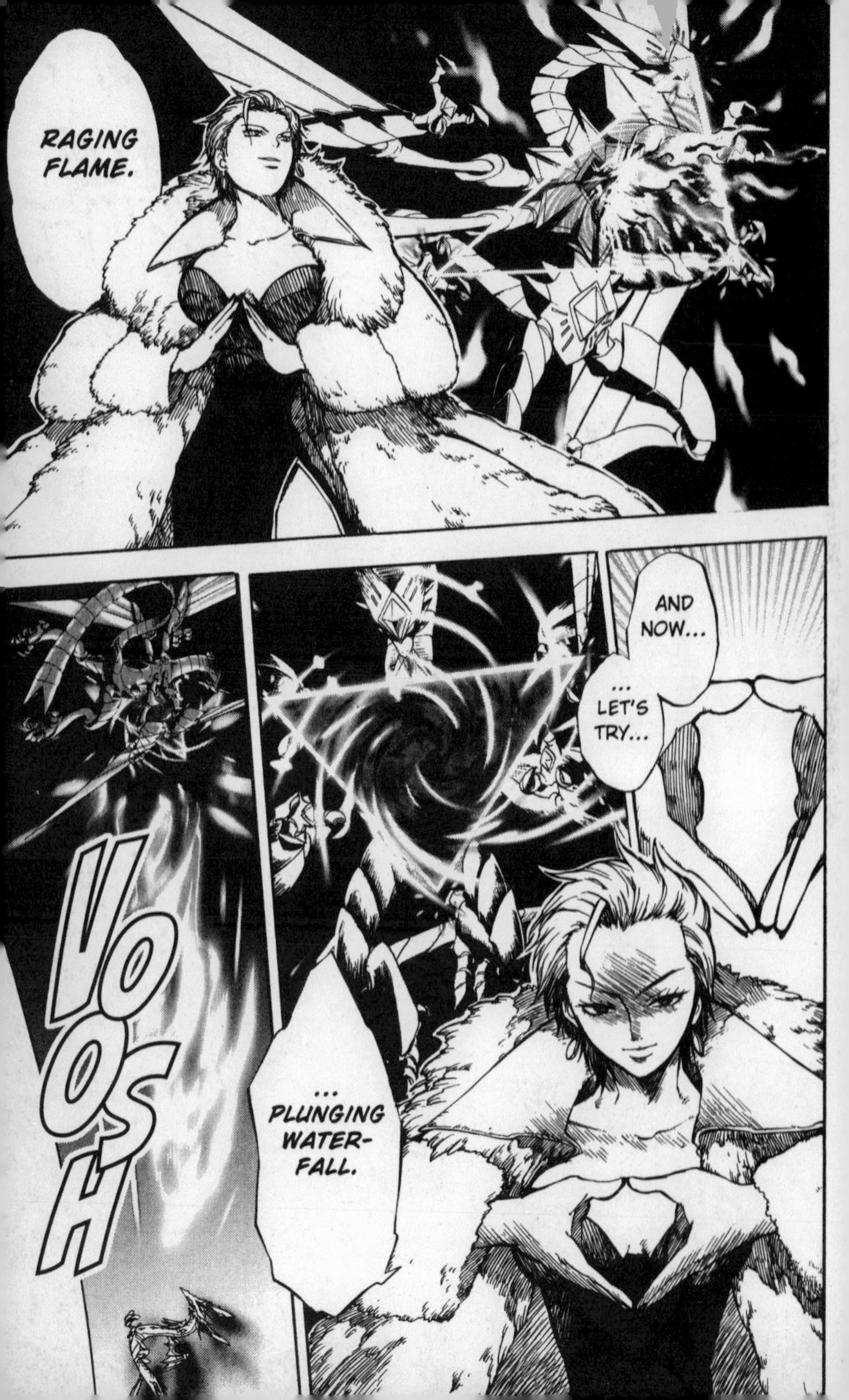
RAGING FLAME.
AND NOW...
...LET'S TRY...
...PLUNGING WATER-FALL.
VOOSH

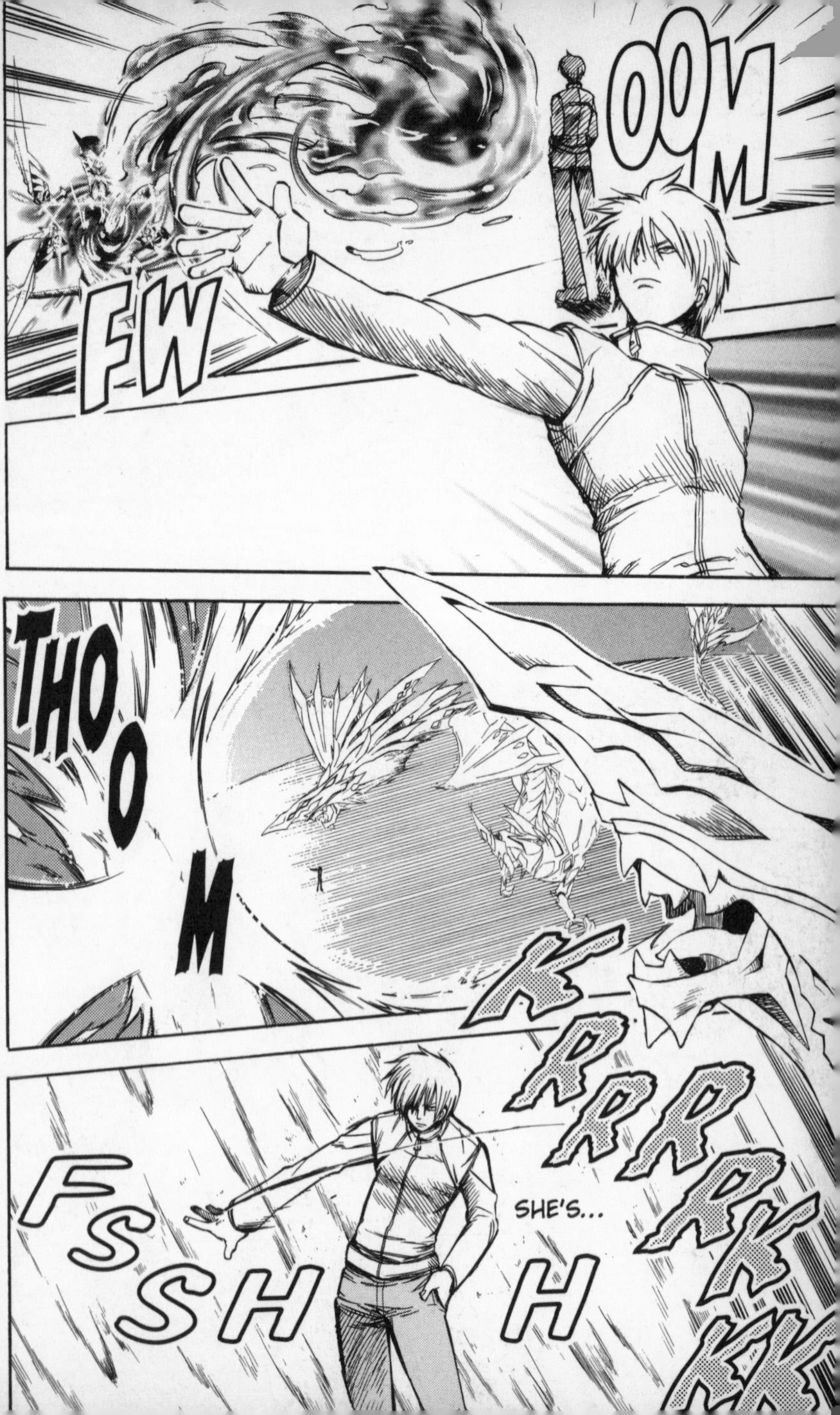
OOMM
FW
KRRRKKK
THOOM
SHE'S...
FSSHH

READ THIS WAY

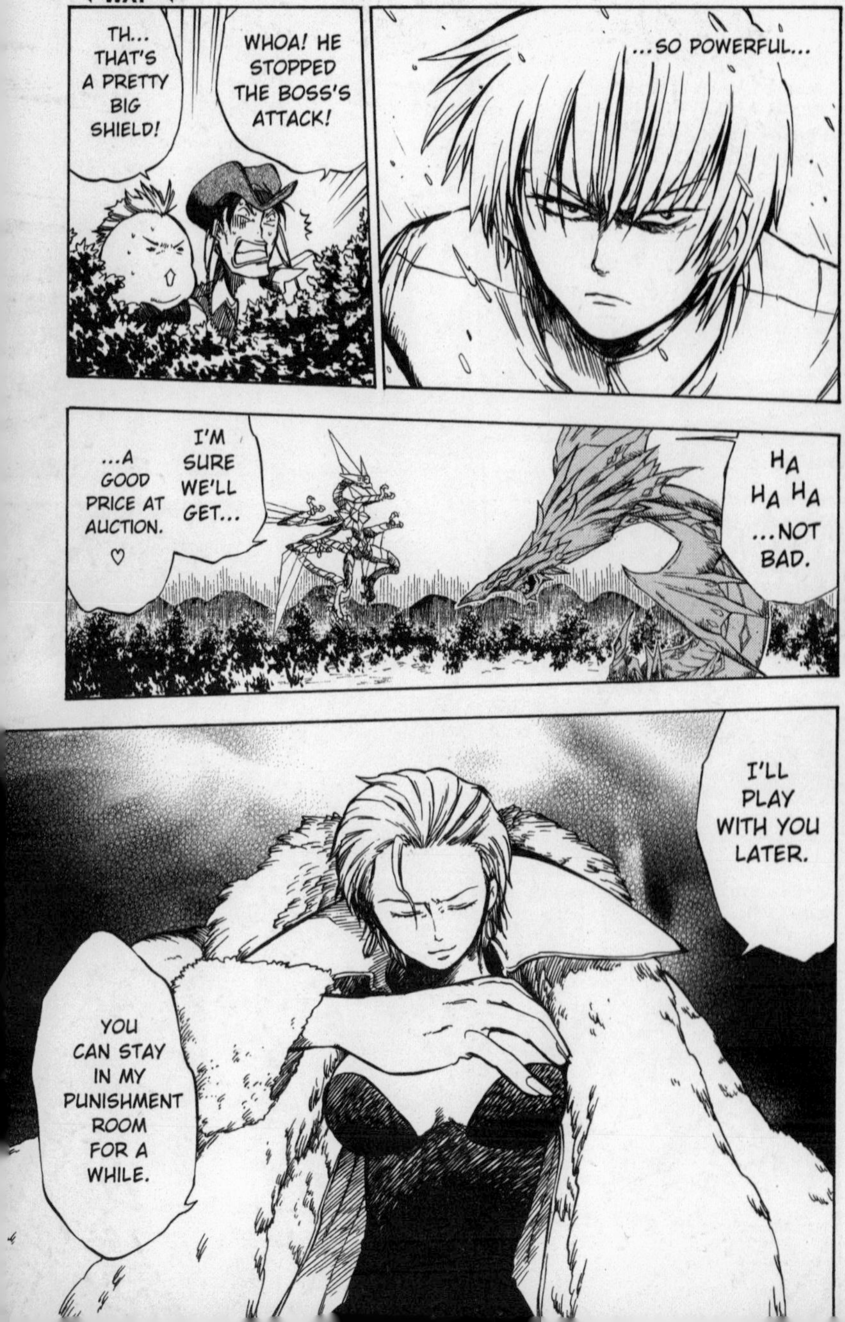
...SO POWERFUL...
WHOA! HE STOPPED THE BOSS'S ATTACK!
TH... THAT'S A PRETTY BIG SHIELD!
HA HA HA ...NOT BAD.
I'M SURE WE'LL GET...
...A GOOD PRICE AT AUCTION. ♡
I'LL PLAY WITH YOU LATER.
YOU CAN STAY IN MY PUNISHMENT ROOM FOR A WHILE.

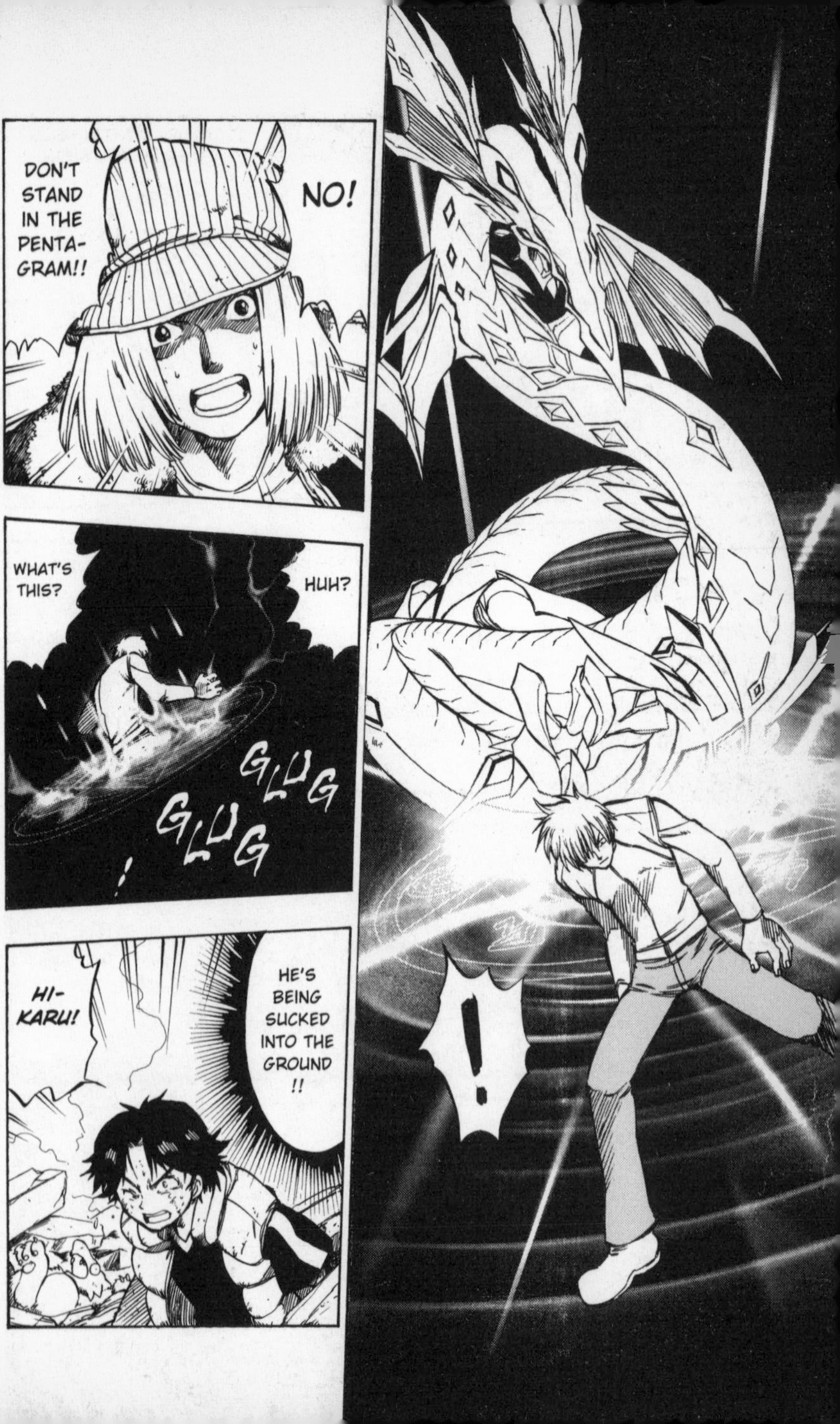
!
NO!
DON'T STAND IN THE PENTA-GRAM!!
HUH?
WHAT'S THIS?
GLUG GLUG
!
HE'S BEING SUCKED INTO THE GROUND !!
HI-KARU!

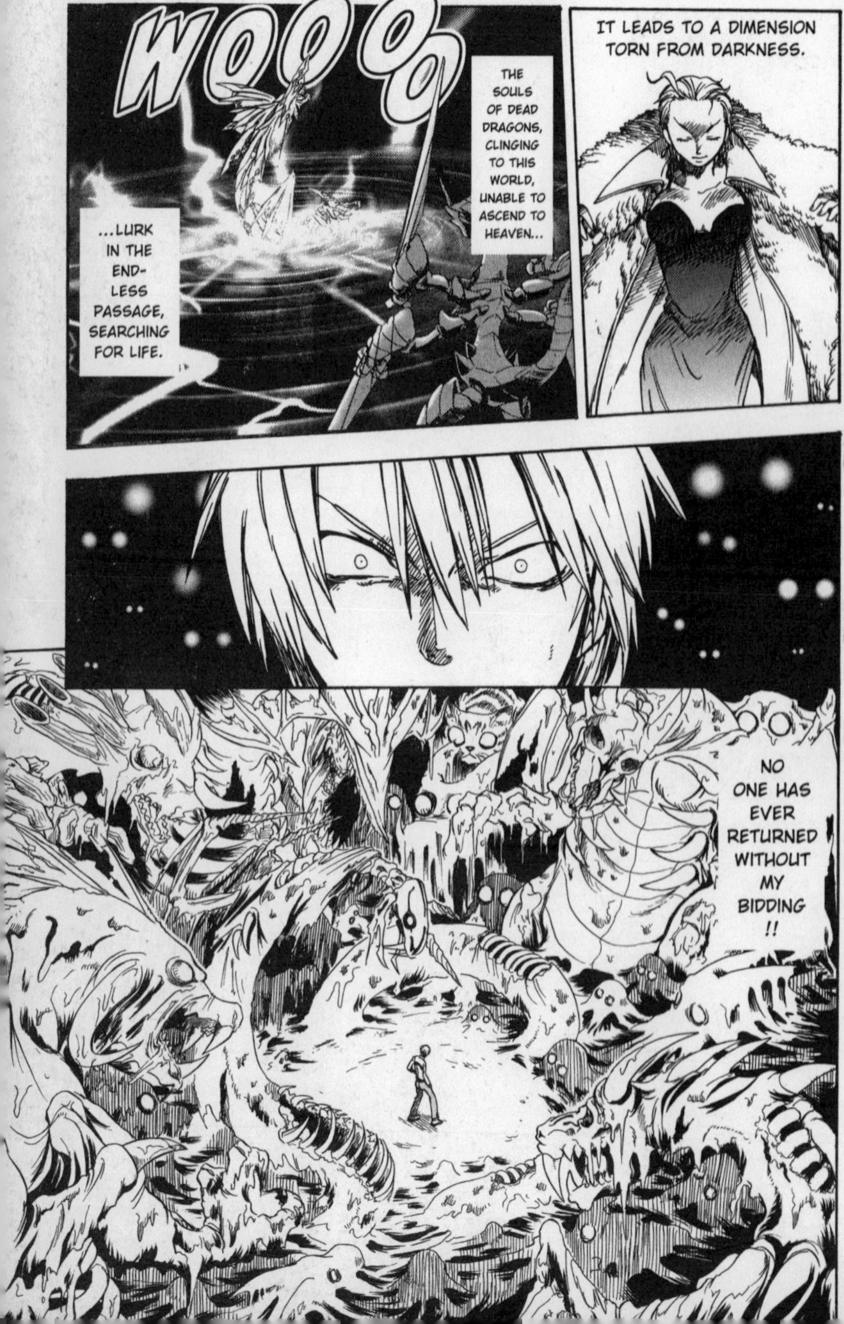
IT LEADS TO A DIMENSION TORN FROM DARKNESS.
WOOOOO
THE SOULS OF DEAD DRAGONS, CLINGING TO THIS WORLD, UNABLE TO ASCEND TO HEAVEN...
...LURK IN THE END-LESS PASSAGE, SEARCHING FOR LIFE.
NO ONE HAS EVER RETURNED WITHOUT MY BIDDING!!

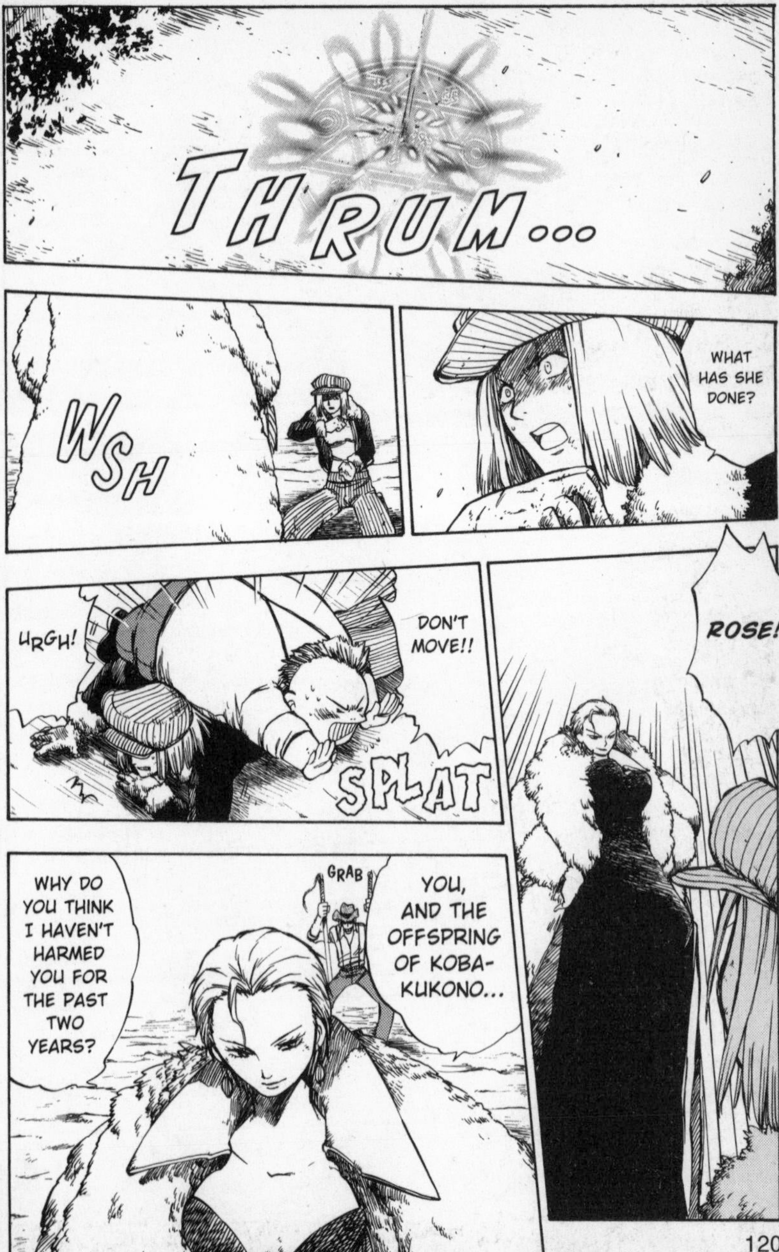
THRUM...
WHAT HAS SHE DONE?
WSH
ROSE!
DON'T MOVE!!
URGH!
SPLAT
GRAB
YOU, AND THE OFFSPRING OF KOBA-KUKONO...
WHY DO YOU THINK I HAVEN'T HARMED YOU FOR THE PAST TWO YEARS?

READ THIS WAY

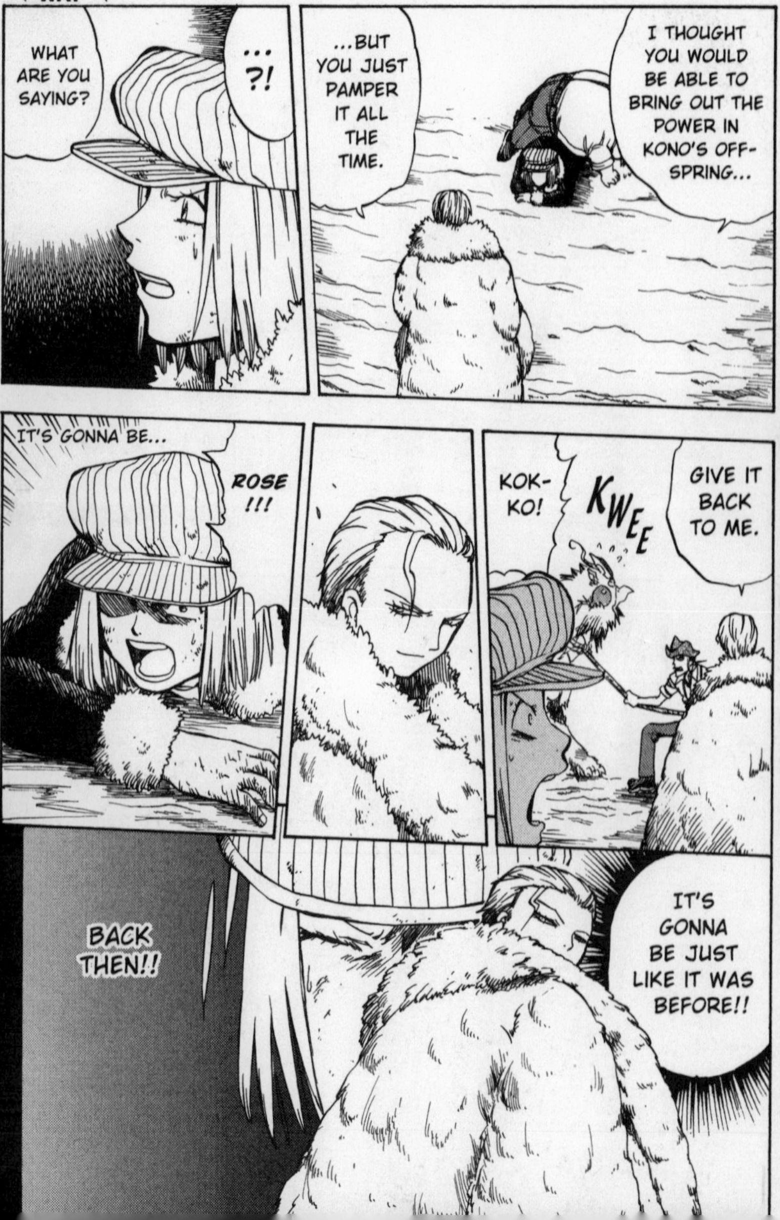

I THOUGHT YOU WOULD BE ABLE TO BRING OUT THE POWER IN KONO'S OFF-SPRING...
...BUT YOU JUST PAMPER IT ALL THE TIME.
...?!
WHAT ARE YOU SAYING?
GIVE IT BACK TO ME.
KWEE
KOK-KO!
ROSE!!!
IT'S GONNA BE...
IT'S GONNA BE JUST LIKE IT WAS BEFORE!!
BACK THEN!!

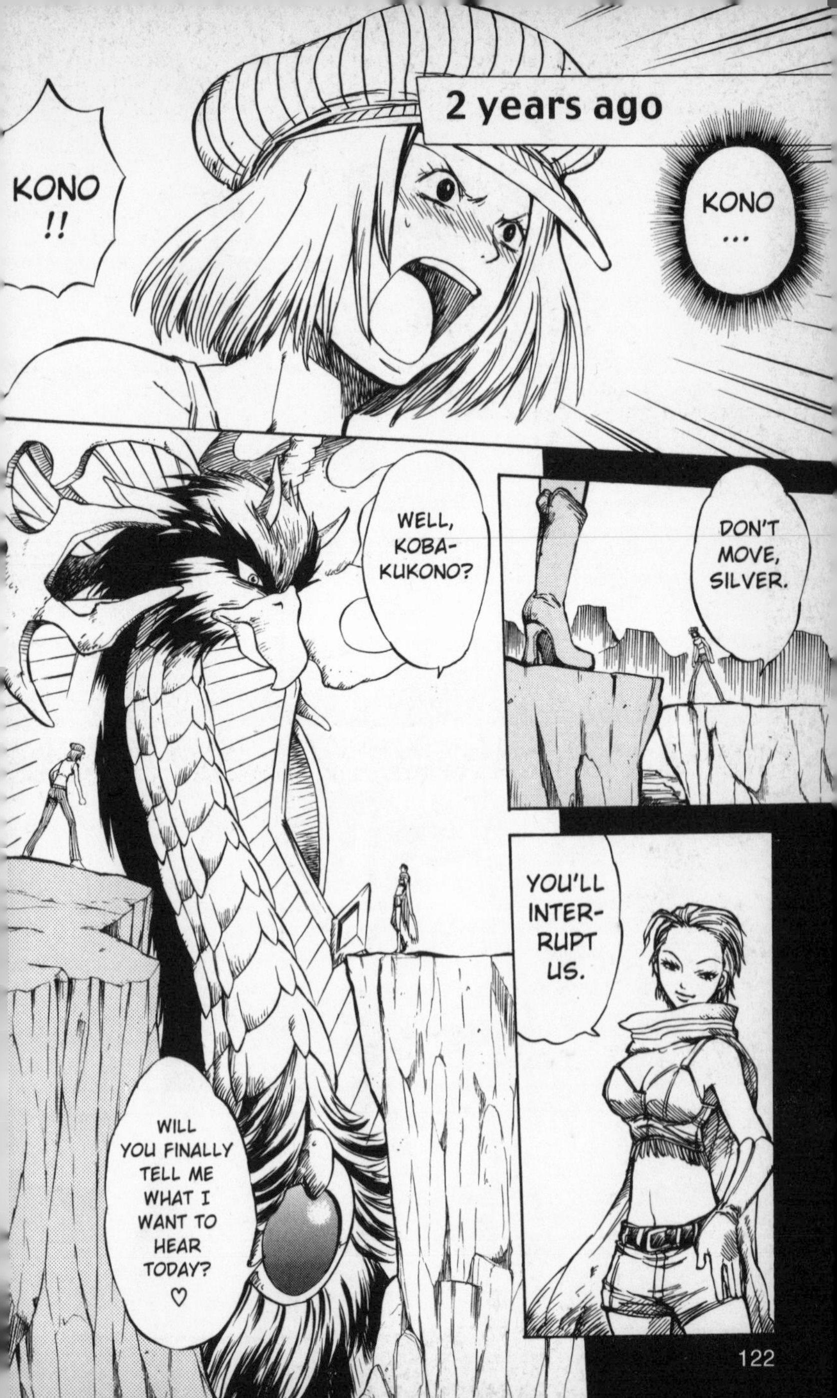
2 years ago
KONO ...
KONO !!
DON'T MOVE, SILVER.
YOU'LL INTER-RUPT US.
WELL, KOBA-KUKONO?
WILL YOU FINALLY TELL ME WHAT I WANT TO HEAR TODAY? ♡

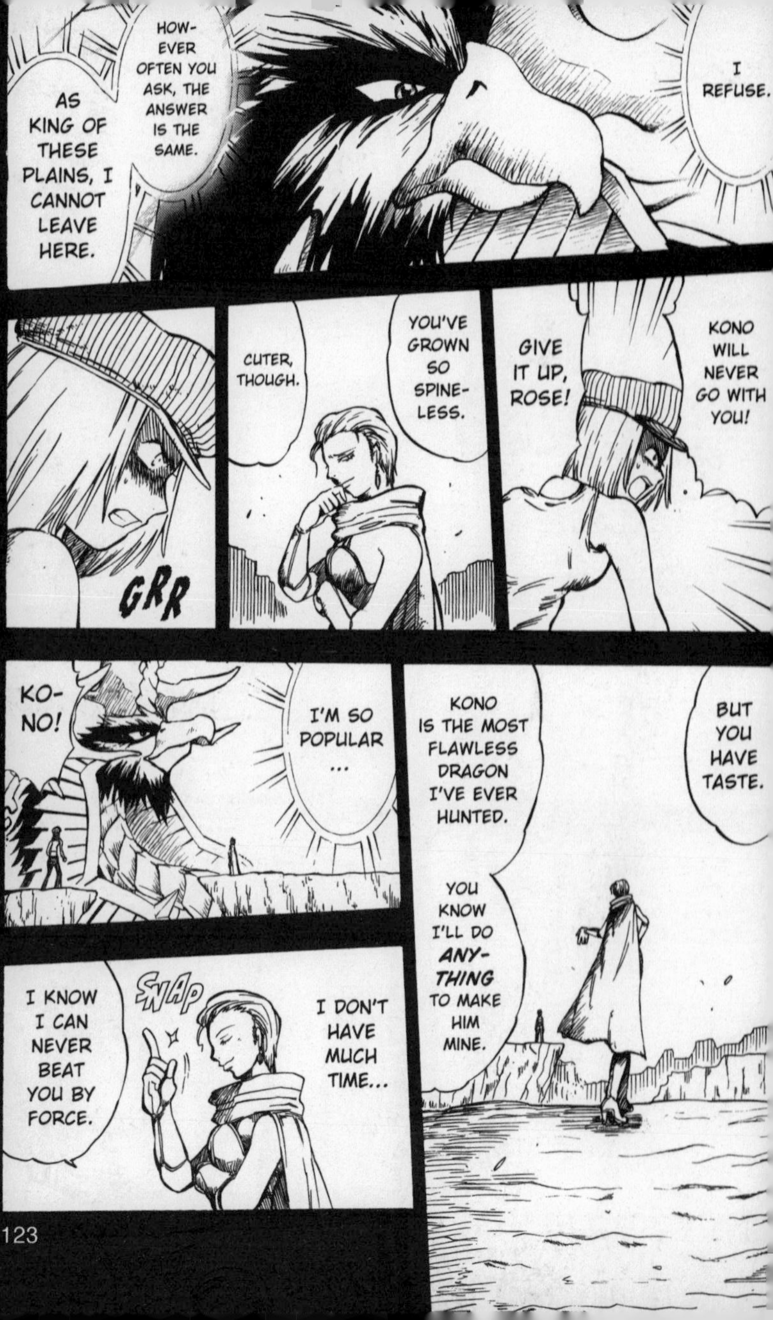
I REFUSE.
HOWEVER OFTEN YOU ASK, THE ANSWER IS THE SAME.
AS KING OF THESE PLAINS, I CANNOT LEAVE HERE.
KONO WILL NEVER GO WITH YOU!
GIVE IT UP, ROSE!
YOU'VE GROWN SO SPINELESS.
CUTER, THOUGH.
GRR
BUT YOU HAVE TASTE.
KONO IS THE MOST FLAWLESS DRAGON I'VE EVER HUNTED.
YOU KNOW I'LL DO ANYTHING TO MAKE HIM MINE.
I'M SO POPULAR ...
KONO!
I DON'T HAVE MUCH TIME...
SNAP
I KNOW I CAN NEVER BEAT YOU BY FORCE.

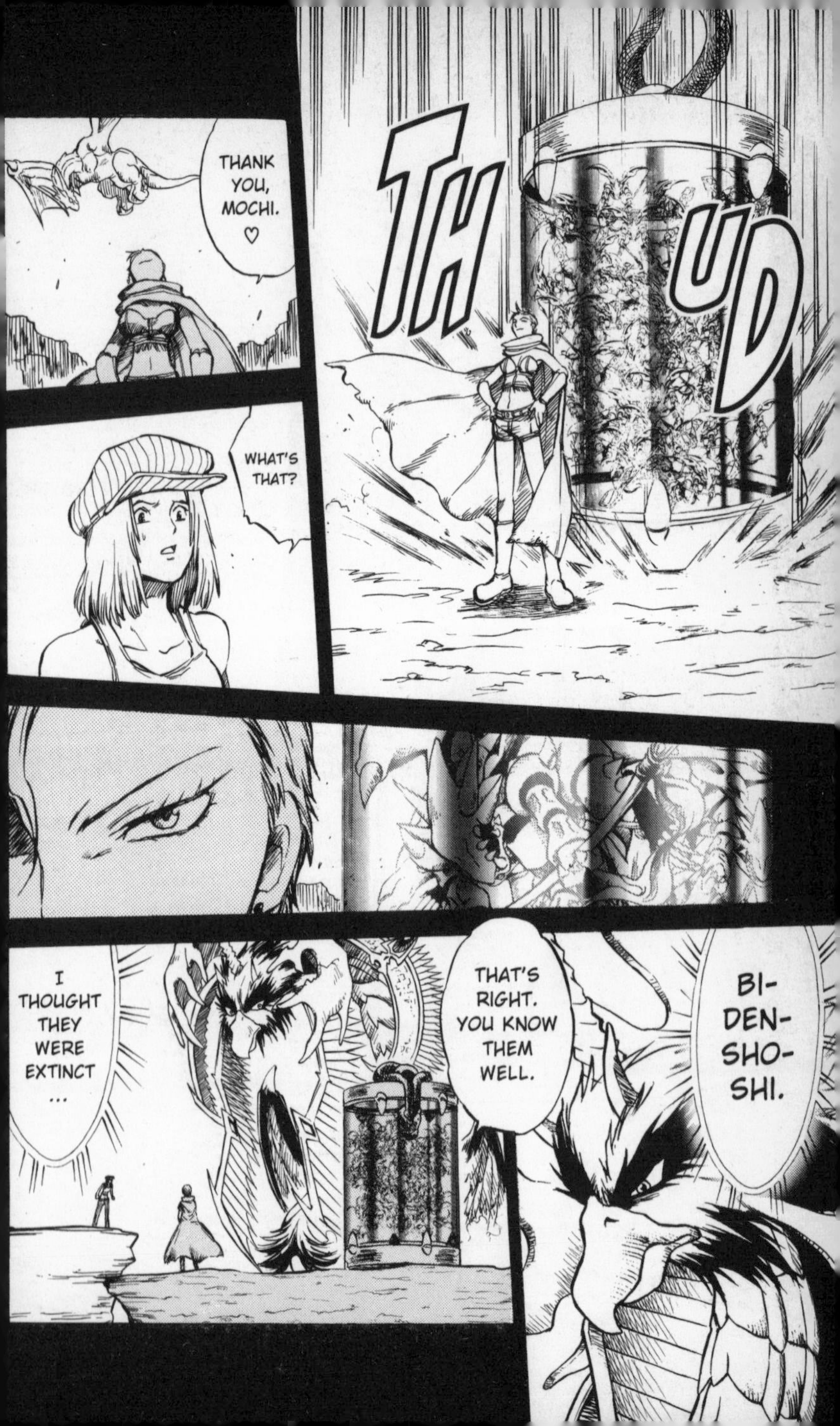
THUD
THANK YOU, MOCHI. ♡
WHAT'S THAT?
BI-DEN-SHO-SHI.
THAT'S RIGHT. YOU KNOW THEM WELL.
I THOUGHT THEY WERE EXTINCT...

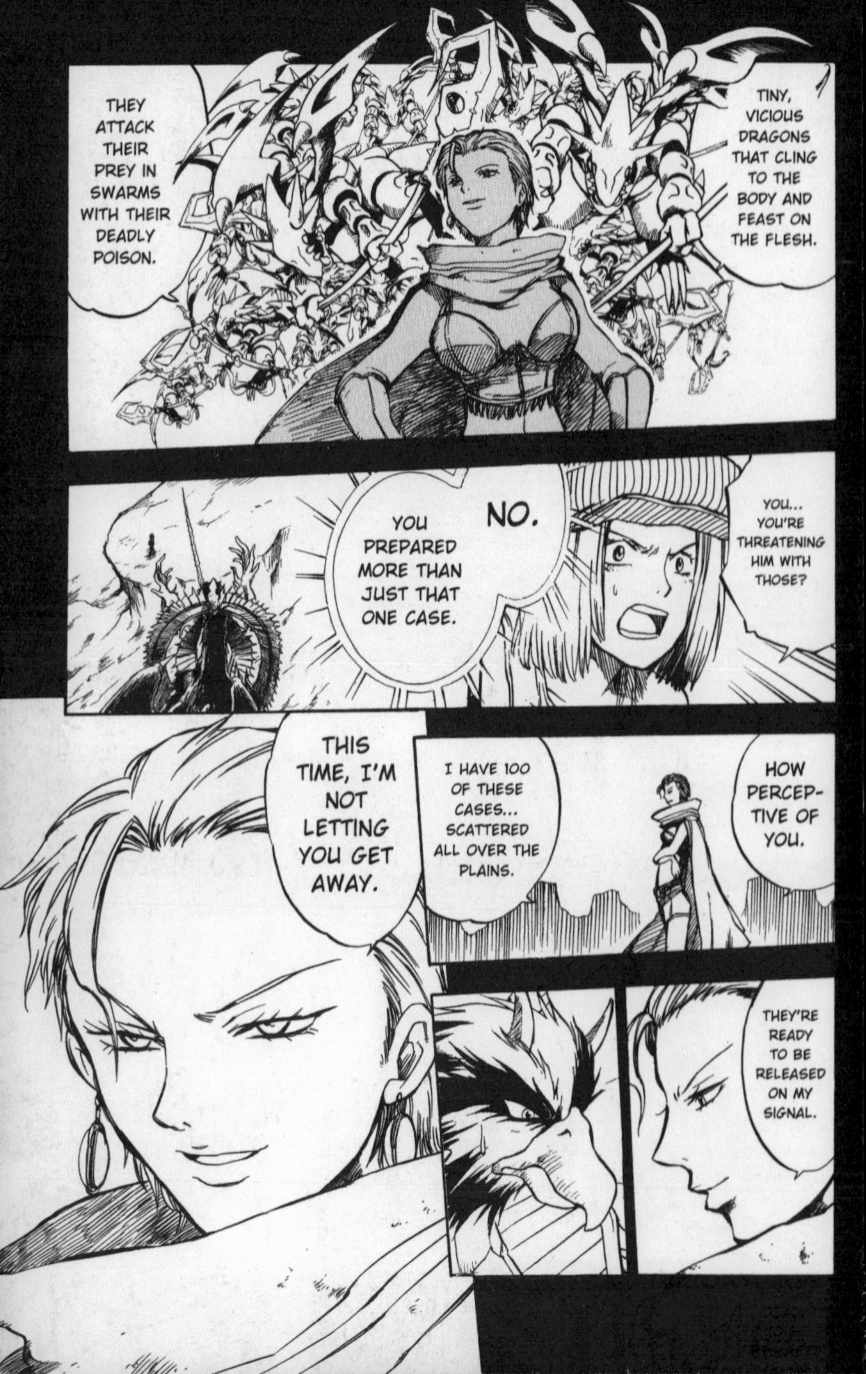
TINY, VICIOUS DRAGONS THAT CLING TO THE BODY AND FEAST ON THE FLESH.
THEY ATTACK THEIR PREY IN SWARMS WITH THEIR DEADLY POISON.
YOU... YOU'RE THREATENING HIM WITH THOSE?
NO.
YOU PREPARED MORE THAN JUST THAT ONE CASE.
HOW PERCEPTIVE OF YOU.
I HAVE 100 OF THESE CASES... SCATTERED ALL OVER THE PLAINS.
THEY'RE READY TO BE RELEASED ON MY SIGNAL.
THIS TIME, I'M NOT LETTING YOU GET AWAY.

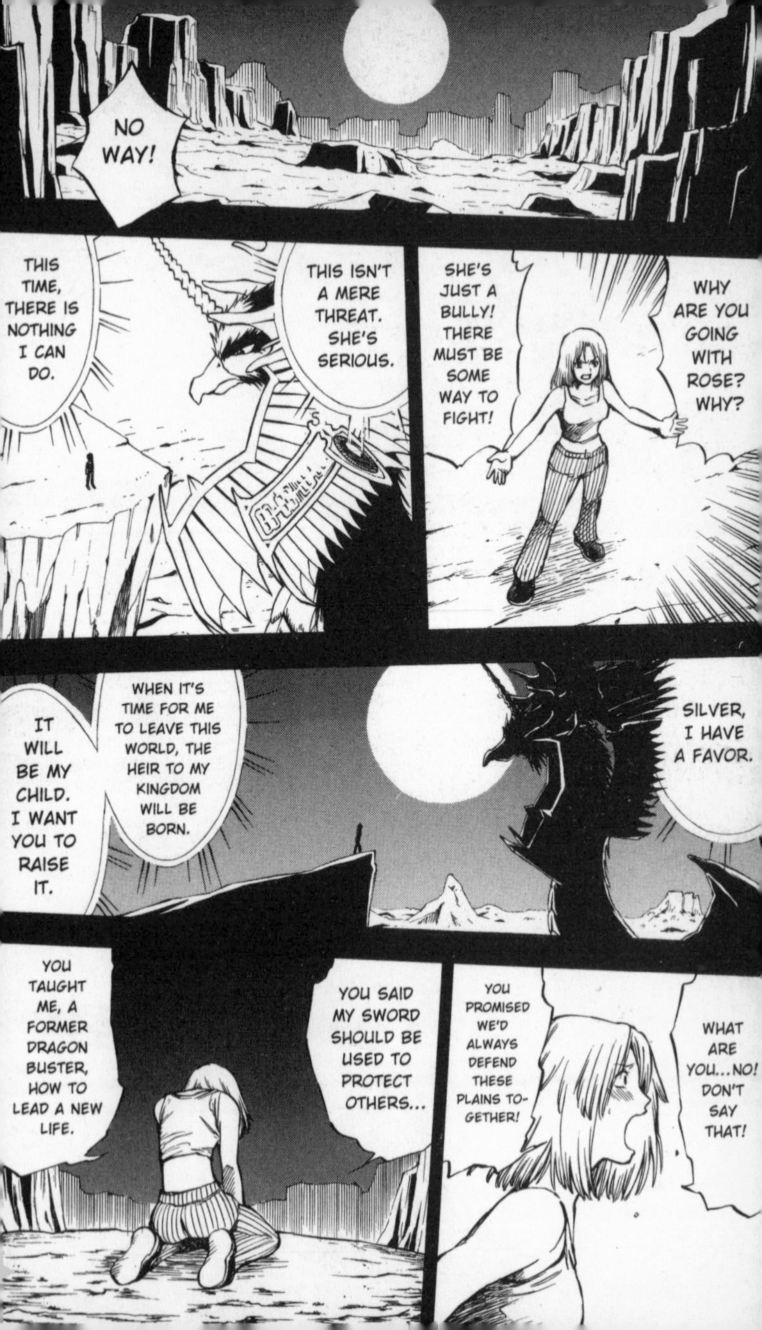
NO WAY!
WHY ARE YOU GOING WITH ROSE? WHY?
SHE'S JUST A BULLY! THERE MUST BE SOME WAY TO FIGHT!
THIS ISN'T A MERE THREAT. SHE'S SERIOUS.
THIS TIME, THERE IS NOTHING I CAN DO.
SILVER, I HAVE A FAVOR.
WHEN IT'S TIME FOR ME TO LEAVE THIS WORLD, THE HEIR TO MY KINGDOM WILL BE BORN.
IT WILL BE MY CHILD. I WANT YOU TO RAISE IT.
WHAT ARE YOU...NO! DON'T SAY THAT!
YOU PROMISED WE'D ALWAYS DEFEND THESE PLAINS TO-GETHER!
YOU SAID MY SWORD SHOULD BE USED TO PROTECT OTHERS...
YOU TAUGHT ME, A FORMER DRAGON BUSTER, HOW TO LEAD A NEW LIFE.

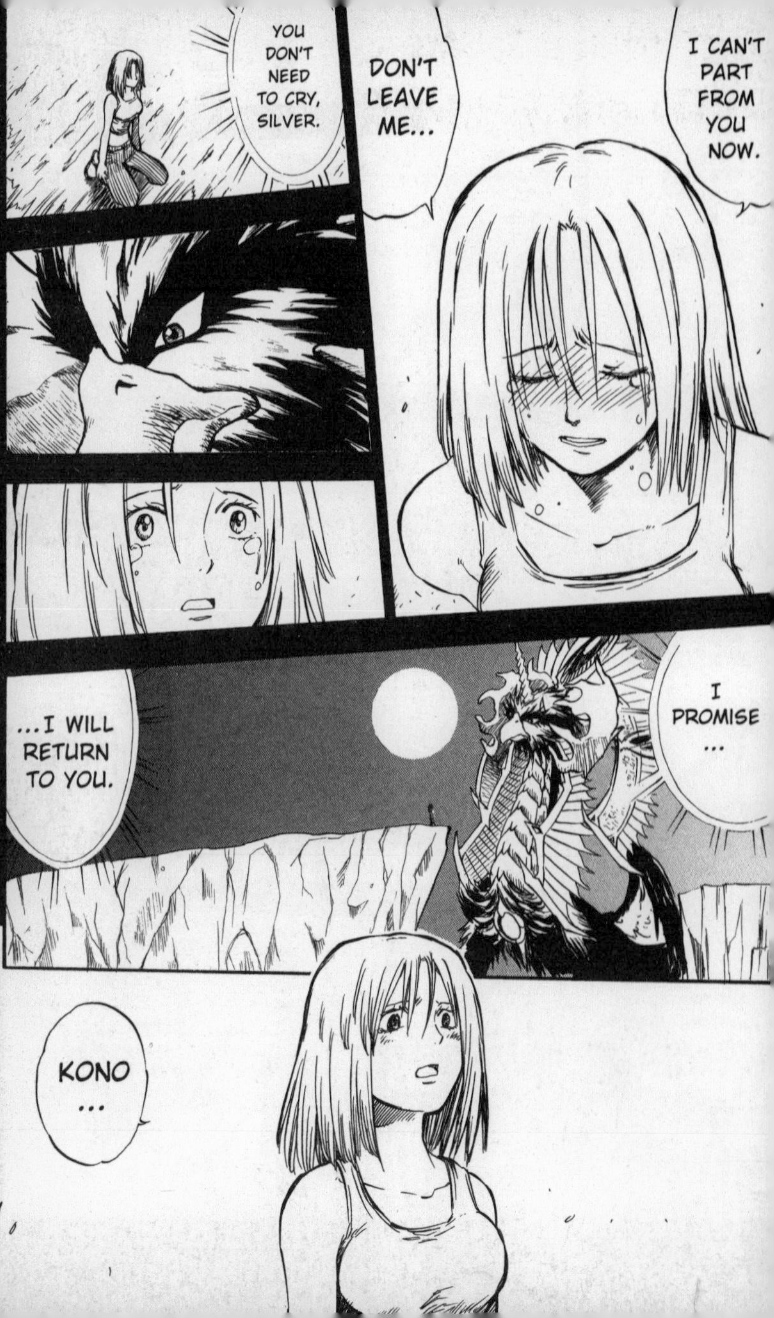
I CAN'T PART FROM YOU NOW.
DON'T LEAVE ME...
YOU DON'T NEED TO CRY, SILVER.
I PROMISE ...
...I WILL RETURN TO YOU.
KONO ...

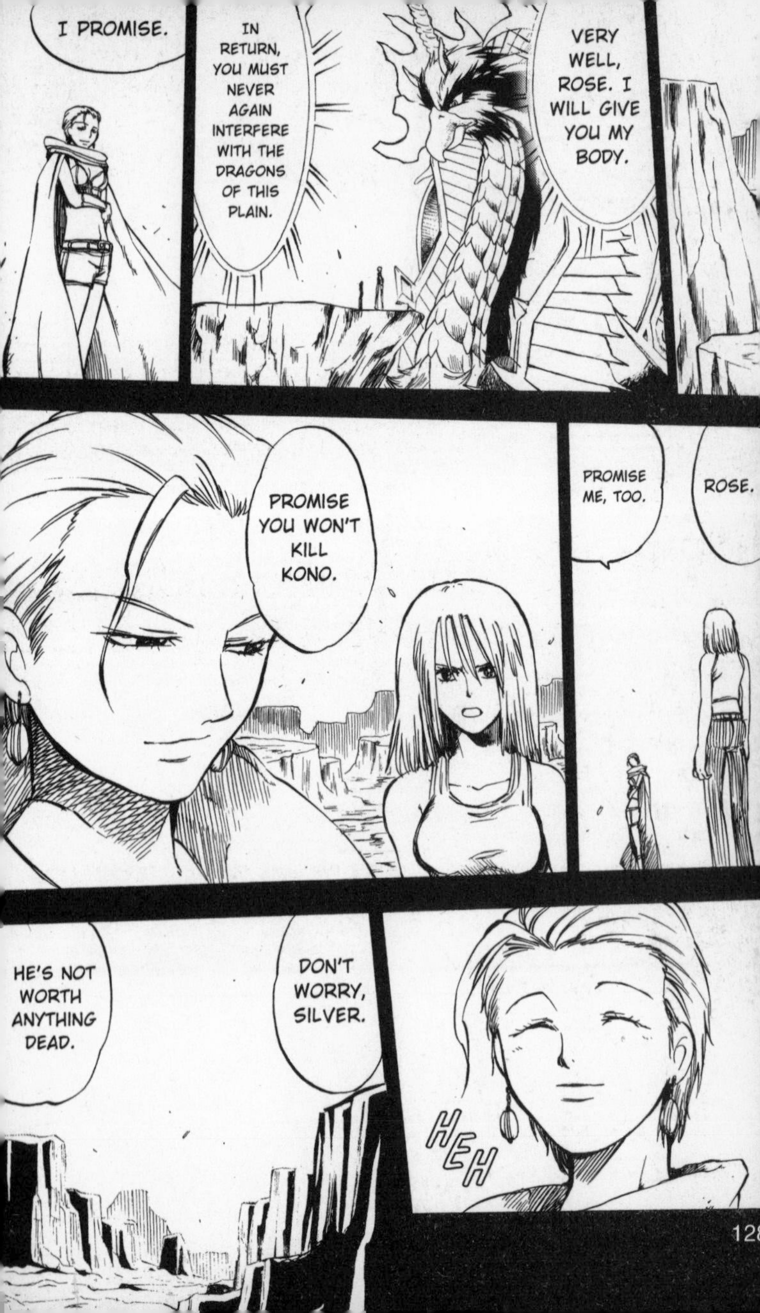
VERY WELL, ROSE. I WILL GIVE YOU MY BODY.
IN RETURN, YOU MUST NEVER AGAIN INTERFERE WITH THE DRAGONS OF THIS PLAIN.
I PROMISE.
ROSE.
PROMISE ME, TOO.
PROMISE YOU WON'T KILL KONO.
HEH
DON'T WORRY, SILVER.
HE'S NOT WORTH ANYTHING DEAD.

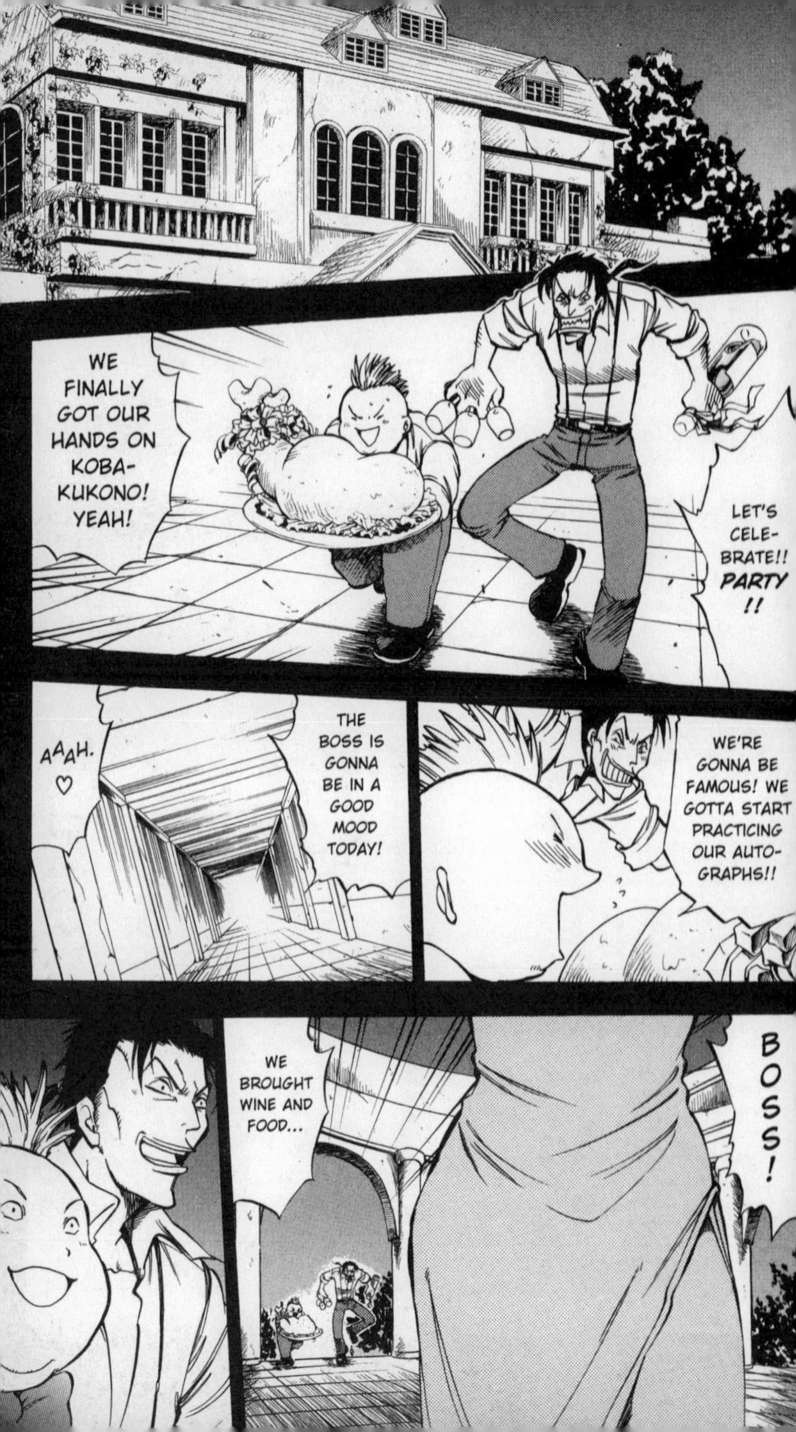
WE FINALLY GOT OUR HANDS ON KOBA-KUKONO! YEAH!
LET'S CELE-BRATE!! PARTY!!
WE'RE GONNA BE FAMOUS! WE GOTTA START PRACTICING OUR AUTO-GRAPHS!!
THE BOSS IS GONNA BE IN A GOOD MOOD TODAY!
AAAH. ♡
BOSS!
WE BROUGHT WINE AND FOOD...

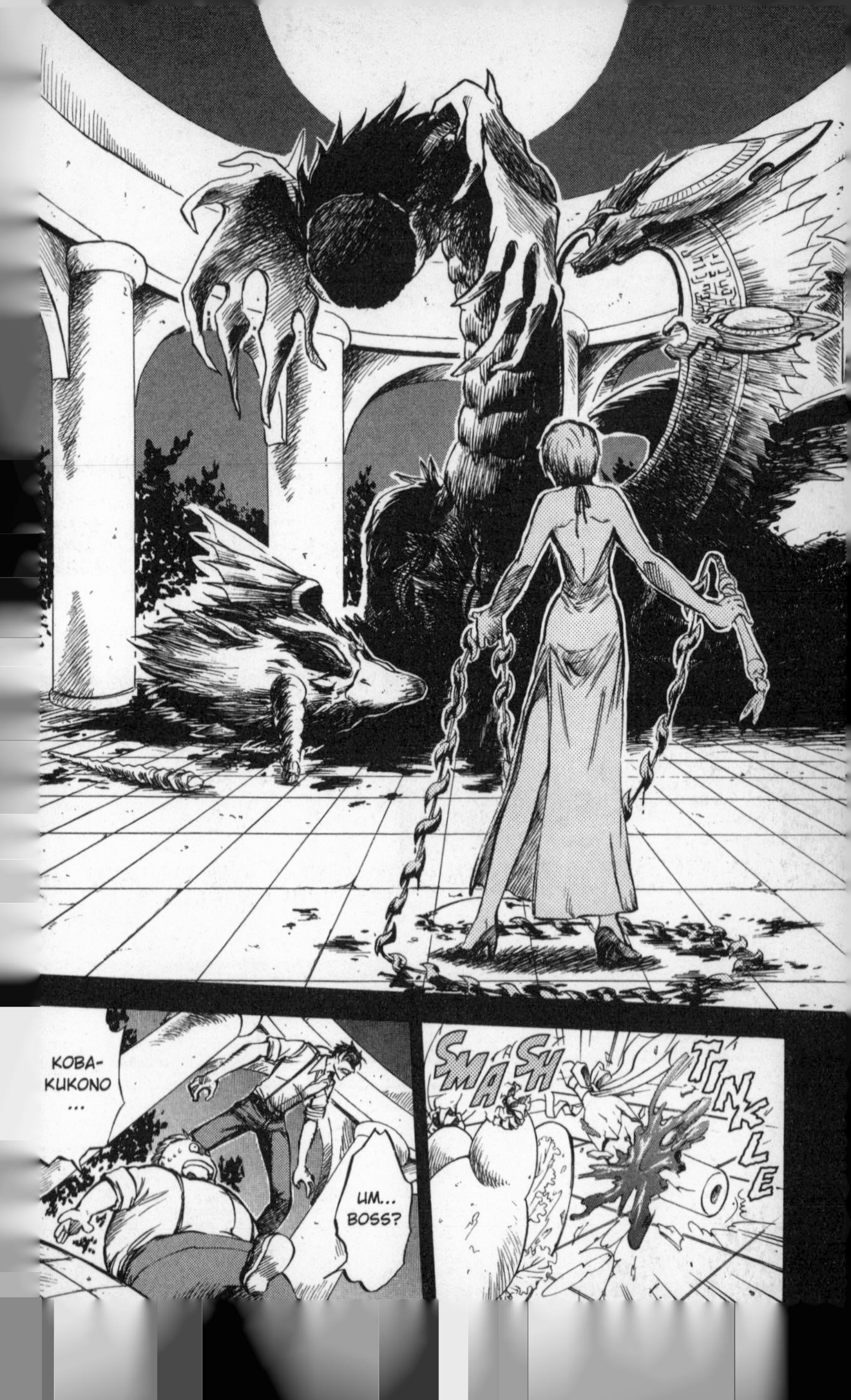
SMASH
TINKLE
KOBA-KUKONO...
UM... BOSS?

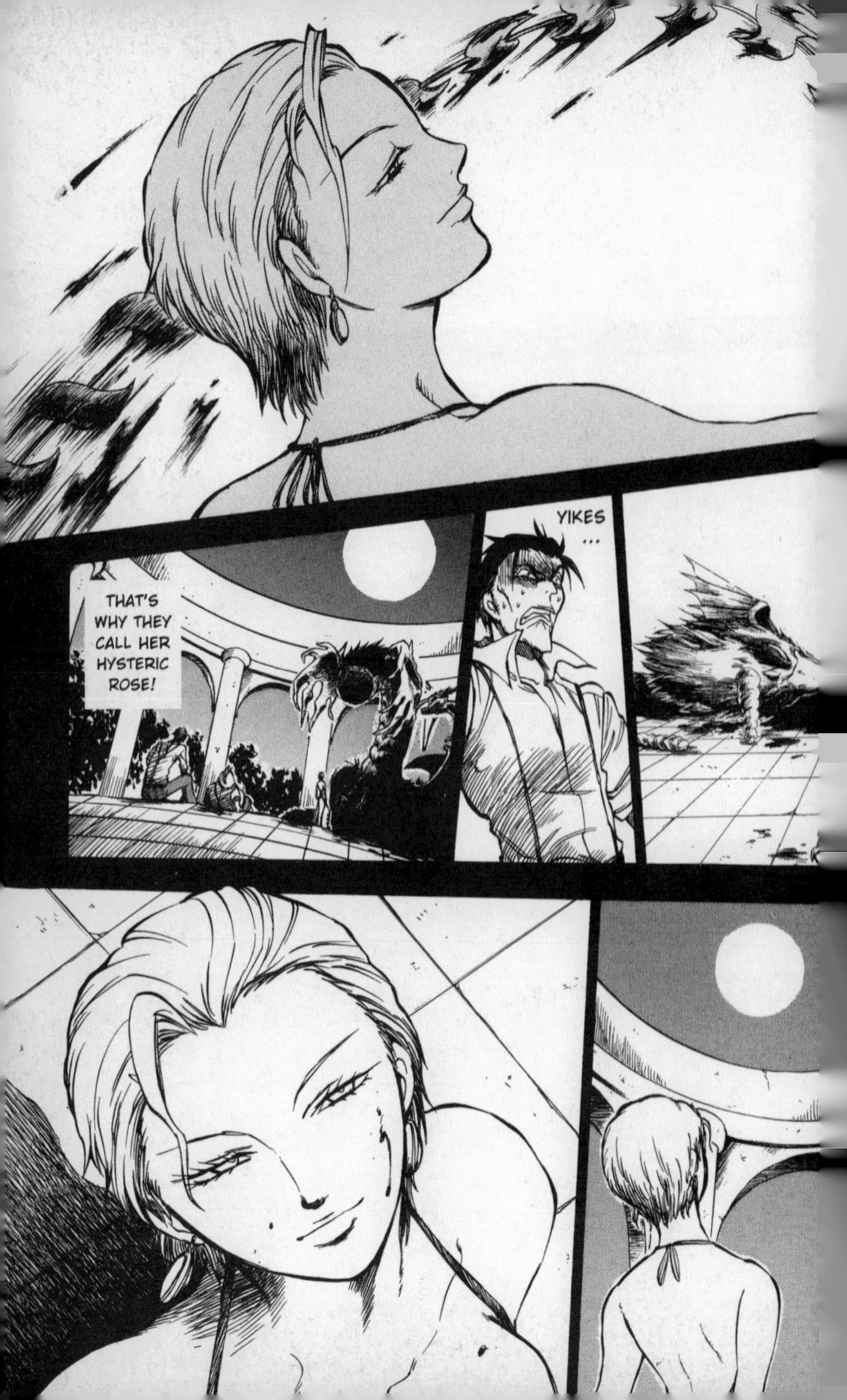
YIKES ...
THAT'S WHY THEY CALL HER HYSTERIC ROSE!

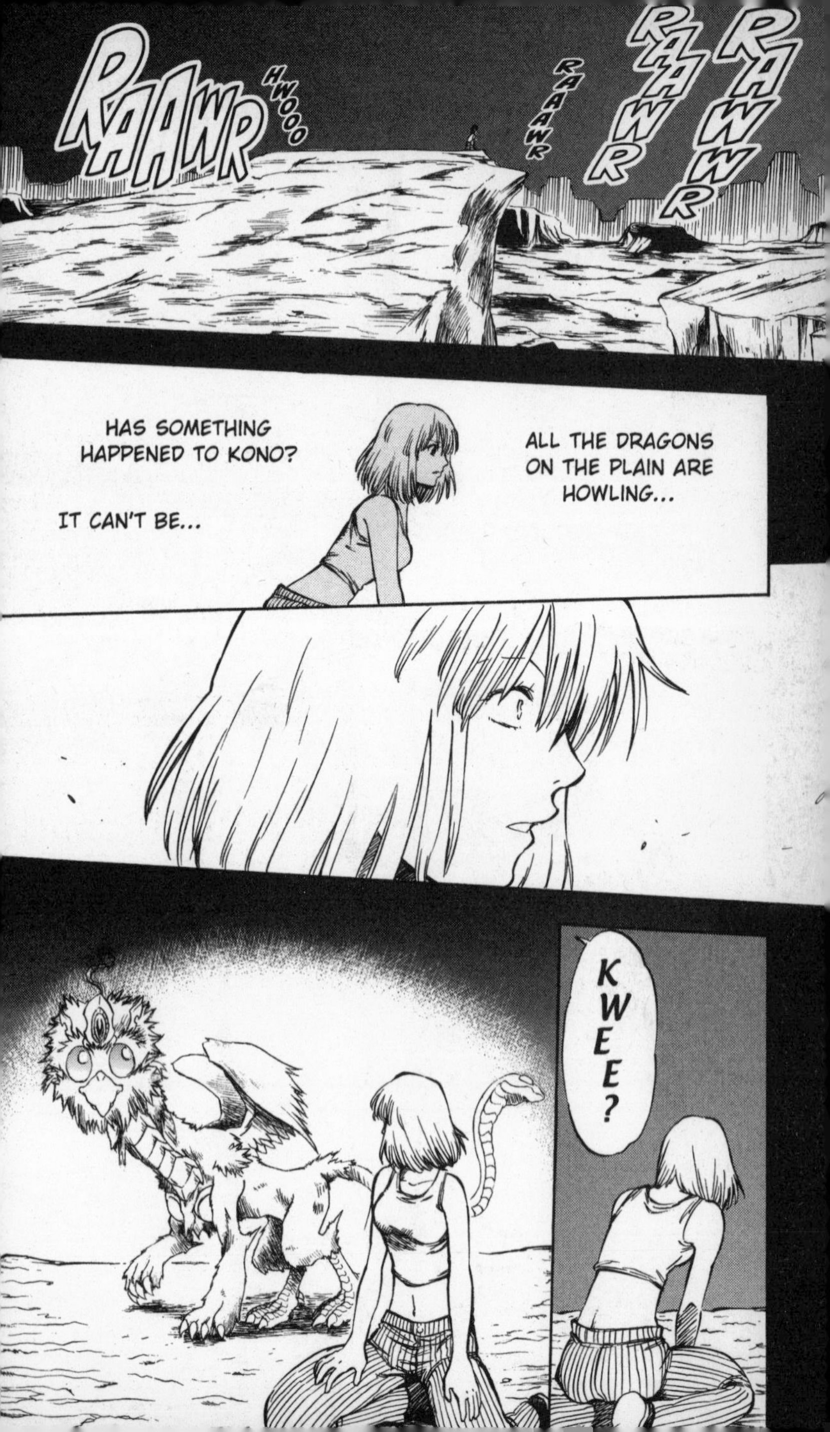
RAWWWR
RAAWR
RAAAAWR
HWOOO
RAAWR
ALL THE DRAGONS ON THE PLAIN ARE HOWLING...
HAS SOMETHING HAPPENED TO KONO?
IT CAN'T BE...
KWEE?

READ THIS WAY

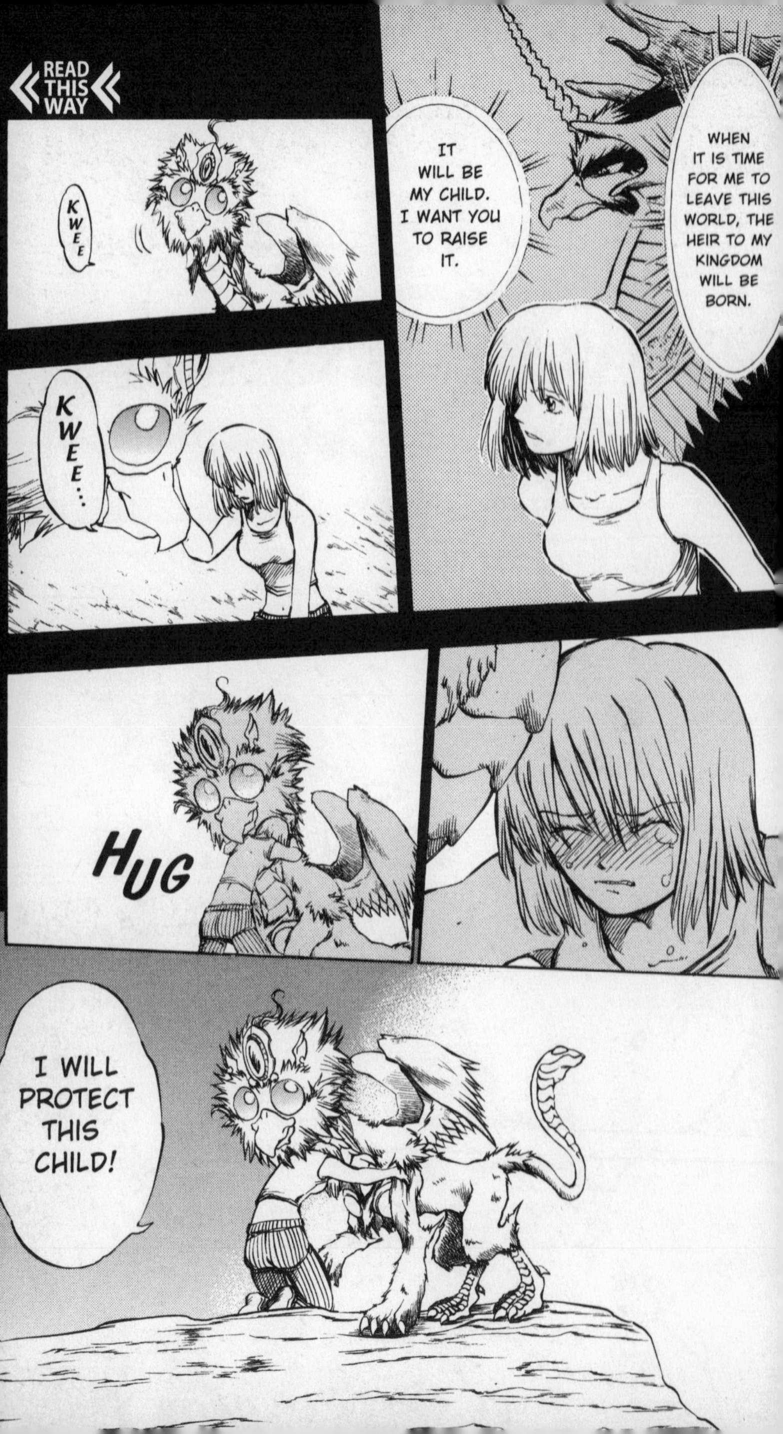
WHEN IT IS TIME FOR ME TO LEAVE THIS WORLD, THE HEIR TO MY KINGDOM WILL BE BORN.
IT WILL BE MY CHILD. I WANT YOU TO RAISE IT.
KWEE
KWEE...
HUG
I WILL PROTECT THIS CHILD!

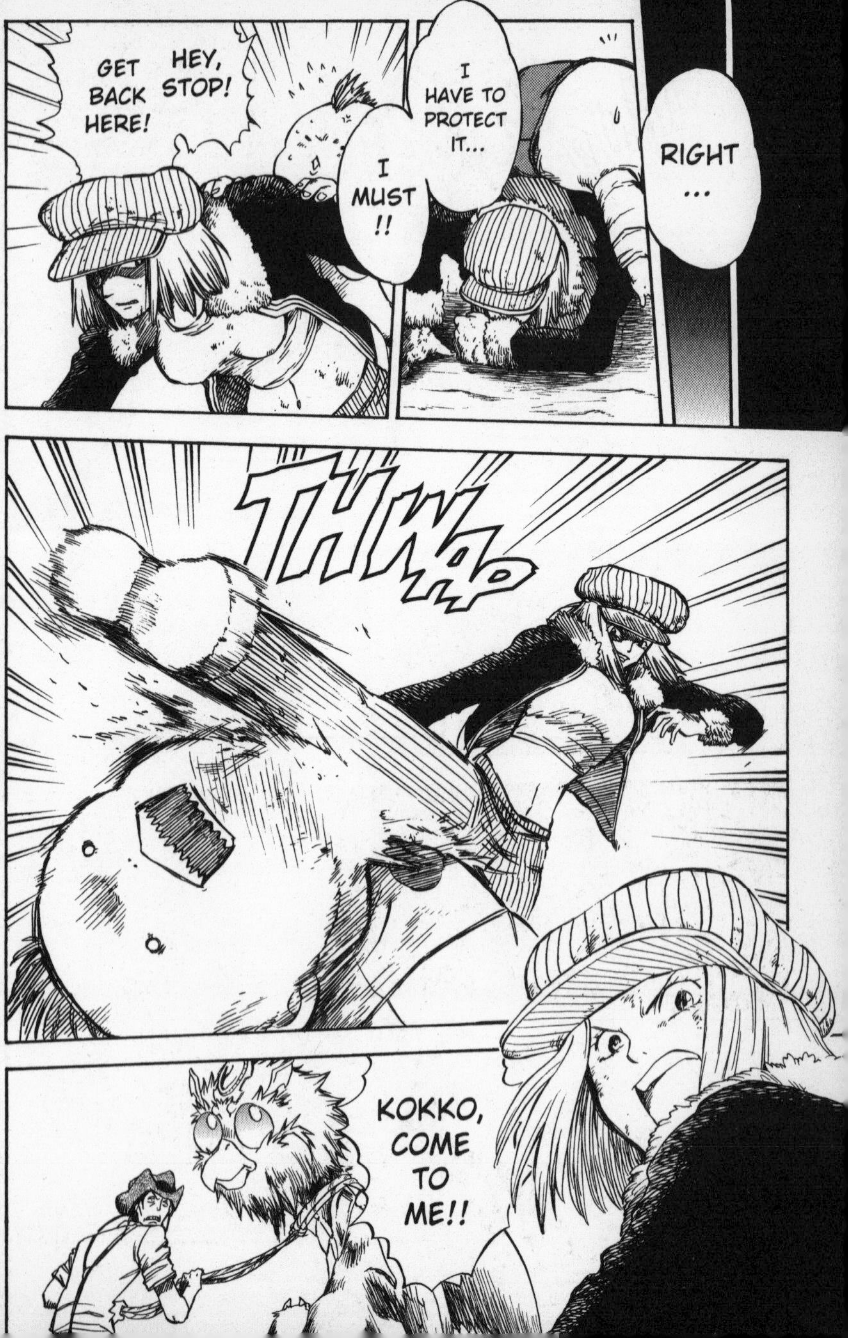
RIGHT ...
I HAVE TO PROTECT IT...
I MUST !!
HEY, STOP!
GET BACK HERE!
THWAP
KOKKO, COME TO ME!!

READ THIS WAY

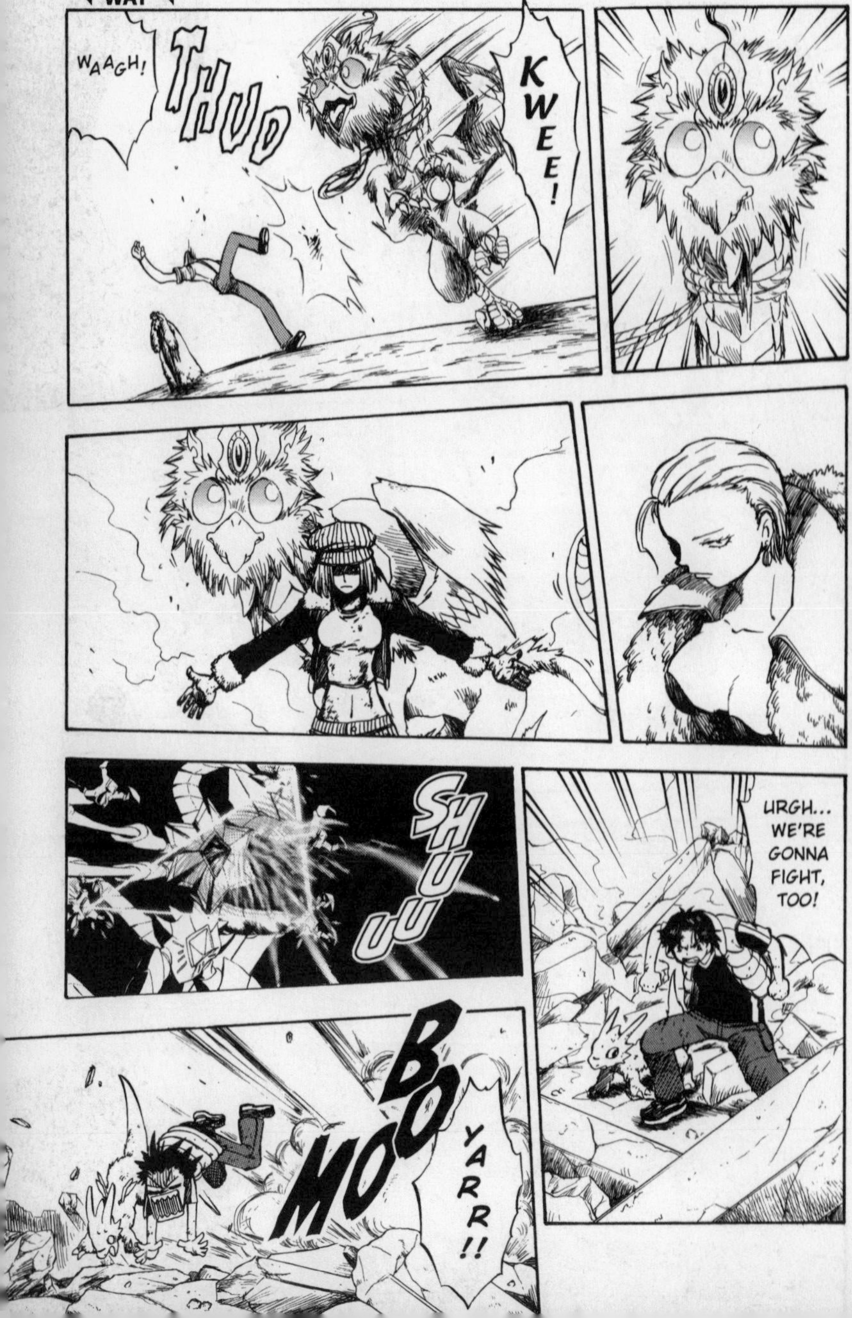
KWEEE!
THUD
WAAGH!
URGH... WE'RE GONNA FIGHT, TOO!
SHUUU
BOOM
YARR!!

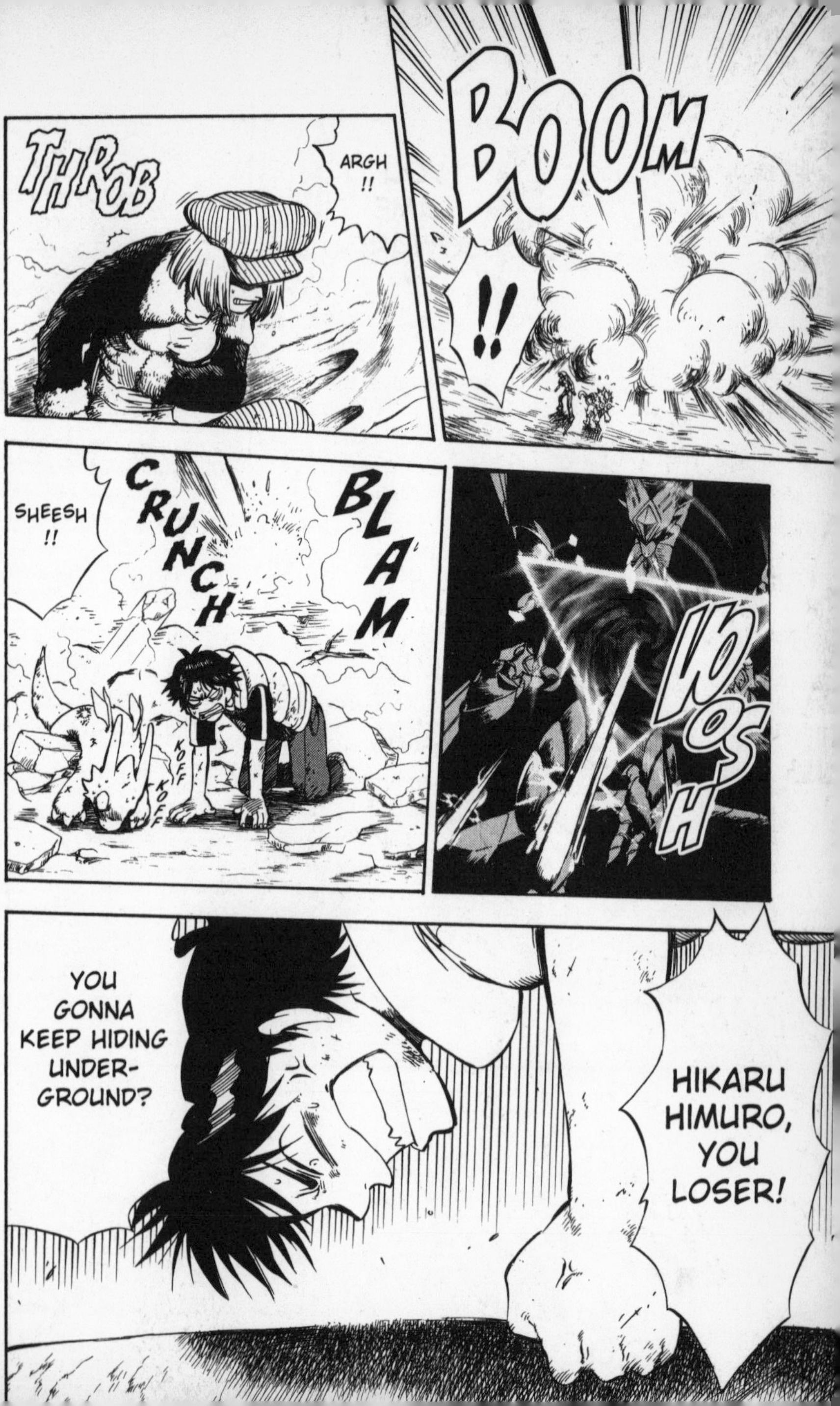
BOOM
!!
THROB
ARGH !!
WOOSH
BLAM
CRUNCH
SHEESH !!
KOFF KOFF
HIKARU HIMURO, YOU LOSER!
YOU GONNA KEEP HIDING UNDER-GROUND?

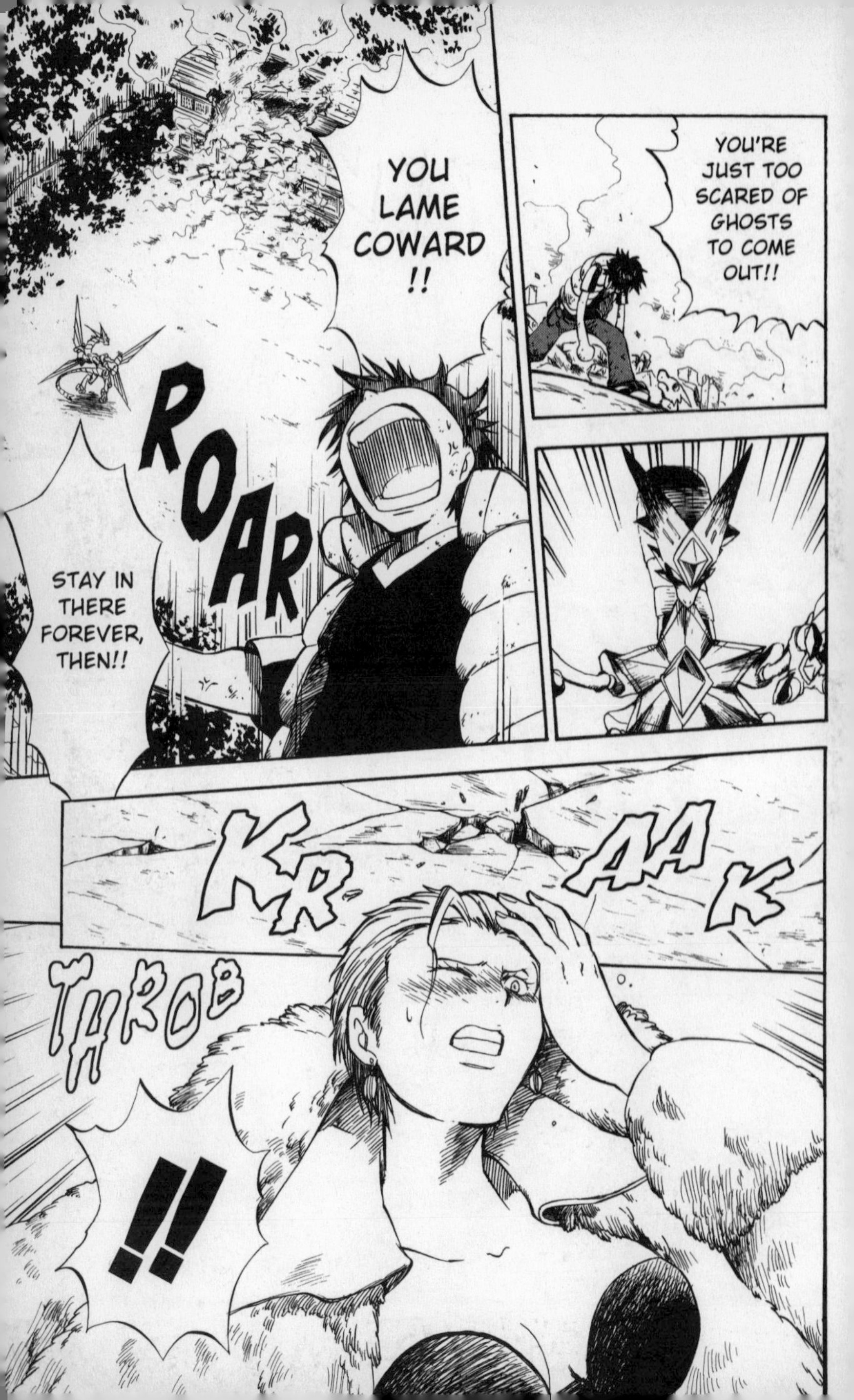
YOU'RE JUST TOO SCARED OF GHOSTS TO COME OUT!!
YOU LAME COWARD!!
ROAR
STAY IN THERE FOREVER, THEN!!
KR-AAK
THROB
!!

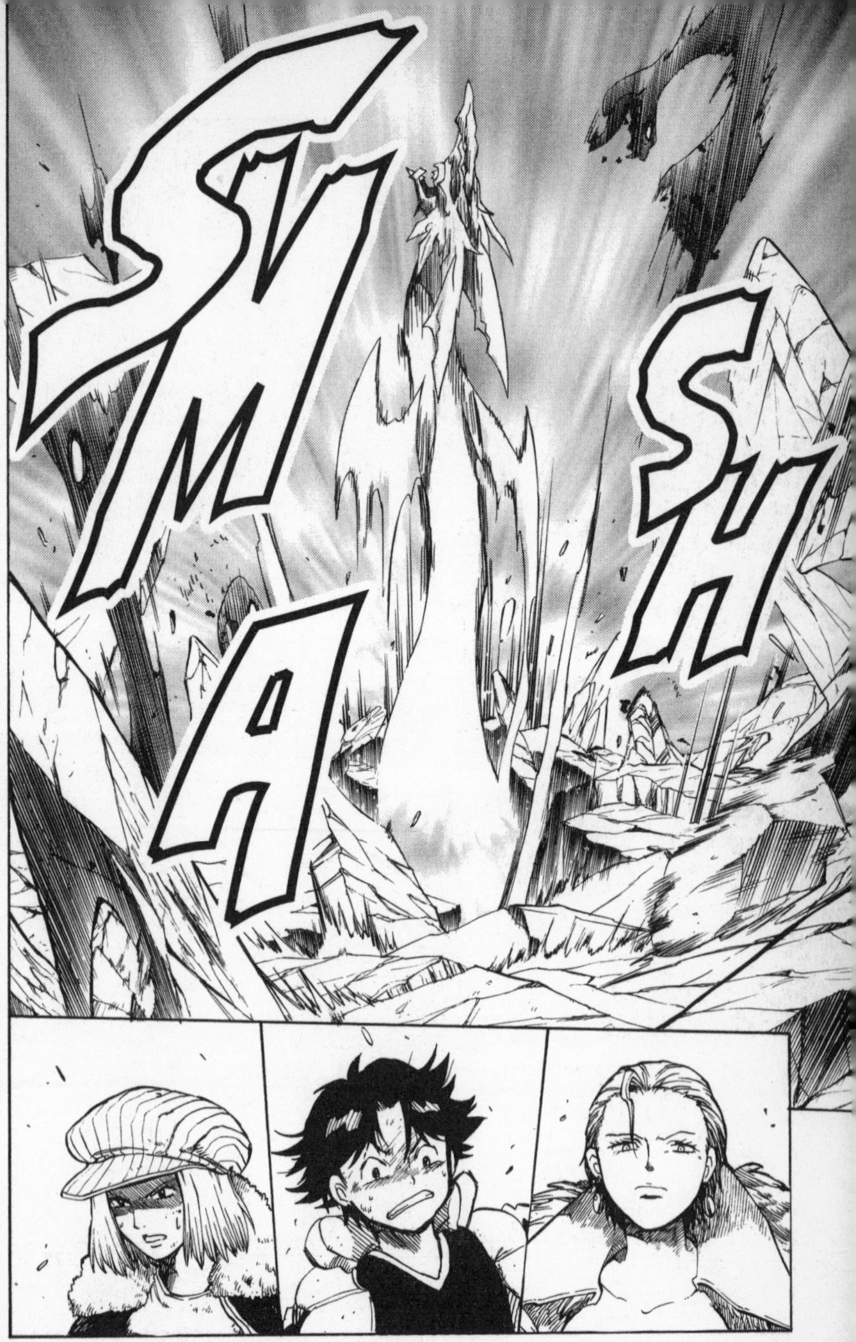
SMASH

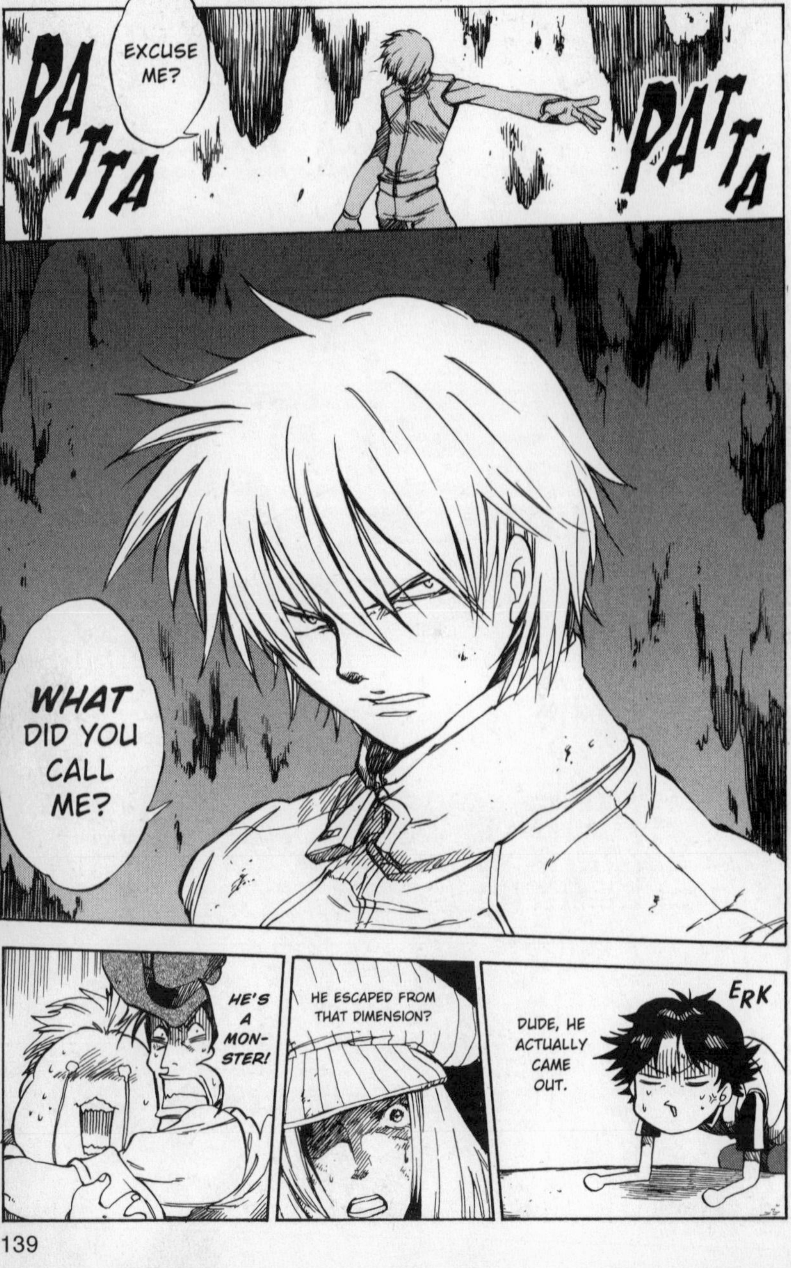
PATTA
EXCUSE ME?
PATTA
WHAT DID YOU CALL ME?
ERK
DUDE, HE ACTUALLY CAME OUT.
HE ESCAPED FROM THAT DIMENSION?
HE'S A MON-STER!

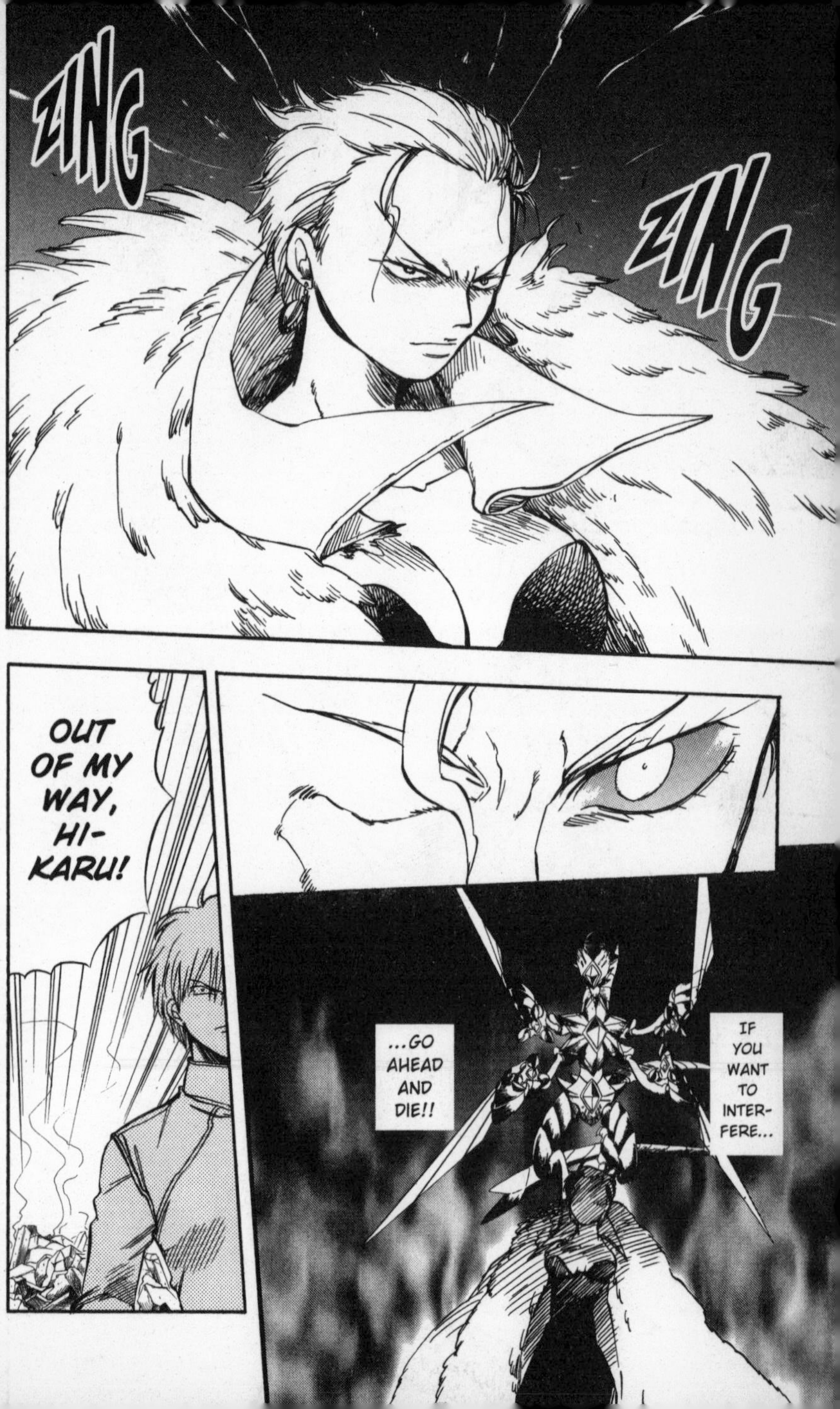
ZING
ZING
IF YOU WANT TO INTER-FERE...
...GO AHEAD AND DIE!!
OUT OF MY WAY, HI-KARU!

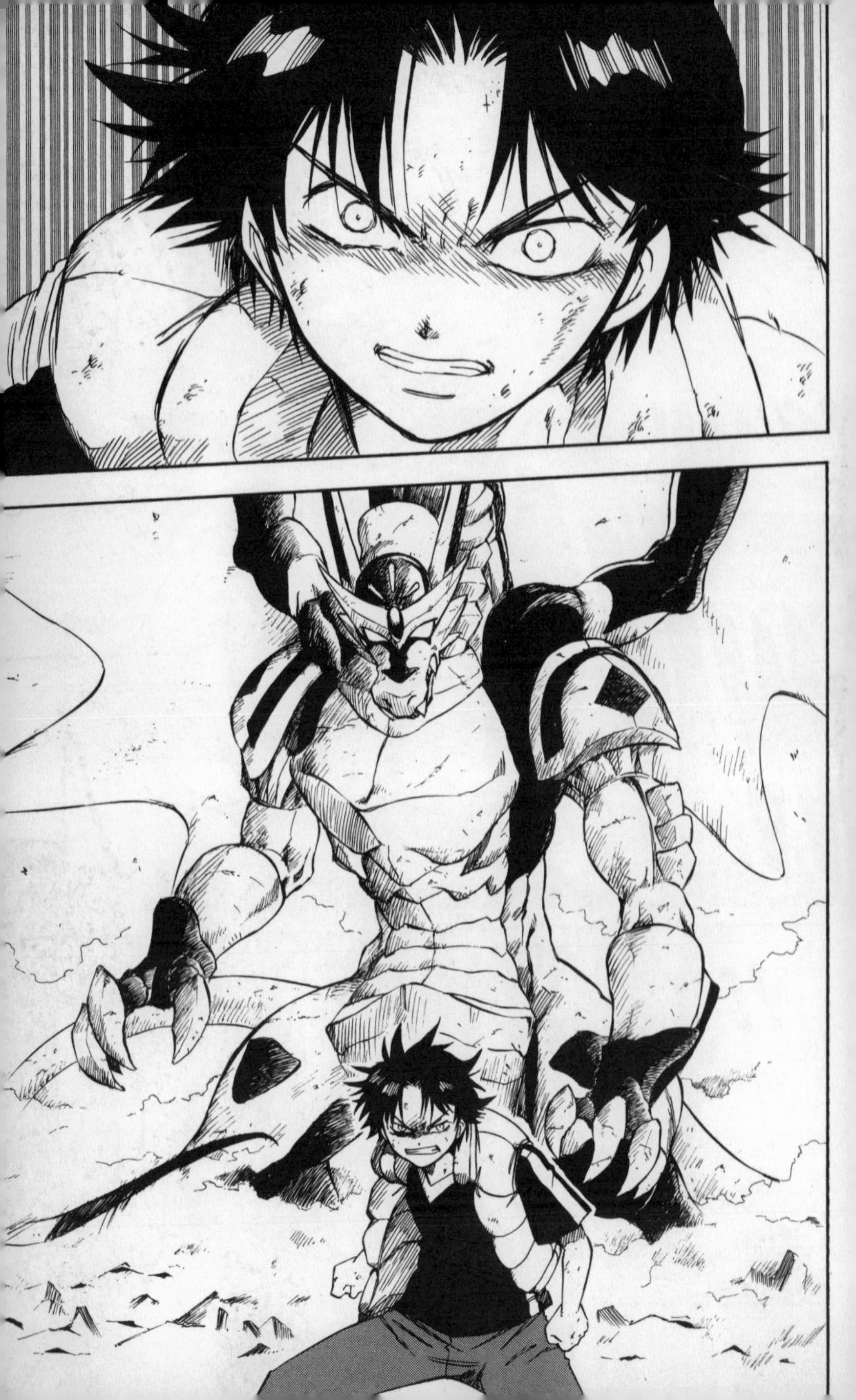

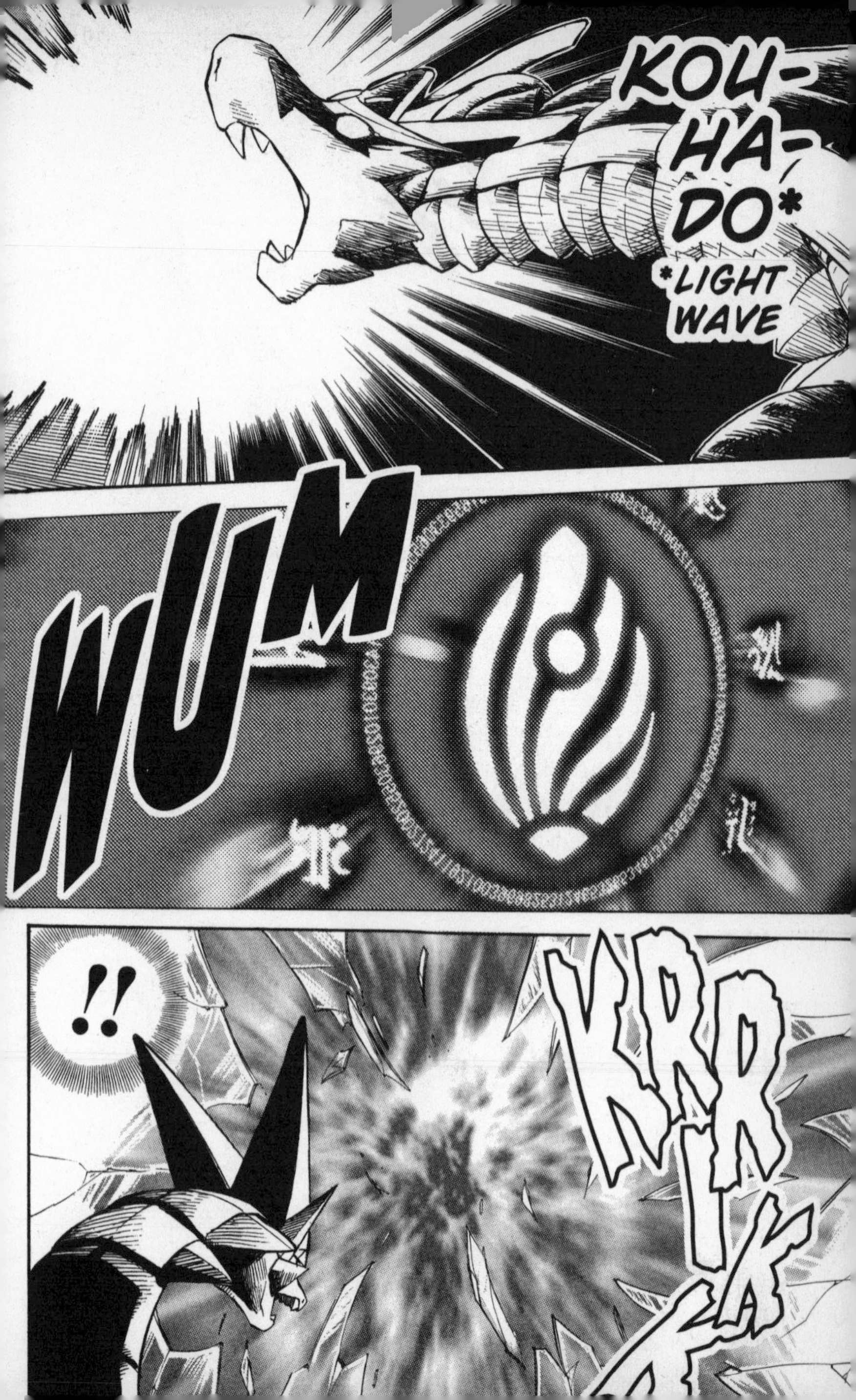
KOU-
HA-
DO*
*LIGHT WAVE
WUM
KRR
!!
K

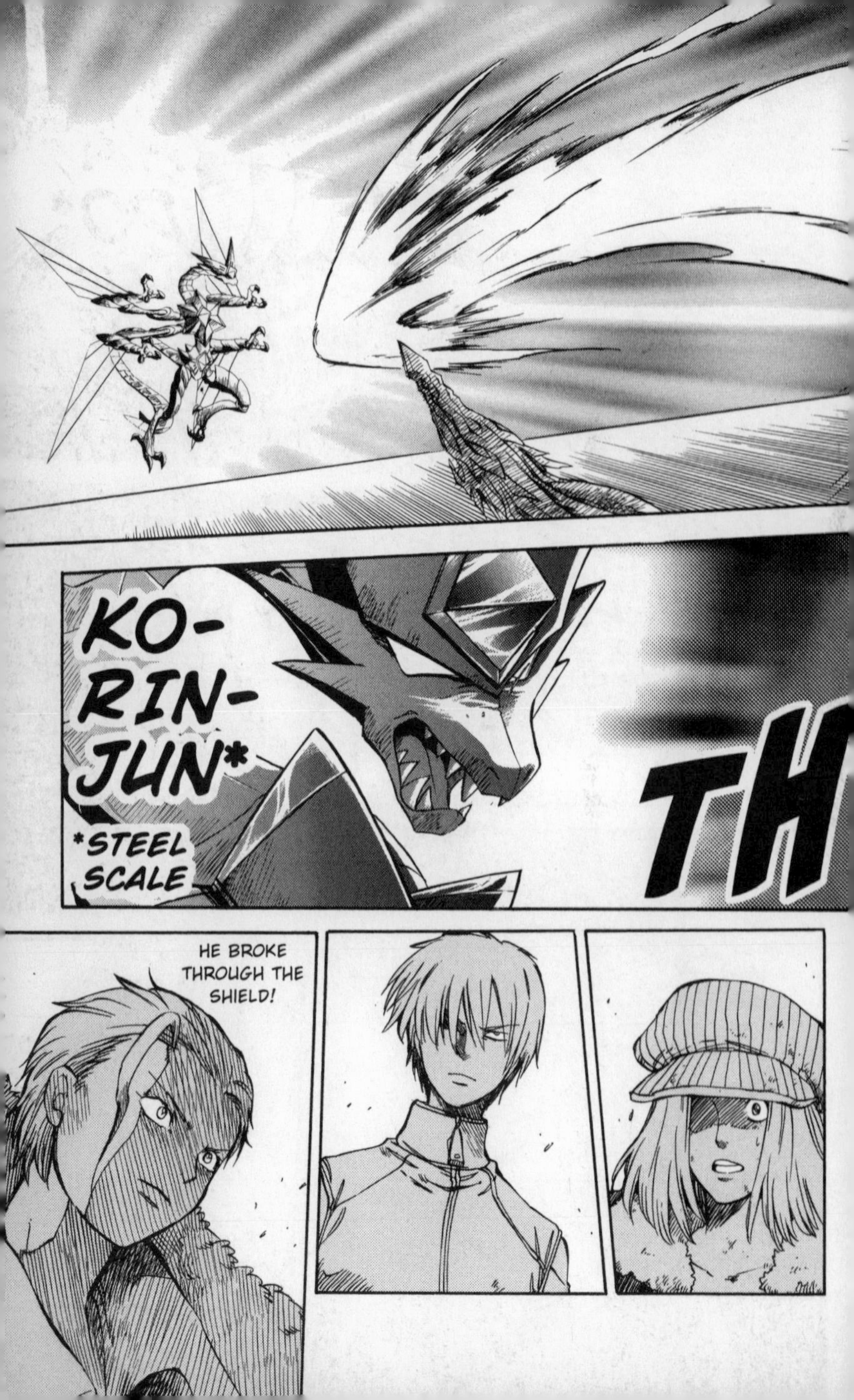
TH
KO-RIN-JUN*
*STEEL SCALE
HE BROKE THROUGH THE SHIELD!

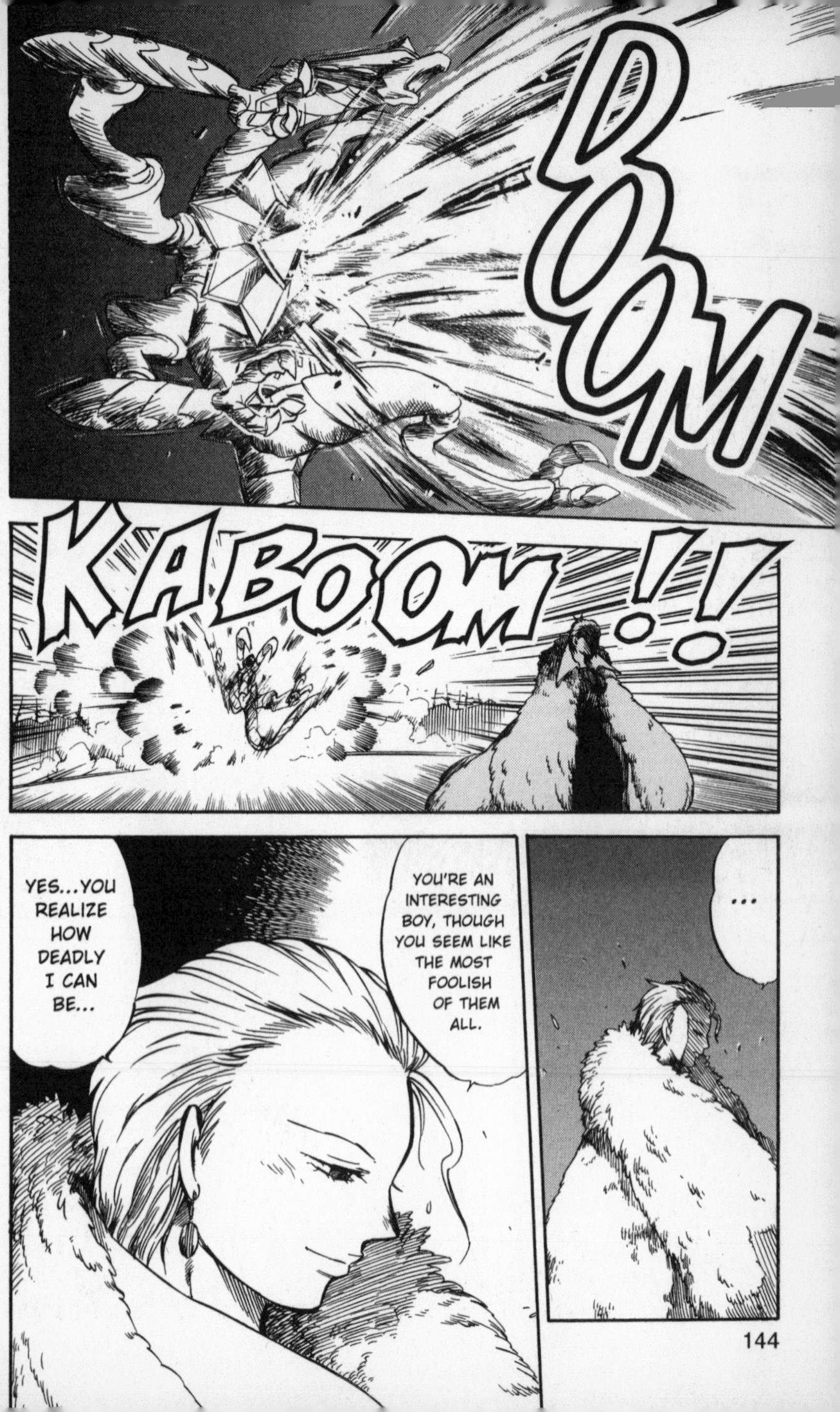
DOOM
KABOOM!!
...
YOU'RE AN INTERESTING BOY, THOUGH YOU SEEM LIKE THE MOST FOOLISH OF THEM ALL.
YES...YOU REALIZE HOW DEADLY I CAN BE...

READ THIS WAY

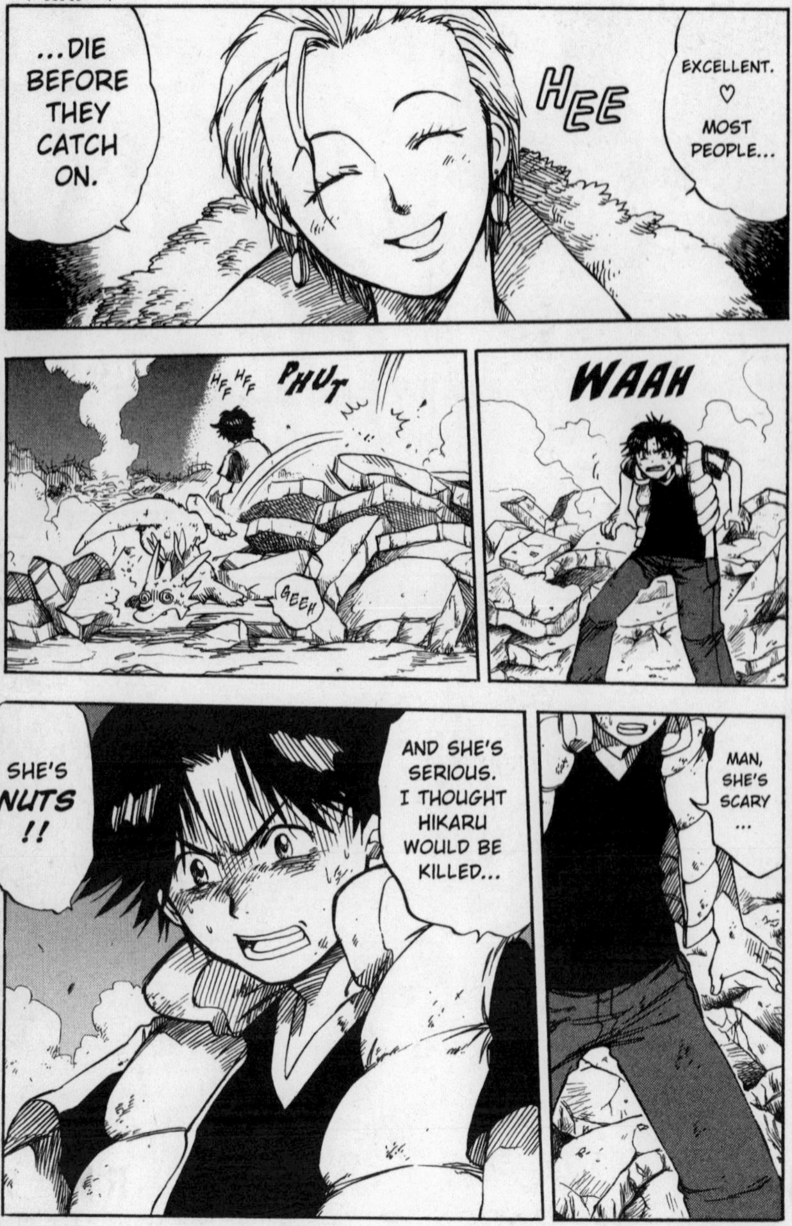

EXCELLENT. ♡ MOST PEOPLE...
HEE
...DIE BEFORE THEY CATCH ON.
WAAH
HFF HFF
PHUT
GEEH
MAN, SHE'S SCARY ...
AND SHE'S SERIOUS. I THOUGHT HIKARU WOULD BE KILLED...
SHE'S NUTS!!

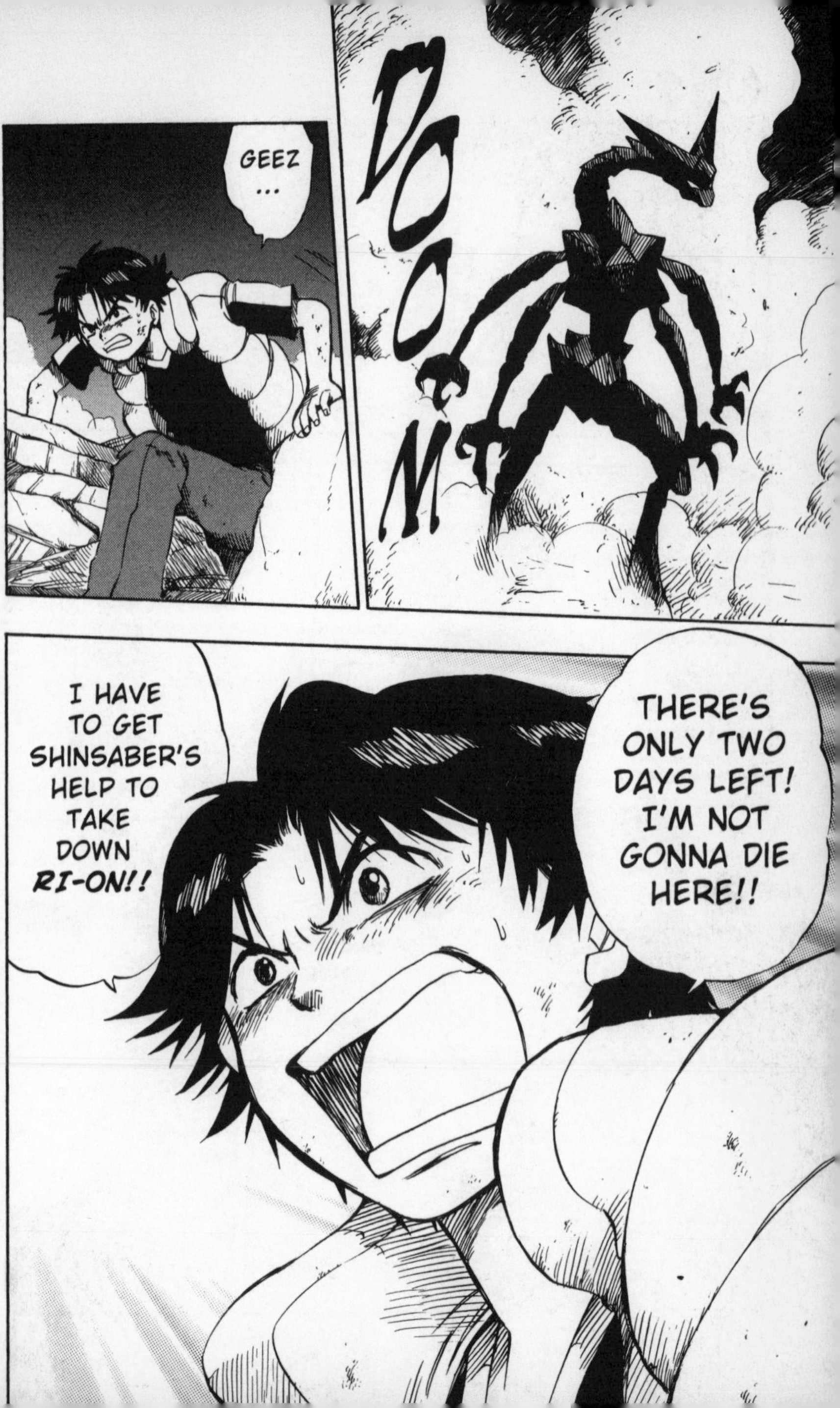
DOOOM
GEEZ ...
THERE'S ONLY TWO DAYS LEFT! I'M NOT GONNA DIE HERE!!
I HAVE TO GET SHINSABER'S HELP TO TAKE DOWN *RI-ON!!*

READ THIS WAY

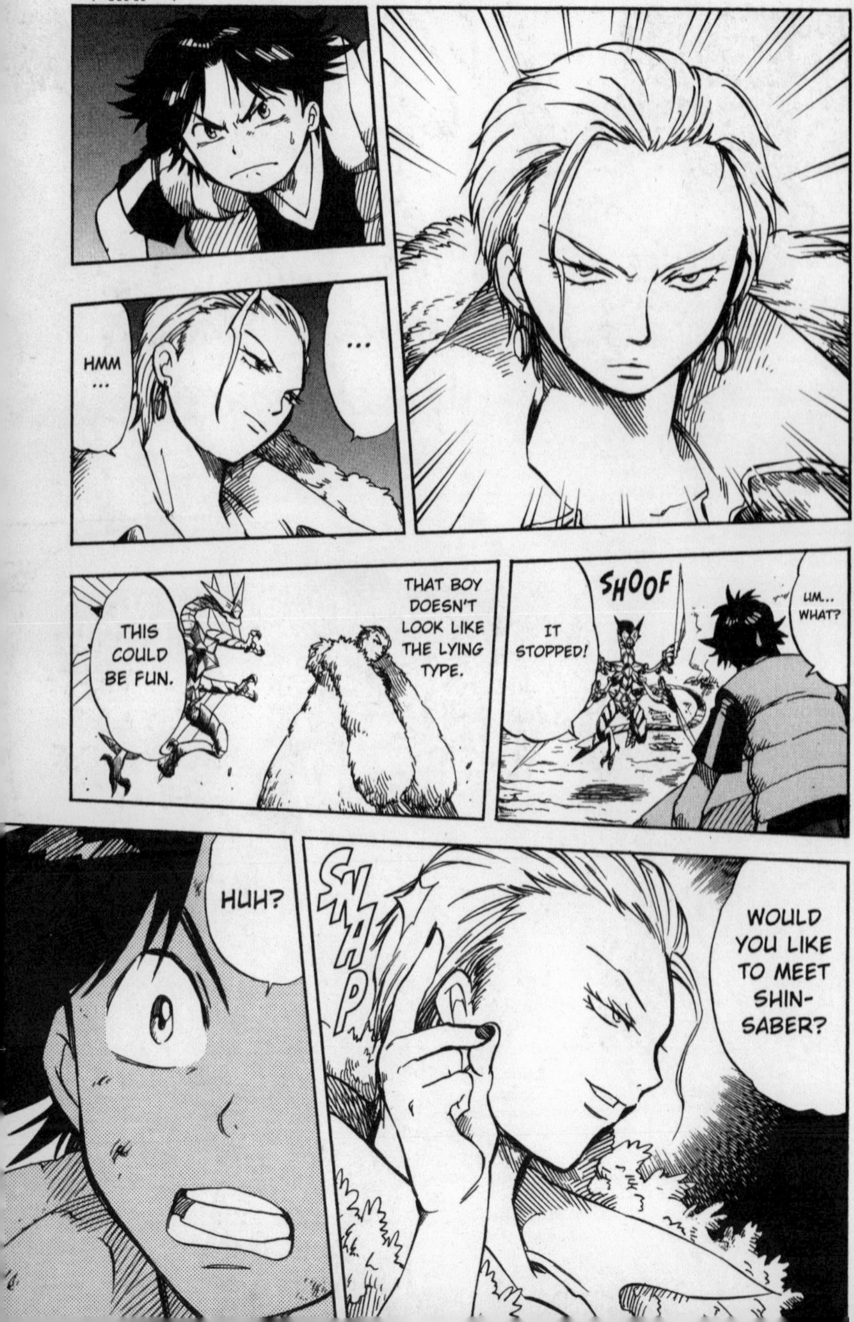
...
HMM ...
UM... WHAT?
SHOOF
IT STOPPED!
THAT BOY DOESN'T LOOK LIKE THE LYING TYPE.
THIS COULD BE FUN.
WOULD YOU LIKE TO MEET SHIN-SABER?
SNAP
HUH?

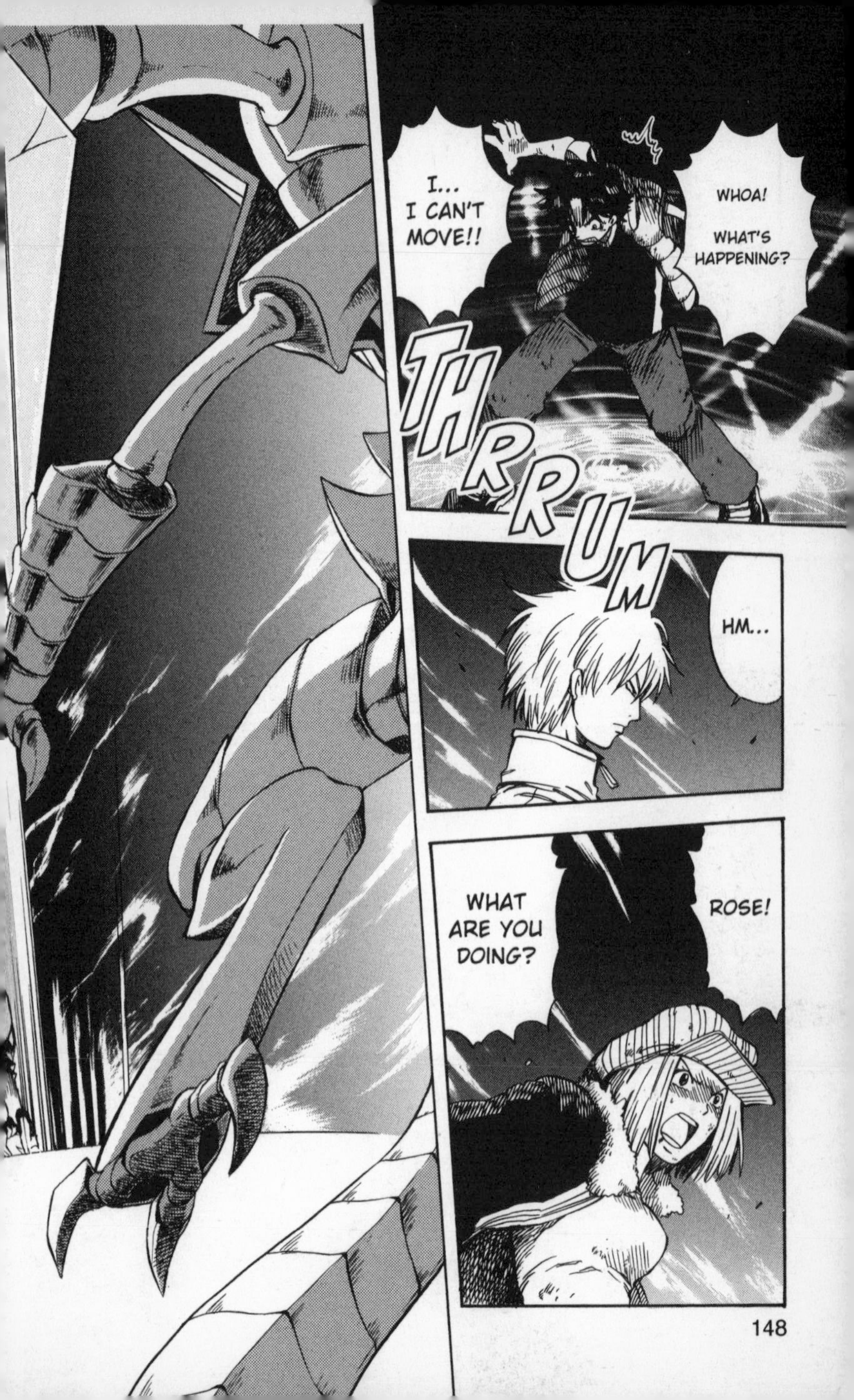
WHOA!
WHAT'S HAPPENING?
I... I CAN'T MOVE!!
THRRUM
HM...
ROSE!
WHAT ARE YOU DOING?

READ THIS WAY

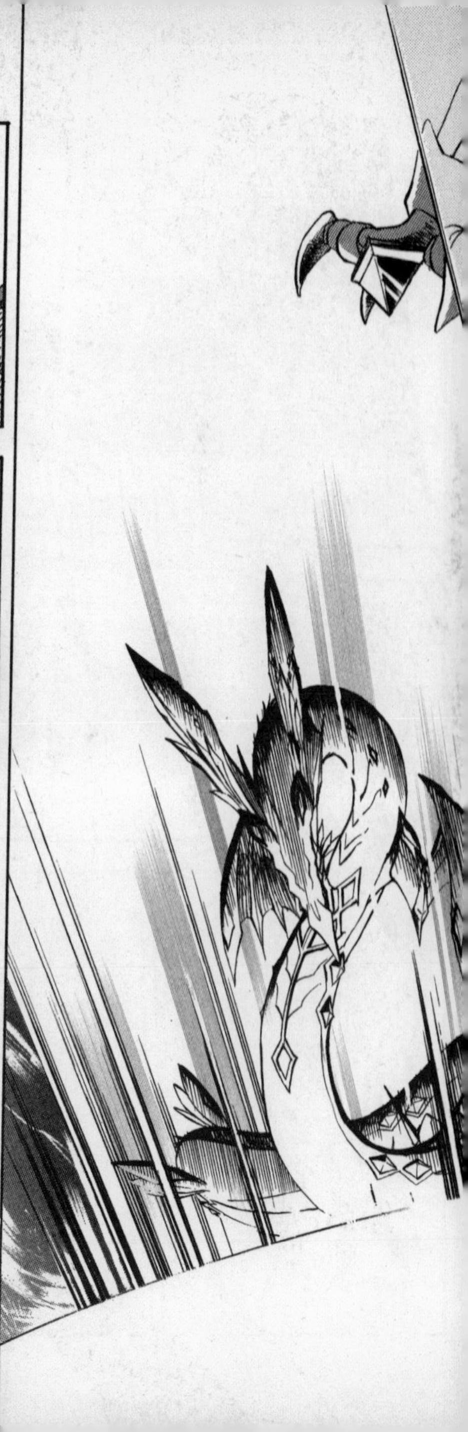

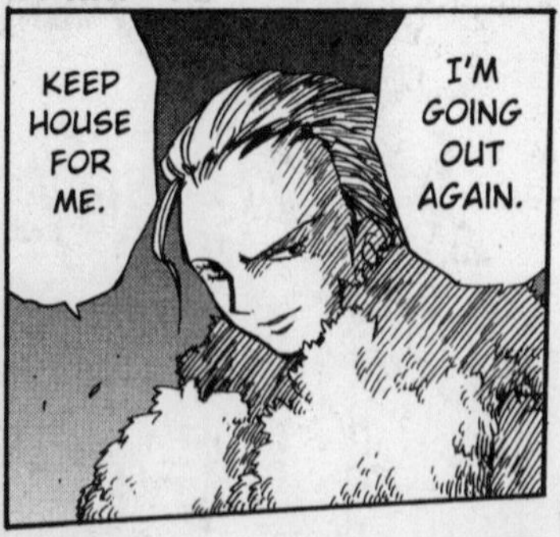
I'M GOING OUT AGAIN.
KEEP HOUSE FOR ME.

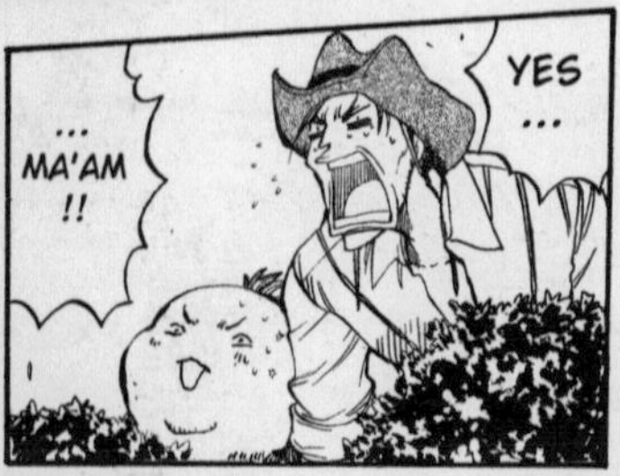
YES ...
... MA'AM !!

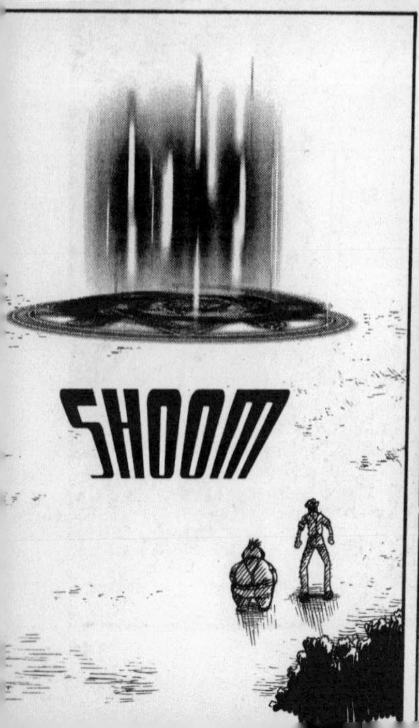
SHOOM

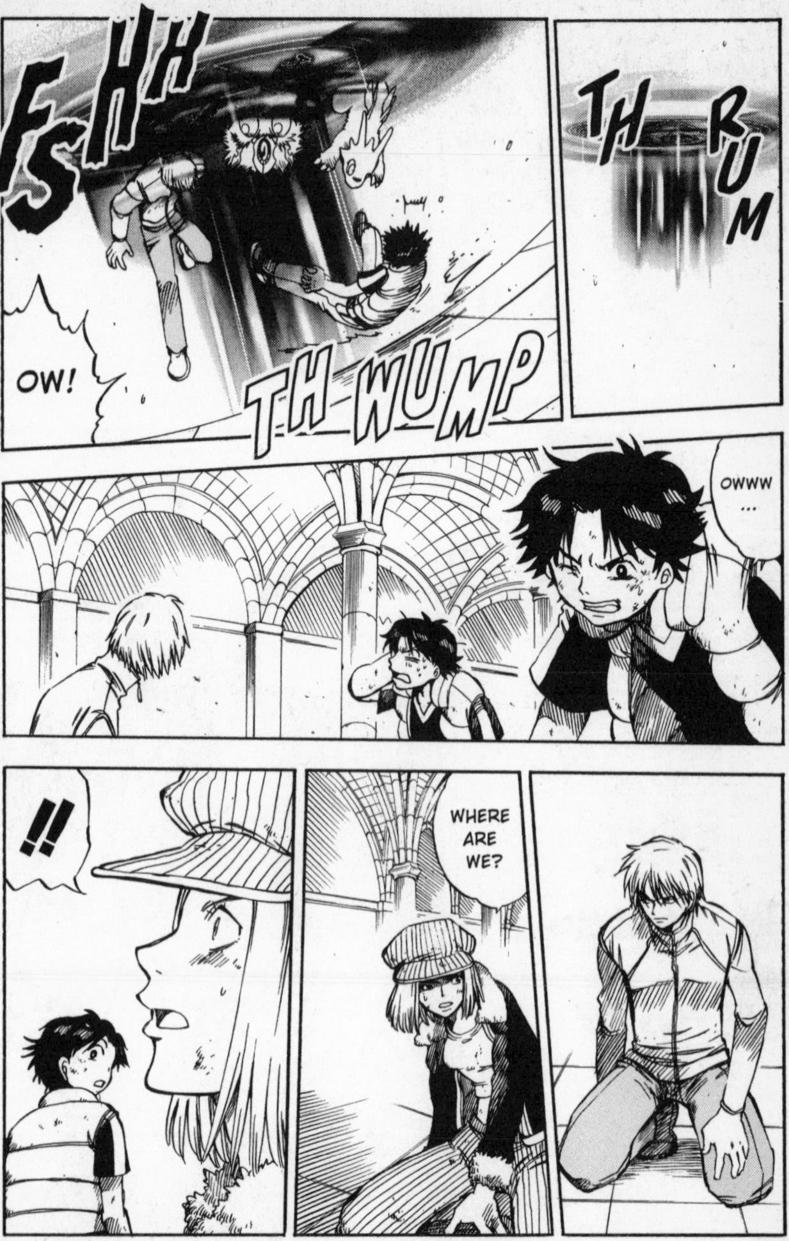
THRUM
FSHH
THWUMP
OW!
OWWW ...
WHERE ARE WE?
!!

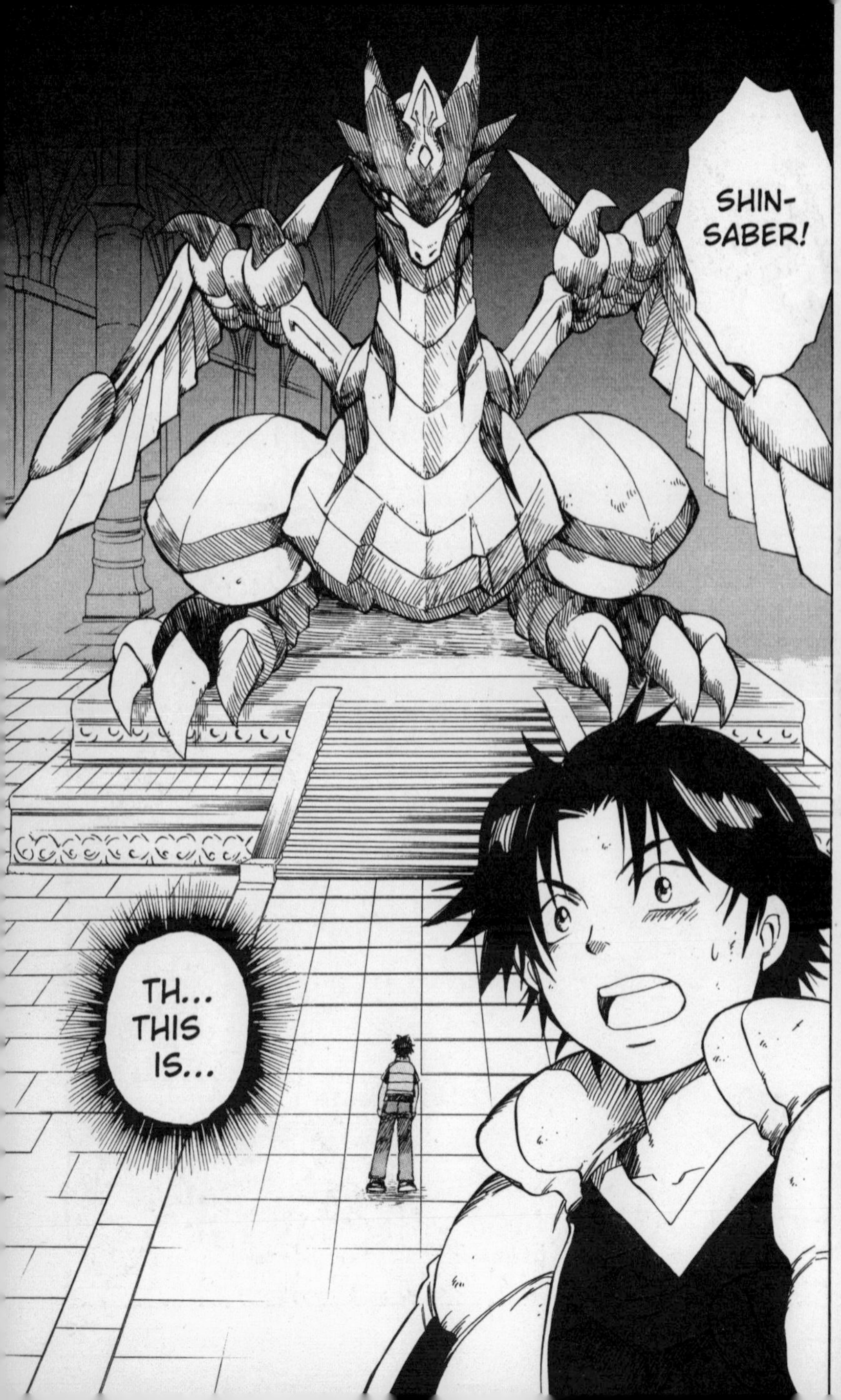
SHIN-SABER!
TH... THIS IS...

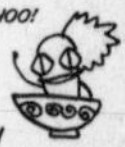
WOO-HOO!

Spaced-Out Silver ②

BY NAGI-CHAN

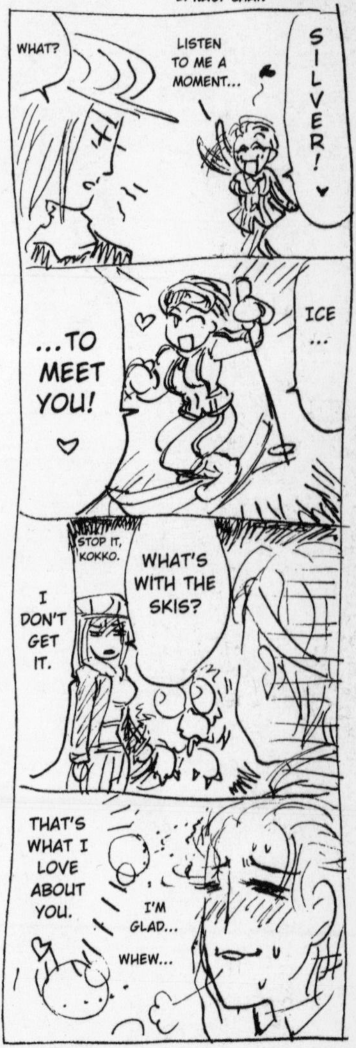
SILVER! ♥
LISTEN TO ME A MOMENT...
WHAT?
ICE ...
...TO MEET YOU! ♥
WHAT'S WITH THE SKIS?
STOP IT, KOKKO.
I DON'T GET IT.
I'M GLAD...
THAT'S WHAT I LOVE ABOUT YOU.
WHEW...

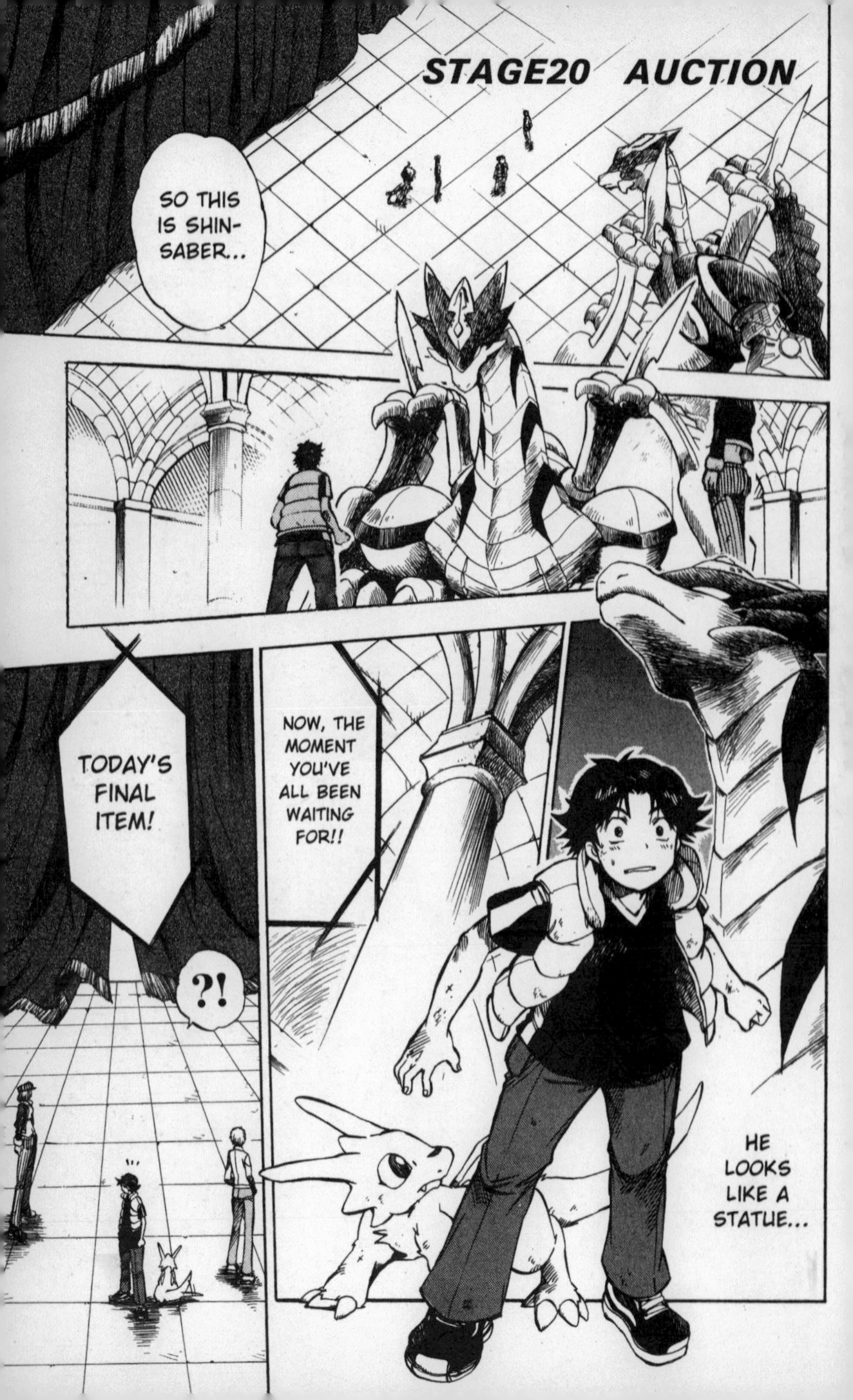
STAGE20 AUCTION
SO THIS IS SHIN-SABER...
NOW, THE MOMENT YOU'VE ALL BEEN WAITING FOR!!
HE LOOKS LIKE A STATUE...
TODAY'S FINAL ITEM!
?!

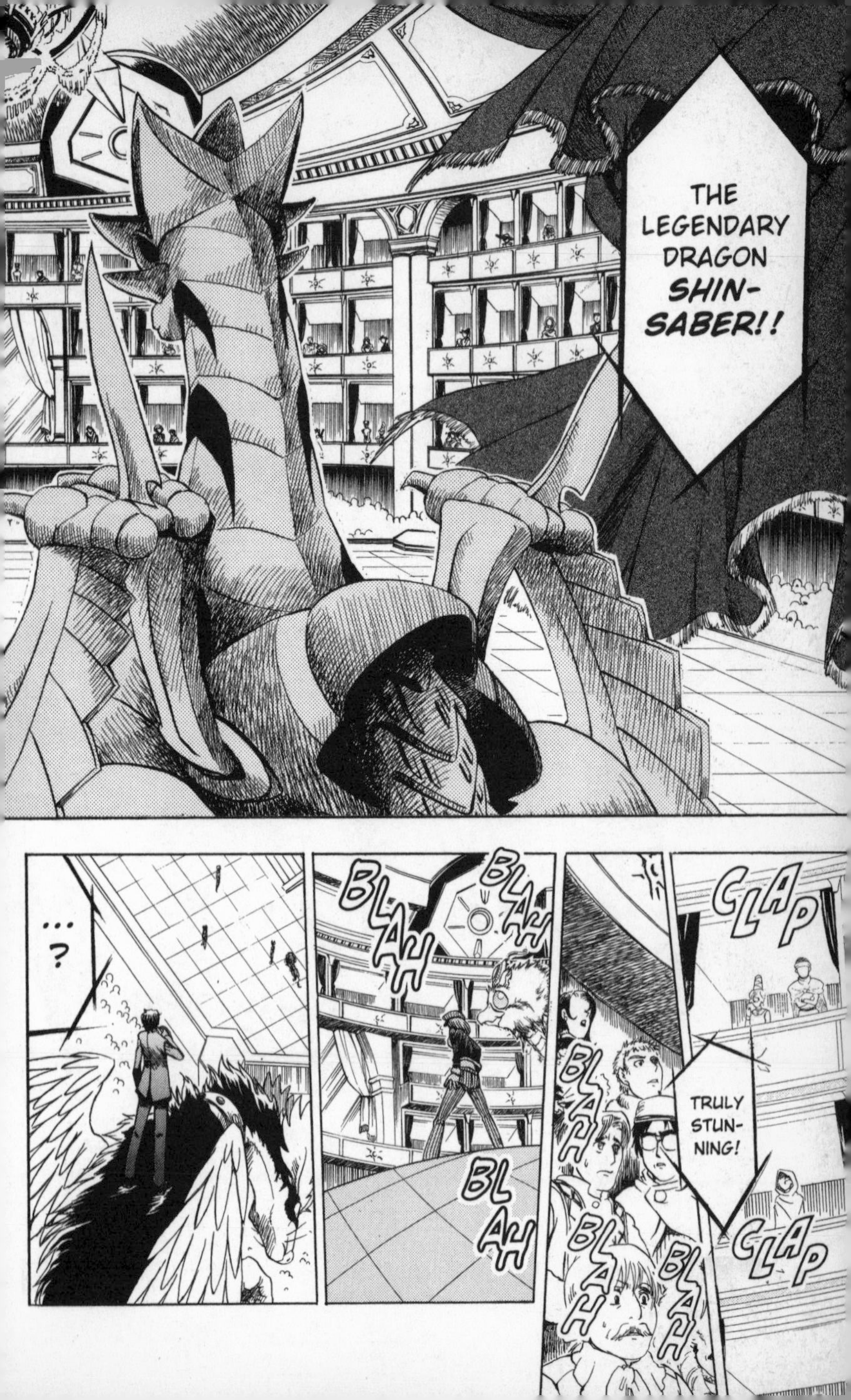
THE LEGENDARY DRAGON SHIN-SABER!!
CLAP
TRULY STUNNING!
CLAP
BLAH
BLAH
BLAH
BLAH
BLAH
BLAH
...?

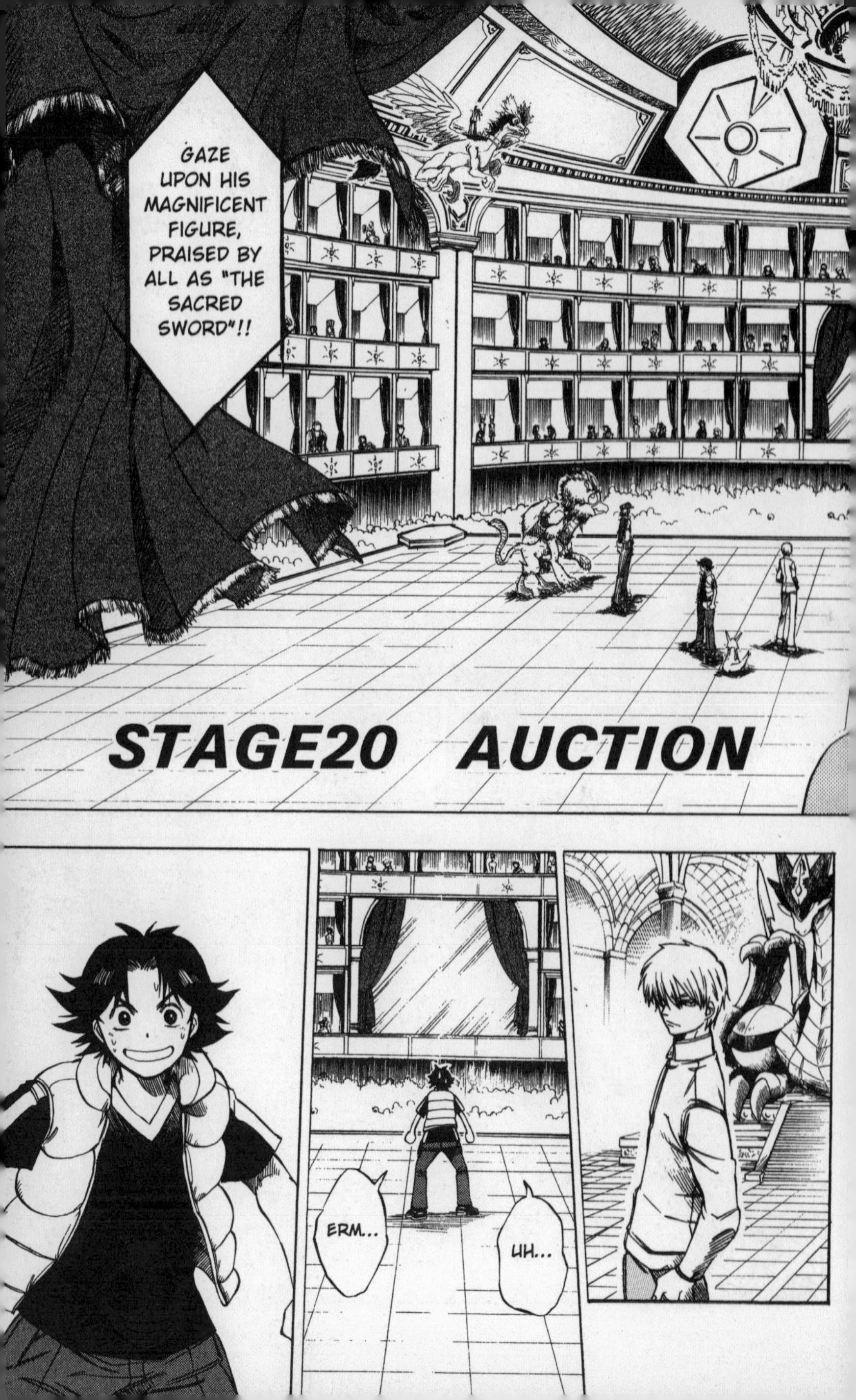
GAZE UPON HIS MAGNIFICENT FIGURE, PRAISED BY ALL AS "THE SACRED SWORD"!!
STAGE20 AUCTION
UH...
ERM...

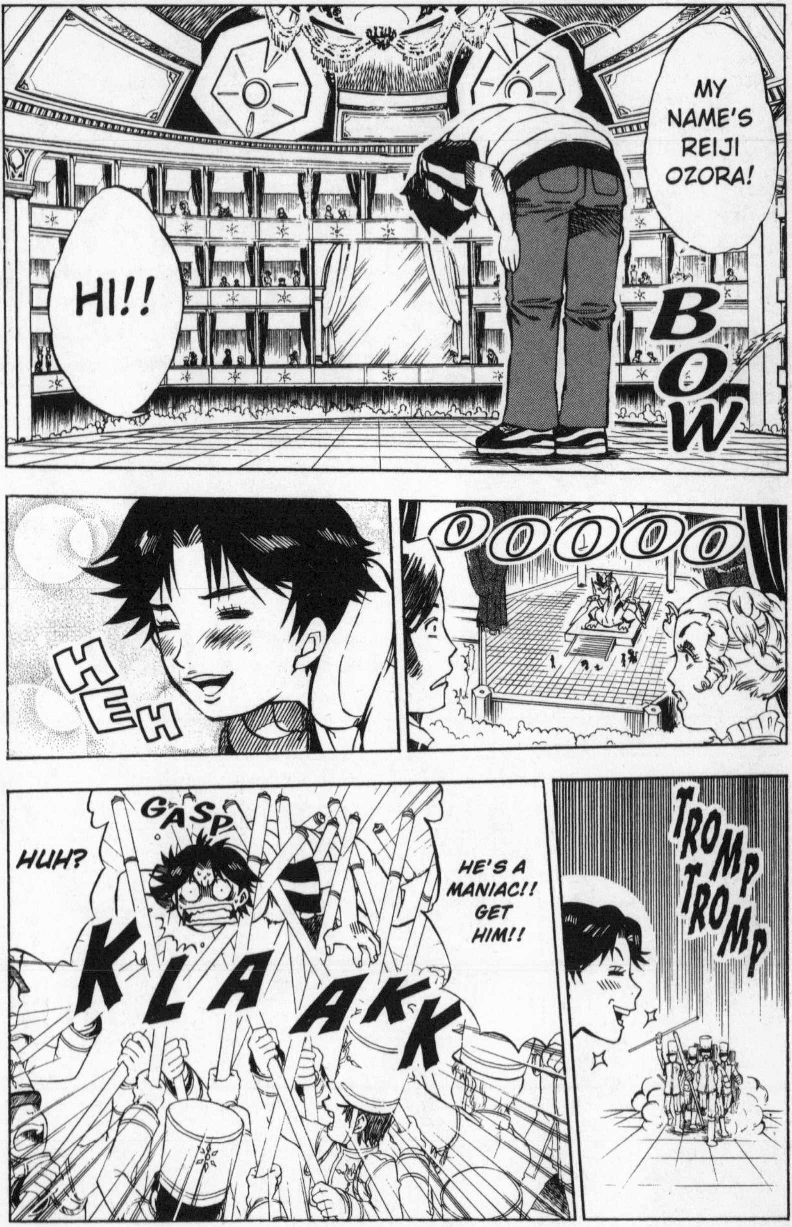
MY NAME'S REIJI OZORA!
BOW
HI!!
OOOOO
HEH
TROMP TROMP
HE'S A MANIAC!! GET HIM!!
GASP
HUH?
KLAAKK

READ THIS WAY

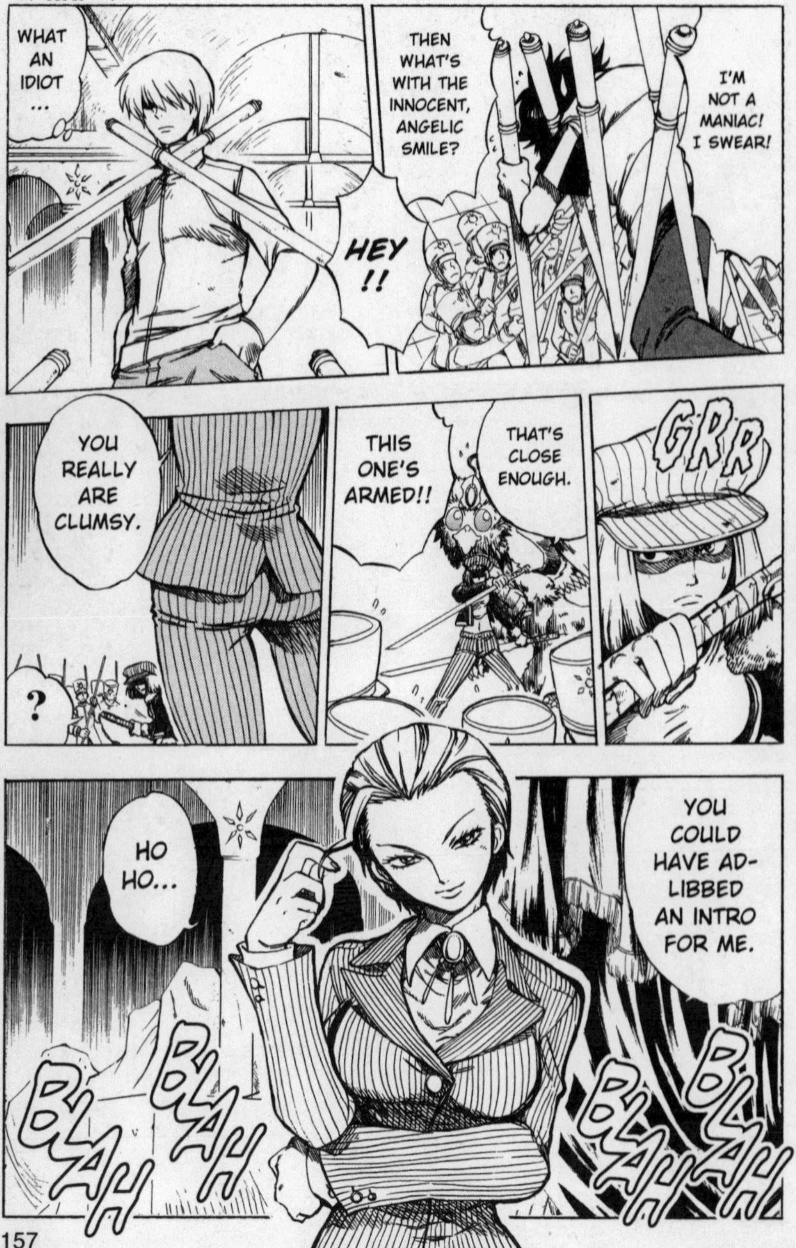
I'M NOT A MANIAC! I SWEAR!
THEN WHAT'S WITH THE INNOCENT, ANGELIC SMILE?
HEY!!
WHAT AN IDIOT...
GRR
THAT'S CLOSE ENOUGH.
THIS ONE'S ARMED!!
YOU REALLY ARE CLUMSY.
?
YOU COULD HAVE AD-LIBBED AN INTRO FOR ME.
BLAH BLAH
HO HO...
BLAH BLAH

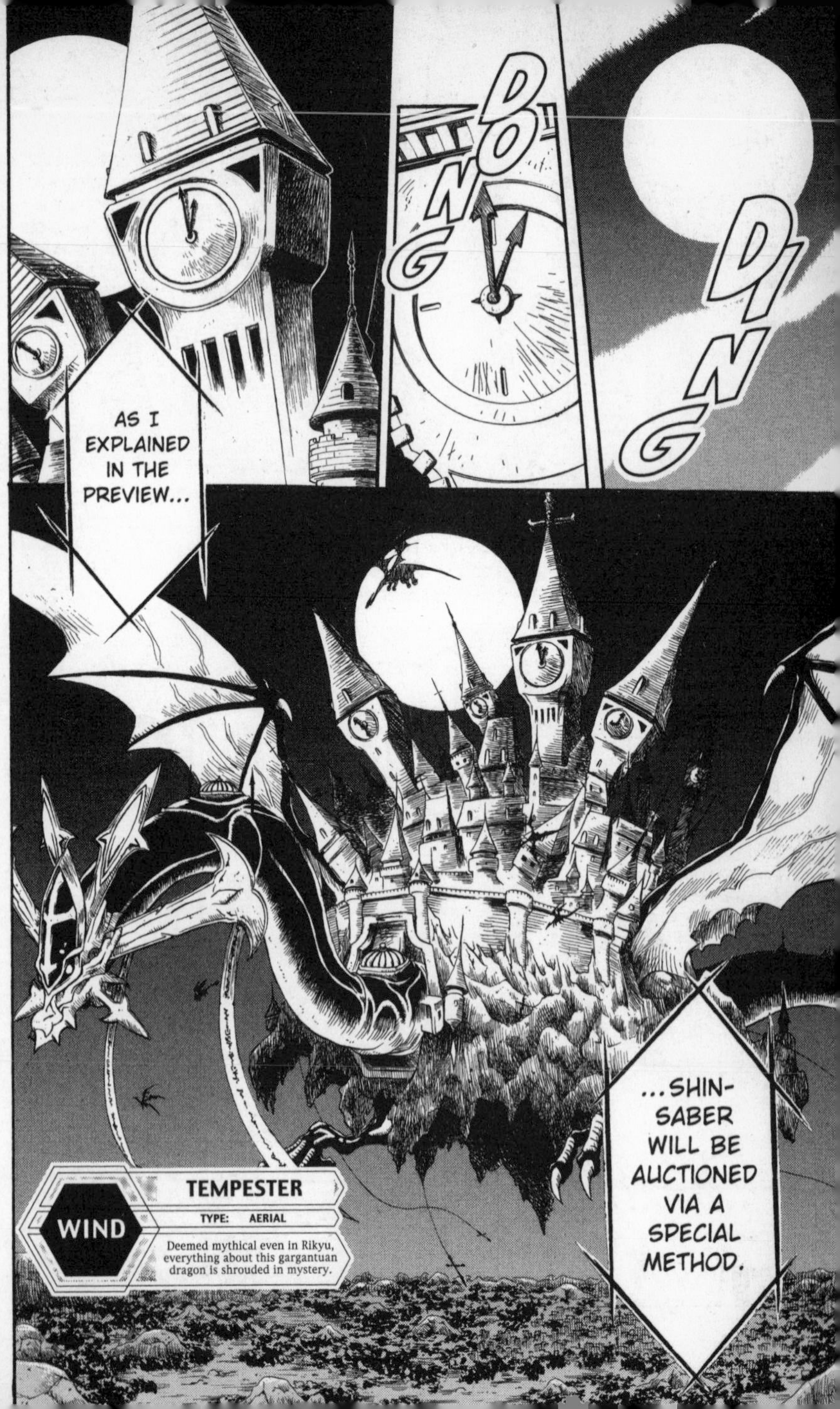
DING
DONG
AS I EXPLAINED IN THE PREVIEW...
...SHIN-SABER WILL BE AUCTIONED VIA A SPECIAL METHOD.
TEMPESTER
WIND
TYPE: AERIAL
Deemed mythical even in Rikyu, everything about this gargantuan dragon is shrouded in mystery.

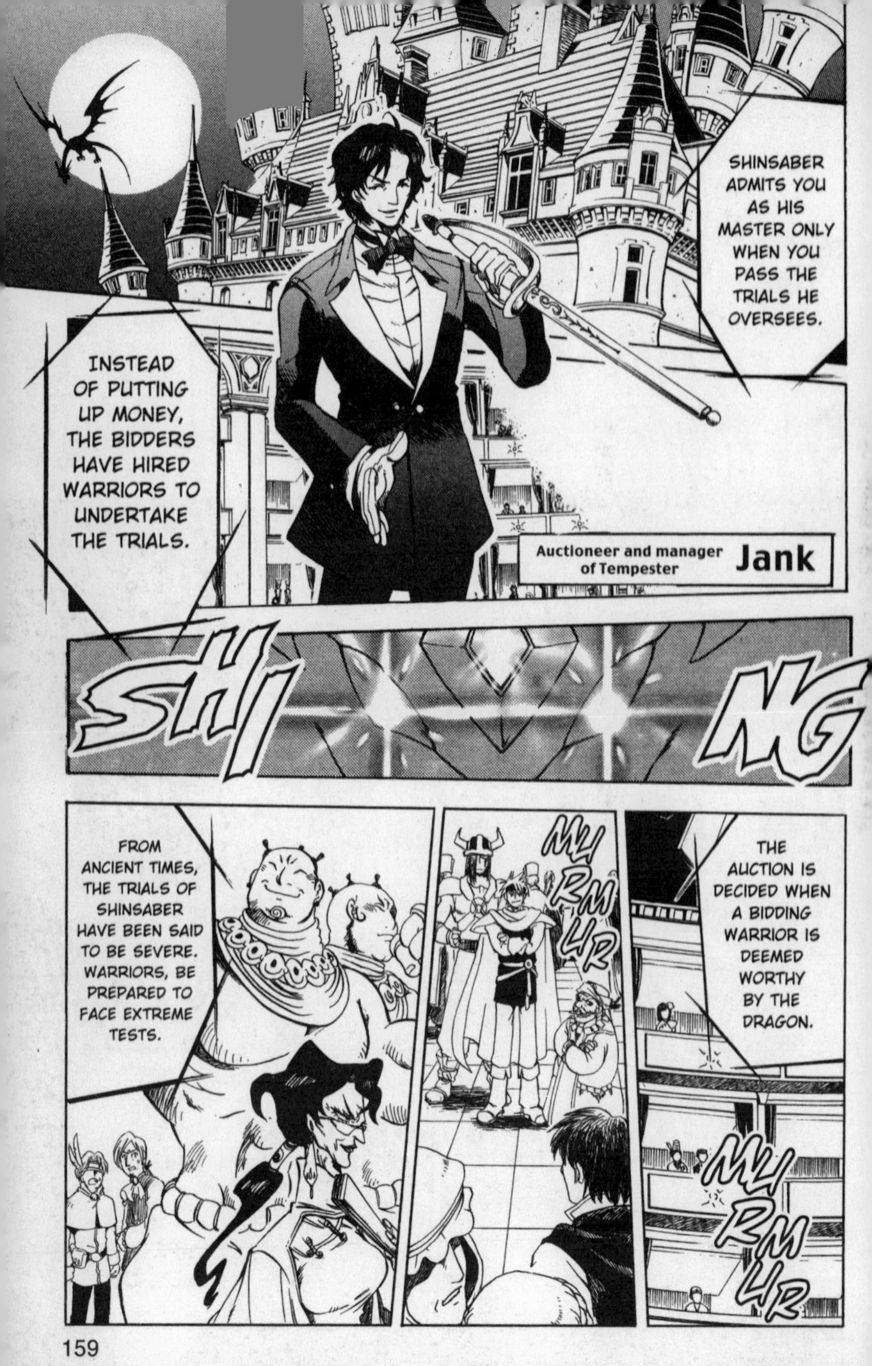
SHINSABER ADMITS YOU AS HIS MASTER ONLY WHEN YOU PASS THE TRIALS HE OVERSEES.
INSTEAD OF PUTTING UP MONEY, THE BIDDERS HAVE HIRED WARRIORS TO UNDERTAKE THE TRIALS.
Auctioneer and manager of Tempester Jank
SHING
THE AUCTION IS DECIDED WHEN A BIDDING WARRIOR IS DEEMED WORTHY BY THE DRAGON.
MURMUR
MURMUR
FROM ANCIENT TIMES, THE TRIALS OF SHINSABER HAVE BEEN SAID TO BE SEVERE. WARRIORS, BE PREPARED TO FACE EXTREME TESTS.

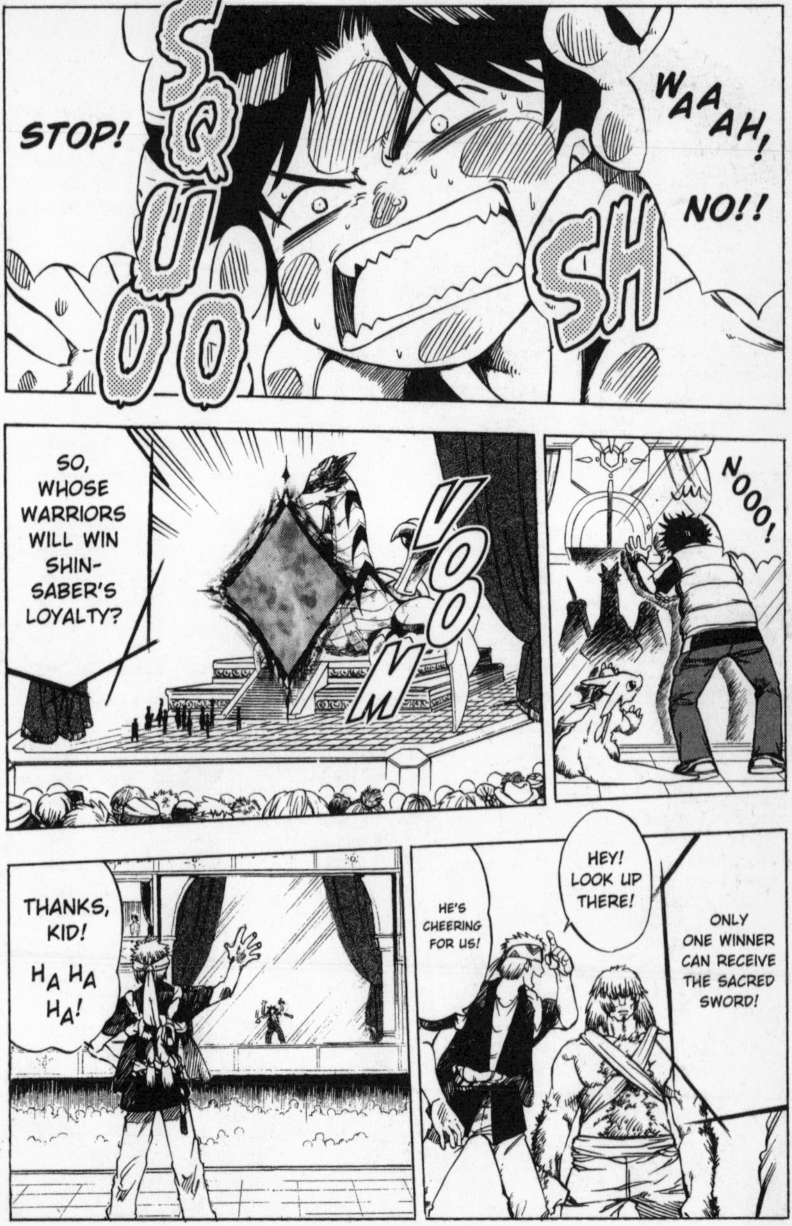
WAAAH, NO!!
SQUOOSH
STOP!
NOOOO!
VOOOM
SO, WHOSE WARRIORS WILL WIN SHIN-SABER'S LOYALTY?
ONLY ONE WINNER CAN RECEIVE THE SACRED SWORD!
HEY! LOOK UP THERE!
HE'S CHEERING FOR US!
THANKS, KID!
HA HA HA!

READ THIS WAY

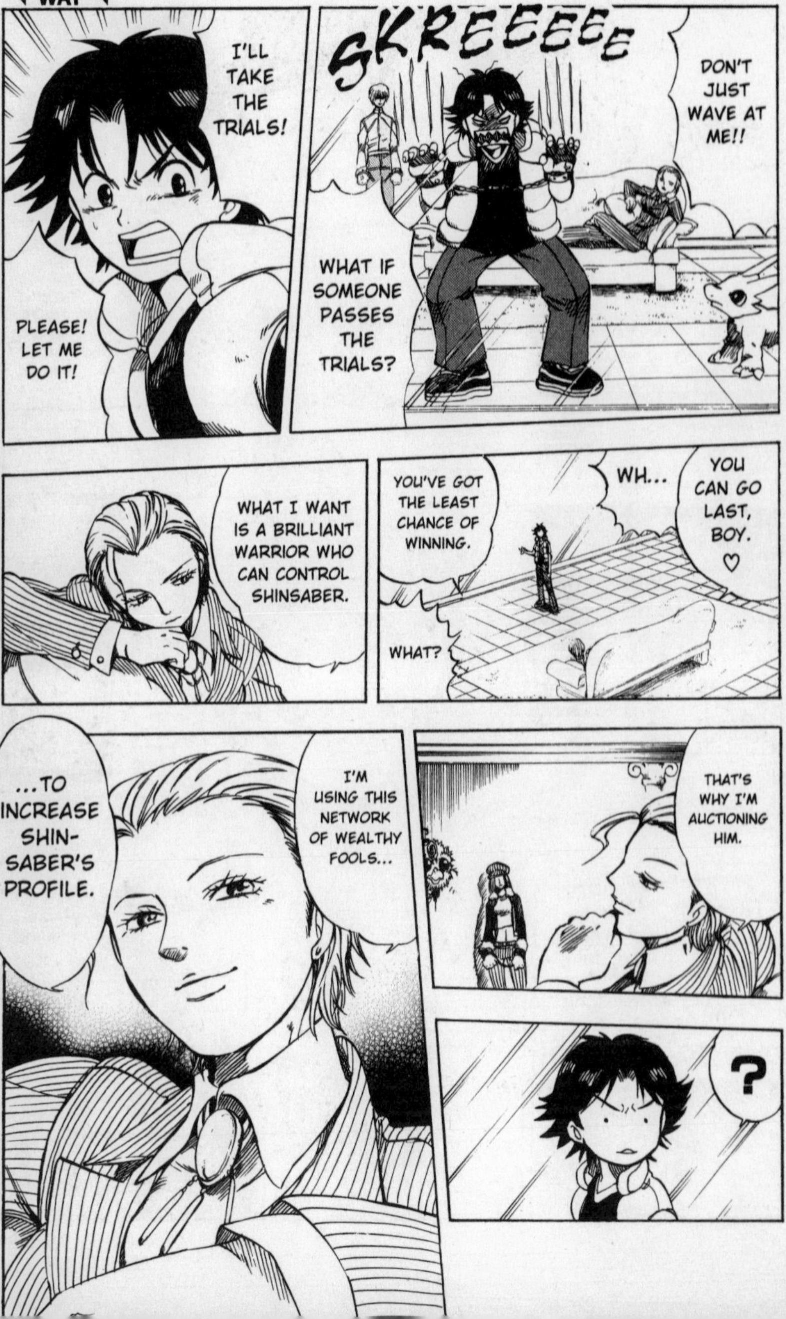
DON'T JUST WAVE AT ME!!
SKREEEEEE
WHAT IF SOMEONE PASSES THE TRIALS?
I'LL TAKE THE TRIALS!
PLEASE! LET ME DO IT!
YOU CAN GO LAST, BOY. ♡
WH...
YOU'VE GOT THE LEAST CHANCE OF WINNING.
WHAT?
WHAT I WANT IS A BRILLIANT WARRIOR WHO CAN CONTROL SHINSABER.
THAT'S WHY I'M AUCTIONING HIM.
?
I'M USING THIS NETWORK OF WEALTHY FOOLS...
...TO INCREASE SHIN-SABER'S PROFILE.

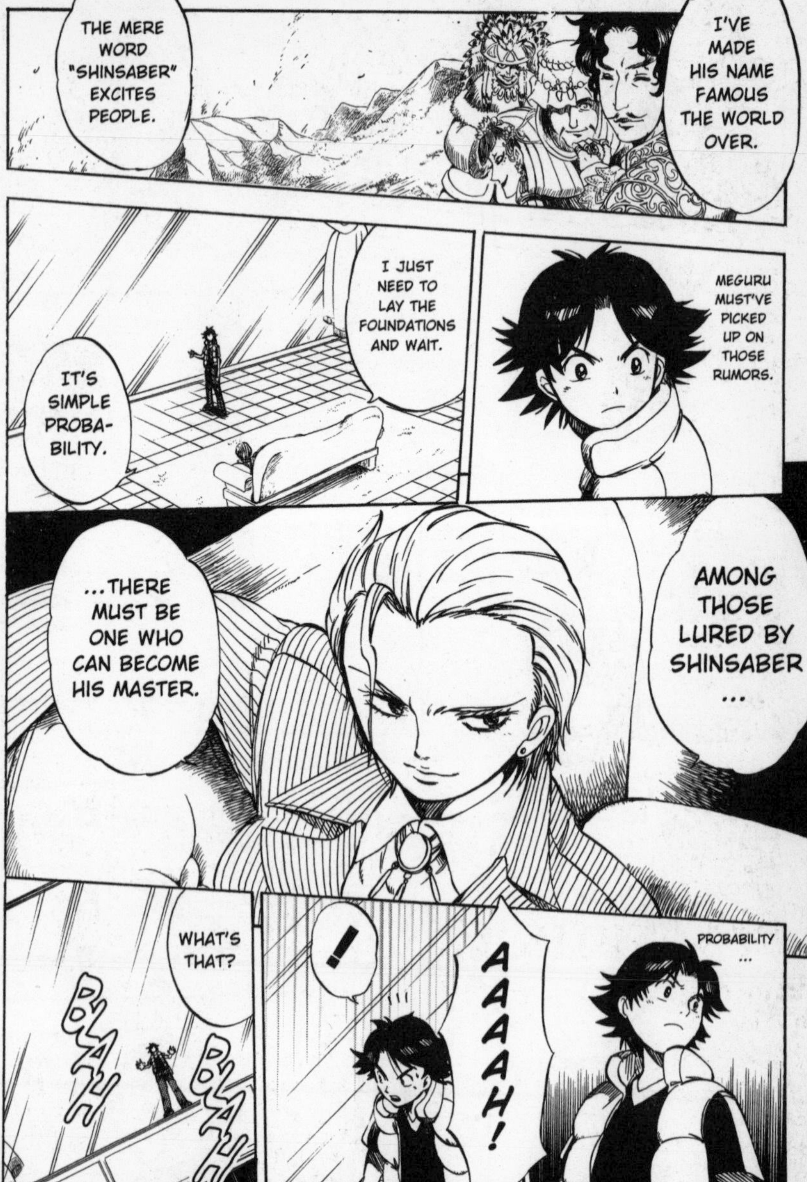
I'VE MADE HIS NAME FAMOUS THE WORLD OVER.
THE MERE WORD "SHINSABER" EXCITES PEOPLE.
MEGURU MUST'VE PICKED UP ON THOSE RUMORS.
I JUST NEED TO LAY THE FOUNDATIONS AND WAIT.
IT'S SIMPLE PROBA-BILITY.
AMONG THOSE LURED BY SHINSABER...
...THERE MUST BE ONE WHO CAN BECOME HIS MASTER.
PROBABILITY...
AAAAH!
!
WHAT'S THAT?
BLAH
BLAH

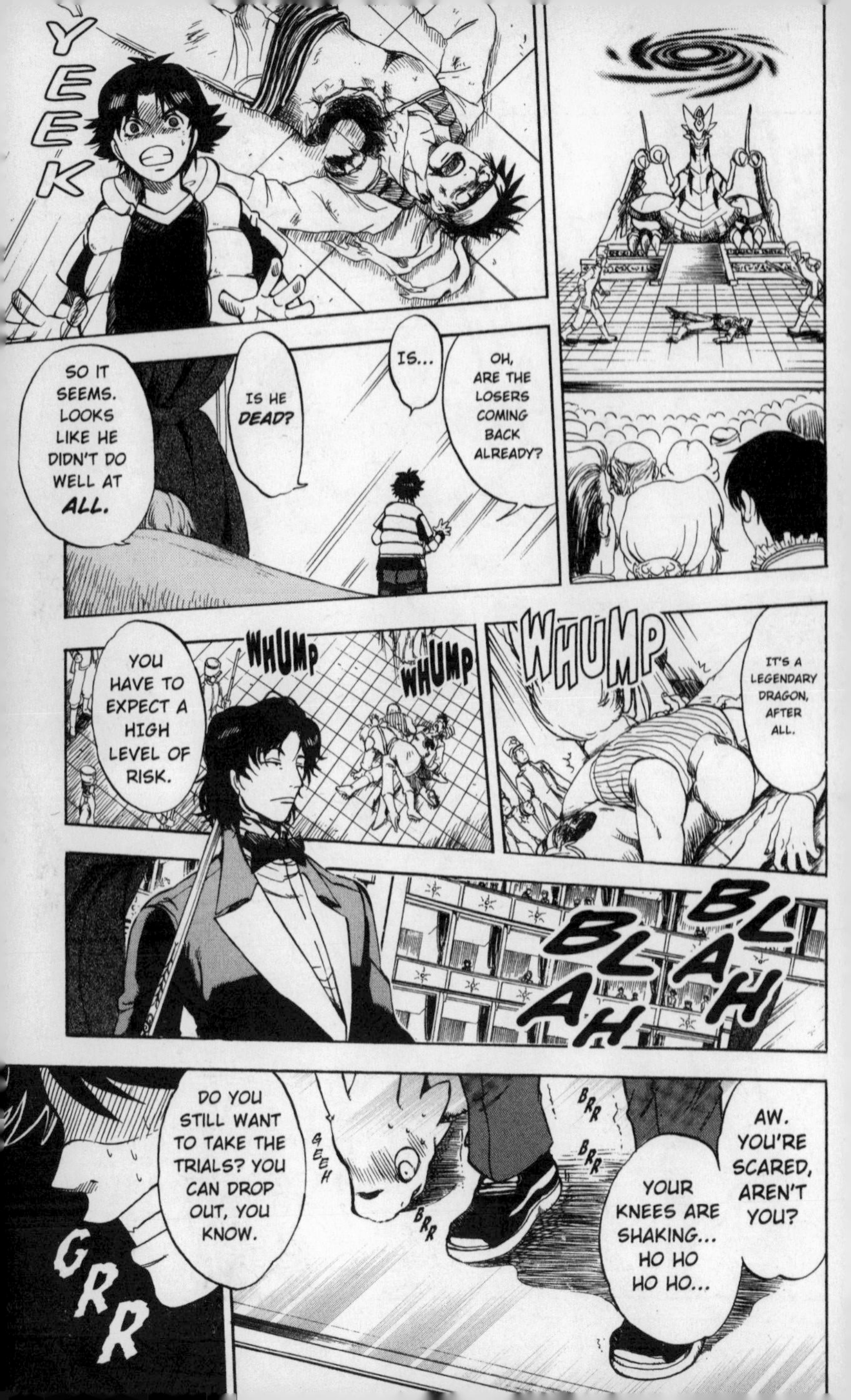
YEEK
OH, ARE THE LOSERS COMING BACK ALREADY?
IS...
IS HE *DEAD?*
SO IT SEEMS. LOOKS LIKE HE DIDN'T DO WELL AT **ALL.**
IT'S A LEGENDARY DRAGON, AFTER ALL.
WHUMP
WHUMP
WHUMP
YOU HAVE TO EXPECT A HIGH LEVEL OF RISK.
BLAH BLAH BLAH BLAH
AW. YOU'RE SCARED, AREN'T YOU?
YOUR KNEES ARE SHAKING... HO HO HO HO...
BRR BRR
BRR
GEEH
DO YOU STILL WANT TO TAKE THE TRIALS? YOU CAN DROP OUT, YOU KNOW.
GRR

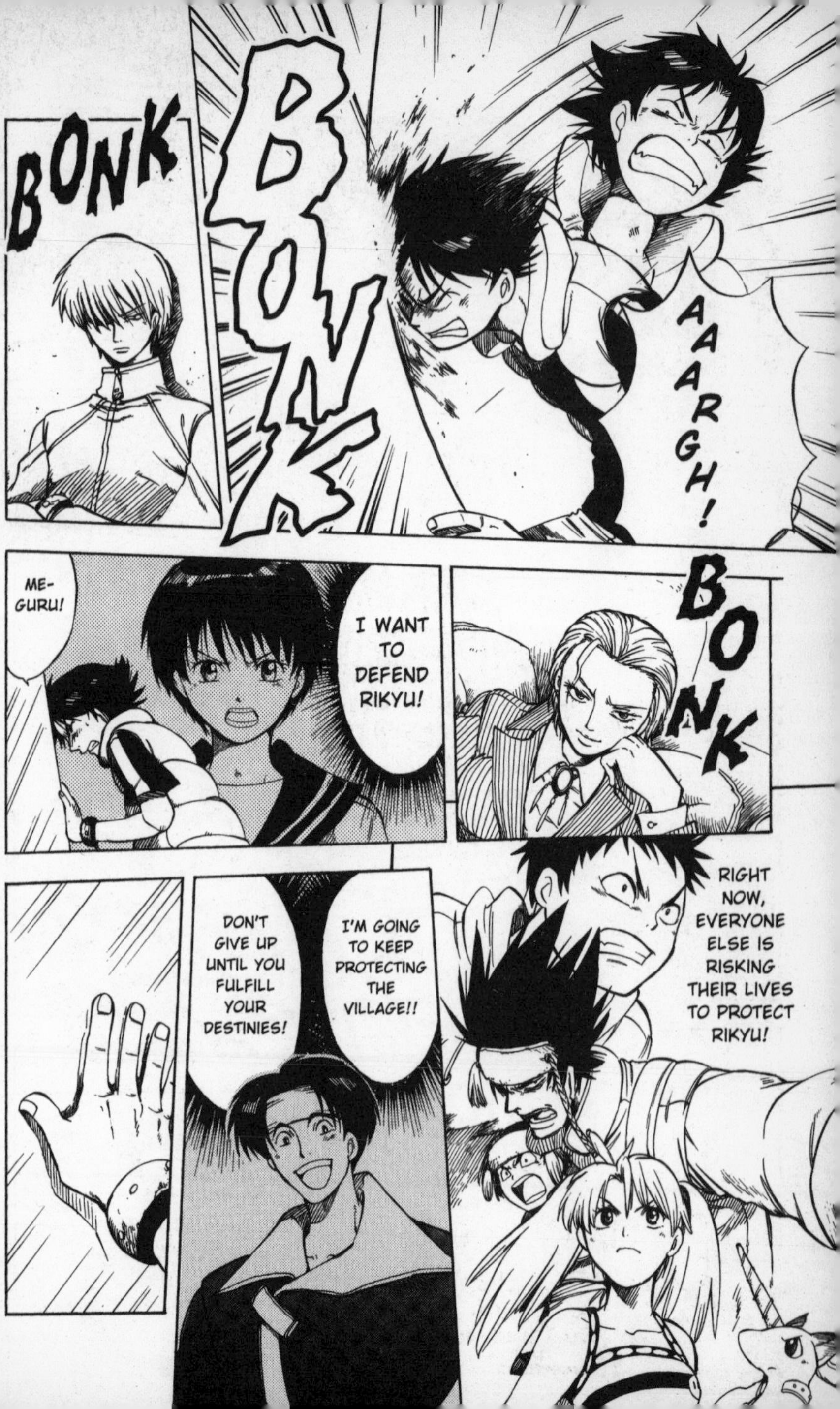
AAARGH!
BONK
BONK
BONK
I WANT TO DEFEND RIKYU!
ME-GURU!
RIGHT NOW, EVERYONE ELSE IS RISKING THEIR LIVES TO PROTECT RIKYU!
I'M GOING TO KEEP PROTECTING THE VILLAGE!!
DON'T GIVE UP UNTIL YOU FULFILL YOUR DESTINIES!

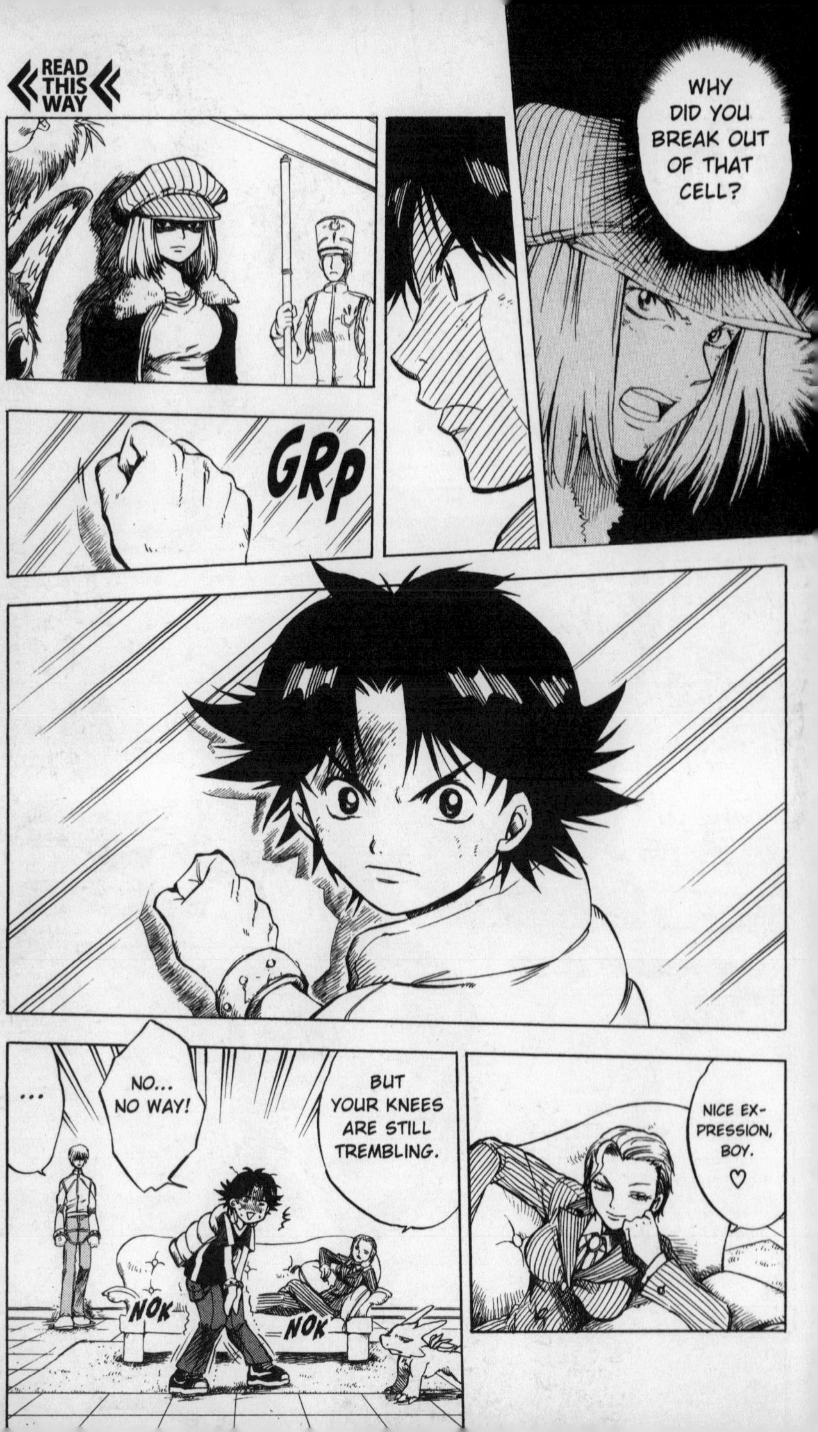
READ THIS WAY
WHY DID YOU BREAK OUT OF THAT CELL?
GRP
NICE EX-PRESSION, BOY. ♡
BUT YOUR KNEES ARE STILL TREMBLING.
NO... NO WAY!
...
NOK
NOK

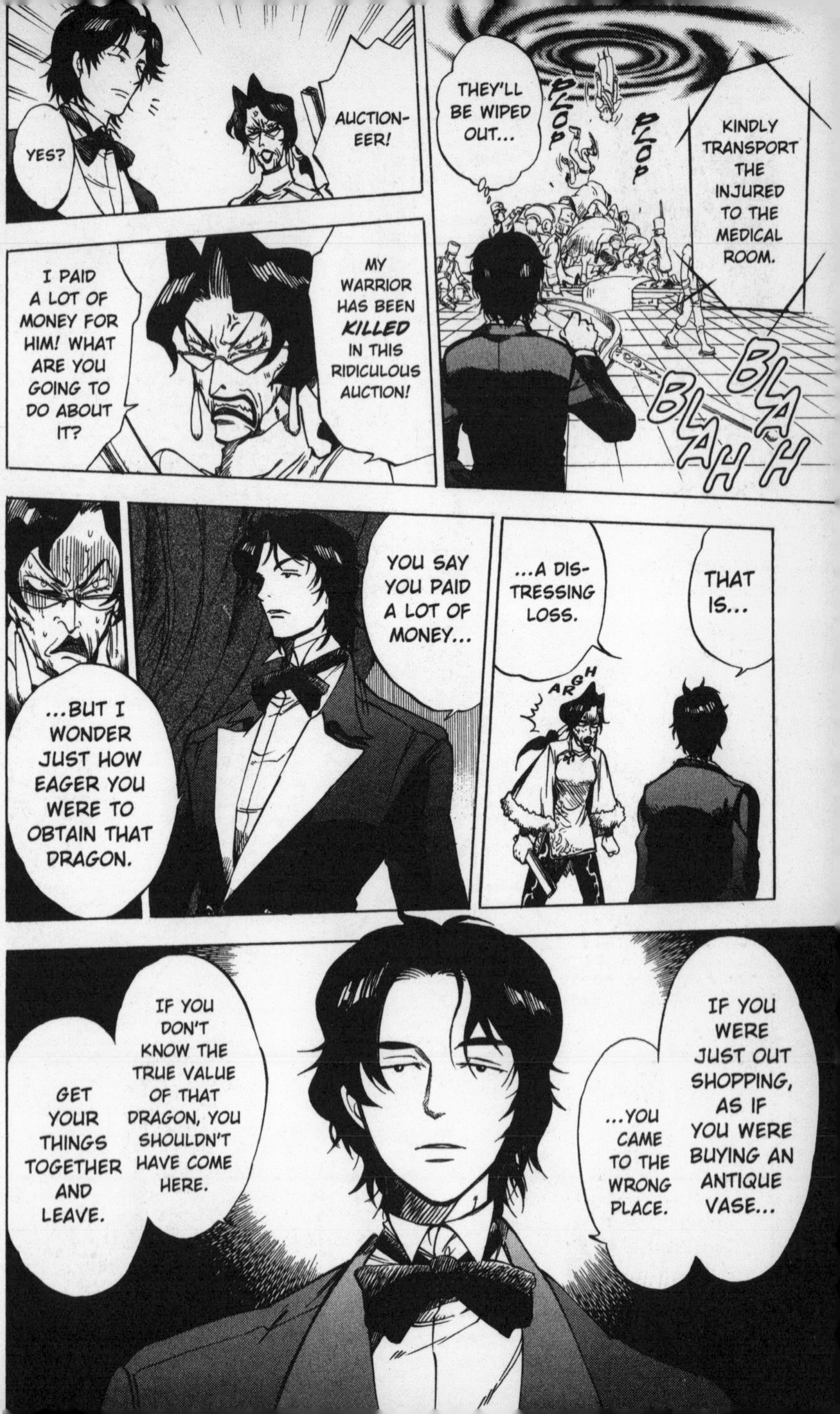
KINDLY TRANSPORT THE INJURED TO THE MEDICAL ROOM.
PLOP
PLOP
THEY'LL BE WIPED OUT...
BLAH BLAH
AUCTION-EER!
YES?
MY WARRIOR HAS BEEN KILLED IN THIS RIDICULOUS AUCTION!
I PAID A LOT OF MONEY FOR HIM! WHAT ARE YOU GOING TO DO ABOUT IT?
THAT IS...
...A DIS-TRESSING LOSS.
ARGH
YOU SAY YOU PAID A LOT OF MONEY...
...BUT I WONDER JUST HOW EAGER YOU WERE TO OBTAIN THAT DRAGON.
IF YOU WERE JUST OUT SHOPPING, AS IF YOU WERE BUYING AN ANTIQUE VASE...
...YOU CAME TO THE WRONG PLACE.
IF YOU DON'T KNOW THE TRUE VALUE OF THAT DRAGON, YOU SHOULDN'T HAVE COME HERE.
GET YOUR THINGS TOGETHER AND LEAVE.

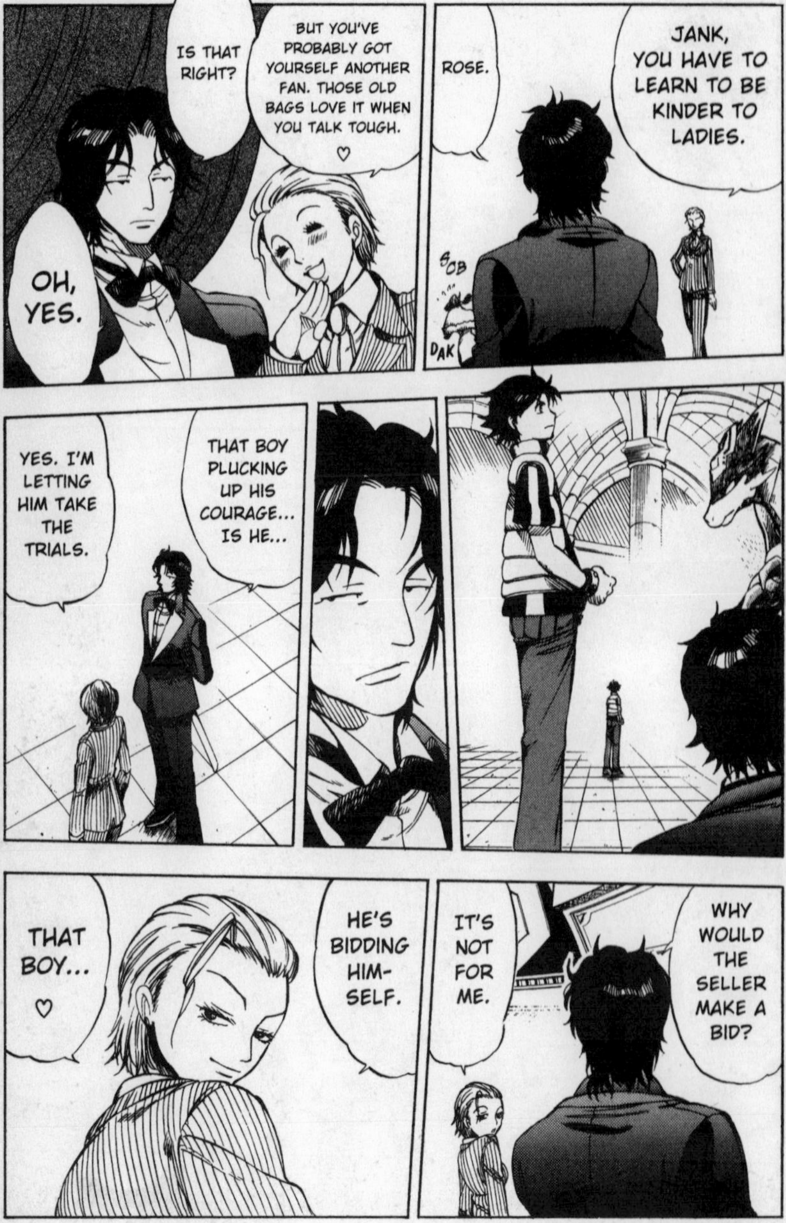
JANK, YOU HAVE TO LEARN TO BE KINDER TO LADIES.
ROSE.
SOB
DAK
BUT YOU'VE PROBABLY GOT YOURSELF ANOTHER FAN. THOSE OLD BAGS LOVE IT WHEN YOU TALK TOUGH. ♡
IS THAT RIGHT?
OH, YES.
THAT BOY PLUCKING UP HIS COURAGE... IS HE...
YES. I'M LETTING HIM TAKE THE TRIALS.
WHY WOULD THE SELLER MAKE A BID?
IT'S NOT FOR ME.
HE'S BIDDING HIMSELF.
THAT BOY... ♡

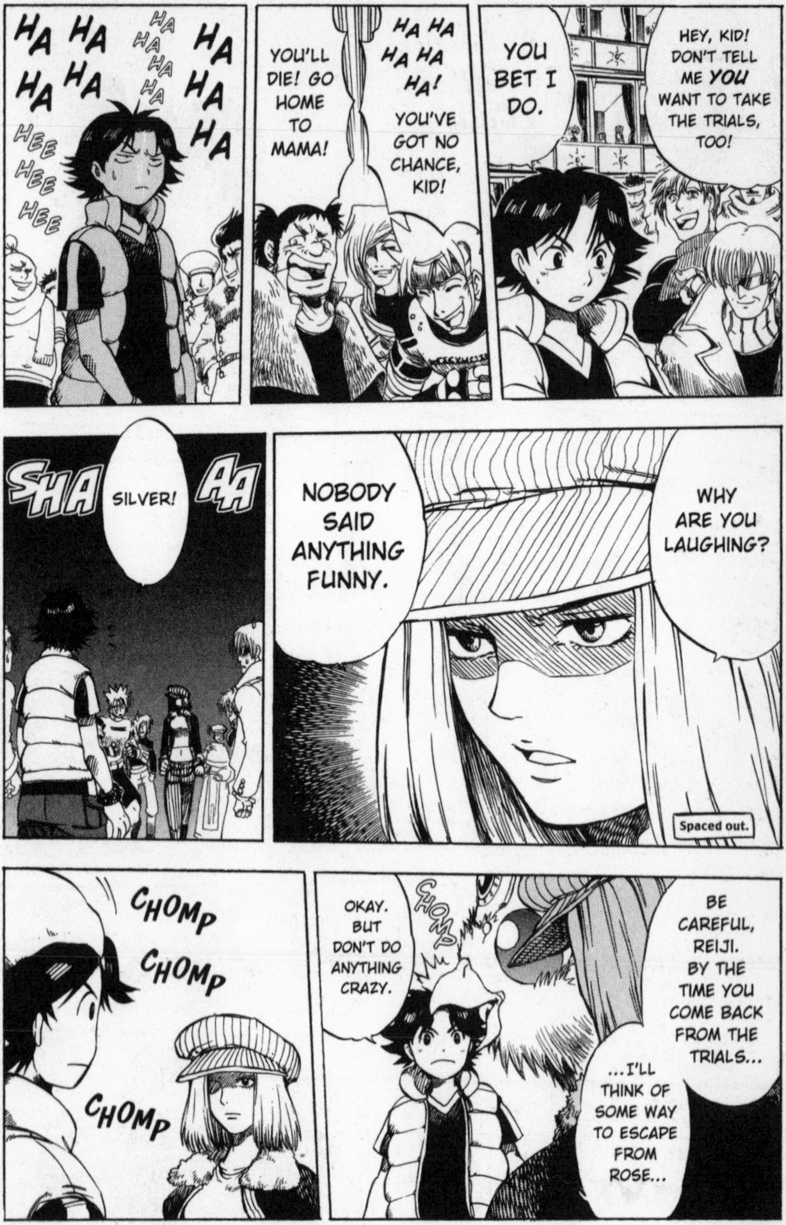
HEY, KID! DON'T TELL ME *YOU* WANT TO TAKE THE TRIALS, TOO!
YOU BET I DO.
HA HA HA HA HA!
YOU'VE GOT NO CHANCE, KID!
YOU'LL DIE! GO HOME TO MAMA!
HA HA HA HA HA HA HA
HA HA HA HA HA
HEE HEE HEE
WHY ARE YOU LAUGHING?
NOBODY SAID ANYTHING FUNNY.
Spaced out.
SHAAA
SILVER!
BE CAREFUL, REIJI. BY THE TIME YOU COME BACK FROM THE TRIALS...
...I'LL THINK OF SOME WAY TO ESCAPE FROM ROSE...
CHOMP
OKAY. BUT DON'T DO ANYTHING CRAZY.
CHOMP
CHOMP
CHOMP

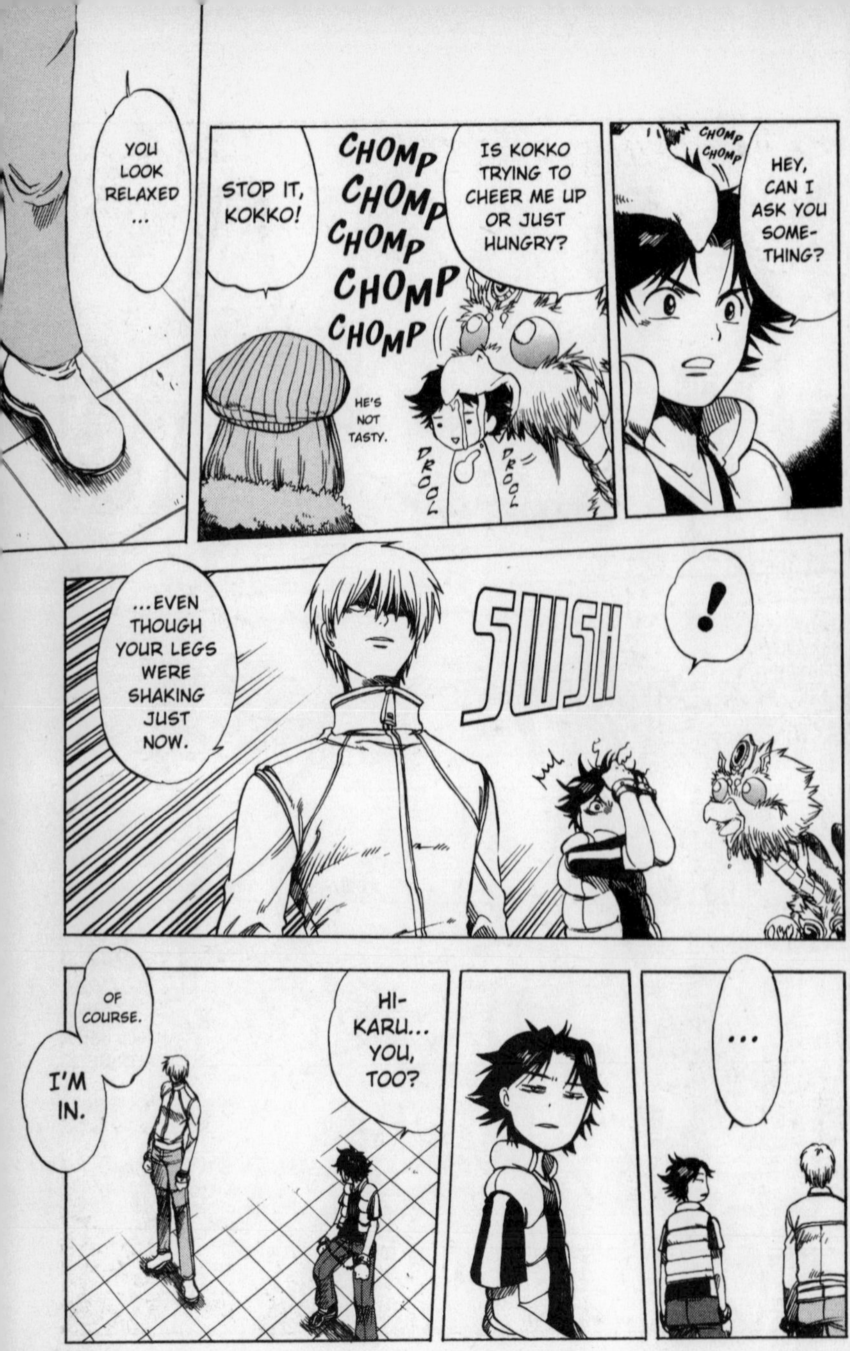
CHOMP CHOMP
HEY, CAN I ASK YOU SOMETHING?
IS KOKKO TRYING TO CHEER ME UP OR JUST HUNGRY?
CHOMP CHOMP CHOMP CHOMP CHOMP
STOP IT, KOKKO!
HE'S NOT TASTY.
DROOL
DROOL
YOU LOOK RELAXED ...
!
SWSH
...EVEN THOUGH YOUR LEGS WERE SHAKING JUST NOW.
...
HI-KARU... YOU, TOO?
OF COURSE.
I'M IN.

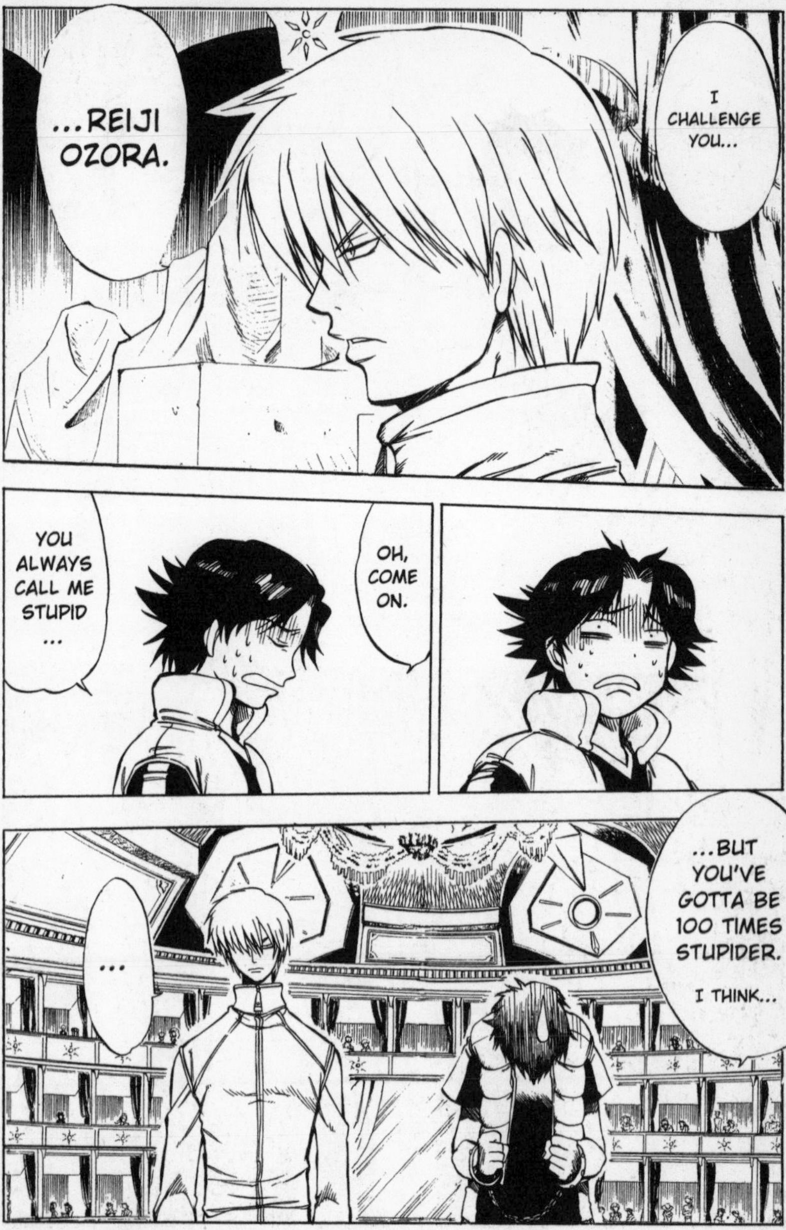
I CHALLENGE YOU...
...REIJI OZORA.
OH, COME ON.
YOU ALWAYS CALL ME STUPID ...
...BUT YOU'VE GOTTA BE 100 TIMES STUPIDER.
I THINK...
...

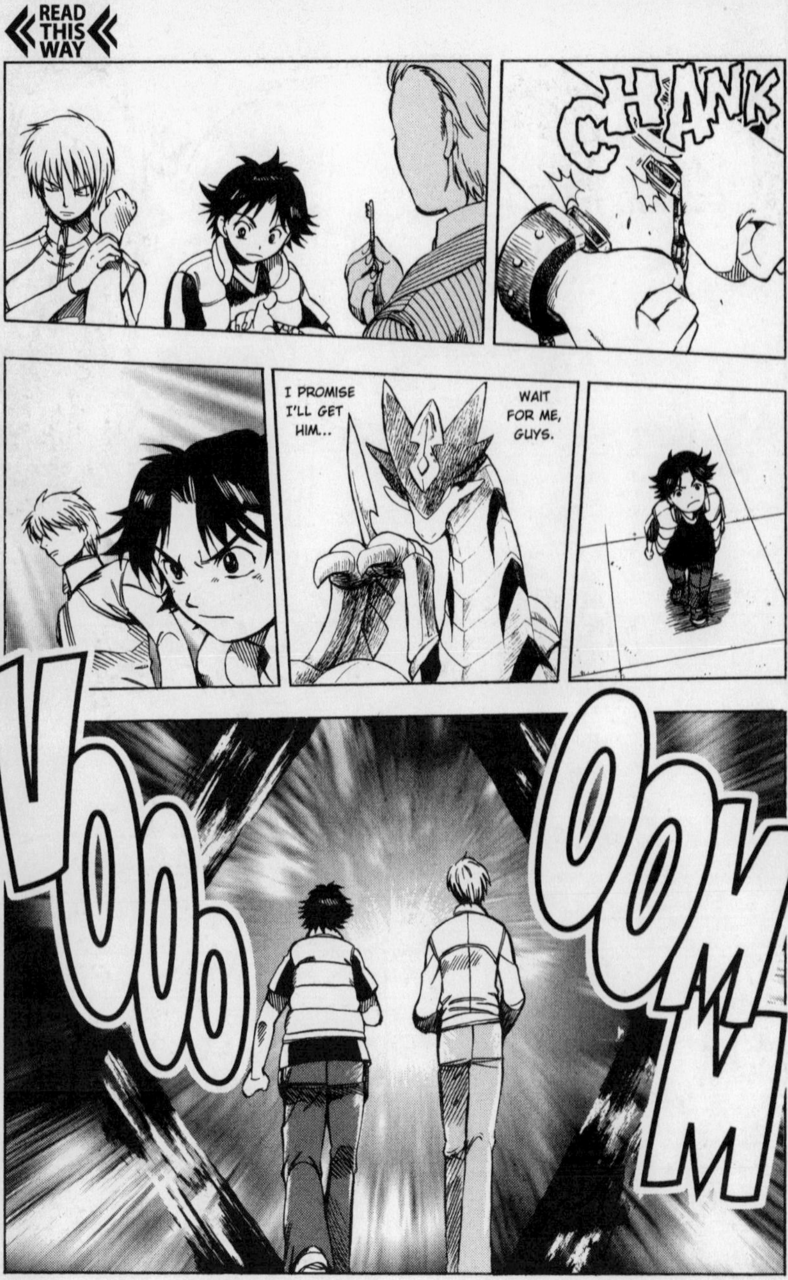
READ THIS WAY
CHANK
WAIT FOR ME, GUYS.
I PROMISE I'LL GET HIM...
VOOOOOOMM

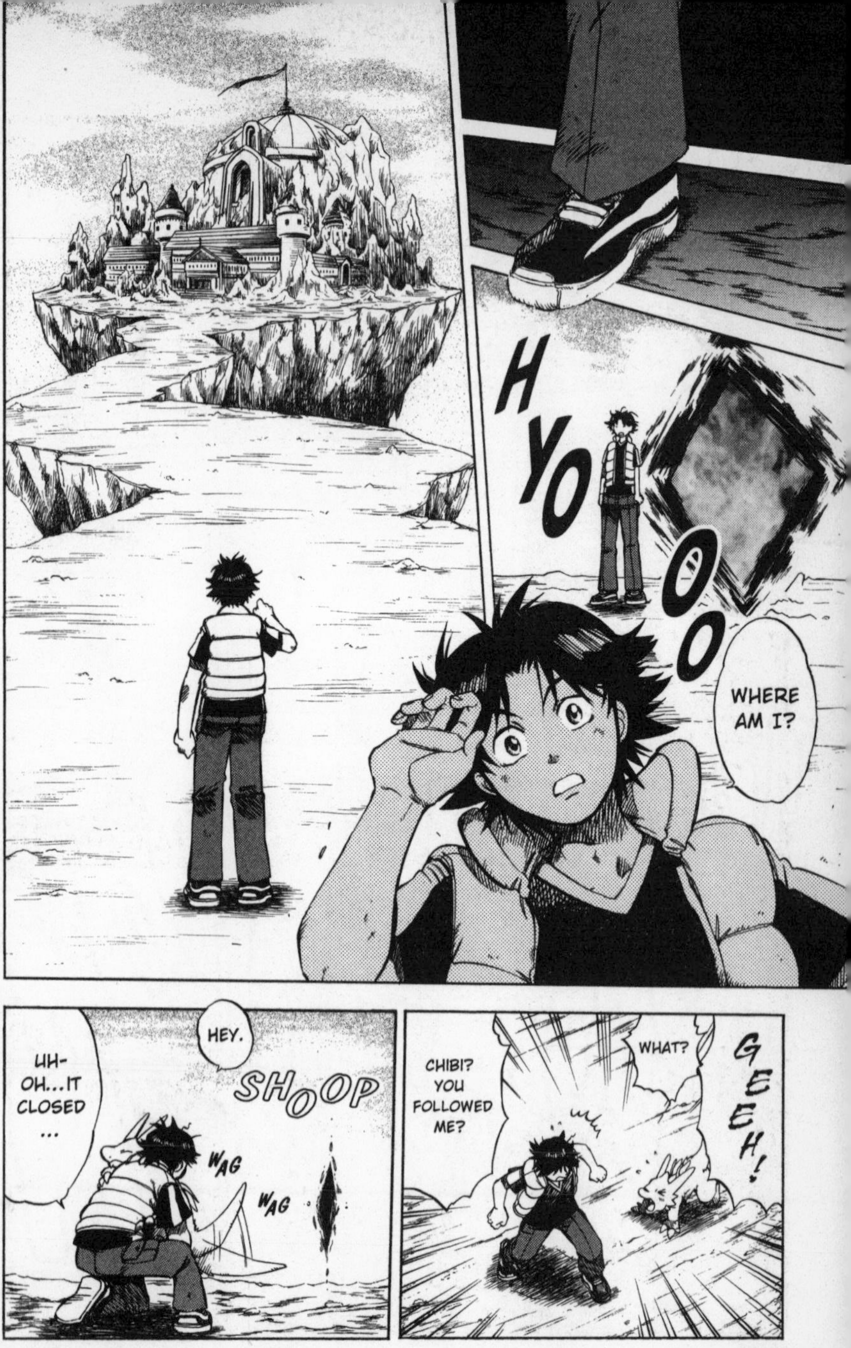
HYOOO
WHERE AM I?
GEEH!
WHAT?
CHIBI? YOU FOLLOWED ME?
HEY.
SHOOP
UH-OH...IT CLOSED...
WAG
WAG

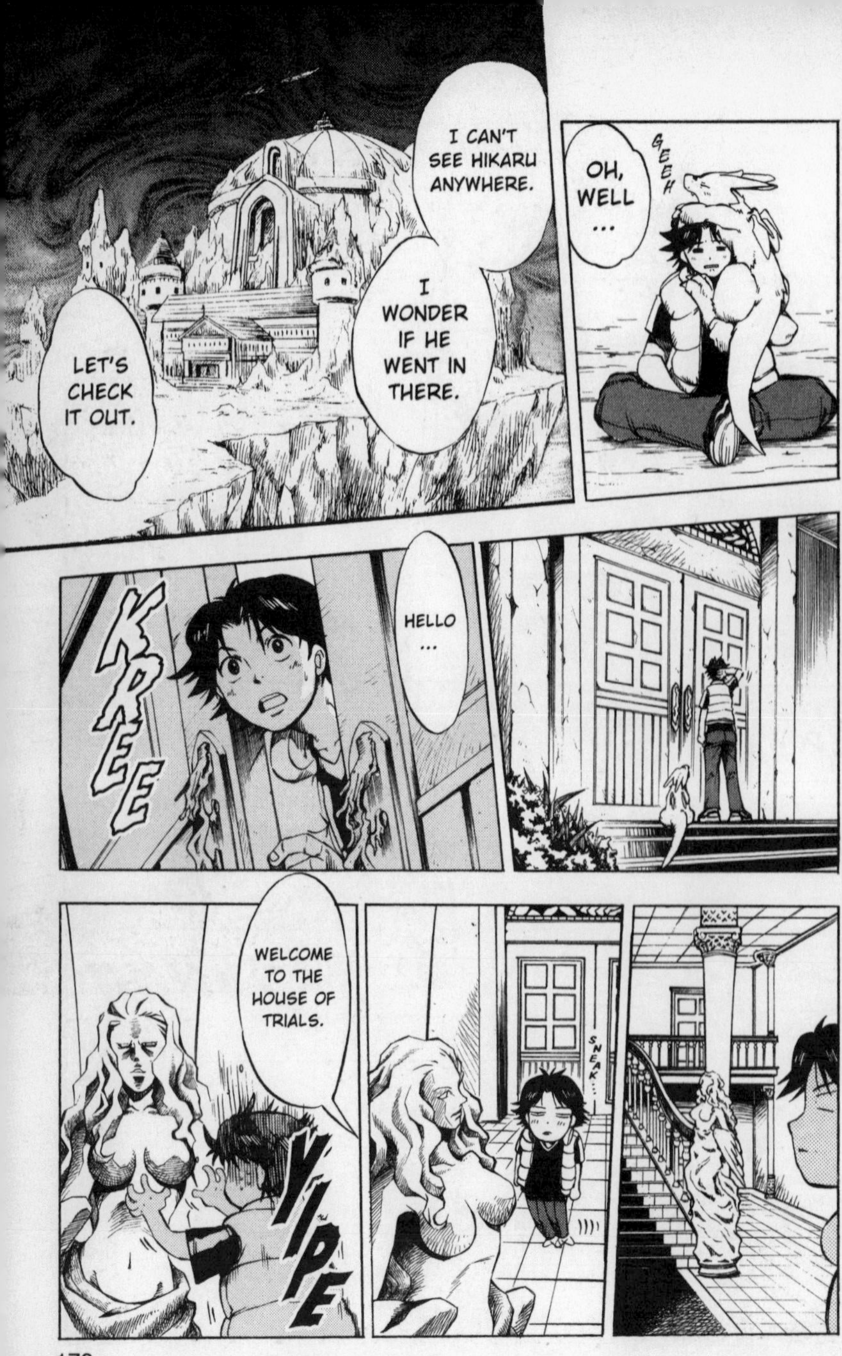
OH, WELL ...
GEEH
I CAN'T SEE HIKARU ANYWHERE.
I WONDER IF HE WENT IN THERE.
LET'S CHECK IT OUT.
HELLO ...
KREE
SNEAK...
WELCOME TO THE HOUSE OF TRIALS.
YIPE

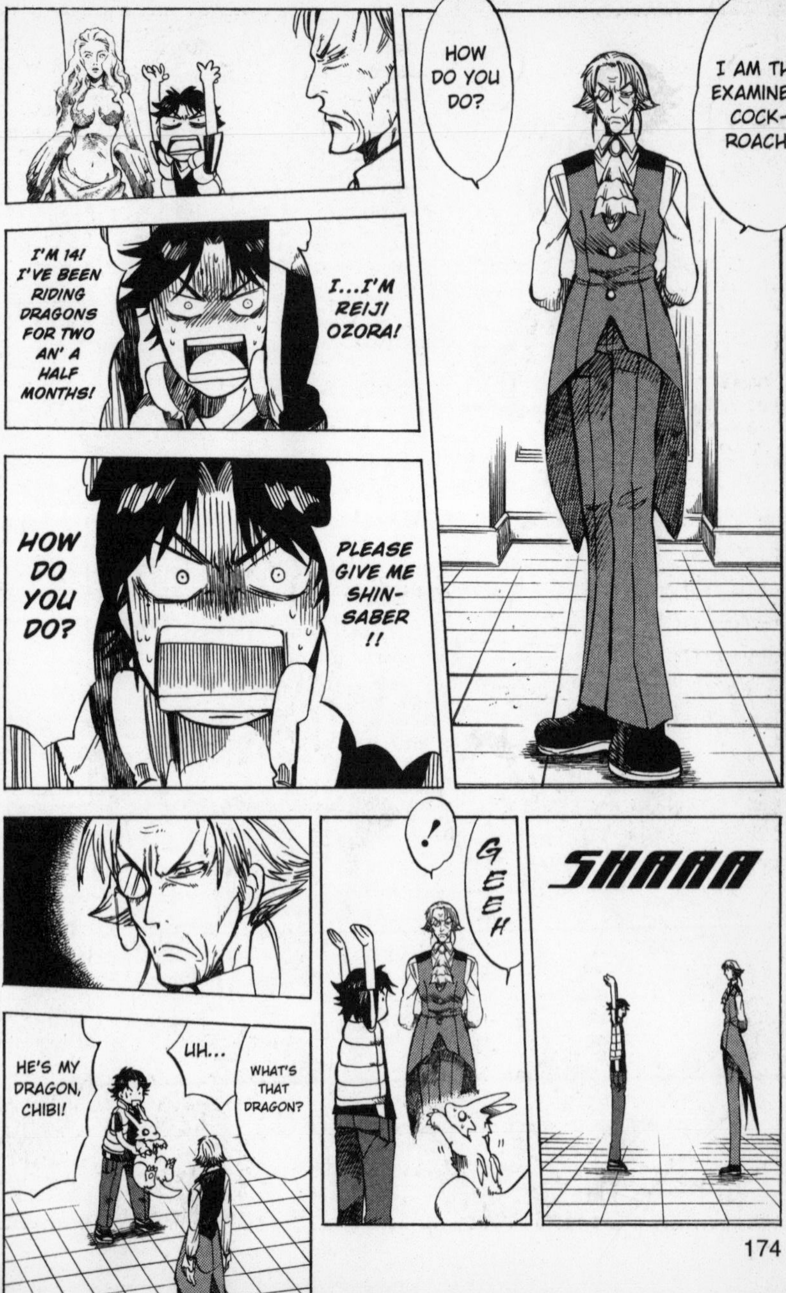
I AM THE EXAMINER, COCK-ROACH.
HOW DO YOU DO?
I...I'M REIJI OZORA!
I'M 14! I'VE BEEN RIDING DRAGONS FOR TWO AN' A HALF MONTHS!
PLEASE GIVE ME SHIN-SABER!!
HOW DO YOU DO?
SHAAA
GEEH
!
WHAT'S THAT DRAGON?
UH...
HE'S MY DRAGON, CHIBI!

READ THIS WAY

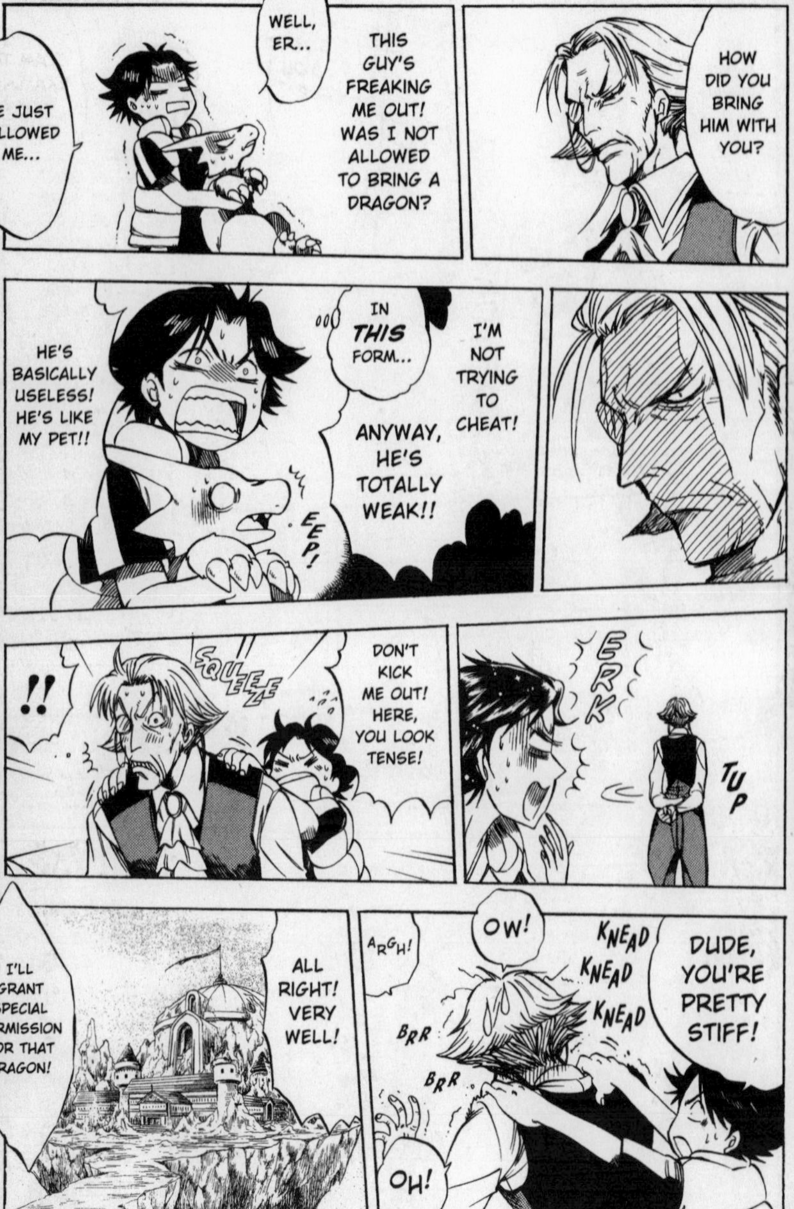
HOW DID YOU BRING HIM WITH YOU?
WELL, ER...
THIS GUY'S FREAKING ME OUT! WAS I NOT ALLOWED TO BRING A DRAGON?
HE JUST FOLLOWED ME...
I'M NOT TRYING TO CHEAT!
IN THIS FORM...
ANYWAY, HE'S TOTALLY WEAK!!
HE'S BASICALLY USELESS! HE'S LIKE MY PET!!
EEP!
ERK
TUP
DON'T KICK ME OUT! HERE, YOU LOOK TENSE!
SQUEEZE
!!
DUDE, YOU'RE PRETTY STIFF!
KNEAD
KNEAD
KNEAD
OW!
ARGH!
BRR
BRR
OH!
ALL RIGHT! VERY WELL!
I'LL GRANT SPECIAL PERMISSION FOR THAT DRAGON!

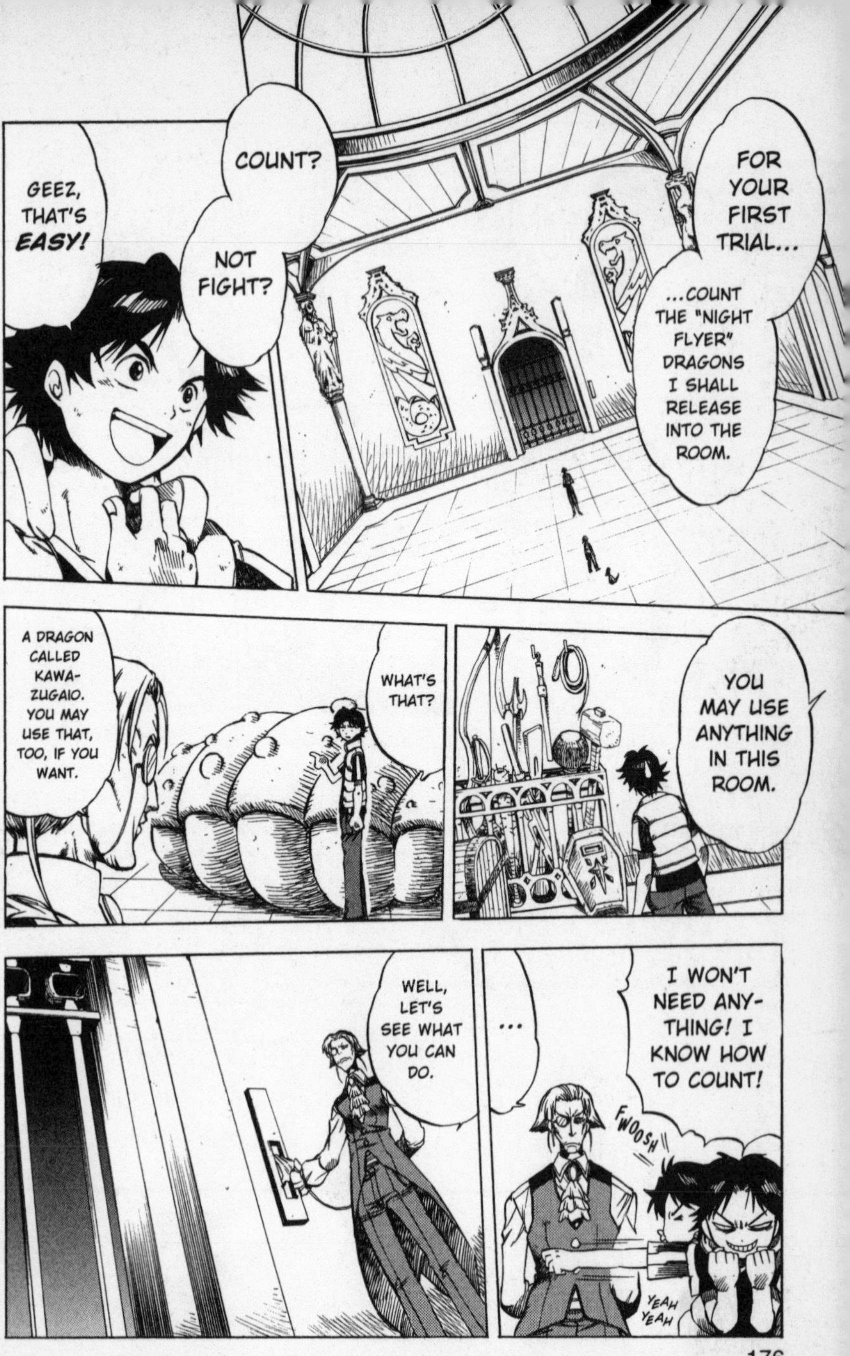
FOR YOUR FIRST TRIAL...
...COUNT THE "NIGHT FLYER" DRAGONS I SHALL RELEASE INTO THE ROOM.
COUNT?
NOT FIGHT?
GEEZ, THAT'S *EASY!*
YOU MAY USE ANYTHING IN THIS ROOM.
WHAT'S THAT?
A DRAGON CALLED KAWA-ZUGAIO. YOU MAY USE THAT, TOO, IF YOU WANT.
I WON'T NEED ANY-THING! I KNOW HOW TO COUNT!
...
FWOOSH
YEAH YEAH
WELL, LET'S SEE WHAT YOU CAN DO.

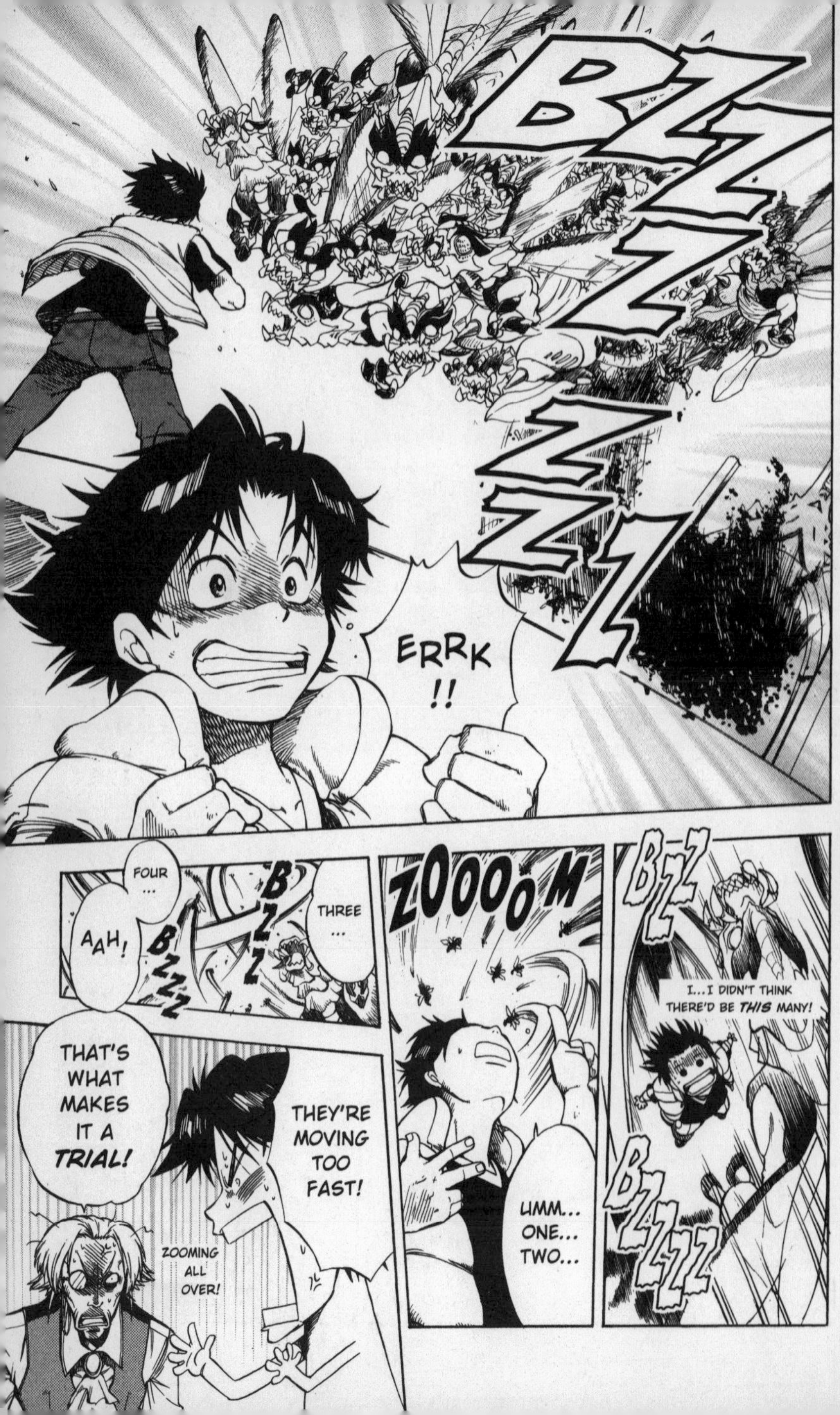
BZZZZZ
ERRK!!
BZZ
I...I DIDN'T THINK THERE'D BE *THIS* MANY!
BZZZZ
ZOOOOM
UMM... ONE... TWO...
THREE...
BZZZ
FOUR...
AAH!
BZZZ
THEY'RE MOVING TOO FAST!
THAT'S WHAT MAKES IT A ***TRIAL!***
ZOOMING ALL OVER!

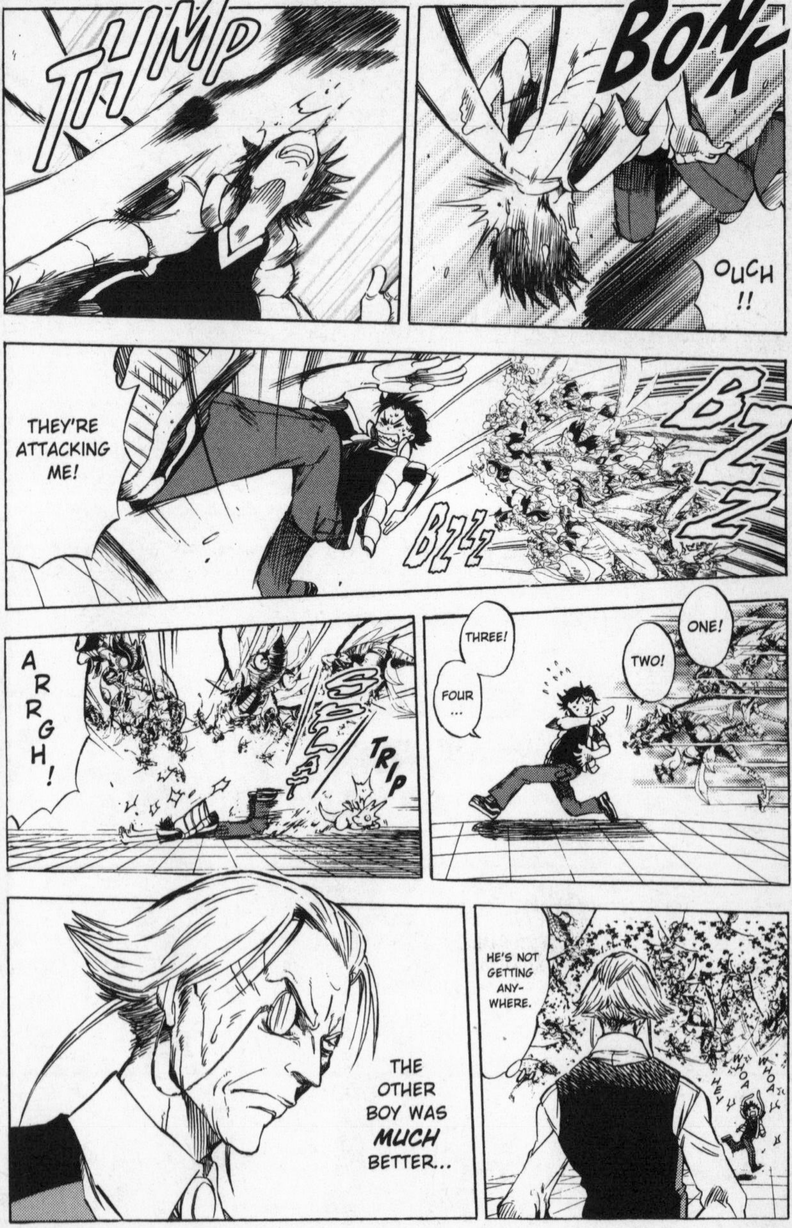
BONK
OUCH!!
THMP
BZZ
BZZZ
THEY'RE ATTACKING ME!
ONE!
TWO!
THREE!
FOUR...
SPLAT
TRIP
ARRGH!
HE'S NOT GETTING ANYWHERE.
WHOA
WHOA
HEY
THE OTHER BOY WAS **MUCH** BETTER...

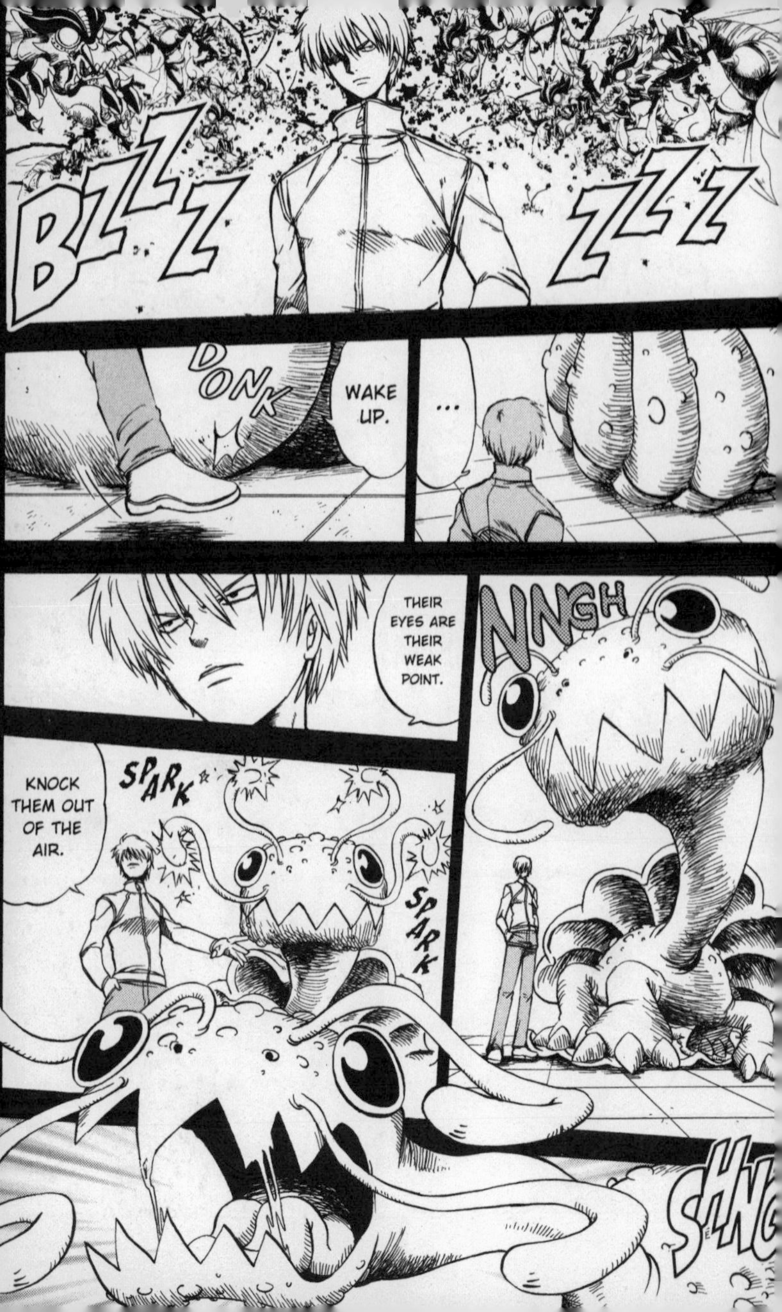
BZZZ
ZZZZ
...
WAKE UP.
DONK
NNGH
THEIR EYES ARE THEIR WEAK POINT.
KNOCK THEM OUT OF THE AIR.
SPARK
SPARK
SHNG

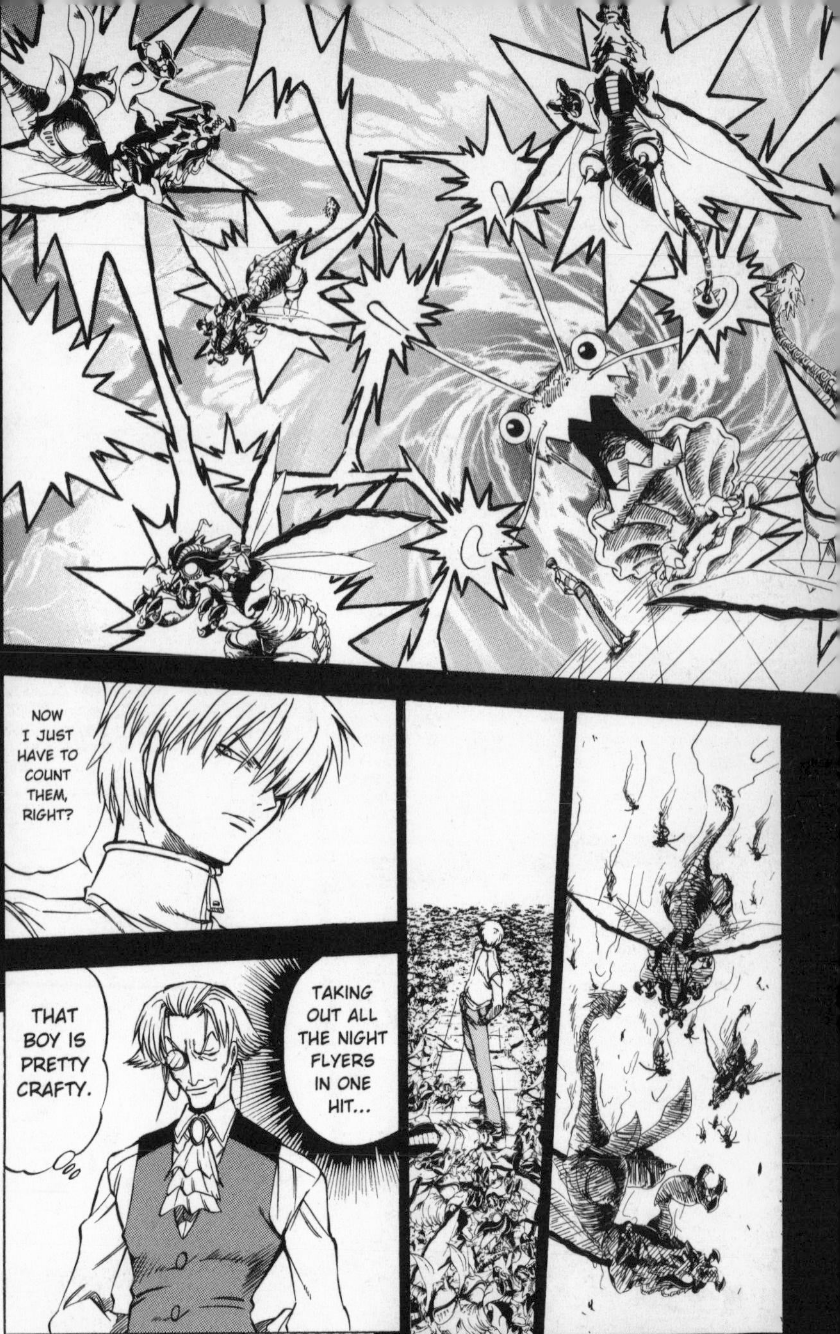
NOW I JUST HAVE TO COUNT THEM, RIGHT?
TAKING OUT ALL THE NIGHT FLYERS IN ONE HIT...
THAT BOY IS PRETTY CRAFTY.

READ THIS WAY

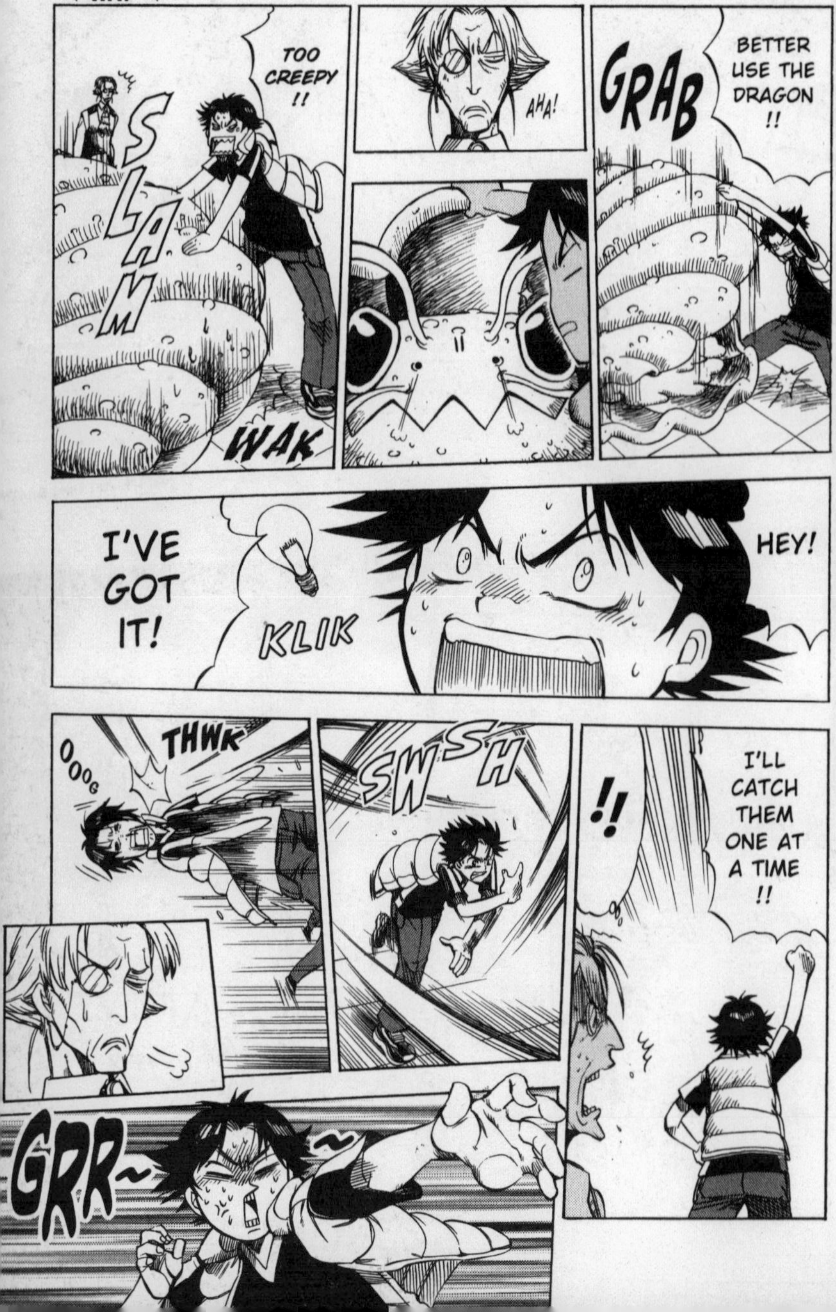
GRAB
BETTER USE THE DRAGON !!
AHA!
TOO CREEPY !!
SLAM
WAK
HEY!
I'VE GOT IT!
KLIK
I'LL CATCH THEM ONE AT A TIME !!
!!
SWSH
THWK
Oooo
GRR~

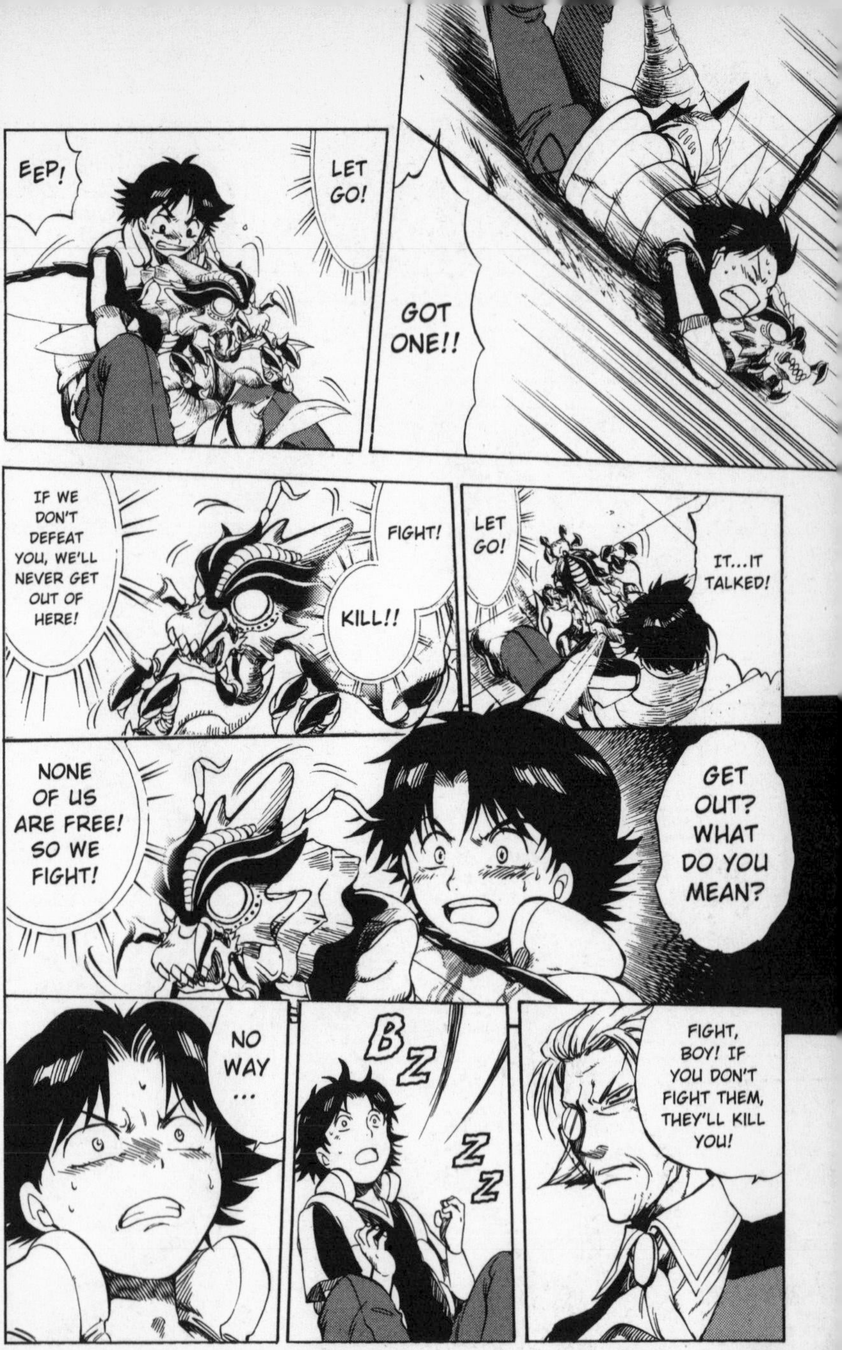
GOT ONE!!
LET GO!
EEP!
IT...IT TALKED!
LET GO!
FIGHT!
KILL!!
IF WE DON'T DEFEAT YOU, WE'LL NEVER GET OUT OF HERE!
GET OUT? WHAT DO YOU MEAN?
NONE OF US ARE FREE! SO WE FIGHT!
FIGHT, BOY! IF YOU DON'T FIGHT THEM, THEY'LL KILL YOU!
BZZZ
NO WAY ...

READ THIS WAY

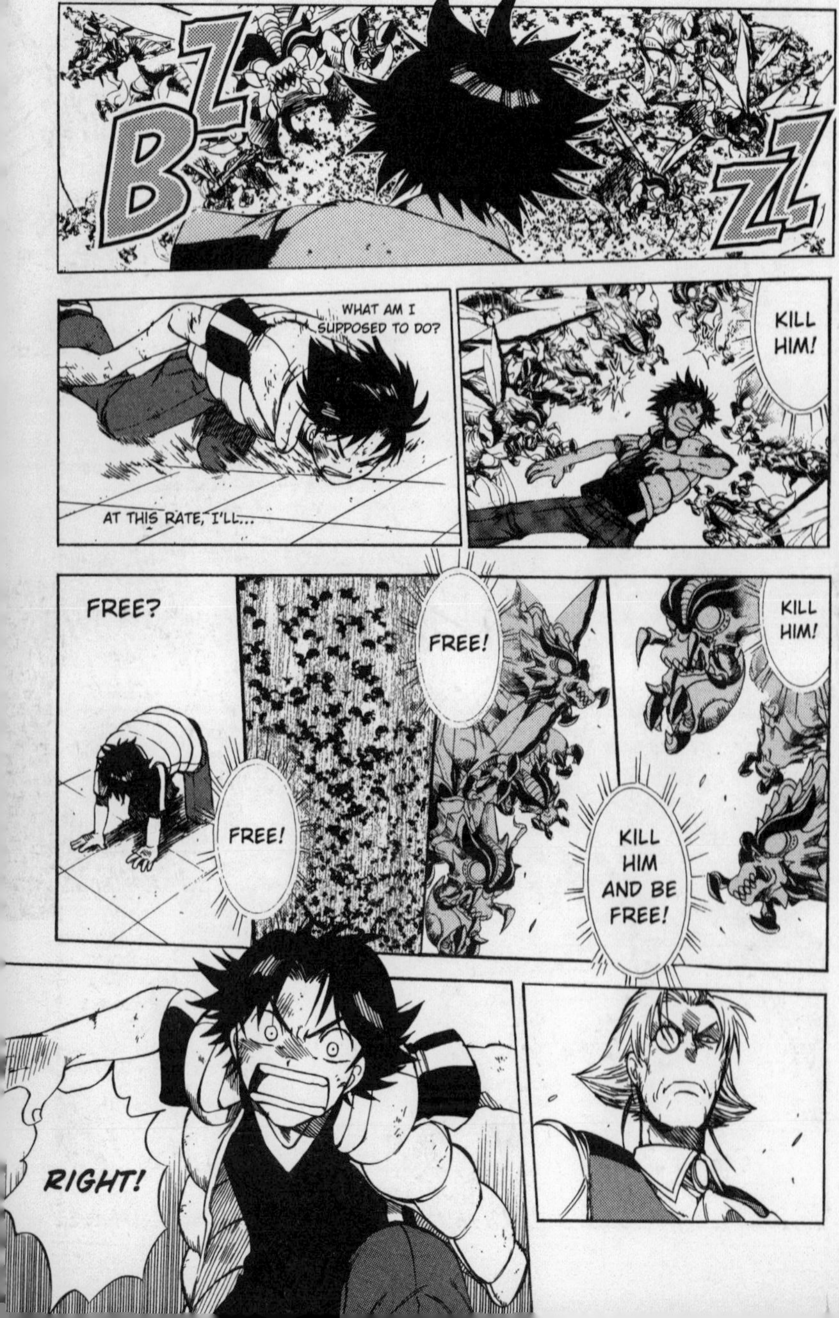
BZZZ
KILL HIM!
WHAT AM I SUPPOSED TO DO?
AT THIS RATE, I'LL...
KILL HIM!
KILL HIM AND BE FREE!
FREE!
FREE!
FREE?
RIGHT!

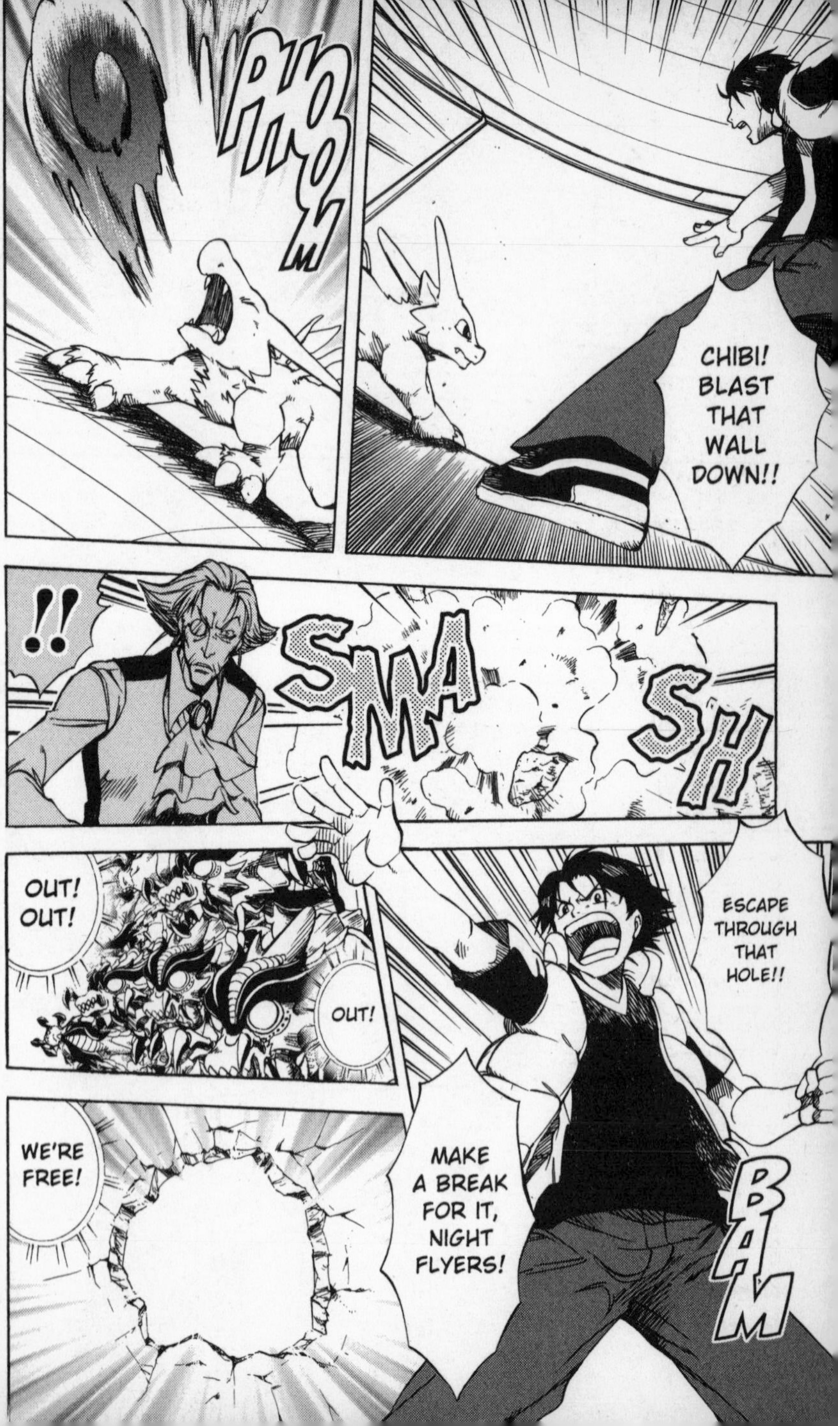
CHIBI! BLAST THAT WALL DOWN!!
PWOOM
!!
SMASH
ESCAPE THROUGH THAT HOLE!!
MAKE A BREAK FOR IT, NIGHT FLYERS!
BAM
OUT! OUT!
OUT!
WE'RE FREE!

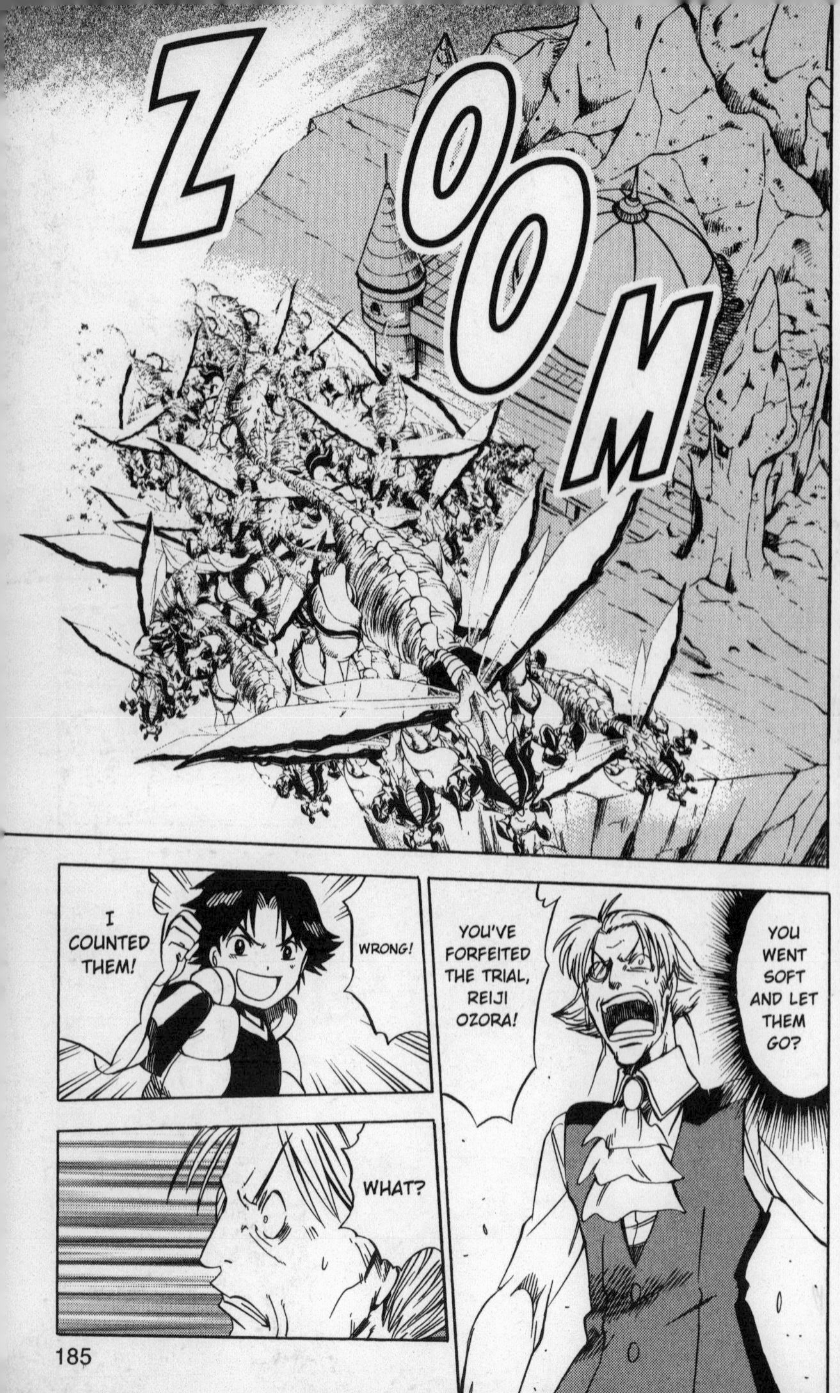
ZOOM
YOU WENT SOFT AND LET THEM GO?
YOU'VE FORFEITED THE TRIAL, REIJI OZORA!
WRONG!
I COUNTED THEM!
WHAT?

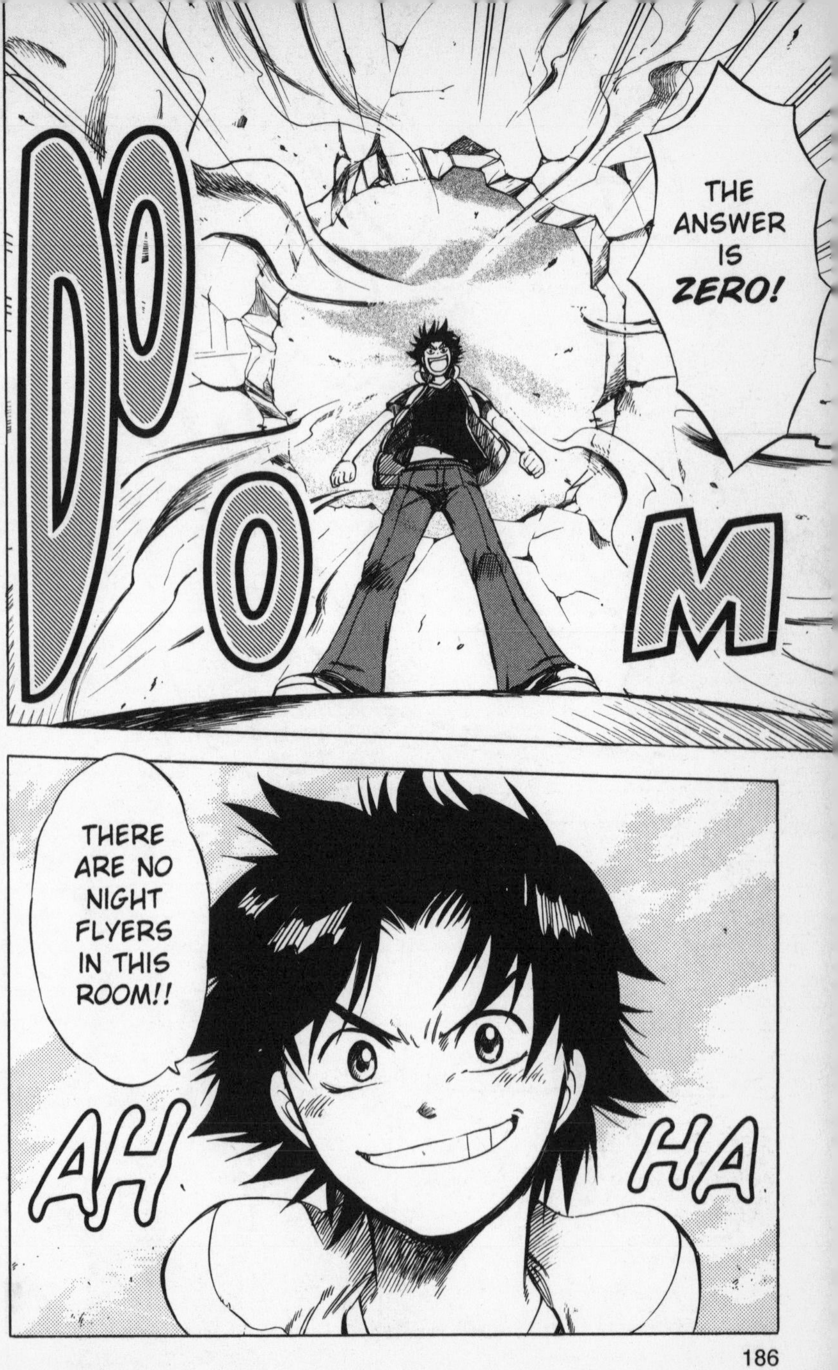
THE ANSWER IS ZERO!
DOOM
THERE ARE NO NIGHT FLYERS IN THIS ROOM!!
AH HA

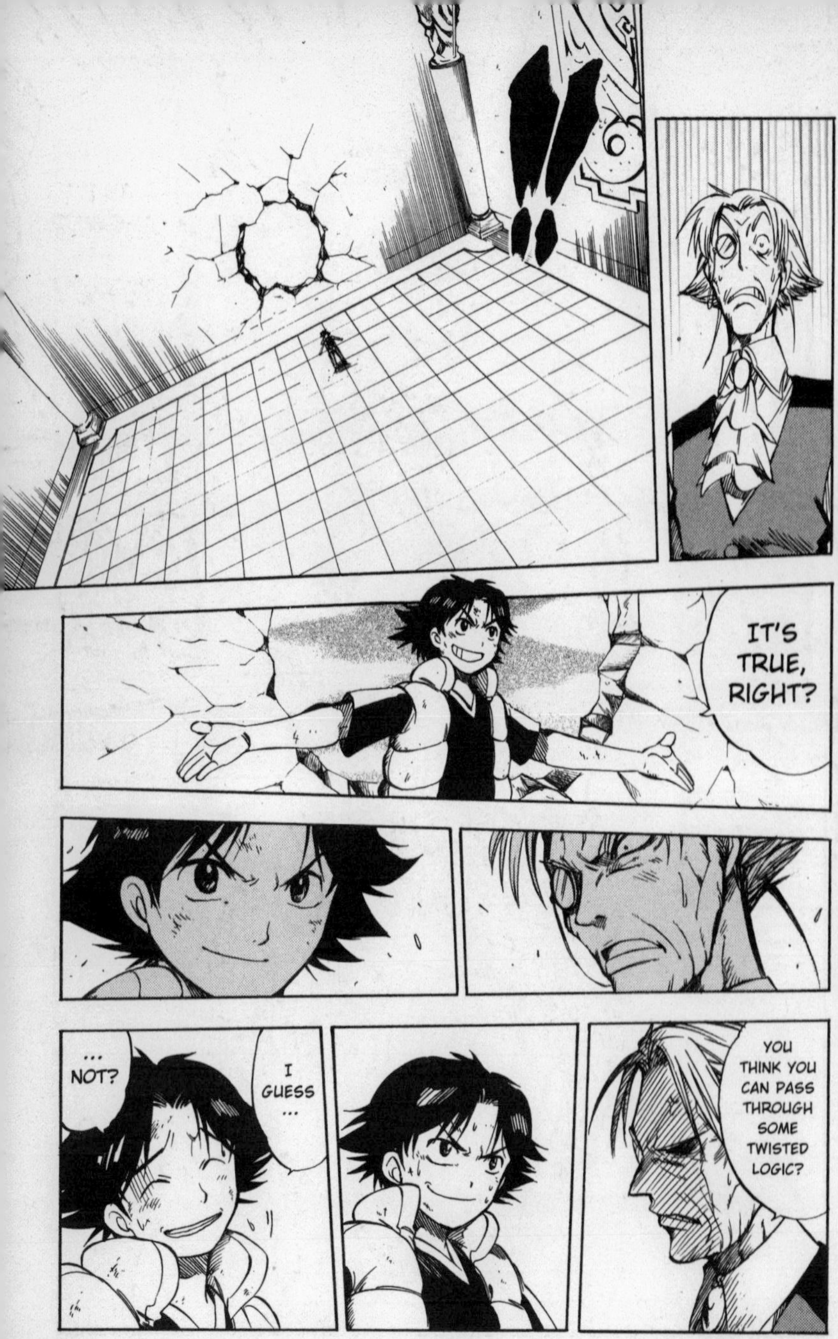
IT'S TRUE, RIGHT?
YOU THINK YOU CAN PASS THROUGH SOME TWISTED LOGIC?
I GUESS ...
... NOT?

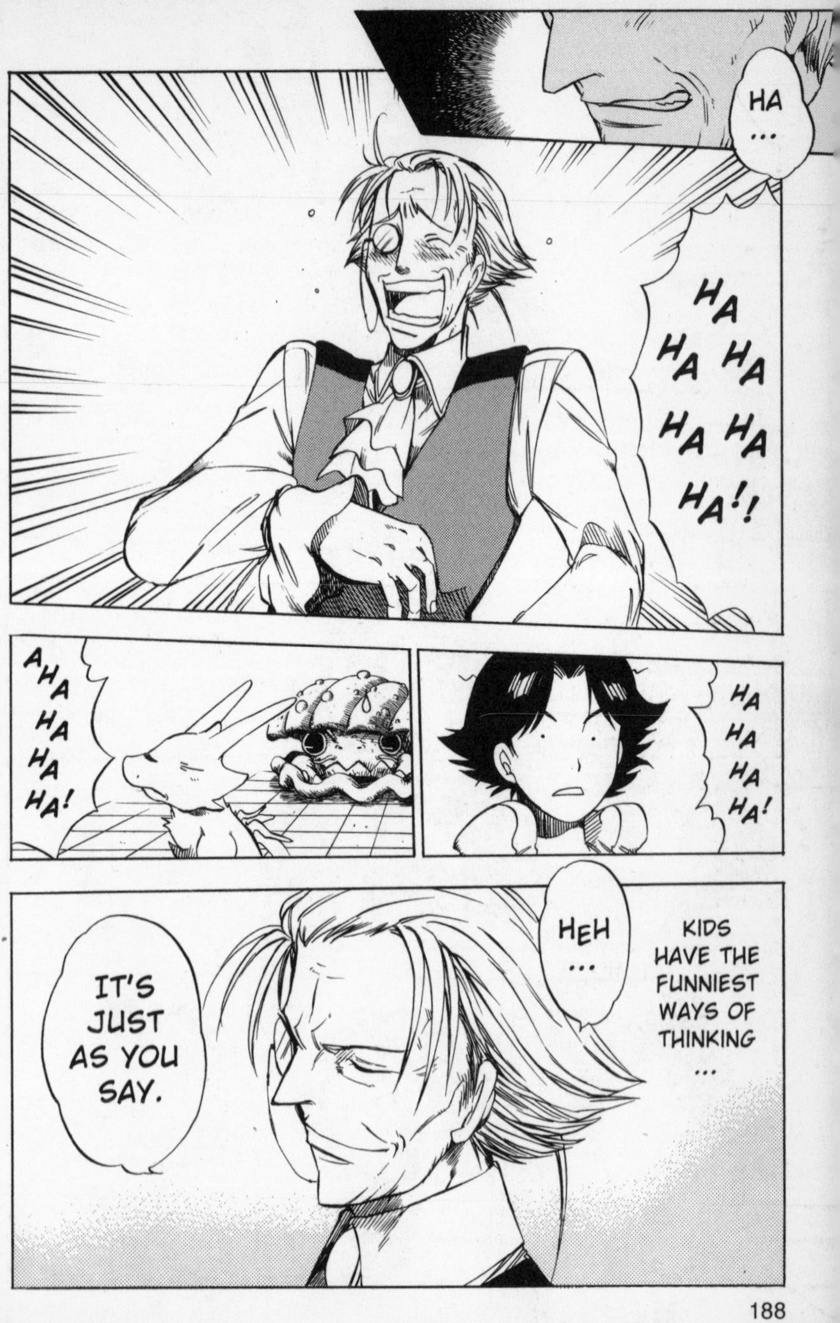

HA ...
HA HA HA HA HA HA HA!!
HA HA HA HA!
AHA HA HA HA!
HEH ...
KIDS HAVE THE FUNNIEST WAYS OF THINKING ...
IT'S JUST AS YOU SAY.

READ THIS WAY

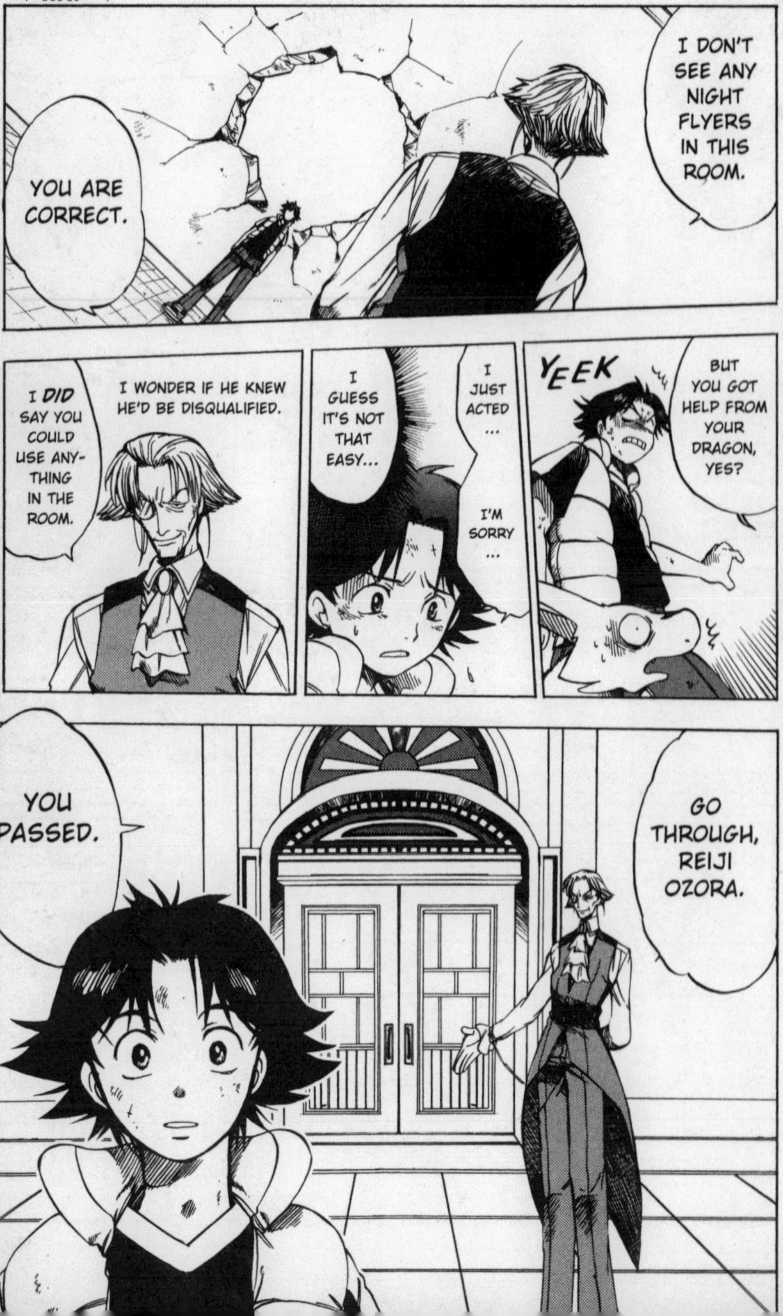
I DON'T SEE ANY NIGHT FLYERS IN THIS ROOM.
YOU ARE CORRECT.
YEEK
BUT YOU GOT HELP FROM YOUR DRAGON, YES?
I JUST ACTED...
I'M SORRY...
I GUESS IT'S NOT THAT EASY...
I WONDER IF HE KNEW HE'D BE DISQUALIFIED.
I *DID* SAY YOU COULD USE ANYTHING IN THE ROOM.
GO THROUGH, REIJI OZORA.
YOU PASSED.

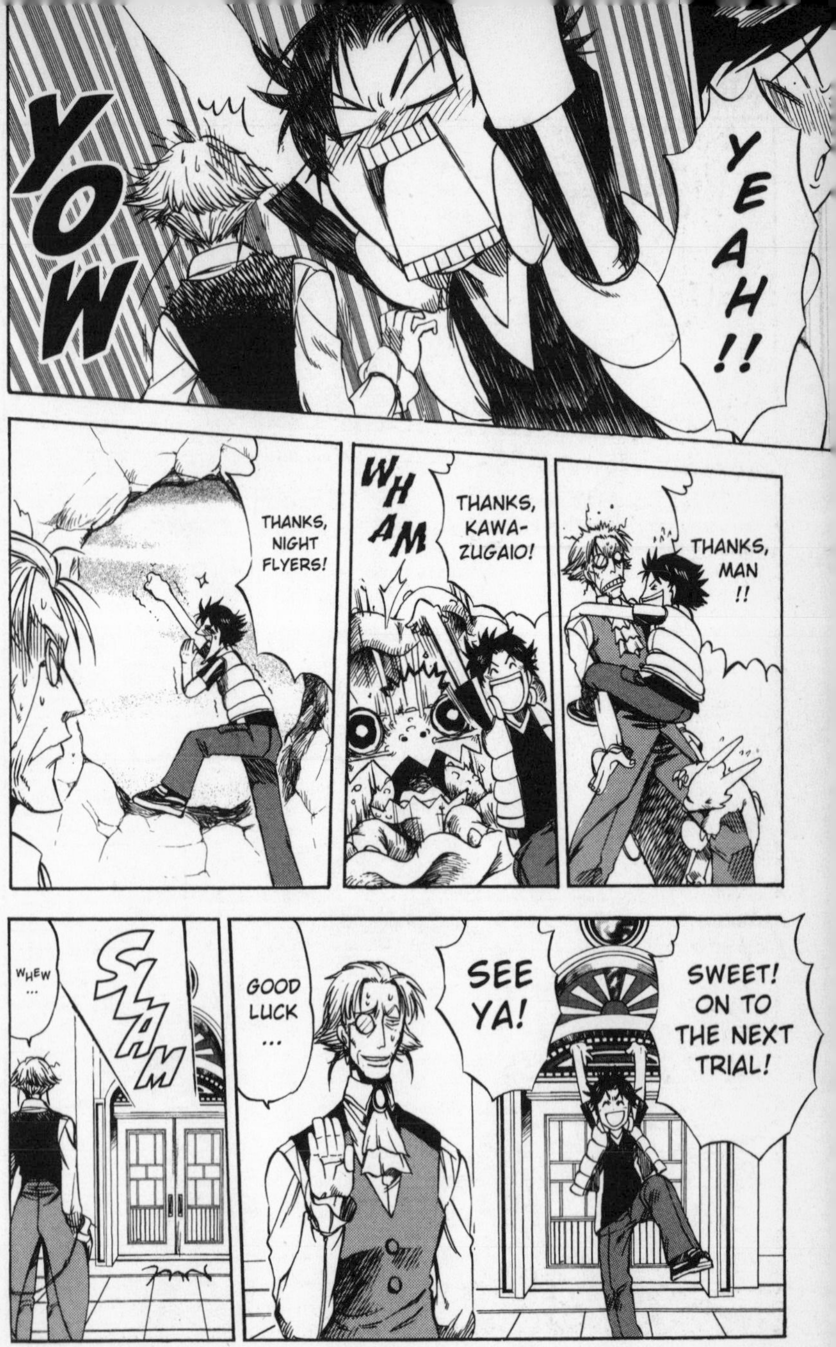
YEAH!!
YOW
THANKS, MAN !!
THANKS, KAWA-ZUGAIO!
WHAM
THANKS, NIGHT FLYERS!
SWEET! ON TO THE NEXT TRIAL!
SEE YA!
GOOD LUCK ...
SLAM
WHEW ...

READ THIS WAY

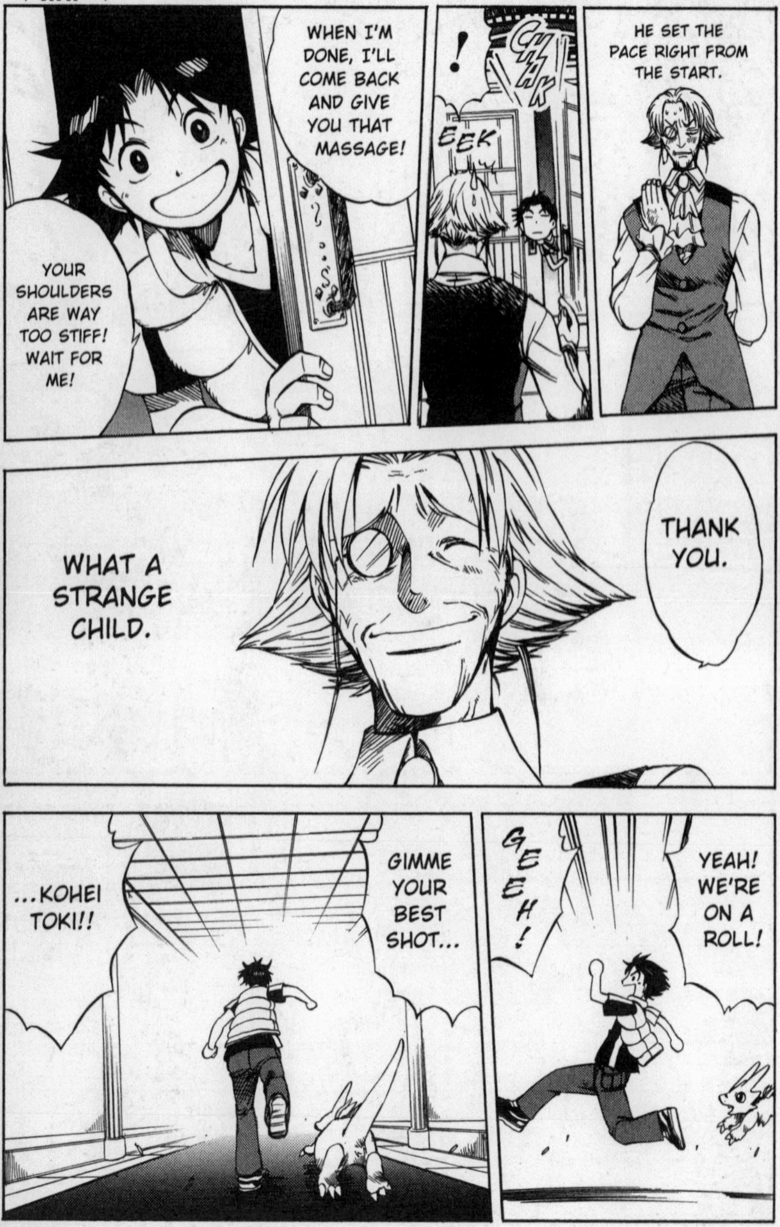
HE SET THE PACE RIGHT FROM THE START.
!
CHAK
EEK
WHEN I'M DONE, I'LL COME BACK AND GIVE YOU THAT MASSAGE!
YOUR SHOULDERS ARE WAY TOO STIFF! WAIT FOR ME!
THANK YOU.
WHAT A STRANGE CHILD.
YEAH! WE'RE ON A ROLL!
GEEH!
GIMME YOUR BEST SHOT...
...KOHEI TOKI!!

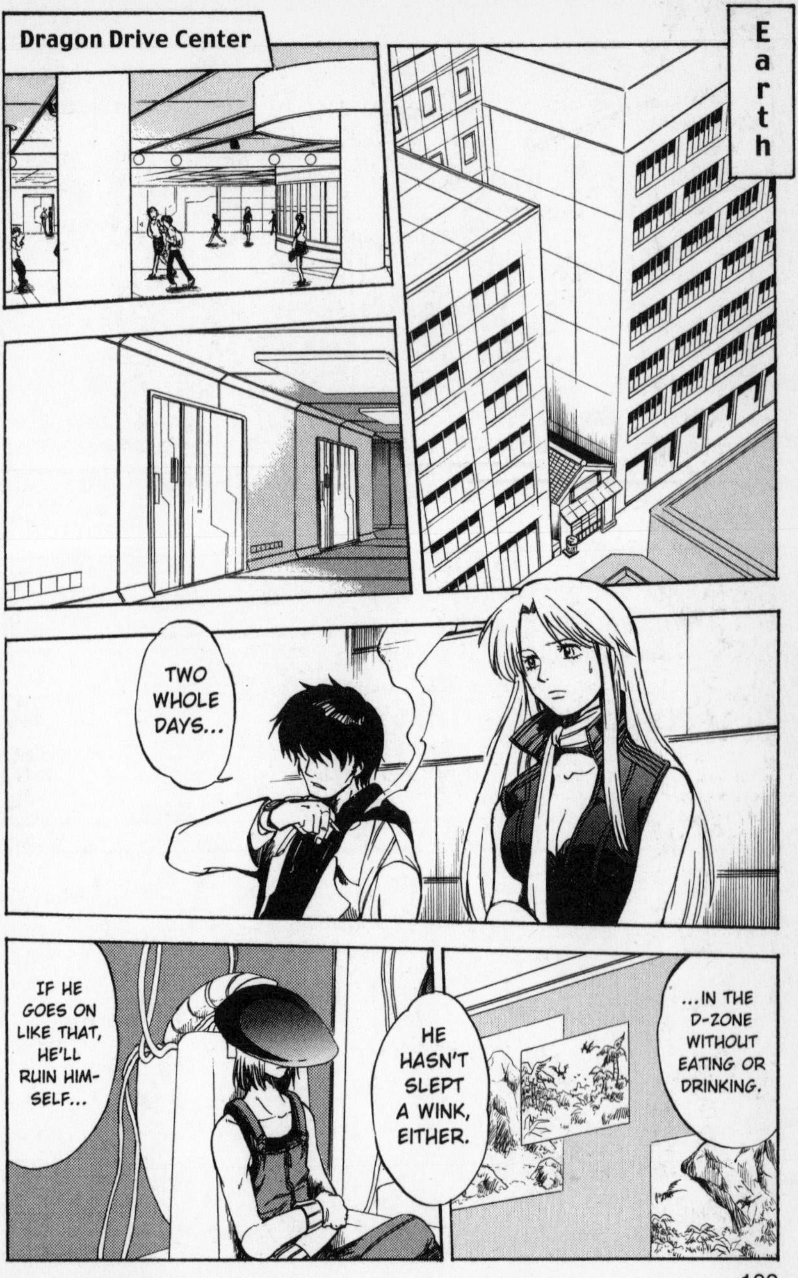
Earth
Dragon Drive Center
TWO WHOLE DAYS...
...IN THE D-ZONE WITHOUT EATING OR DRINKING.
HE HASN'T SLEPT A WINK, EITHER.
IF HE GOES ON LIKE THAT, HE'LL RUIN HIM-SELF...

READ THIS WAY

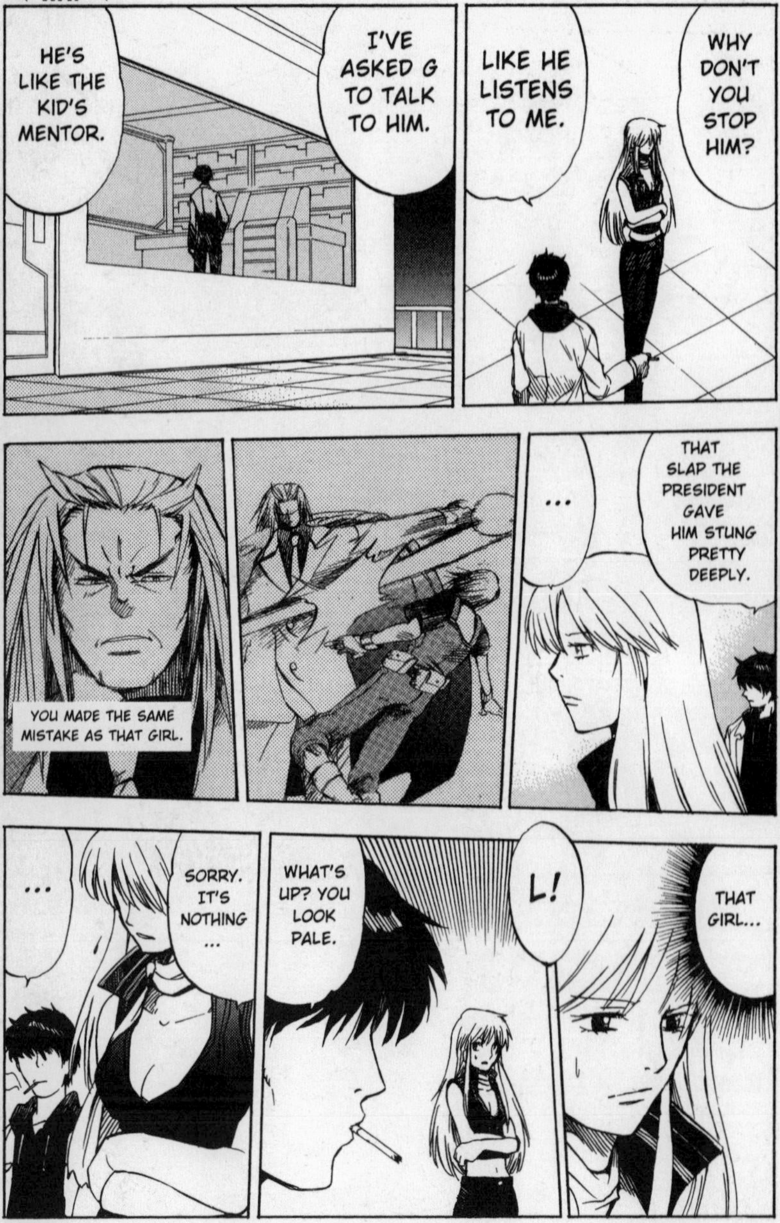

WHY DON'T YOU STOP HIM?
LIKE HE LISTENS TO ME.
I'VE ASKED G TO TALK TO HIM.
HE'S LIKE THE KID'S MENTOR.
THAT SLAP THE PRESIDENT GAVE HIM STUNG PRETTY DEEPLY.
...
YOU MADE THE SAME MISTAKE AS THAT GIRL.
THAT GIRL...
L!
WHAT'S UP? YOU LOOK PALE.
SORRY. IT'S NOTHING ...
...

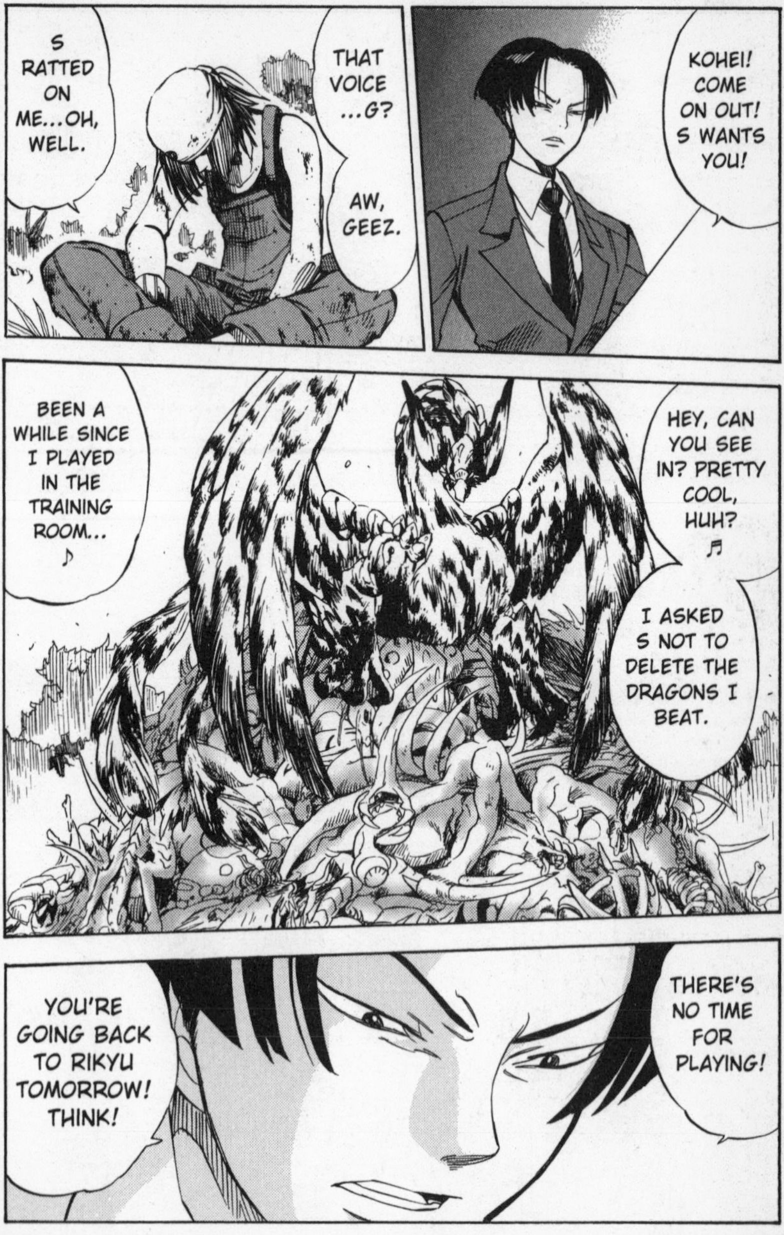
KOHEI! COME ON OUT! S WANTS YOU!
THAT VOICE ...G?
AW, GEEZ.
S RATTED ON ME...OH, WELL.
HEY, CAN YOU SEE IN? PRETTY COOL, HUH? ♬
I ASKED S NOT TO DELETE THE DRAGONS I BEAT.
BEEN A WHILE SINCE I PLAYED IN THE TRAINING ROOM... ♪
THERE'S NO TIME FOR PLAYING!
YOU'RE GOING BACK TO RIKYU TOMORROW! THINK!

READ THIS WAY

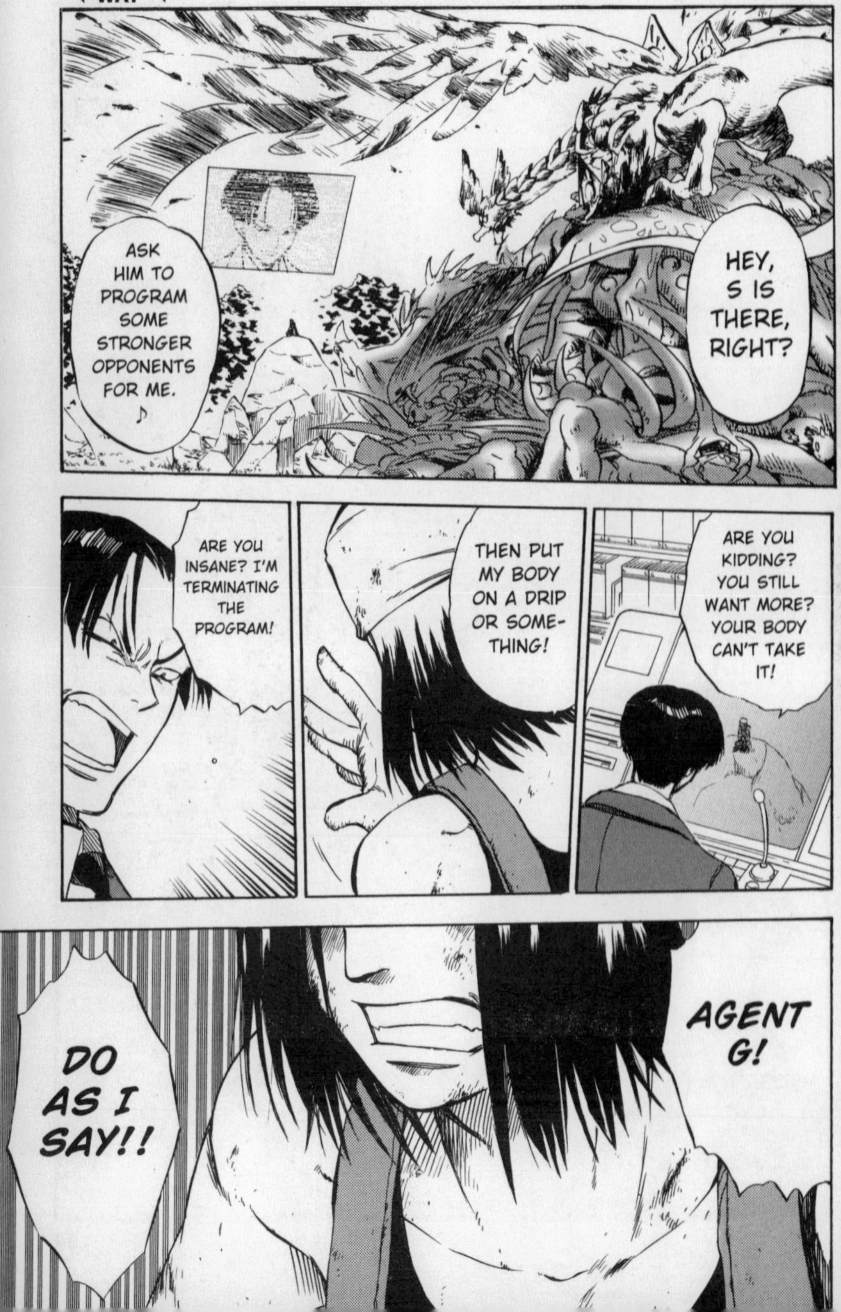
HEY, S IS THERE, RIGHT?
ASK HIM TO PROGRAM SOME STRONGER OPPONENTS FOR ME. ♪
ARE YOU KIDDING? YOU STILL WANT MORE? YOUR BODY CAN'T TAKE IT!
THEN PUT MY BODY ON A DRIP OR SOME-THING!
ARE YOU INSANE? I'M TERMINATING THE PROGRAM!
AGENT G!
DO AS I SAY!!

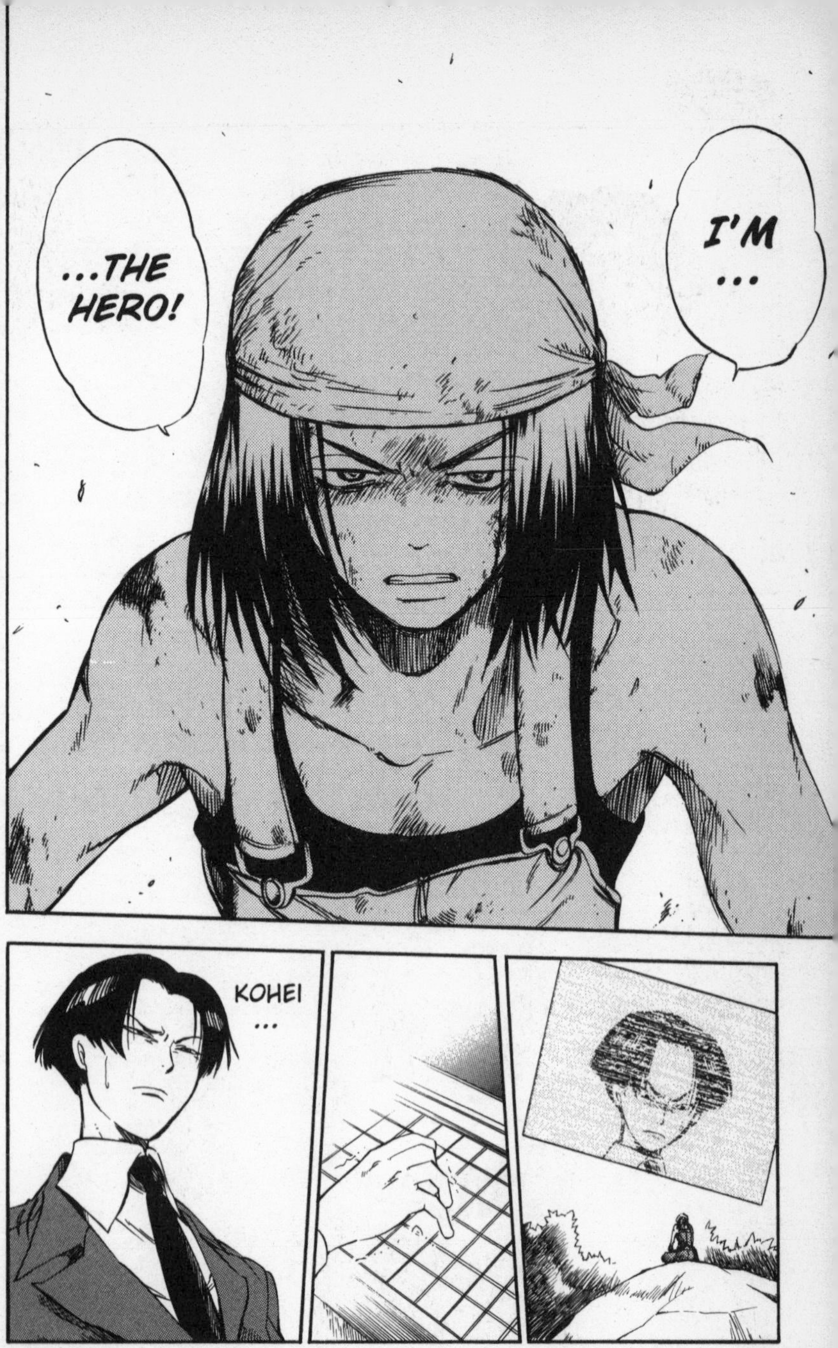
I'M ...
...THE HERO!
KOHEI ...

READ THIS WAY

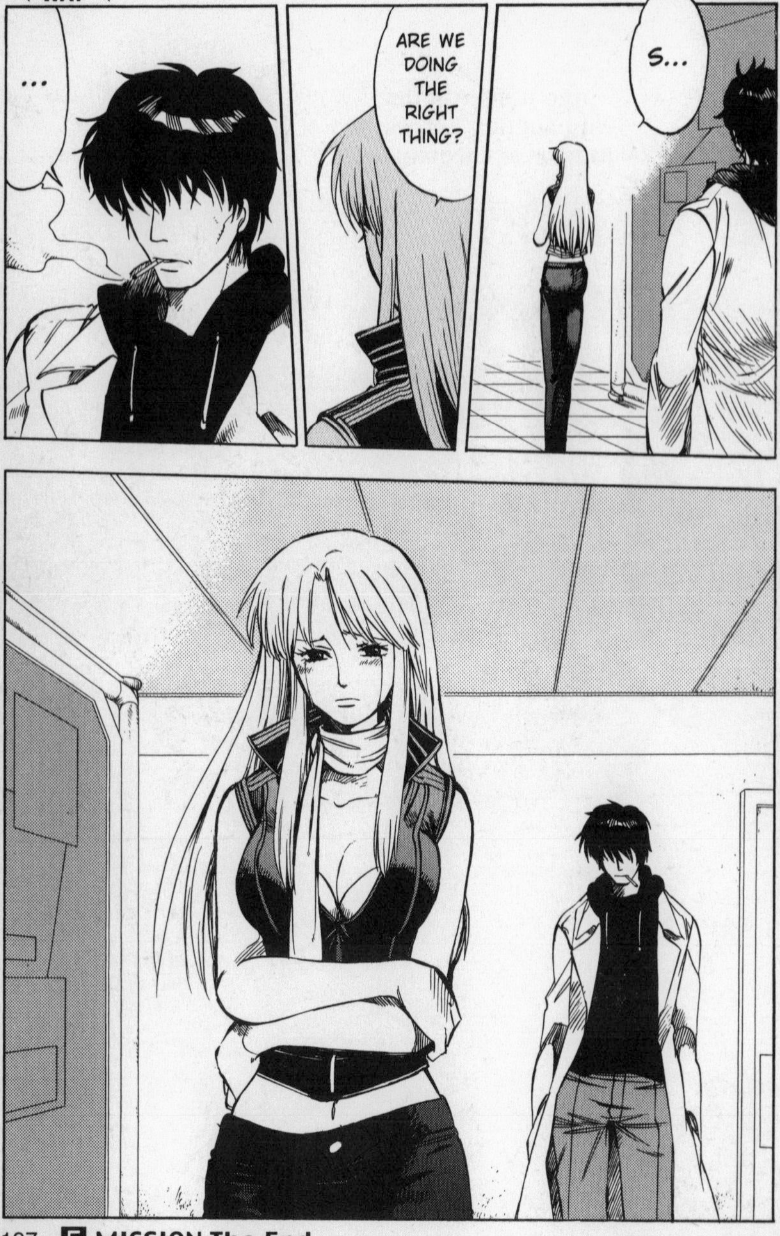
S...
ARE WE DOING THE RIGHT THING?
...

Auctioneer of the Flying Auction Rooms and Master of Ceremonies

Mr. Jank

AGE 28

TOTAL POP STAR MICROPHONE.

A CANE-STYLE MICROPHONE LIKE A SHORT SABER.

← THIS IS THE MIC.

WHEN THE CLOSING BID IS SETTLED, THE AUCTIONEER SWEEPS THE SABER DOWN, ENDING THE BIDDING.

AHHH

ASLEEP?

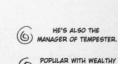

HE'S ALSO THE MANAGER OF TEMPESTER.

POPULAR WITH WEALTHY MIDDLE-AGED WOMEN.

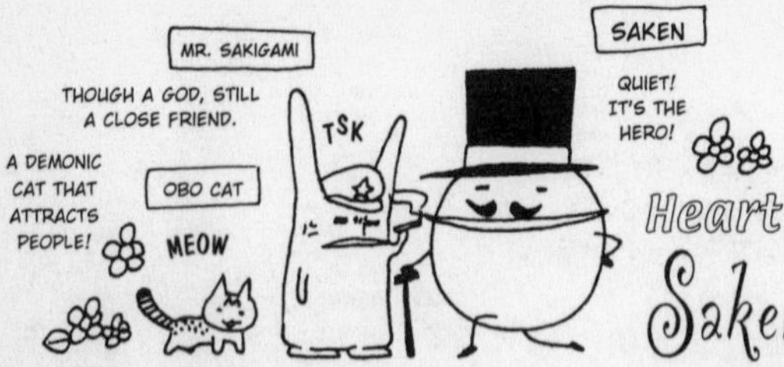
SAKEN
QUIET! IT'S THE HERO!
MR. SAKIGAMI
THOUGH A GOD, STILL A CLOSE FRIEND.
TSK
OBO CAT
A DEMONIC CAT THAT ATTRACTS PEOPLE!
MEOW

Heartwarming Saken Theater

BY KEN-ICHI SAKURA

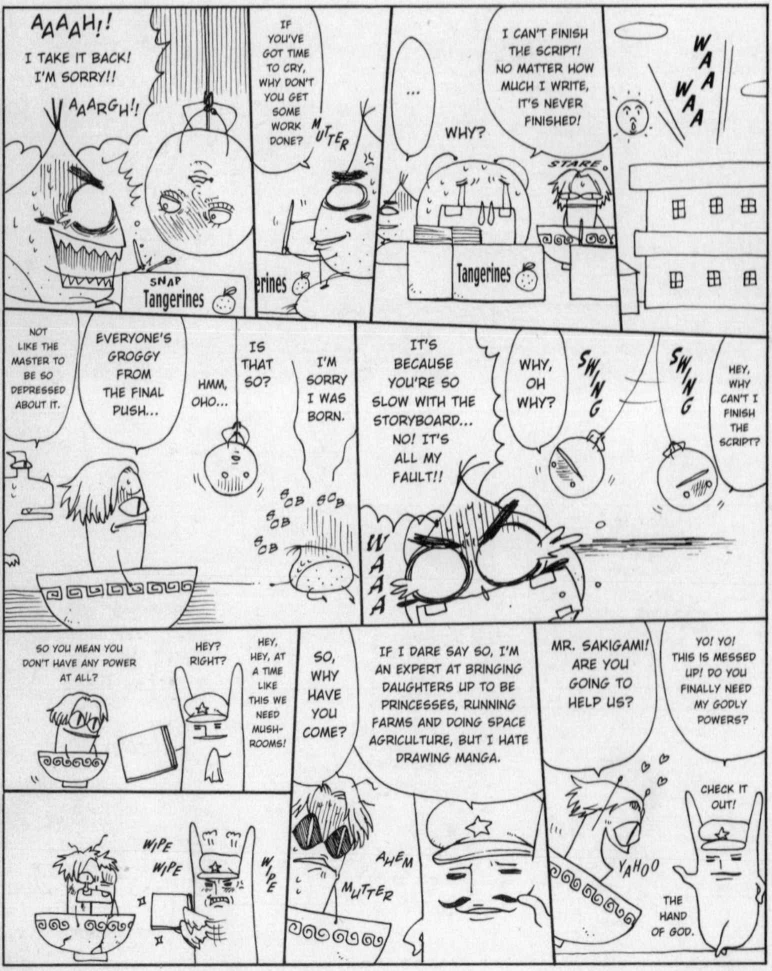
WAA
WAA
I CAN'T FINISH THE SCRIPT! NO MATTER HOW MUCH I WRITE, IT'S NEVER FINISHED!
...
WHY?
STARE
Tangerines
IF YOU'VE GOT TIME TO CRY, WHY DON'T YOU GET SOME WORK DONE?
MUTTER
erines
AAAAH!!
I TAKE IT BACK! I'M SORRY!!
AAARGH!!
SNAP
Tangerines
HEY, WHY CAN'T I FINISH THE SCRIPT?
SWING
WHY, OH WHY?
SWING
IT'S BECAUSE YOU'RE SO SLOW WITH THE STORYBOARD... NO! IT'S ALL MY FAULT!!
WAAAA
I'M SORRY I WAS BORN.
IS THAT SO?
HMM, OHO...
EVERYONE'S GROGGY FROM THE FINAL PUSH...
NOT LIKE THE MASTER TO BE SO DEPRESSED ABOUT IT.
SCB SCB
SCB
SCB
YO! YO! THIS IS MESSED UP! DO YOU FINALLY NEED MY GODLY POWERS?
MR. SAKIGAMI! ARE YOU GOING TO HELP US?
CHECK IT OUT!
YAHOO
THE HAND OF GOD.
IF I DARE SAY SO, I'M AN EXPERT AT BRINGING DAUGHTERS UP TO BE PRINCESSES, RUNNING FARMS AND DOING SPACE AGRICULTURE, BUT I HATE DRAWING MANGA.
SO, WHY HAVE YOU COME?
AHEM
MUTTER
HEY, HEY, AT A TIME LIKE THIS WE NEED MUSH-ROOMS!
HEY? RIGHT?
SO YOU MEAN YOU DON'T HAVE ANY POWER AT ALL?
WIPE
WIPE
WIPE

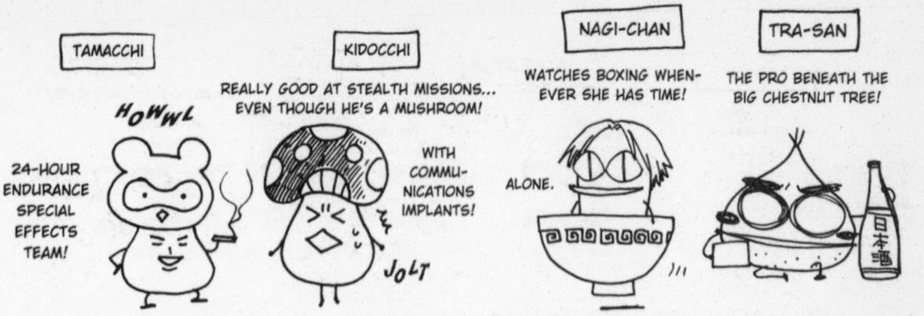
TRA-SAN
THE PRO BENEATH THE BIG CHESTNUT TREE!
NAGI-CHAN
WATCHES BOXING WHENEVER SHE HAS TIME!
ALONE.
KIDOCCHI
REALLY GOOD AT STEALTH MISSIONS... EVEN THOUGH HE'S A MUSHROOM!
WITH COMMUNICATIONS IMPLANTS!
JOLT
TAMACCHI
HOWWL
24-HOUR ENDURANCE SPECIAL EFFECTS TEAM!

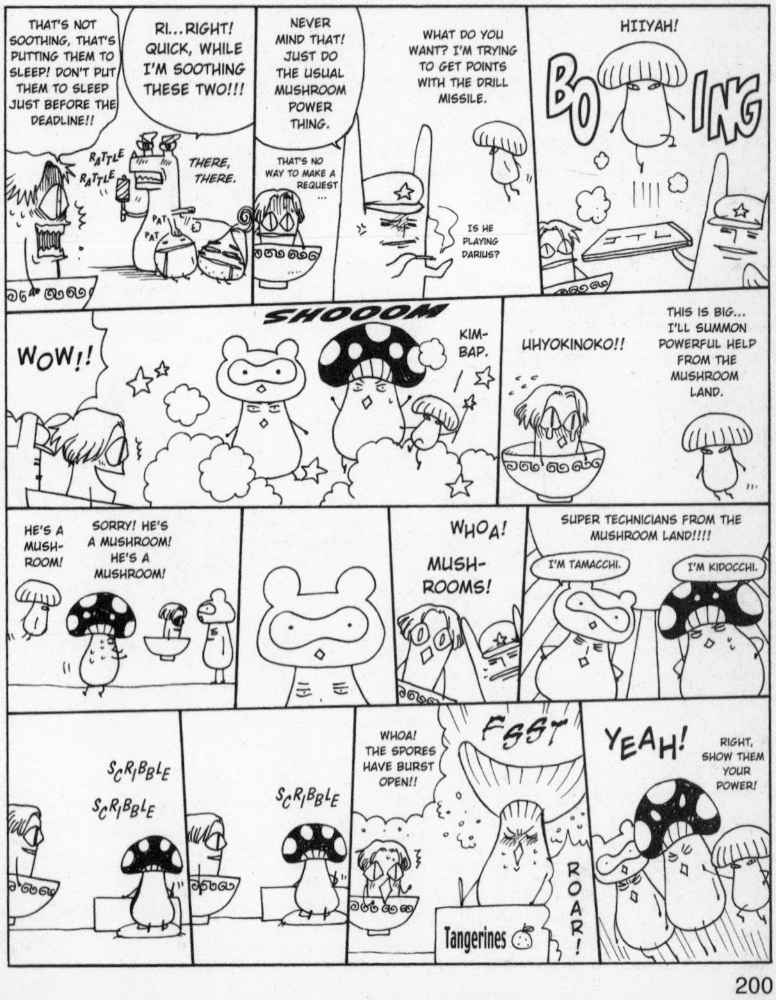
HIIYAH!
BOING
WHAT DO YOU WANT? I'M TRYING TO GET POINTS WITH THE DRILL MISSILE.
IS HE PLAYING DARIUS?
NEVER MIND THAT! JUST DO THE USUAL MUSHROOM POWER THING.
THAT'S NO WAY TO MAKE A REQUEST ...
RI...RIGHT! QUICK, WHILE I'M SOOTHING THESE TWO!!!
THAT'S NOT SOOTHING, THAT'S PUTTING THEM TO SLEEP! DON'T PUT THEM TO SLEEP JUST BEFORE THE DEADLINE!!
THERE, THERE.
RATTLE RATTLE
PAT PAT
THIS IS BIG... I'LL SUMMON POWERFUL HELP FROM THE MUSHROOM LAND.
UHYOKINOKO!!
SHOOOM
KIM-BAP.
WOW!!
SUPER TECHNICIANS FROM THE MUSHROOM LAND!!!!
I'M KIDOCCHI.
I'M TAMACCHI.
WHOA!
MUSH-ROOMS!
SORRY! HE'S A MUSHROOM! HE'S A MUSHROOM!
HE'S A MUSH-ROOM!
YEAH!
RIGHT, SHOW THEM YOUR POWER!
FSST
ROAR!
Tangerines
WHOA! THE SPORES HAVE BURST OPEN!!
SCRIBBLE
SCRIBBLE
SCRIBBLE

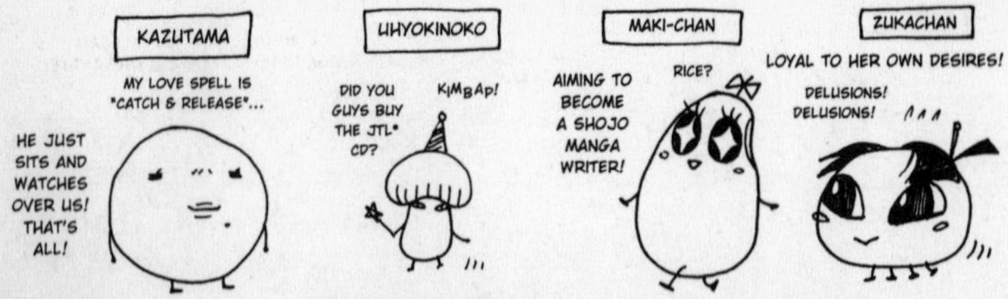
ZUKACHAN
LOYAL TO HER OWN DESIRES!
DELUSIONS! DELUSIONS!
MAKI-CHAN
RICE?
AIMING TO BECOME A SHOJO MANGA WRITER!
UHYOKINOKO
KIMBAP!
DID YOU GUYS BUY THE JTL* CD?
KAZUTAMA
MY LOVE SPELL IS "CATCH & RELEASE"...
HE JUST SITS AND WATCHES OVER US! THAT'S ALL!

*JTL: A KOREAN POP GROUP.

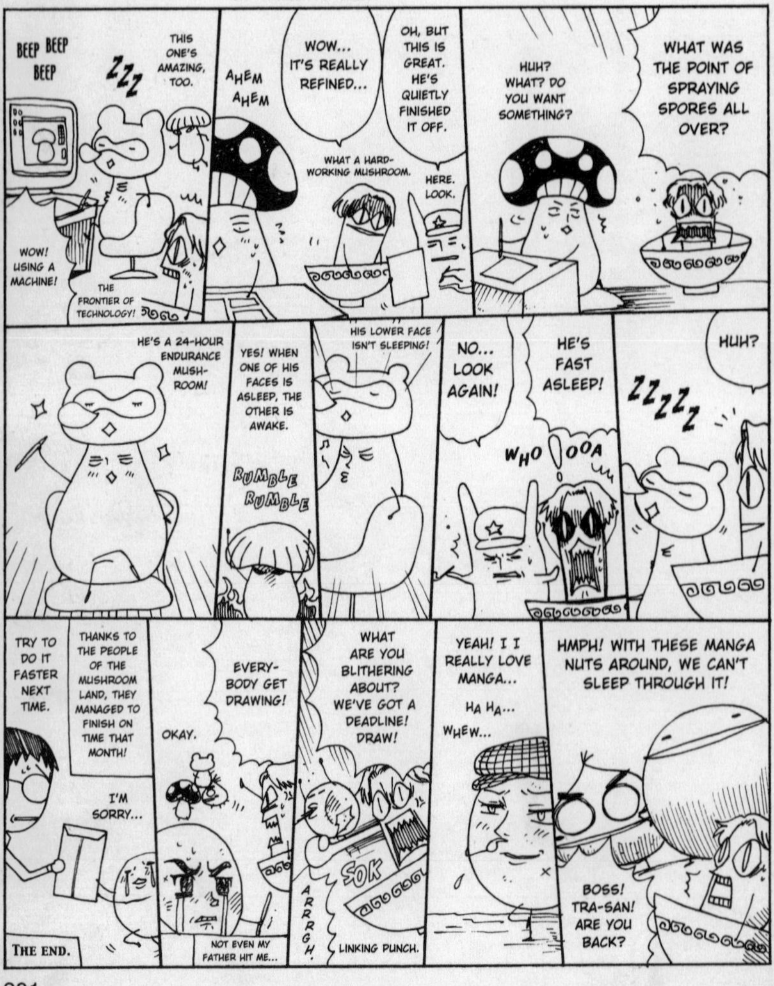
WHAT WAS THE POINT OF SPRAYING SPORES ALL OVER?
HUH? WHAT? DO YOU WANT SOMETHING?
OH, BUT THIS IS GREAT. HE'S QUIETLY FINISHED IT OFF.
WOW... IT'S REALLY REFINED...
AHEM AHEM
HERE. LOOK.
WHAT A HARD-WORKING MUSHROOM.
THIS ONE'S AMAZING, TOO.
ZZZ
BEEP BEEP BEEP
WOW! USING A MACHINE!
THE FRONTIER OF TECHNOLOGY!
HUH?
ZZZZ
HE'S FAST ASLEEP!
NO... LOOK AGAIN!
WHOOOA
HIS LOWER FACE ISN'T SLEEPING!
YES! WHEN ONE OF HIS FACES IS ASLEEP, THE OTHER IS AWAKE.
RUMBLE RUMBLE
HE'S A 24-HOUR ENDURANCE MUSH-ROOM!
HMPH! WITH THESE MANGA NUTS AROUND, WE CAN'T SLEEP THROUGH IT!
BOSS! TRA-SAN! ARE YOU BACK?
YEAH! I I REALLY LOVE MANGA...
HA HA...
WHEW...
WHAT ARE YOU BLITHERING ABOUT? WE'VE GOT A DEADLINE! DRAW!
SOK
ARRRGH.
LINKING PUNCH.
EVERY-BODY GET DRAWING!
OKAY.
NOT EVEN MY FATHER HIT ME...
THANKS TO THE PEOPLE OF THE MUSHROOM LAND, THEY MANAGED TO FINISH ON TIME THAT MONTH!
TRY TO DO IT FASTER NEXT TIME.
I'M SORRY...
THE END.

COMING NEXT VOLUME...

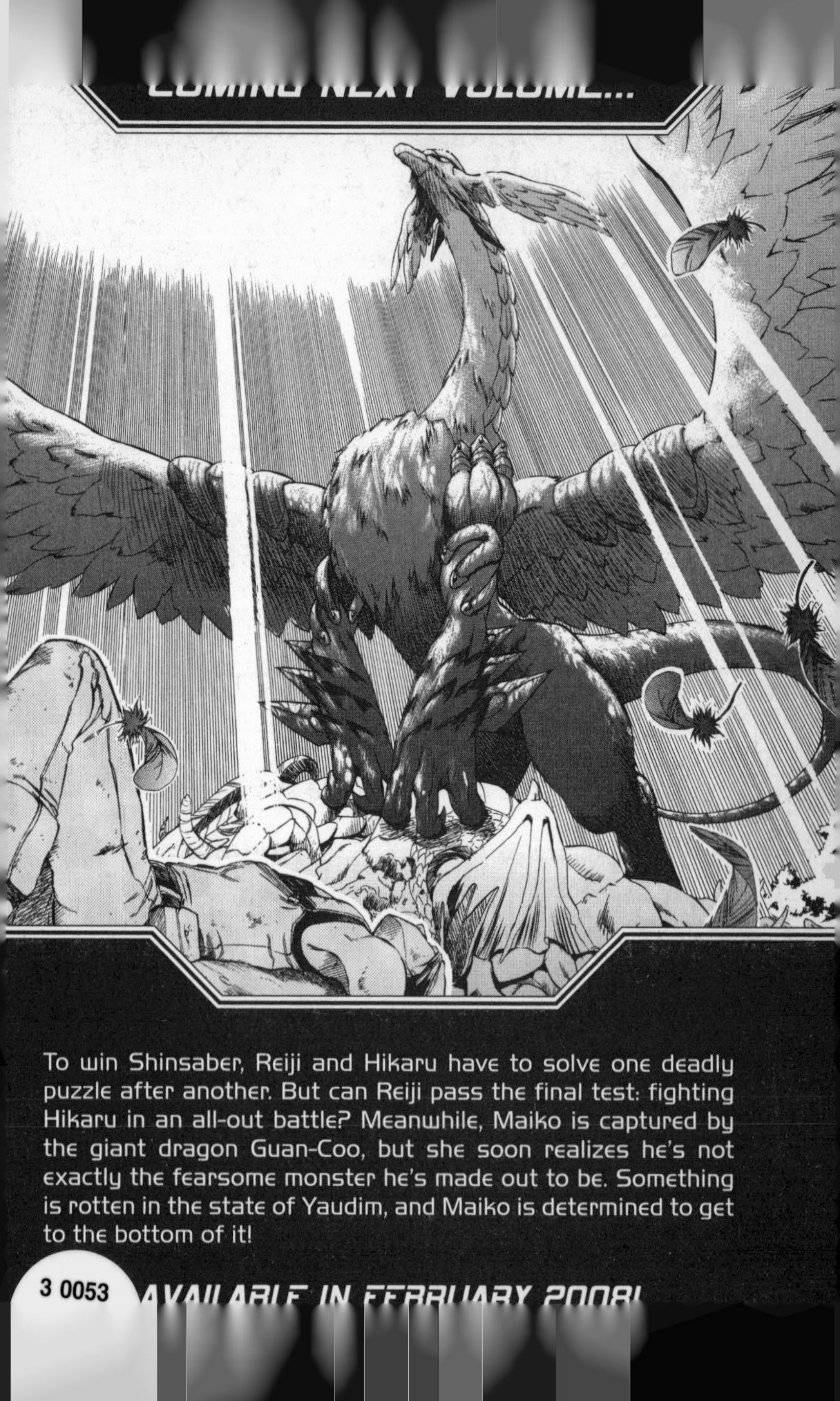

To win Shinsaber, Reiji and Hikaru have to solve one deadly puzzle after another. But can Reiji pass the final test: fighting Hikaru in an all-out battle? Meanwhile, Maiko is captured by the giant dragon Guan-Coo, but she soon realizes he's not exactly the fearsome monster he's made out to be. Something is rotten in the state of Yaudim, and Maiko is determined to get to the bottom of it!

AVAILABLE IN FEBRUARY 2008!

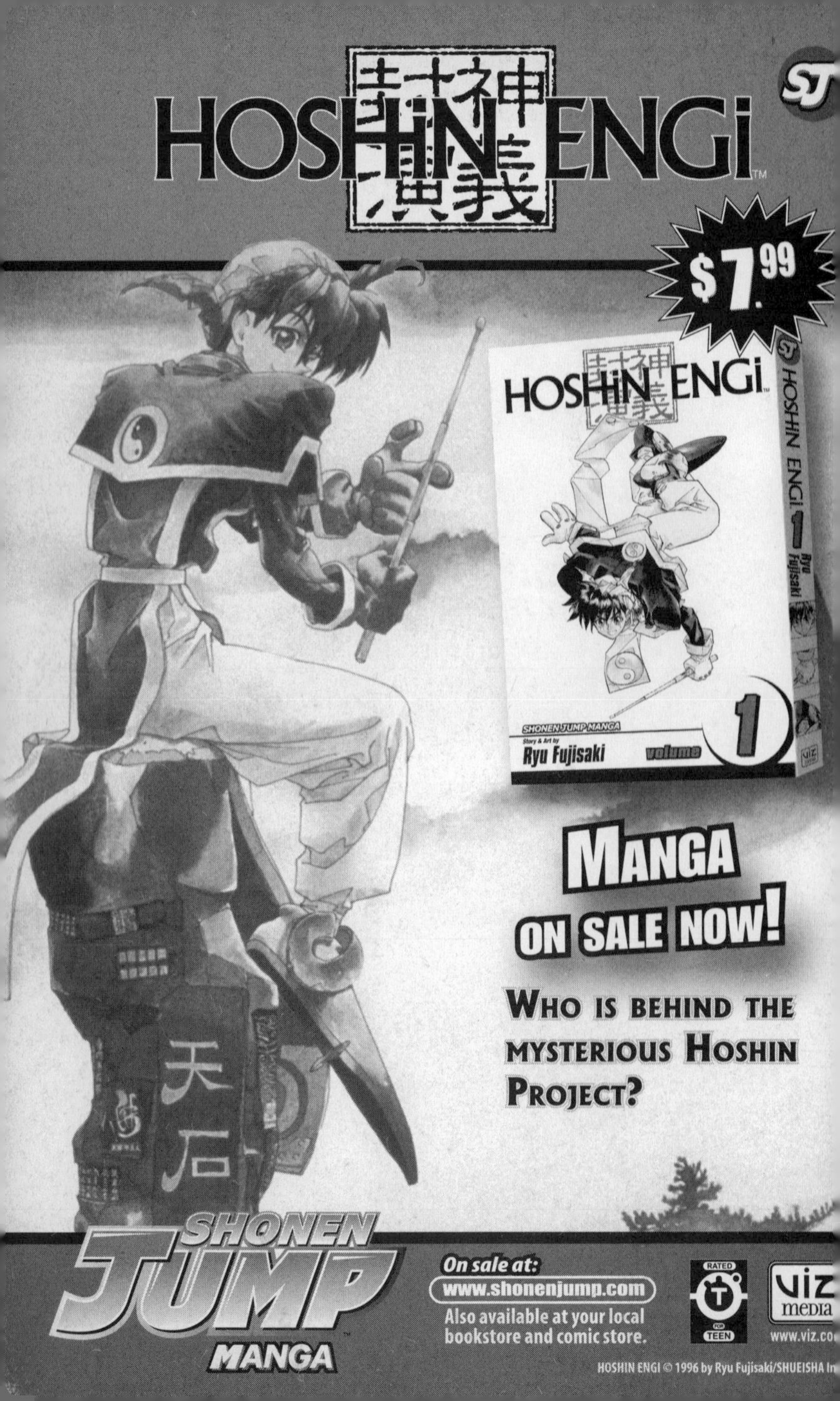
SJ
HOSHiN ENGi
封神演義
$7.99
HOSHiN ENGi
SJ HOSHiN ENGi 1 Ryu Fujisaki
SHONEN JUMP MANGA
Story & Art by
Ryu Fujisaki
volume 1
MANGA
ON SALE NOW!
WHO IS BEHIND THE MYSTERIOUS HOSHIN PROJECT?
天
石
SHONEN JUMP MANGA
On sale at:
www.shonenjump.com
Also available at your local bookstore and comic store.
RATED T FOR TEEN
viz media
www.viz.co
HOSHIN ENGI © 1996 by Ryu Fujisaki/SHUEISHA In

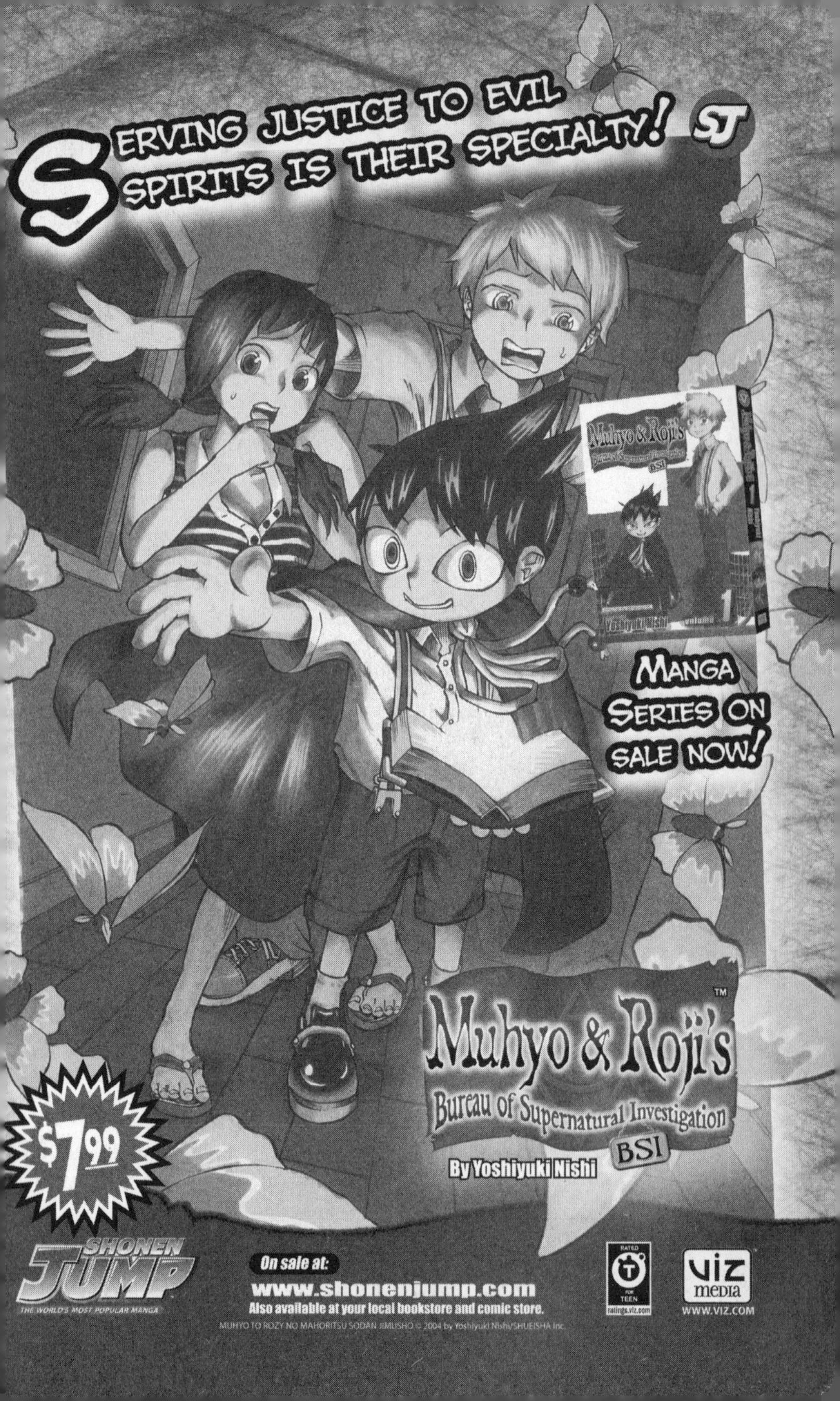

SERVING JUSTICE TO EVIL SPIRITS IS THEIR SPECIALTY!
SJ
MANGA SERIES ON SALE NOW!
Muhyo & Roji's™
Bureau of Supernatural Investigation
BSI
By Yoshiyuki Nishi
$7.99
SHONEN JUMP
THE WORLD'S MOST POPULAR MANGA
On sale at:
www.shonenjump.com
Also available at your local bookstore and comic store.
RATED T FOR TEEN
ratings.viz.com
viz media
WWW.VIZ.COM
MUHYO TO ROZY NO MAHORITSU SODAN JIMUSHO © 2004 by Yoshiyuki Nishi/SHUEISHA Inc.

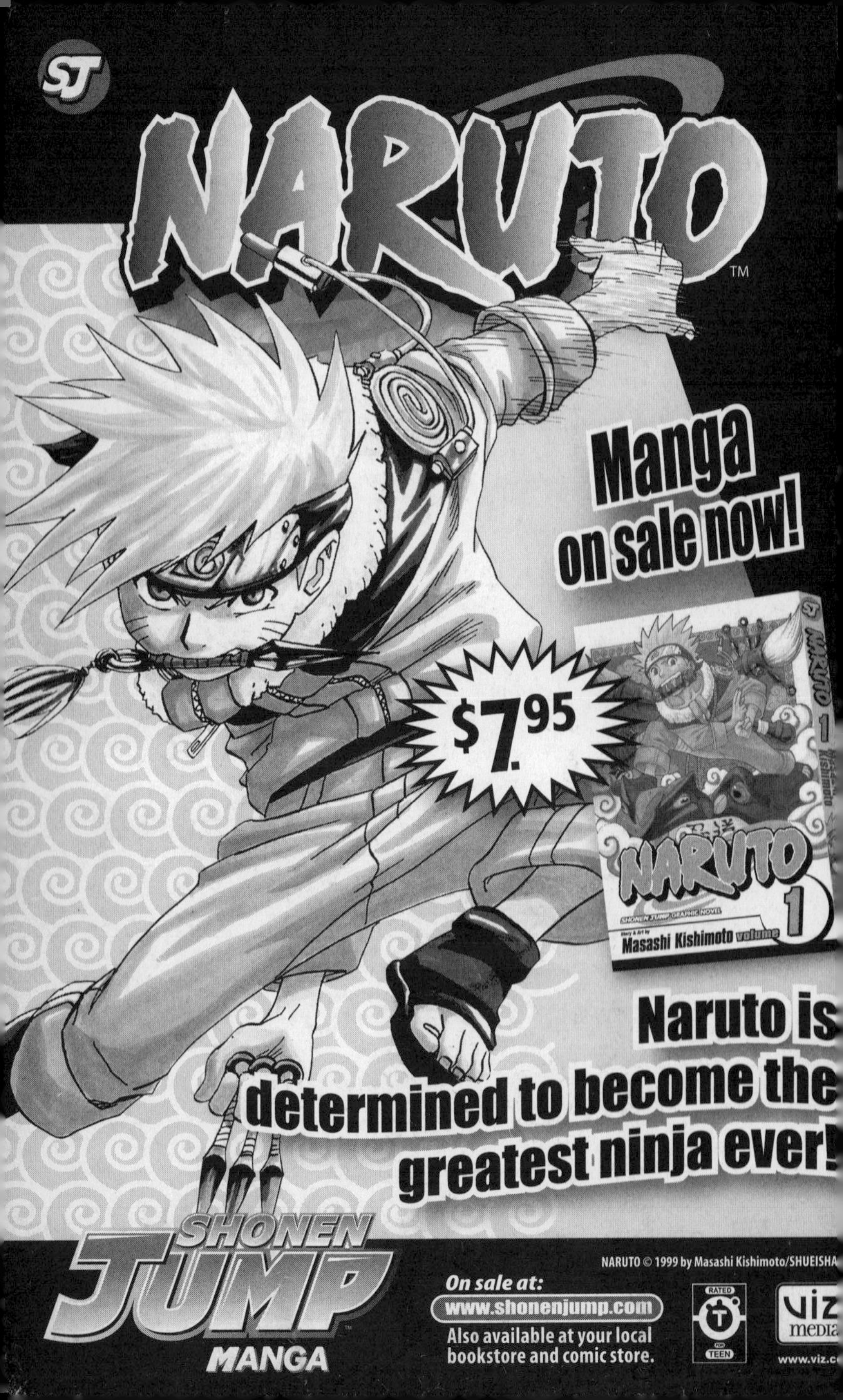
SJ
NARUTO™
Manga on sale now!
$7.95
NARUTO 1
SHONEN JUMP GRAPHIC NOVEL
Masashi Kishimoto volume 1
Naruto is determined to become the greatest ninja ever!
SHONEN JUMP MANGA
NARUTO © 1999 by Masashi Kishimoto/SHUEISHA
On sale at:
www.shonenjump.com
Also available at your local bookstore and comic store.
RATED T FOR TEEN
viz media
www.viz.c

APR 1 3 2010

Save **50% off** the newsstand price!

SHONEN JUMP

THE WORLD'S MOST POPULAR MANGA

SUBSCRIBE TODAY and SAVE 50% OFF the cover price PLUS enjoy all the benefits of the SHONEN JUMP SUBSCRIBER CLUB, exclusive online content & special gifts ONLY AVAILABLE to SUBSCRIBERS!

☑ **YES!** Please enter my 1 year subscription (12 issues) to *SHONEN JUMP* at the INCREDIBLY LOW SUBSCRIPTION RATE of $29.95 and sign me up for the SHONEN JUMP Subscriber Club!

Only **$29⁹⁵!**

NAME

ADDRESS

CITY   STATE   ZIP

E-MAIL ADDRESS

☐ MY   IE LATER

CREDIT   ERCARD

ACCOU   EXP. DATE

SIGNAT

NEN JUMP
scriptions Service Dept.
Box 515
unt Morris, IL 61054-0515

Make checks payable to: **SHONEN JUMP.**
Canada add US $12. No foreign orders. Allow 6-8 weeks for delivery.

P6SJGN   YU-GI-OH! © 1996 by Kazuki Takahashi / SHUEISHA Inc.